Being a Medical Clerical Worker

PRENTICE HALL HEALTH MEDICAL CLERICAL SERIES
Kay Cox-Stevens RN, MA, Series Editor

Being a Medical Clerical Worker: An Introductory Core Text, Third Edition, *Jacquelyn Marshall, BA, MT, MA*
Being a Medical Information Coder, Third Edition, *Laurie Dodson, RRA, MPH*
Being a Medical Records/Health Information Clerk, Third Edition, *Kathryn McMiller, RHIA*

Kay Cox-Stevens, RN, MA, is a Health Careers Specialist and Medical Assistant Program Coordinator at Saddleback College, and the Author of Prentice Hall's *Being a Health Unit Coordinator.*

Being a Medical Clerical Worker:

An Introductory Core Text

Third Edition

Jacquelyn R. Marshall, BA, MT, MA
Kay Cox-Stevens, RN, MA
Series Editor

PEARSON
Prentice
Hall
Upper Saddle River, New Jersey 07458

Library of Congress Cataloging-in-Publication Data

Marshall, Jacquelyn.
  Being a medical clerical worker : an introductory core text /
Jacquelyn R. Marshall.— 3rd ed.
     p. ; cm. — (Prentice Hall Health medical clerical series)
  Includes bibliographical references and index.
  ISBN 0-13-112672-5
  1. Medical secretaries.
  [DNLM: 1. Medical Secretaries. 2. Medical Records. 3. Office
Management. W 80 M368b 2004] I. Title. II. Series.
  R728 .M33 2004
  651'.961—dc21

                         2003004874

Notice: Care has been taken to confirm the accuracy of the information presented in this book. The author, editor, and the publisher, however, cannot accept any responsibility for errors or omissions or for the consequences for application of the information in this book and make no warranty, express or implied, with respect to its contents.

The author and the publisher have exerted every effort to ensure that drug selections and dosages set forth in this text are in accord with current recommendations and practice at time of publication. However, in view of ongoing research, changes in government regulations, and the constant flow of information relating to drug therapy and drug reactions, the reader is urged to check the package inserts of all drugs for any change in indications of dosage and for added warnings and precautions. This is particularly important when the recommended agent is a new and/or infrequently employed drug.

The author and publisher disclaim all responsibility for any liability, loss, injury, or damage incurred as a consequence, directly or indirectly, of the use and application of any of the contents of this volume.

Publisher: Julie Levin Alexander
Assistant to Publisher: Regina Bruno
Executive Editor: Barbara Krawiec
Editorial Assistant: Sheba Jalaluddin
Director of Production and Manufacturing: Bruce Johnson
Managing Production Editor: Patrick Walsh
Production Liaison: Mary C. Treacy
Production Editor: Jessica Balch, Pine Tree Composition
Manufacturing Manager: Ilene Sanford

Manufacturing Buyer: Pat Brown
Design Director: Cheryl Asherman
Cover Designer: Chris Weigand
Senior Marketing Manager: Nicole Benson
Marketing Assistant: Janet Ryerson
Channel Marketing Manager: Rachele Strober
Composition: Pine Tree Composition, Inc.
Printer/Binder: Banta Book Group
Cover Printer: Phoenix Color Corp.

Pearson Education Ltd., *London*
Pearson Education Australia Pty. Limited, *Sydney*
Pearson Education Singapore, Pte. Ltd.
Pearson Education North Asia Ltd., *Hong Kong*
Pearson Education Canada, Ltd., *Toronto*
Pearson Educación de Mexico, S.A. de C.V.
Pearson Education—Japan, *Tokyo*
Pearson Education Malaysia, Pte. Ltd.
Pearson Education, *Upper Saddle River, New Jersey*

10 9 8 7 6 5 4 3
ISBN 0-13-112672-5

To the patient, sincere,
and ethical medical clerical workers
who daily make patients feel comfortable
in a strange, often confusing,
health care environment.

Contents

Contents

Foreword

Choosing a medical clerical career is a smart decision. The U.S. Bureau of Labor and Statistics reports medical clerical occupations to be one of the fastest growing through 2010. Some of the reasons for the continuing demand for medical clerical workers include the aging of America and the rapid increase in the number of medical tests and treatments available. The resultant paperwork requires workers trained to maintain medical records and select and apply codes for insurance billing and statistics gathering. Legal considerations and the scrutiny of managed care, Medicare, third-party payers, regulators, the courts, and consumers have made the proper management of patients' charts increasingly important.

Industry, on the other hand, reports that there are not nearly enough trained medical clerical workers to meet the demand, and many jobs go unfilled. Adequate training opportunities and training tools are in short supply, particularly in some career areas.

The Prentice Hall Health Medical Clerical Series was created in recognition of these needs. Designed as easy-to-understand yet comprehensive texts, this series guides students through the duties and responsibilities of medical clerical workers in their chosen fields. *Being a Medical Clerical Worker: An Introductory Core Text* contains information considered common to all medical areas.

It is hoped that this series will make a significant contribution toward filling the gap of supply and demand for medical clerical workers and that you, the student, will utilize these books to the fullest degree as you embark on your new career.

Kay Cox-Stevens
Series Editor

Preface

There have been dramatic changes in health care since the first edition of *Being a Medical Clerical Worker: An Introductory Core Text* was published in 1990. More than a decade later, the medical clerical worker faces more complex challenges, with the work environment changing rapidly. In this profession, textbooks must be updated on a regular basis to make sure that students receive current information about a dynamic profession.

This latest edition has many new features, formats, and sections. Hopefully, the changes are informative and user-friendly. The chapters have a new look as well as much new material, including:

- Updated information on certification programs
- Explanation of several legal terms not discussed in previous editions, updated due to the increasing importance of medico-legal issues
- Continual emphasis on ethical behavior, especially the importance of confidentiality of patient information
- *Real-Life Scenarios,* a feature in most of the eighteen chapters, gives the students a chance to discuss realistic, on-the-job situations
- Updated information about newer modes of communication and their uses in the medical office, such as electronic transmissions
- Current information on handling medical records
- Updated pharmacology information
- Expanded section on diagnostic testing
- A revamped chapter renamed *Medical Office Information Technology* that stresses critical confidentiality issues concerning the use of such technology
- A revised health insurance chapter emphasizing the latest technology, requirements, and forms required to correctly understand insurance billing
- Latest updated information about computerized billing, collection, and banking
- Updated review questions and learning activities

Being a Medical Clerical Worker continues to be the core textbook in the Prentice Hall Medical Series. The goal of this edition is to familiarize the students with technological advances designed to better serve the patient, reduce errors, and increase efficiency of communications.

However, technology is wasted if the medical clerical worker does not commit him- or herself to ethical and moral excellence in dealing with patients, as well as a firm commitment to being a positive part of the health care team. Being a medical clerical worker brings continual challenges and rewards for the professional who truly wants to be proud of his or her professional accomplishments. Additionally, career advancement continues to be possible for those who excel in their positions.

Jacquelyn R. Marshall

ACKNOWLEDGMENTS

The author wishes to thank the many people who cooperated in the effort involved in publishing this book.

- Kay Cox-Stevens, who continually believes in upholding the highest standards for her medical clerical students as well as for her various clinical publications
- The staff of Prentice Hall Health, especially Barbara Krawiec and her Editorial Assistant Sheba Jalaluddin
- The reviewers who carefully read and made suggestions for the changes in the third edition of this textbook
- The other dedicated authors in the Prentice Hall Medical Clerical series

ABOUT THE AUTHOR

Jacquelyn Marshall, BA, MT, MA, has been a health care worker, serving as a clinical laboratory scientist, for over twenty years. Ms. Marshall has also served as a science curriculum writer/consultant and has developed Model Curriculum Standards for Vocational Health Occupations throughout California. She has also taught vocational health care courses after receiving a teaching credential. Ms. Marshall currently is a freelance medical writer and is author of eight textbooks. She has also developed several instructor's guides and has edited and contributed to three medical series.

ABOUT THE SERIES EDITOR

Kay Cox-Stevens, RN, MA, is Program Coordinator of the Medical Assistant Program at Saddleback College in Mission Viejo, California, and owner of Achiever's Development Enterprises, a consulting and publishing business. She is a former Professional Development Consultant for Special Projects and Curriculum Development for the California Department of Education. She was a Master Trainer for Health Careers Teacher Training through California Polytechnic University of Pomona and served as chairperson of the California Health Careers Statewide Advisory Committee.

Professor Cox-Stevens conceived this series and worked with the authors to develop each book. She is a former Professional Development Consultant with the California Department of Education, Chairperson of the California Health Careers Advisory Committee, and health careers curriculum specialist. She was a critical care nurse and inservice educator. She is currently the Medical Assistant Program Coordinator at Saddleback College in southern California.

Introduction to Being a Medical Clerical Worker

Accreditation	A process that grants recognition to an educational program for maintaining standards qualifying its graduates for professional work.
American Association of Medical Assistants (AAMA)	A national association for medical assistants, medical assistant students, and medical assisting instructors, with both state and local chapters.
Benefits	Compensations for an employee in addition to salary; examples include vacation, holiday, and sick pay, as well as disability insurance and health insurance.
Certification	That which vouches for or affirms that certain standards have been met.
Certified medical assistant (CMA)	Certification earned through examination by an AAMA-accredited program or after appropriate training or work experience as a medical clerical worker in certain institutions.
Commission on Accreditation of Allied Health Education Programs (CAAHEP)	A group of professionals in the field who set standards for education for various health education programs.
Competency	A state of being legally qualified or adequate.
Continuing education (CE)	Education received by a worker that is intended to improve or maintain job competence.
Externship	A transitional period between the classroom and employment where students are placed in potential employment sites under close supervision.
Health maintenance organization (HMO)	Prepaid health care program of group practice with comprehensive medical care being provided and with an emphasis on preventive medicine.
Medical clerical worker	A term denoting or describing one who performs a wide range of clerical functions in the medical environment, including the medical secretary, administrative medical assistant, medical transcriptionist, hospital insurance clerk, medical records clerk, medical admissions clerk, health unit coordinator, medical information coder, and others.

INTRODUCTION

A **medical clerical worker** has many exciting options for employment in today's health care market. Opportunities for advancement are increasingly available as the need for skilled medical clerical workers grows in the expanding medical world. Specialization in the medical clerical field offers challenges and financial rewards.

As technology continues to expand, technical skills and knowledge in the medical clerical field are increasing. Computers have replaced the simple appointment book, and flexibility is needed to adjust to the constant changes such technology brings.

There is one aspect of the medical clerical worker's job that has never changed throughout history. Serving the *patient* remains the most important part of your job. Patience, compassion, and a warm smile are still the most valuable traits of the medical clerical health care worker.

*H*ISTORY OF THE MEDICAL CLERICAL WORKER

Early in the twentieth century, the clerical aspects of a physician's practice were quite simple. A doctor performed his or her own paperwork, or perhaps one assistant would be hired. In more recent times, medical clerical workers have become a necessity, with an enormous volume of paperwork produced by changing technology. The medical clerical health care worker has consistently gained more and more authority, along with increased responsibility. There are now exciting possibilities for variety and specialization.

*P*ERSONAL QUALIFICATIONS

You have chosen to become a medical clerical health care worker. Perhaps you have selected this occupation because you have observed medical clerical workers and have become interested in their profession. You may have read about the many job opportunities and the potentially flexible schedules. There are certain personality traits that will help you become an excellent medical clerical worker. Some people naturally have many such traits, and others can be learned in school and on the job.

The following are qualities that can help you succeed as a medical clerical worker. Review the list and see how many of these traits you already possess. How many could you develop with practice?

- You are dependable and trustworthy.
- You are punctual.
- You like being well organized.
- You enjoy clerical work and pay attention to detail.
- You can be flexible.
- You are thorough.
- You can work under pressure.
- You are a good speller.
- You have pride in yourself and the job you are doing.
- You really like working with people.
- You consider yourself a kind and sympathetic person who likes to listen.
- You try to be tactful.
- You can accept criticism.
- You can follow rules and detailed instructions.
- You welcome a new challenge.
- You project a professional image.

Compassion

The ability to feel compassion for others ranks as one of the most crucial personality traits for the medical clerical worker. You will be coming into contact with ill people, who can often be angry, frightened, and disagreeable. You must be able to put yourself in their place and realize that illness is a great burden on the individual as well as the individual's family. You are an important link between the patient and the busy doctor, and your role often includes providing reassurance.

Punctuality

Employers list punctuality on the top of their list as the most desirable trait for an employee. The office or department in which you work is carefully organized around each person. Your continual absence or tardiness puts pressure on your fellow workers. It is your responsibility to arrive on time each day, solving transportation and family crises before the workday starts. If you must be absent, inform your supervisor as soon as possible so that arrangements can be made to replace your services. Some offices do not have a replacement staff, so work will be reassigned to the other employees.

Accuracy

Every employee in the medical field must understand that accuracy in your work can affect the well-being of others. Attention to the smallest detail is required, whether taking a message from a patient to the doctor, calling in a prescription to the pharmacy, or recording a patient's history. It is important to try to make as few mistakes as possible, admitting the error if it is yours. Always ask for a further explanation if you do not understand.

Flexibility

Flexibility is required of all medical workers in a constantly evolving industry. Technology changes so rapidly that the medical clerical workers may find themselves suddenly dealing with a new computerized billing method or a multiline telephone system. Methods that have been learned and used for years become outdated. The medical clerical worker must adopt a positive attitude toward new challenges, whether it be a new machine or a particularly difficult patient. Today's health care environment may present opportunities for cross-training. A medical clerical worker might be asked to learn a new task not previously stated in his or her job description.

Educational Requirements

The training, job description, and definition of the medical clerical worker have continually changed to keep up with the dramatic changes in the medical environment. The specific knowledge and skills are most frequently obtained through completion of an educational program in a proprietary school, community college, or university. Recommended coursework at such institutions might include:

- Communication skills
- Computer competencies
- Medical terminology
- Office management
- Business courses focusing on billing, accounting, insurance coding, and similar subject matter
- Office machines
- Professionalism/medical ethics

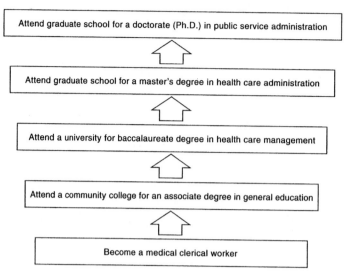

FIGURE 1.1 Career ladder.

Entry level medical clerical workers can look forward to many possibilities for career advancement. An exceptionally motivated worker might possibly aspire to a career ladder illustrated in Figure 1.1.

*C*ERTIFICATION PROGRAMS

The **American Association of Medical Assistants (AAMA)** is an organization founded with three main purposes: **accreditation, certification,** and **continuing education** for persons wishing to be medical clerical workers as well as those who want to be certified in clinical procedures.

Accreditation standards are developed by the American Medical Association (AMA) and the AAMA through the **Commission on Accreditation of Allied Health Education Programs (CAAHEP).** Any training facility that wishes to assure that medical clerical programs are of high quality strive to satisfy CAAHEP standards.

Certification is a voluntary, not mandatory, program for medical clerical workers as well as all medical assistants. An examination is given at the end of the student's training to measure professional **competency.** A passing score on this examination earns the individual the status of being certified and having the title of **certified medical assistant (CMA).** These initials follow the individual's name. In some areas of the United States, a CMA certification is mandatory to be hired as a medical clerical worker.

Recertification is mandatory for the CMA every five years, either by taking the certification examination again or attending educational programs to update skills.

Externships are considered a transition period for the medical clerical worker from the classroom to the employment site. An externship is planned and supervised by a coordinator from a medical clerical program. The facility extending the opportunity is then a partner in the education of the student. Often, a student may be hired by the externship site if the student proves to be a good worker. Additionally, the student receives a realistic view of his or her future profession before committing to this vocational path.

CONTINUING EDUCATION

Once you become a medical clerical worker, employers encourage and often pay for continuing education (CE). One of the best ways to further the medical clerical education is through membership in local, state, and national associations. Hundreds of educational programs are sponsored by local and state AAMA groups throughout the year. Home study courses are also available. Other programs may also be available through local educational institutions and health care facilities.

Continuing education not only enhances the medical clerical worker's skills and knowledge but also gives the worker an opportunity to meet with other members of the profession. Valuable practical information can be obtained by discussing common problems and solutions with people within your field.

JOB DESCRIPTION

Health care institutions and private medical offices use many different names for the medical clerical worker. Doctors' offices and clinics often hire Administrative Medical Assistants, Front Office Medical Assistants, Medical Secretaries, and Medical Receptionists. Larger health care institutions often have job titles such as Medical Office Clerk, Hospital Admitting Clerk, Medical Records Clerk, Insurance Clerk, Medical Transcriptionist, Hospital Unit Secretary, and others. Whatever the label, there are certain tasks that are often common to all of these titles. These tasks include:

- Receiving patients and families
- Information and education resource for patients
- Filing
- Typing/word processing
- Computer data entry
- Scheduling appointments
- Composing and transcribing correspondence
- Mail processing
- Insurance processing
- Maintaining patient records
- Billing
- Public relations
- Ordering and inventory
- Telephone skills
- Banking
- Light bookkeeping
- Physical maintenance and management of the office

During a normal workday, the medical clerical worker comes in contact with a wide variety of people. Besides the enormous diversity found in patient personalities, medical clerical workers also interact with nurses, doctors, pharmacists, laboratory workers, radiology staff, administrators, supervisors, housekeepers, volunteers, and many other people. The medical clerical worker must be prepared to communicate with surgeons, who may use complex technical terms, as well as patients, some of whom may speak little English. Such diversity creates many challenges, some frustrating and some rewarding.

One of the most important things that all medical professionals must remember is that their duties are very specific, known as their **scope of practice.** As set forth in ethical guidelines for various medical professions as well as job descriptions, an employee must be careful never to operate out of his or her proscribed job description. Failure to follow such guidelines can result in losing one's job or even involvement in a lawsuit.

*P*ROFESSIONAL IMAGE

A patient's first and lasting impression of a facility is often gained from interaction with a medical clerical worker. Proper grooming inspires confidence in both patients and fellow workers. A pleasant, orderly, and businesslike appearance must be maintained at all times.

Most employers have an established dress code. If uniforms are worn, they should be clean, pressed, and properly fitted. If street clothes are allowed, they should be comfortable, clean and pressed, and in good condition (no missing buttons, tears, and so on). Shoes should be comfortable, with low heels and nonskid heels and soles. Excessive jewelry is discouraged, and makeup should be applied lightly.

Proper hygiene is very important in the medical office. Such problems as bad breath, unwashed hair, dirty nails, and offensive body odor will not present a professional image and will not instill confidence in the patient or impress the employer. Many patients are either allergic to perfume or dislike heavy fragrances.

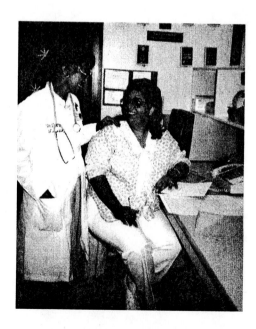

The medical clerical worker should speak in a calm voice, trying never to convey anger to the patient. Any interoffice disputes should never be played out in front of the patient. Bad moods and excessively emotional displays are considered unprofessional behaviors when dealing with patients.

*E*MPLOYMENT OPPORTUNITIES

Employment opportunities have expanded rapidly for the medical clerical worker in the past several decades. Where a physician's office once offered the only jobs for someone interested in the field, the options are now much more extensive.

Medical care has never been more expensive or competitive. Insurance companies are not willing to pay for unnecessary procedures. Many different institutions are competing for patient services. The health care institution, as well as the private medical office, must be run in a cost-effective manner.

There are a number of facilities and agencies that provide medical care. They can be very rewarding places for the medical clerical worker to gain employment. A partial list includes:

- *General acute care hospitals,* where patients are hospitalized for a short time, from a day to a few weeks. These facilities provide a wide range of services, as well as emergency medical care.
- *Specialized hospitals,* which have facilities that provide care for specific problems, such as psychiatric illnesses and orthopedic injuries, as well as chronic disease care such as tuberculosis hospitals.
- *Long-term care hospitals,* also known as convalescent hospitals, are facilities concentrating on care for elderly people who need continual nursing care. They also tend to patients who require care for an extended convalescence.
- *Clinics* are facilities in which several doctors with varied specialties combine their practices. A patient can receive immediate care for a variety of problems.
- *Physician and dental facilities* provide care to keep patients well and diagnose illness. Simple surgery may be performed in these facilities.
- *Rehabilitation centers* operate for patients who require physical therapy and other therapies for the temporary or permanent loss of limb or organ function. Some patients may stay at these facilities, and others may be treated on an outpatient basis.
- ***Health maintenance organizations (HMOs)*** stress preventive health care. They provide health services that include hospitalization, basic medical services, checkups, and so on.
- *Home health care agencies* provide care in the home for patients who need health services but do not require being in the hospital.

Additional sources of employment for the medical clerical worker might include:

- University medical schools
- Research centers
- Pharmaceutical companies
- Medical supplies and equipment companies
- Foundations

- Laboratories
- Health and accident insurance companies
- Freelance (self-employed)

You have many choices for employment as a medical clerical worker. The large institutions often have higher pay scales and better **benefits.** Opportunities for advancement may be more available. You may, however, feel lost in the pressure and fast pace of a hospital setting. You also may not enjoy working weekends and holidays, as many workers do in such institutions.

If you choose a smaller facility, such as a doctor's office, you could have more responsibility and more variety in your job. You may also enjoy the personal touch of getting to know the patient population. However, the pay may be lower with reduced or few benefits. Entry-level salaries may be minimum wage, with salary levels increasing with certification, experience, advanced training, and so on.

Many workers today have the opportunity to work on a freelance basis, contracting with doctors or health care facilities to do insurance billing, medical transcription, collections, and many other medical clerical services. The advantages here include control over your work hours. Disadvantages are lack of benefits and job security.

Full-time employed medical clerical workers can expect benefits in addition to salary. Some part-time employees may also receive partial benefits such as the following:

- *Vacation.* Often a minimum of two weeks with pay after completing a year of full-time employment; increases with tenure.
- *Paid holidays.* Paid holidays generally include New Year's Day, Memorial Day, July 4th, Labor Day, Thanksgiving, and Christmas.
- *Health insurance.* Often available in many forms; some may require an employee co-payment.
- *Disability insurance.* Plan that may cover a percentage of employee's salary if a disabling condition prevents employment.
- *Life insurance.* Usually available as a set amount such as equal to one year of salary.

Additional benefits might include profit sharing and complimentary health care.

*H*EALTH CARE ORGANIZATIONS

The medical clerical worker does not function alone in his or her work environment. The medical clerical worker is a significant member of the health care team, providing patient care. Each member of the health care team should be considered interdependent, each depending on the others for certain areas of expertise to assist in the patient's well-being.

In addition to understanding and respecting various professions in the medical environment, the medical clerical worker must strive continually to build and maintain harmonious relationships.

Health Care Facilities

Health care facilities must be well organized in order to function successfully in today's competitive health care environment. Hospitals and clinics must operate as efficiently as possible without sacrificing a caring environment for the patient.

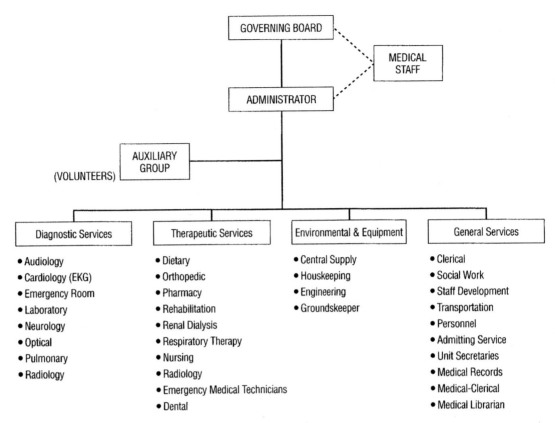

FIGURE 1.2 Hospital organization chart.

An example of a health care facility organization chart is shown in Figure 1.2. Each service has specialized departments, determined by what type of service is given. Separate facilities may have different terms for individual departments.

■ *Diagnostic services* include services that are involved with the diagnosis of illness.
■ *Therapeutic services* are involved in treating the patient.
■ *Environmental and equipment services* include equipment and environmental maintenance.
■ *General services* include support services that are required for the efficient operation of the facility.

Medical Specialties

When working in a hospital, a clinic, or in a physician's office, the medical clerical worker will come into contact with many different medical specialties. A medical specialist is a doctor who devotes herself or himself to a single branch of medical knowledge. You may find yourself working in an area that deals often with one branch of medicine, such as cardiology. Table 1.1 lists definitions of most of the present-day medical specialties and the title of the physician practicing those specialties.

Nurses

Nursing personnel are responsible for carrying out physicians' orders and giving nursing care to patients. Specialized areas of nursing include:

TABLE 1.1	*M*EDICAL SPECIALTIES	
Specialty	**Title of Practitioner**	**Description**
Allergies	Allergist	A subspecialty of internal medicine dealing with diagnosis and treatment of body reactions resulting from unusual sensitivity to foods, pollens, dust, medicines, or other substances
Anesthesiology	Anesthesiologist	Administration of various forms of anesthesia in operations or diagnosis to cause loss of feeling or sensation
Cardiovascular diseases	Cardiologist	A subspecialty of internal medicine involving the diagnosis and treatment of diseases of the heart and blood vessels
Chiropractic	Chiropractor (not physicians; licensed in their field)	Manipulative treatment of disorders originating from misalignment of spinal vertebrae
Dentistry	Dentist (not physicians; licensed in their field)	Diagnosis and treatment of diseases and disorders of the teeth and gums
Dermatology	Dermatologist	Diagnosis and treatment of diseases of the skin
Emergencies	Emergency physician	Deals with immediate-urgent care of patient in emergency rooms and emergency clinics (also called trauma medicine)
Endocrinology	Endocrinologist	Diagnosis and treatment of diseases of the hormone-secreting ductless glands
Family practice	Family practitioner	Diagnosis and treatment of disease by medical and surgical methods for all members of the family, regardless of age
Gastroenterology	Gastroenterologist	A subspecialty of internal medicine concerned with diagnosis and treatment of disorders of the digestive tract
General surgery	Surgeon	The diagnosis and treatment of disease by surgical means without limitation to special systems or body regions
Geriatrics	Gerontologist	Diagnosis and treatment of diseases, disorders, and problems of aging
Gynecology	Gynecologist	Diagnosis and treatment of diseases of the female reproductive organs
Hematology	Hematologist	Diagnosis and treatment of diseases and disorders of blood and blood-forming tissues
Infertility	Infertility specialist	Diagnosis and treatment of problems related to conceiving and maintaining pregnancy
Internal medicine	Internist	Diagnosis and nonsurgical treatment of illnesses of adults
Nephrology	Nephrologist	Diagnosis and treatment of diseases and disorders of the kidney
Neurological surgery	Neurosurgeon	Diagnosis and surgical treatment of brain, spinal cord, and nerve disorders
Neurology	Neurologist	Diagnosis and treatment of diseases of brain, spinal cord, and nerves
Obstetrics	Obstetrician	The care of women during pregnancy, childbirth, and the interval immediately following
Oncology	Oncologist	Diagnosis and treatment of cancer
Ophthalmology	Ophthalmologist	Diagnosis and treatment of diseases of the eye, including prescribing glasses
Optometry	Optometrist (not physicians; licensed in their field)	Measurement of accuracy of vision to determine if corrective lenses are needed
Orthopedics	Orthopedist	Diagnosis and treatment of disorders and diseases of the muscular and skeletal systems
Otolaryngology	Otolaryngologist	Diagnosis and treatment of diseases of the ear, nose, and throat
Pathology	Pathologist	Study and interpretation of changes in organs, tissues, cells, and alterations in body chemistry to aid in diagnosing disease and determining treatment
Pediatrics	Pediatrician	Prevention, diagnosis, and treatment of children's diseases
Physical medicine and rehabilitation	Physiatrist	Diagnosis of disease or injury in the various systems and areas of the body and rehabilitation and treatment by means of physical procedures as well as treatment and restoration of the convalescent and physically handicapped patient
Plastic surgery	Plastic surgeon	Corrective or reparative surgery to restore deformed or mutilated parts of the body
Podiatry	Podiatrist	Diagnosis and treatment of diseases and disorders of the feet
Proctology	Proctologist	Diagnosis and treatment of diseases of the rectum
Psychiatry	Psychiatrist	Diagnosis and treatment of mental disorders
Radiology	Radiologist	Use of radiant energy, including x-rays, in the diagnosis of disease
Sports medicine	S. M. specialist	Diagnosis and treatment of injuries sustained in athletic endeavors
Therapeutic radiology	Radiologist	The use of radiant energy, including x-rays, radium, and other radioactive substances in the treatment of diseases
Thoracic surgery	Thoracic surgeon	Operative treatment of the lungs, heart, or the large blood vessels within the chest cavity
Urology	Urologist	Diagnosis and treatment of diseases or disorders of the kidneys, bladder, ureters, and urethra and of the male reproductive organs

Nurse Practitioner. A nurse practitioner is a registered nurse (RN) who has taken advanced training and has acquired expert knowledge in a special branch of medical practice. A nurse practitioner often has a master's degree. This nurse is often employed by physicians in private practice, clinics, or HMOs.

Registered Nurse. A registered nurse is a professional nurse who has completed a course of study at a state-approved school of nursing and passed a national licensure examination. RNs are licensed to practice by individual states. They are often employed at hospitals, convalescent homes, clinics, and home health care agencies. Some registered nurses have a two- or three-year training program. Others have received a four-year college degree and have a Bachelor of Science degree. These nurses often are in administration and public health nursing. Other registered nurses have done postgraduate work and have master's and doctoral degrees in nursing education or other specialties.

Licensed Vocational Nurse. Also known as licensed practical nurses, these nurses are trained in basic nursing techniques and direct patient care. They practice under the direct supervision of a registered nurse. They have usually completed a one-year training program (some programs are longer). They are often employed by hospitals, convalescent hospitals, physicians in private practice, and in clinics.

Nursing Assistant. Also known as CNAs (certified nursing assistants), nurses' aides, or nursing assistants, these nurses complete a basic nursing procedures training course that may last up to a year. These nurses perform basic treatments and bedside tasks for the patient under the supervision of a registered nurse.

Patient treatment areas of a hospital are divided into nursing units. Table 1.2 illustrates several common nursing units.

Specialized Units

A large hospital may include even more divisions than those already listed. Some specialized units, where a medical clerical worker might be employed, may care for a patient and then transfer the patient to one of the nursing units listed in Table 1.2. Some specialized units are listed in Table 1.3. As a medical clerical worker, it is important that you be aware of all the different ways that service is provided in a medical facility.

TABLE 1.2   Nursing Units

Unit	Function
Alcoholic Rehabilitation	Care of patients receiving treatment for alcoholic abuse
Gynecology (GYN)	Care of women with diseases of the female reproductive system
Intensive Care Unit (ICU)	Care of patients who are critically ill and in need of constant supervision and specialized nursing care. May be further divided into:
	■ *Coronary care unit (CCU):* Care of critically ill patients with heart and related diseases
	■ *Medical intensive care unit (MICU):* Care of critically ill medical patients
	■ *Pediatric intensive care unit (PICU):* Care of critically ill children
	■ *Surgical intensive care unit (SICU):* Care of critically ill surgical patients
Medical (Med)	Care of patients with medical (nonsurgical) conditions
Neurology (Neuro)	Care of patients with diseases of the nervous system
Nursery	Care of newborns
Obstetrics (OB)	Care of women who are having, or have had, babies
Orthopedics (Ortho)	Care of patients with injury or disease of the musculoskeletal system
Pediatrics (Peds)	Care of children
Psychiatry (Psych)	Care of patients with mental and emotional disorders
Rehabilitation (Rehab)	Care of patients receiving treatment for physical handicaps
Surgical (Surg)	Care of patients who will undergo or have undergone surgery
Urology	Care of patients with diseases of the urinary system and males with diseases of the reproductive tract

TABLE 1.3 SPECIALIZED UNITS	
Unit	**Function**
Emergency Room (ER)	Care of patients needing emergency treatment for diseases or injuries that have occurred outside the hospital
Labor and Delivery (L&D)	Care of women who are in labor or are delivering babies
Operating Room (OR)	Care of patients undergoing surgery
Outpatient Department (OPD)	Care of patients seen in a clinic setting for disorders not requiring hospitalization
Outpatient Surgery	Care of patients having minor surgery that does not require overnight hospitalization
Recovery Room (RR)	Care of patients immediately after surgery until condition stabilizes and can return to nursing unit
Renal Dialysis	Care of patients with kidney disorders who require artificial devices to maintain kidney function and sustain life
Trauma Unit	Immediate surgical care of injured patients by special team of physicians and nurses

PROFESSIONAL ASSOCIATIONS

The medical world is constantly changing, and to keep up with the pace of research and technology the medical clerical worker needs to read professional magazines and take advantage of educational seminars. Many associations have been formed around the country to help the medical clerical worker keep up with the changing trends and opportunities in the field. Belonging to such an association can put you in touch with other members of your profession through newsletters, seminars, workshops, and conventions. Membership also allows you to have a voice in legislated stands and regulations that affect your job.

American Association of Medical Assistants
20 North Wacker Drive, Suite 1575
Chicago, IL 60606-2963
(312) 899-1500
http://www.aama.ntl.org

Registered Medical Assistant of AMI
710 Higgins Road
Park Ridge, IL 60068
(847) 823-5169
http://www.amtl.com

International Association of Administrative Professionals
P.O. Box 20404
Kansas City, MO 64195-0404
(816) 891-6600
http://www.iaap-hq.org

American Association for Medical Transcription
100 Sycamore Avenue
Modesto, CA 95354
(209) 527-9620
http://www.aamt.org

National Association of Health Unit Coordinators
1947 Madron Road
Rockford, IL 61107
(888) 22NAHUC
http://www.nahuc.org

SUMMARY

The medical clerical field is rapidly changing, filled with increasing responsibilities and opportunities for the medical clerical worker.

Specialization may appeal to you in this field, or perhaps you are attracted to a position where you have a wide variety of duties and responsibilities. After completing a training program, the medical clerical profession has much to offer someone who is determined to be an excellent employee. Certification programs assure high standards of excellence for your field, as well as continuing education opportunities.

LEARNING ACTIVITIES

1. Interview a medical clerical worker at a local health care facility, asking such questions as:
   (a) What do you like most about your job?
   (b) What do you like least about your job?
   (c) How much training have you had for your position?
   (d) Do you have any opportunities for advancement?
   (e) What benefits do you receive?

2. Call three human resource departments at local health care facilities and ask questions like:
   (a) Are there often medical clerical openings at your facility?
   (b) What type of training do you prefer for such positions?
   (c) What salary range is offered to medical clerical workers?

3. List six personality traits you possess that might be valuable to an employer. Do they match the list in this chapter describing the effective medical clerical worker?

4. Identify jobs using the classified section of the local paper.

5. Contact a professional medical assistant organization to see what is offered to the medical clerical worker.

6. List seven desirable personality traits for a medical clerical worker.

7. Name four titles that can pertain to a medical clerical worker.

8. Explain why a neat personal appearance and good hygiene are important for the medical clerical worker.

9. In most cases, what is the minimum educational requirement for the medical clerical worker?

10. What is the most important part of the medical clerical worker's job?

11. List six duties that a medical clerical worker might perform.

12. Name seven potential employers for a medical clerical worker.

13. Draw a typical organization chart of a hospital.

14. What is the difference among diagnostic, therapeutic, environmental and equipment, and general services?

15. Name a national professional association of medical assistants.

16. Name three specialized areas of nursing.

17. Explain the term *scope of practice*.

CHAPTER 2

Medical Ethics and Legal Responsibilities

VOCABULARY

Advanced directive (AD)	A legal document in which an individual gives written instructions expressing his or her wishes regarding health care in the event that person can no longer make those decisions.
Arbitration	Method of resolving malpractice disputes; both parties waive the right to a court trial, with the dispute presented before an impartial panel.
Assault	An unlawful threat or attempt to do bodily injury to another.
Battery	Unlawful touching of another person without his or her consent with or without resultant injury.
Bioethics	Branch of ethical study resulting from technological advances and medical research; centers on moral issues and problems that arise in medical practice.
Civil law	A statute that enforces private rights and liabilities, as differentiated from criminal law.
Confidentiality	Information the health care team obtains from and about the patient that is considered to be privileged; such information cannot be disclosed to a third party without patient consent.
Contract	An agreement between two or more parties for the doing or not doing of some definite thing.
Defamation	Attack on a person's reputation—called *libel* when written and *slander* when spoken.
Durable power of attorney	A legal document that allows an individual named in the document to act on behalf of another. A durable power of attorney for health care (DPAHC) allows the patient to express his or her health care decisions and the amount of authority he or she wishes the agent to assume.
Duty of care	The obligation under law for a health care worker to perform services for a patient that meet the common standards of practice expected for a comparable worker; the *patient* is protected by recognition of the health worker's responsibility for duty of care.
Emancipated minor	A person who is underage but has established through legal action that he or she is living apart from the parents and is financially responsible and able to consent to treatment.
Ethics	A code of conduct that represents ideal behavior.
Euthanasia	An act by an individual to assist a person to die when that person is suffering from an incurable condition.
Felony	A major crime for which greater punishment is imposed than for a misdemeanor.
Good Samaritan laws	Laws (differing in various states) that protect a health care worker from a malpractice suit when coming to the aid of a person in an emergency situation.

Guardian	A court-appointed person whose duty it is to make decisions for and protect the interests of another person who cannot make his or her own decisions.
Incompetent	Wanting in physical or mental fitness.
Informed consent	The patient is informed of the risks and alternatives to a medical procedure; the patient signs a consent form, acknowledging the assumed risks.
Invasion of privacy	To make public knowledge any private or personal information without the individual's consent.
Libel	Written defamation.
Licensure	Authorization by the state to practice one's profession or vocation; involves control of educational standards, licensing examinations, means for revocation of license, and prohibitions for the unlicensed.
Living will	A written agreement between the patient and physician to withhold heroic measures if the patient's condition is such that it cannot be reversed.
Malpractice	Literally "bad practice" by a professional; care below the expected community standard, which has led to injury.
Negligence	Failure to do something a reasonable person *would do* under ordinary circumstances, or doing something a reasonable person *would not do* under ordinary circumstances; negligence can work in two ways, by action or by omission.
Patient's bill of rights	A document produced by the American Hospital Association stating what a patient has the right to expect during medical treatment.
Plaintiff	One who institutes a lawsuit.
Reasonable care	The health care worker is protected by law if it can be determined that he or she acted reasonably as compared with fellow workers.
Slander	Oral or spoken defamation.
Statute of limitations	The time established for filing lawsuits.

OBJECTIVES

After completing this chapter, the student is responsible for performing the following objectives:

- Explain the difference between medical ethics and medical law.
- Discuss the American Association of Medical Assistants Code of Ethics.
- List four examples of ethical behavior for the medical clerical worker. Discuss the Patient's Bill of Rights.
- Identify the need for licensing of medical personnel.
- Define *duty of care, reasonable care, negligence,* and *medical malpractice.*
- Discuss the Rule of Personal Liability.
- Identify the Good Samaritan laws.
- Demonstrate your knowledge of patient consent forms.
- List several points to remember about maintaining a patient's record.

*I*NTRODUCTION

The laws and ethical codes of conduct for the medical profession must be understood by the medical clerical worker. These laws and ethical codes protect all members of the medical profession, as well as the patient.

Medical ethics have been important in the study of medicine since 400 B.C., with the advent of the Hippocratic Oath, a document developing standards of medical conduct and ethics. Today, the many professional associations have codes of ethics to govern their health care workers. Health unit coordinators, medical records technicians, medical transcriptionists, and other medical clerical workers all have ethical codes that provide guidelines for professional behavior.

During the past twenty years, patients have brought lawsuits against physicians in dramatically increasing numbers. The practice of medicine exists within a framework of laws. Such laws governing medical practices vary from state to state, so it is important to know your state's laws governing the medical clerical worker, as well as federal and local statutes.

*E*THICS VS. LAW

Medical **ethics** are concerned with whether the medical worker's actions are right or wrong, whereas *medical law* focuses on whether the medical worker acted legally or illegally. *Ethical behavior* refers to behavior that represents ideal conduct for a certain group. Each group of health care professionals requiring a license has drafted and adopted a specific code of ethics. These ethics are based on moral principles and practices. If accused of unethical behavior by a medical worker's professional association, you can be issued a warning or expelled from the association. Medical assistants follow a code of ethics adopted by the American Association of Medical Assistants (see next section).

The term **bioethics** refers to the branch of ethics dealing with issues arising in the practice of medical research. Transplanting organs, artificially maintaining life, and genetic engineering are examples of bioethical issues. This is a very complex field drawing on such disciplines as science, medicine, philosophy, sociology, and theology.

Medical law governs the legal conduct of the members of the medical profession. There are federal, state, and local laws to be followed, and violation of such laws subjects the offender to civil or criminal prosecution. **Civil law** is law that enforces private rights and liabilities, not criminal behavior. Professional licenses can be taken away, fines can be levied, and prison sentences can be given. Often, the line between what is unethical and what is illegal can be unclear. If you, as a medical clerical worker, decided you were going to be rude to an AIDS patient, that is unethical behavior. But if you decided to inform the AIDS patient's neighbor of his or her disease, that is illegal behavior. In addition, you can be sued by a patient for **defamation,** which is considered an attack on a person's reputation. This is called libel when written and slander when spoken.

Another example of the difference between unethical and illegal behavior concerns the viewing of a friend's chart in a part of the hospital where you do not work. If you read it out of curiosity, that is unethical. If you talk about it, that is illegal. If an action is illegal, it is always unethical. However, it can be unethical without being illegal. Ethics represent the highest standards of behavior.

TABLE 2.1	AMERICAN ASSOCIATION OF MEDICAL ASSISTANTS CODE OF ETHICS

Preamble

The Code of Ethics of AAMA shall set forth principles of ethical and moral conduct as they relate to the medical profession and the particular practice of medical assisting.

Members of the AAMA dedicated to the conscientious pursuit of their profession, and thus desiring to merit the high regard of the entire medical profession and the respect of the general public which they serve, do pledge themselves to strive always to:

a. Render service with full respect for the dignity of humanity;
b. Respect confidential information obtained through employment unless legally authorized or required by responsible performance of duty to divulge such information;
c. Uphold the honor and high principles of the profession and accept its disciplines;
d. Seek to continually improve the knowledge and skills of medical assistants for the benefit of patients and professional colleagues;
e. Participate in additional service activities aimed toward improving the health and well-being of the community.

Copyright by the American Association of Medical Assistants, Inc. Reprinted by permission.

AAMA CODE OF ETHICS

The American Association of Medical Assistants has adopted a code of ethics that provides guidelines for professional behavior (see Table 2.1).

The creed of the American Association of Medical Assistants reads as follows:

AAMA CREED*

I believe in the principles and purposes of the profession of medical assisting.
I endeavor to be more effective.
I aspire to render greater service.
I protect the confidence entrusted to me.
I am dedicated to the care and well-being of all people.
I am loyal to my employer.
I am true to the ethics of my profession.
I am strengthened by compassion, courage and faith.

ETHICAL BEHAVIOR

As a medical clerical worker, you must display ethical behavior at all times. To maintain a high level of ethical conduct as a medical clerical worker, you would:

- Respect the rights of all patients to have opinions, lifestyles, and beliefs that are different from yours. Never degrade or malign a patient.
- Always remember that everything seen, heard, or read about a patient is *confidential* and does not leave the job site. Never discuss a patient's condition within hearing distance of others. Violating a patient's personal information is an **invasion of privacy.**
- Be conscientious in doing your work, doing the best you can at all times. Pay special attention to accuracy in all tasks.

*Copyright by the American Association of Medical Assistants, Inc. Revised 1996. Used with permission.

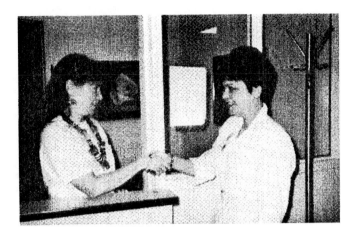

- Be ready to be of service to patients and fellow workers at any time of the workday.
- Let the patient know that it is a privilege for you to assist him or her.
- Follow closely the specific rules of ethical conduct prescribed by your employer.
- Maintain courteous relations with everyone in your facility, as well as those who visit or telephone.
- Never leave a patient's record exposed on your desk.
- Never touch a patient without his or her consent. Unlawful touching can be defined as **battery**. **Assault** is a threat to do bodily harm or actually injuring someone.
- **Libel** is a punishable offense where someone writes something that defames (injure one's reputation). **Slander** is when someone speaks something that harms a person's reputation. The medical clerical must guard against both offenses.

$\mathcal{T}$HE PATIENT'S BILL OF RIGHTS

The American Hospital Association produced a document called a **Patient's Bill of Rights** (Table 2.2). The intent of the bill of rights is to make both medical personnel and patients aware of what the patient has a right to expect.

$\mathcal{M}$EDICAL LICENSES

The medical profession is legally regulated in the United States by the issuing of licenses. All fifty states require the licensing of hospitals, and many groups of health care workers are also licensed.

Licenses can be revoked legally when a medical professional is found to have violated various statutes involved in the licensing process. Grounds for losing a medical license include serious crimes such as murder, rape, and arson; "moral turpitude" crimes, such as income tax crimes, minor sexual offenses, and false statements while applying for a license; incapacity due to insanity; or excessive use of intoxicants or drug addiction.

Although the medical clerical worker is not licensed, you might be asked by your employer to keep a record of all continuing education units the physician must earn as a part of physician license renewal.

TABLE 2.2	*P*ATIENT'S BILL OF RIGHTS

1. The patient has the right to considerate and respectful care.
2. Patients have the right to obtain from their physician complete current information concerning their diagnosis, treatment, and prognosis in terms they can be reasonably expected to understand.
3. An informed consent should include knowledge of the proposed procedure, along with its risks and probable duration of incapacitation. In addition, the patient has a right to information regarding medically significant alternatives.
4. The patient has the right to refuse treatment to the extent permitted by law, and to be informed of the medical consequences of his action.
5. Case discussion, consultation, examination, and treatment should be conducted discretely. Those not directly involved must have the patient's permission to be present.
6. The patient has the right to expect that all communication and records pertaining to his care should be treated as confidential.
7. The patient has the right to expect the hospital to make a reasonable response to his request for services. The hospital must provide evaluation, service, and referral as indicated by the urgency of the case.
8. The patient has the right to obtain information as to any relationship of his hospital to other health care and educational institutions, insofar as his care is concerned. The patient has the right to obtain information as to the existence of any professional relationships among individuals, by name, who are treating him.
9. The patient has the right to be advised if the hospital proposes to engage in or perform human experimentation affecting his care or treatment. The patient has the right to refuse to participate in such research projects.
10. The patient has the right to expect reasonable continuity of care.
11. The patient has the right to examine and receive an explanation of his bill regardless of the source of payment.
12. The patient has the right to know what hospital rules and regulations apply to his conduct as a patient.

*P*ATIENT AND MEDICAL WORKER LEGAL PROTECTION

When a patient and a physician enter into a relationship, this is considered a **contract.** The practice of medicine is carried out within a framework of laws. The medical clerical worker *must* be aware of basic legal ground rules of the profession. Laws pertain both to the protection of patients, employees, and health care institutions. It is mandatory to have the knowledge to avoid legal trouble as a result of something you do during your workday.

    Licensure and certification help to ensure that certain health care workers have the knowledge to practice their vocations. Additionally, there are many terms that are relevant to the medical clerical worker that are legal protections in the health care environment.

Duty of Care

The patient absolutely is entitled to safe care. **Duty of care** is defined as treating the patient by meeting the common or average standards of practice expected in the community under similar circumstances.

Reasonable Care

Reasonable care protects the health care worker by law if it can be proven that he or she acted reasonably as compared to fellow workers. If the health care worker is judged to fail to meet such a standard with harm coming to the patient, negligence may be proven.

Negligence

Negligence refers to the failure to give reasonable care or the giving of unreasonable care. The patient is harmed because of the health care worker's doing something wrong or failing to do something that he or she should have done under the circumstances.

Statute of Limitations

When a patient feels that something has been done to him or her that is possibly grounds for a lawsuit, there is a **statute of limitations** concerning the amount of time that can go by before any action is taken. After a proscribed time period, a lawsuit may not be filed.

Guardian

Occasionally, a patient may not be able to make his or her own decisions due to mental and/or physical incapacity. In this case, a court-appointed **guardian** may make decisions for and protect the interests of another person. A guardian may be assigned to a patient who has been declared **incompetent** by a court.

Emancipated Minor

Parents are required to sign consent forms for children under 18 years of age in most states. However, there is a legal term known as the **emancipated minor.** This is a person under 18 years of age who has established through legal action that he or she does not live with parents, is financially and legally responsible for himself or herself, and is able to consent to treatment.

Living Will

A **living will** is written agreement between the patient and physician to withhold heroic measures if the patient's condition is such that it cannot be reversed. Medical offices will often have such agreements to give to patients at their request.

Advanced Directive (AD)

The **advanced directive** is a legal document in which an individual gives written instructions expressing his or her wishes regarding health care in the event that person can no longer make those decisions.

Durable Power of Attorney

The **durable power of attorney** is yet another legal document that allows a person named in the document to act on behalf of another. The *Durable Power of Attorney for Health Care (DPAHC)* allows the patient to express his or her health care decisions and the amount of authority he or she wishes the agent to assume. This power is often granted to a family of an elderly relative.

Good Samaritan Laws

Good Samaritan laws are designed to protect people from legal action when giving emergency medical aid, without charging, within the areas of their training. These laws, while not always clearly written, are designed to encourage health care professionals to render first aid in an emergency situation without fear of being sued for negligence.

$\mathcal{M}$EDICAL MALPRACTICE

Medical **malpractice,** also called *medical professional liability,* is a term that appears in newspapers throughout the country. Everyone has heard of huge financial settlements that certain patients have been awarded due to a mistake made by one of the members of the medical community, usually a physician. The higher the educational level and requirements of health workers, the greater the likelihood that they may be held responsible for their actions.

Malpractice is defined as any misconduct or lack of skill that results in patient injury. A patient who thinks that a medical worker has been negligent in diagnosing and treating an illness or accident may file a medical malpractice claim. Most claims are made against physicians, but any medical employee, including nurses, laboratory technologists, and medical clerical workers, can be named in a malpractice suit. Most medical malpractice insurance policies allow physicians to cover their employees as well, but medical office employees may wish to purchase their own policies, which are usually very inexpensive.

Sometimes medical malpractice suits filed by patients will not go to court, but will be settled by **arbitration.** Often both parties (physician and patient) have agreed before (and sometimes after) treatment that both will waive the right to a court trial in case of a dispute. Arbitration can help resolve any controversy before an impartial panel (*grievance committee*). This process allows for less expense, greater privacy for both parties, and it may be fairer.

The medical clerical worker may be asked to present the arbitration agreement to patients for signature. If a lawsuit is in fact instituted, the medical clerical worker can be asked to contact the physician's insurance carrier promptly and to include an arbitration agreement signed by the patient. Physicians are responsible for the medical clerical workers in doctors' offices. Hospitals are responsible for medical clerical workers in hospital settings.

In a hospital setting, a patient may sue the entire hospital, including more than one staff member. This process can become more complicated, and the medical clerical worker may be expected to be a part of the process.

Physicians are liable for the actions of their employees when the employees are on duty. For example, a medical clerical worker accepts throat culture specimens from two patients and mislabels the specimens. The patient who has a serious streptococcus infection of the throat is told that the culture is normal, and the normal patient is put on antibiotics. Subsequently, the strep throat patient without treatment develops heart valve damage from the strep infection. A physician could be sued for the negligence of an employee in this case.

Additional terms that apply to legal situations that the medical clerical worker might come across follow.

Plaintiff

A **plaintiff** is a person who institutes a lawsuit. In the case of a medical employee being sued, the plaintiff is the patient who feels he or she has grounds for a suit. The employee would be the defendant.

Euthanasia

If an individual, including a medical professional, a family member, or friend, assists a person to die when that person is suffering from an incurable condition, the person may be prosecuted for assisting in **euthanasia.**

Felony

A **felony** is a major crime for which greater punishment is imposed than for a misdemeanor. Many situations listed in this chapter are considered felonies by the courts.

You can also be held jointly responsible if you work for a doctor who is involved in an illegal act and you are aware of the crime. Physicians must also report crimes that they learn about when practicing medicine, such as a shooting, child abuse, or stabbings. Medical clerical workers can be held jointly responsible if such reports are not made. Patient confidentiality, protecting the patient's right to complete privacy of his/her records, does not apply in certain situations. Births, deaths, communicable diseases, and crimes are examples of occurrences that a physician is required to report. Medical clerical workers can be held jointly responsible if such reports are not made.

$\mathcal{S}$EXUAL HARASSMENT

Sexual harassment can occur in any workplace. According to the U.S. Equal Employment Opportunity Commission (EEOC), sexual harassment is a form of sex discrimination. Employers should have a process in place so that they can take immediate steps when they receive such a complaint.

Should you become a victim of unwelcome sexual advances or other forms of behavior of an offensive sexual behavior, you should report the behavior to a supervisor immediately. During your training and in your training manual for the workplace, definitions of sexual harassment should be clearly set forth, along with measures to stop the offensive behavior. You may also not realize that something you say in an offhanded way might also be considered such behavior.

Real-Life Scenario

Rebecca was hired as a medical clerical worker recently at the office of Dr. Jones. She is absolutely delighted to get this job. The salary and hours are perfect for Rebecca and her family, and the office is located a few blocks from her apartment so that she can walk to work. Additionally, Dr. Jones and his staff seem very pleasant and easy to work with.

About two weeks after Rebecca finished training, Dr. Jones complimented her on her sweater, commenting that it was very flattering to her figure. Rebecca blushed, but took the compliment well. The next week, Dr. Jones patted Rebecca lightly on the rear end (or was it just her lower back?) after Rebecca had helped Dr. Jones with a problem. A few weeks later, Dr. Jones asked Rebecca when they found themselves alone in the office if she was happy with her marriage. He also inquired if she had a good life. After these three incidents, Rebecca is feeling very uncomfortable in Dr. Jones's presence and is not sure what to do. She loves her job!

1. Should Rebecca report these incidents to her supervisor, the Office Manager?
2. Should Rebecca just stay away from Dr. Jones whenever possible?
3. Should Rebecca tell Dr. Jones how she feels and try to work it out with him?
4. Is Rebecca being sexually harassed?

CONFIDENTIALITY

In the age of computerization where privacy is increasingly threatened, the issue of **confidentiality** has never been more important. Often, information disclosed in the diagnosis or treatment of a case could be destructive to the patient's reputation. Mental illness, drug and alcohol addiction, sexually transmitted diseases, and other types of problems could be misunderstood and unfairly judged by people ignorant of such problems. AIDS patients have lost employment opportunities, been denied access to insurance, and even lost their places of residence because of diagnosis information becoming public. Although laws are now in place to protect AIDS sufferers from such unfairness, problems still occur.

Medical clerical workers are bound ethically and legally as employees of physicians to protect the privacy and confidentiality of patient-physician interactions. Physicians can share information about patient confidences *only* if required by law to share information. Rarely a physician may feel that certain information must be divulged to protect society or keep the patient from serious harm. Breaches in confidentiality can result in a lawsuit against the physician and his or her employees, or against a hospital.

In a hospital setting, the medical clerical worker can be exposed to a wide range of confidential information about many patients. Discretion is absolutely mandatory.

PATIENT CONSENT

When a physician makes a diagnosis and recommends a specific treatment, the patient has the responsibility to decide whether to accept the diagnosis and method of treatment. The physician must inform the patient, in words that the patient can understand, of the risks and alternatives to any suggested procedure. The patient must decide whether to accept all the explained risks. A consent form (Figure 2.1) is then signed, with the patient accepting the risk of the procedure. This is called **informed consent.** The medical clerical worker may be expected to prepare a consent form for any type of surgery, whether in-office or at the hospital. Consents are also required before an experimental procedure or other unusual procedure is performed, or before experimental drugs are taken.

If the patient has difficulty with the English language, the consent form must be translated for the patient or prepared in the patient's native language. A patient can sue if the process of informed consent has not been performed properly. Additional details concerning consent forms include:

- The patient must be able to understand the consent form fully so that he or she realizes what is being signed. Mentally handicapped patients should be given explanations that can be understood completely, with as few confusing terms as possible.
- The patient must be of sound mind and not forced to sign the consent form. A patient should not be allowed to sign when under the influence of alcohol or drugs.
- All signatures must be in ink. Full legal names must be used. All signatures must be witnessed and dated.
- Any adult over 18 years of age may sign his or her own consent unless the patient is incompetent and has a guardian, or there is an emergency, when two physicians must sign.
- Married minors may sign their own consent for treatment.

**AUTHORIZATION FOR AND CONSENT TO SURGERY OR
SPECIAL DIAGNOSTIC OR THERAPEUTIC PROCEDURES**

To _____
Name of Patient

Your admitting physician is_____ , M.D.

Your surgeon is_____ , M.D.

1. The hospital maintains personnel and facilities to assist your physicians and surgeons in their performance of various surgical operations and other special diagnostic and therapeutic procedures. These surgical operations and special diagnostic or therapeutic procedures all may involve calculated risks of complications, injury or even death, from both known and unknown causes and no warranty or guarantee has been made as to result or cure. Except in a case of emergency or exceptional circumstances, these operations and procedures are therefore not performed upon patients unless and until the patient has had an opportunity to discuss them with his physician. Each patient has the right to consent or refuse any proposed operation or special procedure (based upon the description or explanation received).

2. Your physician and surgeons have determined that the operations or special procedures listed below may be beneficial in the diagnosis or treatment of your condition. Upon your authorization and consent, such operations or special procedures will be performed for you by your physician and surgeons and/or by other physicians and surgeons selected by them. The persons in attendance for the purpose of administering anesthesia or performing other specialized professional services, such as radiology, pathology and the like, are not the agents, servants or employees of the hospital or your physician or surgeon, but are independent contractors performing specialized services on your behalf and, as such, are your agents, servants or employees. Any tissue or member severed in any operation will be disposed of in the discretion of the pathologist, except _____

3. Your signature below the operations or special procedures listed below constitutes your acknowledgment (i) that you have read and agreed to the foregoing (ii) that the operations or special procedures have been adequately explained to you by your attending physicians or surgeons and that you have all of the information that you desire, and (iii) that you authorize and consent to the performance of the operations or special procedures.

Operation or Procedure

_____
_____
_____
_____

SIGNATURE _____ DATE _____ TIME _____
Patient

SIGNATURE _____ DATE _____ TIME _____
Witness

(If patient is a minor or unable to sign, complete the following):

Patient is a minor, or is unable to sign, because _____

_____   _____
Father   Guardian

_____   _____
Mother   Other Person and Relationship

FIGURE 2.1 Consent form.

- Unmarried minors must have a consent signed by one parent or legal guardian. Consent of both parents is suggested. A stepparent may not sign a consent form.
- Emancipated minors may sign their own consent forms. These are people under 18 who have been declared by a court of law to be legally responsible for themselves.
- Any break in the skin may be considered an operation. A consent form must be signed to avoid liability for battery.
- Telephone consents are valid in an emergency situation, provided that the telephoned consent is witnessed by two people. Written confirmation must follow immediately.
- Consents are valid for a reasonable time after signing, as long as there are no changes in the anticipated procedure.

> JM
> 9/5/04
>
> 9/4/04 1400 Has called the office repeatedly seeking Dr. Grover's advice concerning
> ~~asmatic~~ *asthmatic* condition. Refuses to make an appointment to see Dr. Grover.

FIGURE 2.2 Properly corrected document.

𝒫ATIENT RECORDS

The patient's chart (medical record) is a legal document and is the property of the physician for the outpatient, and the property of the hospital when a patient enters the hospital. It is crucial that the records be as accurate, complete, up to date, and neat as possible to protect medical personnel from litigation, as well as to provide evidence of truth if there is a court case.

Always use permanent ink to eliminate the possibility of alterations, and accurately document every instance of failure to keep an appointment or follow the physician's advice. Any part of a patient's medical record is confidential unless a release-of-information form has been signed by the patient. Confidentiality does not apply in the case of crime, when an insurance carrier wishes information about an industrial injury, or when a patient has certain communicable diseases.

The proper method of making corrections in a record is to line out the original entry so that it can be read (Figure 2.2). Then the correction is made, initialed, and dated. *No erasures* are acceptable, as the record with erasures will automatically be rejected as legal evidence.

𝒮UMMARY

Everyone is aware of how often lawsuits are filed in this country. As a medical clerical worker, you must be aware of medical ethics and legal responsibilities of your position. One of the most important concepts to be learned from this chapter is the importance as well of confidentiality, protecting and respecting the privacy of each patient. Failure to do so can result in dismissal and even legal action. The medical clerical worker must strive continually to act on behalf of the patient's best interest by acting in a responsible, ethical, and legal manner.

𝓛EARNING ACTIVITIES

1. Contact a local health facility and report on safeguards taken to ensure that HIV positive patients' rights to privacy are not violated.

2. Divide into small groups and choose a situation that a medical clerical worker can encounter in a health care facility where a breach of ethics or medical law might occur. Report your discussion to the class, perhaps using role playing to illustrate your situation. Examples:

   ■ You hear a fellow worker telling a patient that he or she is probably an alcoholic and should get treatment.

- You overhear another medical clerical worker on the phone telling her best friend that a patient they both know just had an abortion.
- You see a co-worker put prescription medicine into his pocket. The medicine is not his.
- You hear a fellow worker laughing with a patient about the doctor's weight problem.
- You overhear a fellow worker suggest a prescription medication to a patient.

3. Find in a newspaper or magazine an example of unethical or illegal conduct by a health care worker. Report to the class.

4. Contact a guest speaker for your class: for example, an attorney dealing with medical ethics or a member of a licensing board that reviews malpractice complaints.

5. Match each legal term with the correct definition.

___ **(a)** reasonable care	**(1)** Unlawful touching of a patient
___ **(b)** negligence	**(2)** Moral standards and principles
___ **(c)** ethics	**(3)** Acting appropriately in giving aid to a patient
___ **(d)** battery	**(4)** Failing to give a patient appropriate care
___ **(e)** duty of care	**(5)** Health worker must provide safe patient care
___ **(f)** defamation	**(6)** Attacking a person's reputation
___ **(g)** slander	**(7)** Oral or spoken defamation

6. Name the document discussed in this chapter drawn up by the American Hospital Association.

7. What does AAMA stand for?

8. Who is the person protected by "reasonable care"?

9. State the rule of personal liability.

10. Who is protected by the Good Samaritan Laws?

11. Define *negligence* and *medical malpractice.*

12. List four situations where a patient consent form would be necessary.

13. Indicate whether each statement is true or false.
    - ___ **(a)** The patient record is not a legal document.
    - ___ **(b)** Patient confidentiality does not apply if you do not agree with the patient's moral values.
    - ___ **(c)** You are required to report any crimes you learn about while on duty as a medical clerical worker.
    - ___ **(d)** Consents can be signed in pencil or pen.
    - ___ **(e)** Married minors have to have their consent forms signed by one parent.
    - ___ **(f)** One adult can never make medical decisions for another adult.

14. Multiple choice (select the correct answer).
    - **(a)** Reasonable care protects the:
      - **(1)** Doctor.
      - **(2)** Patient.
      - **(3)** Health care worker.
      - **(4)** Supervisor.

(b) The association formed to represent medical assistants is abbreviated:
   (1) AMA.
   (2) ADA.
   (3) AAMA.
   (4) AMAA.

(c) If a health worker were to ask a doctor for an illegal prescription, this would be considered:
   (1) Unethical.
   (2) Illegal.
   (3) Battery.
   (4) Negligence.

(d) If you took some medication meant for a patient, this would be considered:
   (1) Unethical.
   (2) Illegal.
   (3) Malpractice.
   (4) Both 1 and 2.

(e) A patient consent form is not valid when:
   (1) The patient is intoxicated.
   (2) The patient is 16 and unmarried.
   (3) The patient is declared insane.
   (4) All of the above.

(f) Arbitration involves:
   (1) The Good Samaritan Act.
   (2) Ethics and the medical clerical worker.
   (3) Settling a dispute between patient and doctor or hospital outside the courts.
   (4) Informed consent.

(g) Sexual harassment:
   (1) Should be reported immediately to a supervisor.
   (2) Does not usually occur in health care institutions.
   (3) Is not a punishable offence.
   (4) All of the above.

Medical Terminology

Abbreviation   A shortened form of a word or phrase used to represent the complete word or phrase.

Acronym   A word or abbreviation formed by combining the first letter of several words, such as AIDS for *acquired immunodeficiency syndrome* or CBC for *complete blood count*.

Combining form   Created by joining the other word elements and the combining vowel together.

Combining vowel   Usually an "o" is added for ease of pronunciation.

Prefix   A word element, combined with a root, changing or adding to the root word's meaning. A prefix is always placed in the beginning of the word.

Root   A body or main part of the word, referring to the primary meaning of the word as a whole.

Suffix   A word element used to change or add to the meaning of a root word, always placed at the end of the root.

Word elements   Five word elements make up the basis of medical terminology: prefix, suffix, root, combining vowel, and combining form.

After completing this chapter, the student is responsible for performing the following objectives:

- Correctly spell, define, and pronounce the medical terms in this chapter.
- Understand the following five word elements: prefix, root, suffix, combining vowel, and combining form.
- Recognize the variations in medical terminology construction.
- Be familiar with certain medical abbreviations.

INTRODUCTION

The health care industry has a professional language of its own. To be an effective employee and communicator, it is crucial that the medical clerical worker fully understand this language. Correct spelling, definition, and pronunciation of words are vitally important in any medical environment. Patients, fellow workers, and employers will depend on you to understand and use medical terminology competently. Time, thought, and practice will be required to become proficient in the language of the medical world.

*W*ORD ELEMENTS

Medical terms are formed by putting word elements together. **Word elements** include **prefixes, suffixes, roots, combining vowels,** and **combining forms.** The following are examples of word elements combined to create medical terms:

prefix   root   suffix

poly (many) + *arthr* (joint) + *itis* (inflammation)

Definition: *Polyarthritis,* inflammation of many joints

prefix   root   combining vowel   suffix

electro (electric) + *cardi* (heart)   +   *o*   +   *gram* (record)

Definition: *Electrocardiogram,* a record of the electrical activity of the heart
Electrocardiogram is an example of a combining form.

Word elements of medical terms are very much like word elements of familiar English words in our language. Many medical terms are derived from foreign languages, mostly Latin and Greek. You will find it necessary to learn common word elements in medical terminology before putting them together to make new words.

Keep in mind also that medical terms, as with many common English words, do not necessarily contain all five word elements: the *prefix, root, suffix, combining vowel,* and *combining form.* A medical term can contain a prefix, root, and suffix, or a prefix and root only:

prefix   root   suffix

peri (around) + *cardi* (heart) + *al* (pertaining to)

Definition: *Pericardial,* around the heart

prefix   root

pyro (fever) + *genic* (producing)

Definition: *Pyrogenic,* fever producing

A medical term can include a root, combining vowel, and suffix, or a root and suffix only:

root   combining vowel   suffix

path (disease) + *o* + *logy* (study of)

Definition: *Pathology,* the study of disease

root   suffix

mast (breast) + *ectomy* (surgical removal)

Definition: *Mastectomy,* surgical removal of the breast

A medical term can also include a prefix and suffix alone:

prefix   suffix

poly (much) + *uria* (urine)

Definition: *Polyuria,* excessive urination

prefix   suffix

ex (out) + *cise* (cut)

Definition: *Excise,* to cut out

A medical term can be formed by combining two roots and a combining vowel and suffix:

	root	combining vowel		root/suffix	
	gastr (stomach)	+	*o* +	*enter* (intestine)	*itis* (inflammation)

Definition: *Gastroenteritis*, inflammation of the stomach and the intestine

	root	combining vowel		root/suffix	
	oste (bone)	+	*o* +	*arthr* (joint)	*itis* (inflammation)

Definition: *Osteoarthritis*, inflammation of the bones and joints

L IST OF WORD ELEMENTS

A list of word elements arranged alphabetically is provided in Table 3.1. Word elements that are used as prefixes are followed by a hyphen (*auto-*). Those that are used as suffixes are preceded by a hyphen (*-cise*). It is wise to study this list carefully:

- By repeating aloud each of the word elements and its meaning.
- By reading aloud the example words and determining their meanings by referring to the word element list.

TABLE 3.1	COMMON WORD ELEMENTS USED IN HEALTH CARE		
Prefix, Suffix, Root, Combining Form	**Meaning**	**Example**	**Pronunciation**
a-, an-	without, lack of deficient, absent	asepsis anemia	a/SEP/sis an/e/mi/a
ab-, abs-	from, away	abnormal abscess	ab/NORM/al ABS/cess
ad-	near, toward	adrenal	Ad/REN/al
adeno-	gland	adenopathy	ad/en/OP/a/thy
aero-	air	anaerobe	an/A/er/obe
alb-	white	albuminuria	al/Bu/min/uri/a
-algia	pain	analgesia	an/al/GE/si/a
ambi-	both	ambidextrous	am/bi/DEX/trous
angio-	vessel	angioma	an/gi/O/ma
ano-	anus	anoscope	A/no/scope
ante-	before	antenatal	an/te/NAT/al
anti-	against	antiseptic	an/ti/SEP/tic
arterio-	artery	arteriosclerosis	ar/ter/i/o/scler/O/sis
arthro-	joint	arthroplasty	Ar/thro/plas/ty
-ase	enzyme	peptase	PEP/tase
-asethenia	weakness	myasthenia	my/as/THE/ni/a
auto-	self	autopathy	au/to/PATH/y
bi-	two, twice	bicellular	bi/SEL/ul/lar
bio-	life	biology	bi/ol/ogy
brady-	slow	bradycardia	brad/i/CAR/di/a
broncho-	bronchus	bronchitis	bron/CHI/tis
carcin-	cancer of epithelial tissue	carcinogen	car/CIN/o/gen
cardio-	heart	myocardium	my/o/CAR/di/um
-cele	tumor, swelling	enterocele	EN/ter/o/cele
-centesis	puncture	thoracentesis	tho/ra/cen/TE/sis
cephal-	head	hydrocephaly	hy/dro/CEPH/a/ly
chole-	gall	cholelithiasis	chol/e/lith/i/a/sis
cholecysto-	gallbladder	cholecystectomy	cho/le/cys/tect/o/my
choledocho-	common bile duct	choledochostomy	chol/ed/o/CHOS/to/my
chondro-	cartilage	chondroma	chon/DRO/ma
-cide	kill	germicide	GERM/i/cide
circum-	around	circumcision	cir/cum/CI/sion
-cise	cut	excise	ex/CISE
colo-	colon	colitis	co/Li/tis
colpo-	vagina	colporrhaphy	col/POR/rha/phy
contra-	against	contraception	con/tra/CEP/tion
costo-	rib	intercostal	in/ter/COS/tal

(continued)

TABLE 3.1	COMMON WORD ELEMENTS USED IN HEALTH CARE (CONT.)		
Prefix, Suffix, Root, Combining Form	**Meaning**	**Example**	**Pronunciation**
cranio-	skull	craniotomy	cra/ni/OT/o/my
cyano-	blue	cyanotic	cy/an/OT/ic
cysto-	urinary bladder	cystogram	CYS/to/gram
cyto-	cell	monocyte	MON/o/cyte
dactyl-	fingers	dactylitis	DAC/tyl/itis
de-	down, from	decubitus	de/CU/bi/tus
dent-	tooth	dentistry	DEN/tis/try
derma-	skin	dermatology	derm/a/TOL/o/gy
dextro-	right	dextrocardia	dex/tro/CARDI/a
di-	two	diplopia	dip/LOPI/a
dia-	through, between	diarrhea	di/a/RRHE/a
dis-	apart	dissect	dis/SECT
dys-	painful, difficult	dysmenorrhea	dys/men/o/RRHE/a
ecto-	outer	ectocytic	ect/o/SI/tic
-ectomy	surgical removal	prostatectomy	pros/ta/TEC/to/my
-emesis	vomiting	hematemesis	hem/at/EM/e/sis
-emia	blood	leukemia	leu/KE/mi/a
en-	in, inside	encapsulated	en/CAP/su/la/ted
encephalo-	brain	encephalitis	en/ceph/a/LI/tis
endo-	within, inner	endometrium	en/do/ME/tri/um
entero-	intestine	enteritis	en/ter/I/tis
epi-	above, over	epigastric	ep/i/GAS/tric
erythro-	red	erythrocyte	er/yth/RO/cyte
-esthesia	sensation	anesthesia	an/es/THE/si/a
eu-	well	euphoric	eu/PHOR/ic
ex-, extra-	out	extrahepatic	ex/tra/HEP/a/tic
febr-	fever	afebrile	a/FEB/rile
fibro-	connective tissue	fibroma	FI/bro/ma
fore-	before, in front of	forearm	FORE/arm
gastro-	stomach	gastrocele	GAS/tro/cele
-gene, -genic	production, origin	neurogenic	neu/ro/GEN/ic
glosso-	tongue	glossalgia	glos/SAL/gi/a
gluco-, glyco-	sugar, sweet	glycosuria	glyco/SUR/i/a
-gram	record	myelogram	MY/e/lo/gram
-graph	machine	encephalograph	en/CEPH/al/o/graph
-graphy	practice, process	ventriculography	ven/tri/cu/LOG/ra/phy
gyne-	woman	gynecology	gy/ne/COL/o/gy
hema-, hemato-, hem-	blood	hematology	hem/at/OL/o/gy
hemi-	half	hemiplegia	hem/i/PLE/gi/a
hepa-, hepato-	liver	hepatitis	hep/a/TI/tis
herni-	rupture	hernioplasty	HER/ni/o/plas/ty
hetero-	other, dissimilarity	heterogenous	het/er/o/GE/ne/us
histo-	tissue	histology	his/TOL/o/gy
homo-, homeo-	same, similar	homogenous	ho/mo/GEN/ous
hydro-	water	hydronephrosis	hy/dro/neph/RO/sis
hyper-	over, above, increased	hypertension	hy/per/TEN/sion
hypo-	under, beneath, decreased	hypotension	hy/po/TEN/sion
hyster-	uterus	hysterectomy	hys/ter/ECT/o/my
-iasis	condition of	urolithiasis	u/ro/lith/I/as/is
ictero-	jaundice	icterogenic	IC/ter/o/gen/ic
idio-	peculiar to the individual	idiopathic	id/i/o/PATH/ic
ileo-	ileum (part of small intestine)	ileitis	il/e/I/tis
ilio-	ilium (bone)	iliosacrum	il/i/o/SA/crum
inter-, intra-	within	intramuscular	in/tra/MUS/cu/lar
-itis	inflammation of	appendicitis	ap/pen/di/CI/tis
lact-	milk	lactation	LAC/ta/tion
laparo-	abdomen	laparotomy	la/par/OT/o/my
latero-	side	lateroposition	LAT/er/o/po/sit/ion
-lepsy	seizure, convulve	narcolepsy	NAR/co/lep/sy
leuko-	white	leukorrhea	leu/KO/RRHE/a
lipo-	fat	lipoma	lip/O/ma
lith-	stone	lithocystomy	lith/o/cys/TOT/o/my
-lysis	loosen, dissolve	hemolysis	hem/OL/y/sis
macro-	large, long	macrocyte	MAC/ro/cyte
mal-	bad, poor	malabsorption	mal/ab/SORP/tion
-mania	insanity	kleptomania	klep/to/MAN/ia

(continued)

TABLE 3.1	COMMON WORD ELEMENTS USED IN HEALTH CARE (CONT.)		
Prefix, Suffix, Root, Combining Form	Meaning	Example	Pronunciation
mast-	breast	mastectomy	mas/TEC/to/my
mega-	large	splenomegaly	splen/o/MEG/a/ly
melan-	black	melanoma	MEL/an/om/a
men-	month	menstruation	men/stru/A/tion
meso-	middle	mesocardia	mes/o/CAR/di/a
-meter	measure	thermometer	ther/MOM/e/ter
metro-	uterus	metrorrhagia	met/ror/RHA/gia
micro-	small	microscope	MIC/ro/scope
mono-	single, one	monocyte	MON/o/cyte
muco-	mucous membrane	mucocutaneous	mu/co/cu/TA/ne/ous
myco-	fungus	mycosis	my/CO/sis
myelo-	spinal cord, bone marrow	myelomeningocele	my/el/o/men/IN/go/cele
myo-	muscle	myopathy	my/OP/a/thy
narco-	stupor	narcotic	nar/COT/ic
naso-	nose	nasopharynx	nas/o/PHA/rynx
-natal	birth	prenatal	pre/NA/tal
necro-	death	necropsy	NEC/rop/sy
neo-	new	neoplasm	NE/o/plasm
nephro-	kidney	nephritis	ne/PHRI/tis
neuro-	nerve	neuralgia	neu/RAL/gi/a
non-	no, not	nontoxic	non/TOX/ic
ob-	against	obstruction	ob/STRUC/tion
oculo-	eye	oculomycosis	oc/u/lo/my/CO/sis
-ology	study of	bacteriology	bac/ter/i/OL/o/gy
-oma	tumor	carcinoma	car/ci/NO/ma
oophor-	ovary	oophorectomy	o/opho/REC/to/my
ophthalmo-	eye	ophthalmoscope	oph/THAL/mo/scope
-opia	vision	photopic	pho/TOP/ic
-opsy	study of	autopsy	au/TOP/sy
orchi-	testicle	orchipexy	ORCH/i/pex/y
-orrhaphy	to repair a defect	herniorrhaphy	her/ni/OR/raph/y
ortho-	straight	orthopedics	orth/o/PED/ics
-oscopy	look into, see	esophagoscopy	e/soph/a/GOS/co/py
-osis	condition of	neurosis	neu/RO/sis
osteo-	bone	osteoma	os/te/O/ma
-ostomy	surgical opening	colostomy	col/OST/o/my
oto-	ear	otolith	OT/o/lith
-otomy	incision	gastrotomy	gas/TROT/o/my
para-	alongside, abnormal	paraplegia	par/a/PLE/gi/a
path-	disease	pathology	pa/THOL/o/gy
ped-	(Latin) foot	pedograph	PED/o/graph
ped-	(Greek) child	pediatrics	pe/di/AT/rics
-penia	too few	leukopenia	leu/ko/PEN/i/a
peri-	around, covering	pericarditis	pe/ri/car/DI/tis
-pexy	to sew up in position	nephropexy	NEPH/ro/pex/y
pharyngo-	throat	pharyngoplasty	pha/RYN/go/plas/ty
phlebo-	veins	phlebitis	phle/BI/tis
-phobia	fear, dread	photophobia	pho/to/PHO/bi/a
photo-	light	photolysis	pho/TOL/is/is
-plasty	operative revision	rhinoplasty	RHI/no/plas/ty
-pnea	breathing	orthopnea	or/thop/NE/a
pneumo-	air, lungs	pneumonia	pneu/MO/ni/a
poly-	much, many	polyuria	po/ly/U/ri/a
post-	after	postpartum	post/PAR/tum
pre-	before	preoperative	pre/OP/er/a/tive
procto-	rectum	proctoscopy	proc/TOS/co/py
pseudo-	false	pseudotumor	pseu/do/tum/or
psych-	the mind	psychology	psy/CHOL/o/gy
-ptosis	falling	nephroptosis	neph/rop/TO/sis
pyelo-	pelvis, of the kidney	pyelonephritis	py/el/o/neph/RI/tis
pyo-	pus	pyogenic	py/o/GEN/ic
pyro-	heat, temperature	pyrexia	py/REX/i/a
-renal	kidney	suprarenal	su/pra/RE/nal
retro-	behind, backward	retrosternal	ret/ro/STER/nal
-rhage	hemmorrhage, flow	hemorrhage	HEM/or/rhage
-rhea	flow	diarrhea	di/a/RRHE/a
rhino-	nose	rhinopathy	rhi/NOP/a/thy

(continued)

Prefix, Suffix, Root, Combining Form	Meaning	Example	Pronunciation
salpingo-	oviduct	salpingectomy	sal/pin/GEC/to/my
sclero-	hardening	scleroderma	scle/ro/DER/ma
-scopy	sight	microscopy	mi/cro/sco/py
semi-	half	semicircular	sem/i/CIR/cu/lar
septic-	poison, infection	septicemia	sep/ti/CEM/ia
spleno-	spleen	splenocele	SPLE/no/cele
stomato-	mouth	stomatitis	sto/ma/TI/tis
sub-	under	subacute	sub/a/CUTE
-therapy	treatment	hydrotherapy	hy/dro/THER/a/py
-thermy	heat	diathermy	DI/a/therm/y
thoraco-	chest	thoracotomy	thor/a/COT/o/my
thrombo-	clot	thrombosis	throm/BO/sis
thyro-	thyroid gland	thyroxin	thy/ROX/in
trans-	across	transfusion	trans/FU/sion
uni-	one	unicellular	u/ni/CELL/u/lar
uro-	urine	uremia	u/RE/mi/a
-uria, -uric	condition of, presence in urine	uremia	u/RE/mi/a
vaso-	blood vessel	vasoconstriction	vas/o/con/STRIC/tion

This list is by no means complete. These are very common word elements used in most medical environments. You will find it necessary to refer to a complete list in a good medical dictionary frequently. You may also work in a specialized medical setting where additional medical terms and abbreviations are used.

PRONUNCIATION

Medical terms are often difficult to pronounce because you may have never heard of the words. The following hints may help you better understand the pronunciation of common medical terms.

ch   Often sounds like *k.*
Examples: chronic (KRO/nic)
            chondro (KON/dro)
g   Pronounce this *j* when the *g* comes before *e, i,* and *y.*
Examples: genetics (je/NE/tics)
            genitals (JE/ne/tals)
i   Pronounce this as *eye* when added to the end of a word to form a plural.
Examples: bacilli (ba/SIL/eye)
            alveoli (al/VI/o/L/eye)
pn   Pronounce this *n,* as though the *p* were absent.
Examples: pneumonia (nu/MO/ni/a)
            pneumothorax (nu/mo/THOR/ax)
ps   This is pronounced like an *s,* ignoring the *p.*
Examples: psychiatrist (si/KI/a/trist)
            pseudomonas (sue/do/MO/nas)

WORD VARIATION

As with all languages, there are some rules of usage for medical terminology that may confuse you and others that may seem inconsistent. It is important to review some additional aspects of medical terminology to avoid unnecessary confusion.

- A word that has been made from the combination of many word elements not only may have certain letters added but also may have letters changed or omitted. Often this is done to conform to rules of spelling and pronunciation. This can be challenging for the best of spellers!

  Example: laparotomy *laparo* (abdomen) - *o* + *tomy* (incision)

  Explanation: An *o* has been taken out of the word to make the word less awkward.

  Example: suprarenal *super* (above) + *renal* (kidney)

  Explanation: Super is changed to *supra* before combining with *renal.*

- There are also groups of *suffixes* that contain very similar word elements and may be confused, but each suffix has a different meaning.

  Example: -*gram* a record, -*graph* a machine, -*graphy* a process

  A cardio*gram* is a record of heart action. A cardio*graph* is a machine that makes a record. Cardio*graphy* is the process of making a record.

- Perhaps the most misunderstood group of suffixes in medical terminology are the following:

  Example: -*ectomy* surgical removal

  -*stomy* surgical opening

  -*tomy* surgical incision

  If you swallow a sharp object, your surgeon might do a gastro*tomy* (surgical incision into the stomach) to remove the object. If you developed bleeding ulcers, your surgeon might have to remove the stomach, or do a gastr*ectomy.* If you were not able to take food by mouth, your surgeon might do a gastro*stomy,* where a feeding tube would lead directly to the stomach. Remember, *tomys* are sewn up again, whereas *stomys* are left open (stomy = stoma = open).

- To add to the confusion, some word elements that are in common use in everyday speech and spelled the same way may have different meanings in medical terminology. Table 3.1 lists word elements that often cause difficulty. Make sure that you know these terms.

$\mathcal{M}$EDICAL ABBREVIATIONS

You will also come into frequent contact with medical **abbreviations.** It is essential that medical clerical workers become familiar with the most common abbreviations in the medical environments where they work, and are able to use them accurately. Many of the most common medical abbreviations that you may encounter are listed in Table 3.2. Although this list is comprehensive, it is not complete.

As a medical clerical worker, you will encounter additional abbreviations in specialized settings and will always be challenged to learn new terms. For example, if you work for a cardiologist, you would encounter abbreviations that are specific references to the heart (i.e., ASHD: arteriosclerotic heart disease). Some abbreviations such as ASHD and AIDS are **acronyms** (words formed from the first letters of other words or parts of words). Medical terminology includes many acronyms that are sometimes very confusing, especially to patients. Each new medical environment that you encounter will probably require that you learn some different terms and abbreviations. This is part of the challenge of a continually changing job atmosphere.

Medical terminology is often linked to anatomical references that are the basis of diagnostic and therapeutic terms. It is important that the medical clerical worker be able to recognize common diagnostic, therapeutic, and anatomical terms. Health care funding or reimbursement is based on patient diagnosis and treatment, and using the correct terminology can guarantee that the patient will get proper insurance coverage for the particular diagnosis.

TABLE 3.2 MEDICAL ABBREVIATIONS AND SYMBOLS

Abbreviation	Meaning	Abbreviation	Meaning	Abbreviation	Meaning
ac	before meals	emul.	emulsion	mm	millimeter
ad	add	ENT	ear, nose, and throat	mn or MN	midnight
ad lib	as desired	ER	emergency room	MRI	magnetic resonance imaging
Adm.	admission	esp.	especially	Na	sodium
AIDS	acquired immune deficiency syndrome	et	and	N.A.	Nursing Assistant
		etiol.	etiology	neg	negative
AKA	also known as	FBS	fasting blood sugar	N.G.T.	nasogastric tube
AMA	American Medical Association	FDA	Food Drug Administration	NKA	no known allergies
amb.	ambulatory	Fe	iron	NPO	nothing by mouth
ant.	anterior	FF	forced feeding or forced fluids	NS	normal saline
AP	anteroposterior	FH	family history	OB/GYN	obstetrics/gynecology
A.P.&L.	anterior, posterior, and lateral	fld.	fluid	occ.	occasionally
aqua	water; H_2O	FSH	follicle-stimulating hormone	o.d.	right eye
ASAP	as soon as possible	FUO	fever of undetermined origin	OD	overdose
ASHD	arteriosclerotic heart disease	fx.	fracture	O.P.	outpatient
B.I.D.	twice a day	g	grain	OR	operating room
B.M.	bowel movement	GB	gallbladder	Ortho.	orthopedics
BMR	basic metabolic rate	GI	gastrointestinal	o.s.	left eye
B/P	blood pressure	GM, gm	gram	O.T.	occupational therapy
B.R.	bed rest	gt (gtt)	drop (drops)	o.u.	both eyes
B.R.P.	bathroom privileges	G.T.T.	glucose tolerance test	oz	ounce
B.S.	blood sugar	GU	genitourinary	PAP	Papanicolaou smear
C.	centigrade; Celsius	gyn	gynecology	Path.	pathology
c	with	H.A.	headache	pc	after meals
Ca	calcium	HBD	has been drinking	Peds.	pediatrics
ca	cancer	HBP	high blood pressure	per	by, through
cap.	capsule	Hgb	hemoglobin	PID	pelvic inflammatory disease
cath	catheter or catheterization	H&P	history and physical	PKU	phenylketonuria
CBC	complete blood count	hs	bedtime	PO	by mouth
CBR	complete bed rest	HSV	herpes simplex virus	post	after
cc	cubic centimeter	HX	history	post.	posterior
CCU	coronary care unit	hyper	above or high	post-op	postoperative
CHF	congestive heart failure	hypo	below or low	PP	postprandial
chr.	chronic	ICU	intensive care unit	PPM	parts per million
cm	centimeter	IM	intramuscular	pre-op	before surgery
CNS	central nervous system	inhal.	inhalation	prep.	prepartion
C/o	complains of	inj.	injection	P.R.N.	as needed
compd.	compound	int.	internal	prog.	prognosis
cont.	continuous	I&O	intake and output	pt.	patient
COPD	chronic obstructive pulmonary disease	irrig.	irrigation	PTA	prior to admission
		isol.	isolation	q.	every
CPR	cardiopulmonary resuscitation	IUD	intrauterine device	qAM	every morning
CSF	cerebrospinal fluid	IV	intravenous	qd	every day
CT scan	computerized axial tomography scan	IVP	intravenous pyelogram	qh	every hour
		IVPB	intravenous piggyback	qid	four times a day
CVA	cerebrovascular accident	K+	potassium	qod	every other day
D	dose	KUB	kidney, ureter, bladder	qs	quantity sufficient
DAT	diet as tolerated	L or l	liter	qt	quart
dc	discontinue	lab	laboratory	RLQ	right lower quadrant
D/c	discharge	lb.	pound	R.N.	Registered Nurse
D&C	dilatation and curettage	liq.	liquid	R/O	rule out
Dim	half	LLQ	left lower quadrant	ROM	range of motion
dist.	distilled	LLX	lower left extremities	R.R.	recovery room
DNA	does not apply	LP.	lumbar puncture	R.T.	respiratory therapist
DOA	dead on arrival	L.P.N.	Licensed Practical Nurse	RUQ	right upper quadrant
dr	dram	Lt.	left	RX	prescription
DRG	diagnosis related group	LUQ	left upper quadrant	s, s	without
drsg.	dressing	L.V.N.	Licensed Vocational Nurse	s.c.	subcutaneous
D/S	dextrose and normal saline	MA	Medical Assistant	sign	directions
D/W	dextrose and water	mcg.	microgram	sol	solution
DX	diagnosis	MD	Doctor of Medicine	spec.	specimen
E	enema	med	medicine	ss, s̅s̅	half
ea	each	mEq.	milliequivalents	staph.	staphylococcus
ECG, EKG	electrocardiogram	mg	milligram	stat	immediately
elix.	elixir	MI	mycardial infarction	STD	sexually transmitted disease
EMG	electromyogram	ml	milliliter		

(continued)

TABLE 3.2	MEDICAL ABBREVIATIONS AND SYMBOLS (CONT.)				
Abbreviation	**Meaning**	**Abbreviation**	**Meaning**	**Abbreviation**	**Meaning**
syr.	syrup	TKO	to keep open	ung.	ointment
T.	temperature	T.P.R.	temperature, pulse, respiration	URI	upper respiratory infection
T&A	tonsillectomy and adenoidectomy	Trx.	traction	UTI	urinary tract infection
		T.U.R.	transurethral resection	UV	ultraviolet
Tab.	tablet	T.U.R.P.	transurethral resection prostate	VD	venereal disease
TAH	total abdominal hysterectomy	T.V.	tidal volume	vs.	vital signs
		Tx.	treatment	w/a	while awake
T&CM	type and cross-match	U.	unit	w/b	weight bearing
THR	total hip replacement	UA	urinalysis	WBC	white blood count
TIA	transient ischemic attack	UCR	usual, customary, and reasonable	wc.	wheelchair
tid	three times a day			wt.	weight
tinc.	tincture	uncon.	unconscious		

Note: Some of these abbreviations may be written with either capitals or lowercase letters and with or without periods.

SUMMARY

As you can see, mastering medical terminology is not easy. You should always have an up-to-date medical dictionary handy so that you do not have to rely solely on your memory. New terms appear frequently; a few years ago, many of the terms connected with the AIDS epidemic would not have been recognized by medical professionals.

It is important to remember that as a medical clerical worker, you must be comfortable with the language of your field and be able to use the terminology accurately. You will be required to learn the new terms and abbreviations that develop throughout your medical career.

LEARNING ACTIVITIES

1. Referring to the list of word elements in this chapter, select ten words from the "example" of the listing. Write a sentence using each of the ten words in proper context.

2. Divide the class into two teams. Have your instructor write medical terms on the board, one at a time. See which team can identify the term first.

3. Using a medical dictionary, find 20 words that are not on the word element list in Chapter 3. Share the words with your class.

4. If your class has access to computers and medical terminology software, use the software to improve your grasp of medical terminology.

5. Find at least five examples of medical terminology in the newspaper.

6. Make and use flash cards to increase proficiency.

7. List and define three types of word elements used in medical terminology.

8. State the two languages from which most medical terms are derived.

9. List three examples of medical terms combining a prefix, suffix, and root.

10. Give two examples of medical terms combining a prefix and suffix.

11. Give two examples of medical terms combining two root words and a combining vowel.

12. Define an acronym.

13. The following letters can be pronounced in a unique way when used in medical terms. Describe the pronunciation and give examples of medical words with these sounds.
    (a) *pn*
    (b) *ps*
    (c) *ch*

14. Referring to the word element list in Table 3.1, define the following terms, dividing words into parts and combining forms.
    (a) pathology
    (b) lipoma
    (c) afebrile
    (d) carcinoma
    (e) necropsy
    (f) postpartum

15. Identify the following suffixes from the word element list.
    (a) *-ectomy*
    (b) *-stomy*
    (c) *-tomy*
    (d) *-gram*
    (e) *-graph*
    (f) *-graphy*

16. List ten medical abbreviations found in Table 3.2 and define them.

17. Form medical words for the following definitions.
    (a) inflammation of the stomach
    (b) study of cells
    (c) study of disease
    (d) surgical removal of the uterus
    (e) surgical removal of the stomach

CHAPTER 4

Safety and Emergency Care

Cardiac arrest	The sudden stopping of the heart and therefore the circulation.
Cardiopulmonary resuscitation (CPR)	A method to save lives of people in cardiac and respiratory distress and failure. Training in CPR is available through many venues, including the American Red Cross and the American Heart Association.
Carpal tunnel syndrome	Symptoms associated with entrapment of the median nerve within the carpal bones and the transverse ligament at the wrist; often caused by repetitive wrist motion such as working with a computer keyboard.
Combustible	Easily capable of burning.
Crash cart	An emergency cart kept on nursing units and in other patient care areas that contains emergency equipment and supplies to be used only in emergency situations.
Ergonomics	The science of fitting the job to the worker.
Fire extinguisher	Canisters of materials designed to put out all types of fires, including burning liquids, electrical, paper, wood, and cloth.
Infection control	In health care institutions, a constant effort to prevent the spread of infectious organisms.
International hospital code system	A system of codes used to alert the staff in a medical facility to major emergency situations: fire, cardiac and respiratory arrest, uncontrolled persons, and disaster team alert.
Isolation	An area, usually a hospital room, where a patient who has an infection that could spread to other patients is placed, or where a patient is placed when incapable of fighting infection and must be protected from possible sources of infection.
Nosocomial infection	Hospital-acquired infection.
OSHA	Occupational Safety and Health Administration.
Pathogens	Microorganisms that cause infection in human beings.
Quality occurrence report	Also known as an *incident report;* a written report of an unusual occurrence.
Proper body mechanics	Ways of standing and moving one's body to make the best use of strength and avoid injury and fatigue.
Respiratory arrest	When a person suddenly stops breathing.
Standard precautions	OSHA guidelines to treat all potentially infectious materials as infectious regardless of the perceived health status of the patient or co-worker.
Triage	To sort or prioritize care for a group of patients.
Work-related musculoskeletal disorders (WMSDs)	All disorders resulting from workers performing repetitive motions or doing work in an uncomfortable position.

After completing this chapter, the student is responsible for performing the following objectives:

- List general rules of safety in the medical environment.
- Explain why well-designed office furniture helps maintain the health and safety of the medical clerical worker.
- Discuss the importance of good body mechanics.
- Identify ways to control infection in the medical workplace, including handwashing and wearing gloves.
- Explain the importance of properly filled out incident reports.
- List some responsibilities the medical clerical worker might have in case of a medical emergency.
- Discuss what to do in case of fire and an earthquake in a health care facility.
- Explain the International Hospital Code System.

1 NTRODUCTION

Whether the medical clerical worker is employed in a huge hospital or in a small office setting, he or she is part of a team. One of the most important duties of the team is to ensure the safety of each patient as well as of the team members themselves. This requires paying strict attention to any safety hazards that might be present, following all infection control guidelines set up by the employer, avoiding employee workplace injuries, and knowing how to respond to various emergencies that can take place in a medical setting.

G ENERAL SAFETY MEASURES IN THE MEDICAL ENVIRONMENT

There are several general safety measures that must be taken in a health care setting to avoid injury to both patients and health care workers.

- Keep *floors* free of clutter. If you see spilled liquid, wipe it up immediately. Freshly washed floors should be mopped dry. Sweep up glass immediately and avoid picking up glass with your fingers. Wrap glass particles in heavy paper and label for disposal. Glass that shatters into tiny pieces can be blotted up with damp toweling.
- *Walk, don't run!* There are often situations that require a quick response, but refrain from running, especially down corridors. Collisions can be avoided by remembering this rule.
- Walk on the right side of the hall, with no more than two abreast. Be very cautious of intersections (Figure 4.1). Especially in a hospital environment, you will avoid traffic jams, collisions, and injury to yourself and others by following these rules.
- Know location of exits in hospitals and medical buildings. Elevators cannot be used in a fire.
- To avoid injury, use handrails when using stairs.

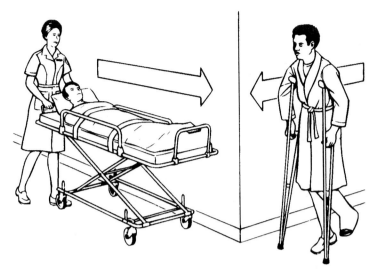

FIGURE 4.1 Use caution at intersections.

- Watch out for swinging doors, which can hit you or someone else, causing injury (Figure 4.2).
- Help keep stairs and halls clear of equipment and obstructions. Often in the medical environment a great deal of equipment is being used for patient care, and it should be returned to its proper place as soon as possible. Housecleaning equipment must not be left where people might trip over it.
- Supplies that arrive in boxes should be unloaded immediately and the boxes disposed of. Many accidents occur when offices become cluttered, and people may stumble over boxes stacked in areas where there is traffic.
- Have burned-out light bulbs replaced immediately.
- Never try to repair or adjust any electrical equipment yourself. Call the designated maintenance person in your office or medical complex.
- If you are using electrical extension cords, never suspend or drape the cord so that it hangs over heating vents, steam pipes, or anything sharp. Be sure that cords are not pinched off by a closed door. Make sure that no one can trip over the extension cord.
- Be careful not to sit too far back in your chair or on the edge of your chair.

FIGURE 4.2 Watch out for swinging doors.

- Keep desk and file drawers closed when not in use.
- If you are required to help transport a patient into or around the workplace, be sure that you set the brakes on the wheels when moving the patient into or out of the wheelchair.
- If you are injured or a patient is injured, even slightly, while in your sight, report the injury to whomever is in charge and complete a form called an *incident* (or *accident*) *report.*
- If you see unsafe conditions, report them at once.

The most important thing for members of a health team to remember is that *everyone is responsible for patient safety.* As a medical clerical worker, you may think that it is the nurse's responsibility to pick up a needle he or she dropped on the floor, or that it is the janitor's duty to remove a mop from the hall. But if you see a hazard that others may overlook, it is your duty either to remove the hazard or to call on someone immediately to take care of the problem.

*E*RGONOMICS

Ergonomics is the science that deals with people's performance and good health while carrying out job tasks, operating office equipment, and generally interacting in the work environment. As applied to the medical clerical worker, the following points are pertinent:

- The medical clerical worker must have a chair that fits him or her while sitting for long periods of time. The height and back need to be adjustable. The use of a footrest may also aid in avoiding posture problems. The worker should relax periodically by standing and moving the body. Variety in the workplace helps keep the medical clerical worker mentally alert and allows physical movement away from the computer.
- At the computer station, glare should not be present on the screen. Employees using a computer screen for an extended period of time should look away from the screen at intervals of one to three minutes at least once an hour. A vertical document holder (Figure 4.3), attached to a flexible equipment arm or free standing, eases eyestrain and improves posture.

FIGURE 4.3 Drawing of a vertical document holder.

■ A good wrist support should be available to keep your wrists as straight as possible. It should have rounded edges, be padded, and be about two inches high. **Carpal tunnel syndrome** can be prevented with proper wrist position while you are operating a computer keyboard. The fingers should be lower than the wrist.

The name used in health care today for all disorders (including carpal tunnel syndrome) resulting from workers performing repetitive motions or do their work in an uncomfortable position is **work-related musculoskeletal disorders (WMSDs).** Simple changes in the work environment often can reduce such problems.

*P*ROPER BODY MECHANICS

Proper body mechanics can be defined as ways to stand and move one's body to make best use of strength and to avoid injury and fatigue. It is important to understand the rules of good body mechanics and to learn to apply them in your job. You will be less tired at the end of the day, and more important, you will avoid injury. Such injuries can affect your body for a lifetime and render you unable to perform your job. Employers are also very interested in avoiding injuries in employees and should encourage you to practice good body mechanics.

Some valuable rules to follow are listed below.

■ When you lift an object (Figure 4.4)
  ■ Squat down close to the load.
  ■ Keep your back straight.
  ■ Grip the object firmly.
  ■ Hold the load close to your body.
  ■ Lift smoothly by pushing up on your strong leg muscles.
  ■ If the load is too heavy, get help!

■ When you have to move a heavy object, it is better to push, pull, or roll the object rather than to lift and carry.

■ Use good posture, keeping your body aligned properly. Stand with your feet about six to eight inches apart to increase the base of your support. Keep your head erect, put your shoulders back, and tuck in your abdomen and buttocks. This will tilt the pelvis forward, help straighten the curve of the back, and decrease muscle strain.

■ When sitting in a chair for extended periods, choose a chair with good back support. Sit with your buttocks pushed back in the chair. Try to position

FIGURE 4.4 Proper lifting.

your body so that your knees are slightly raised and your back remains straight. Stand up and stretch occasionally to relax muscles that may become tense (see Ergonomics section).

■ When you need to lower yourself to pick up something from the floor, widen your base of support by putting your feet six to eight inches apart with one foot slightly forward. Bend at the knees, not at the waist, keeping your back straight, and balancing your weight evenly on both feet. You will provide yourself with the stability to keep your balance, making use of stronger thigh and leg muscles. Remember, back muscles are weaker and can get injured if you bend at the waist.

■ When you want to change the direction of movement (Figure 4.5):
  ■ Turn with your feet.
  ■ Turn with short steps.
  ■ Turn your entire body without twisting your back or neck.

*I*NFECTION CONTROL

A continuous battle goes on in health care facilities to prevent the spread of infectious organisms, known as **pathogens,** to human beings. Both patients and employees are the focus of efforts to control infection. Many health care facilities have separate departments devoted exclusively to **infection control.**

Elaborate methods are used in health care facilities to eliminate hospital-acquired infections, called **nosocomial infections.** The housekeeping staff works constantly to keep all surfaces clean. Patients with infectious diseases are put in **isolation.** But despite such efforts, there are always some harmful microorganisms around us. Common health facility infectious organisms include *staphylococcus* and *pseudomonas* (bacteria), and *Candida albicans* (a fungus).

As a medical clerical worker, you must keep in mind constantly the need to practice the most important way to control infection from spreading: *handwashing* (Figure 4.6). You should wash your hands between glove changes, after visiting the restroom, before and after eating, and throughout the day between patient interactions.

In today's medical environment, the medical clerical worker must wear *protective gloves* when handling specimens that patients bring into a medical facility after collecting a specimen at home. These specimens can include urine, stool, sputum (coughed up from the lungs), throat swabs, sperm, and other body fluids. ALL

FIGURE 4.5 Changing direction of movement.

1. Assemble your equipment, which is found at all times at every sink in all health care institutions.

   a) Soap or detergent.

   b) Paper towels.

   c) Warm, running water.

   d) Wastepaper basket.

2. Turn the faucet on with a paper towel held between your hands and the faucet. Adjust the water to a temperature comfortable for you.

3. Discard the paper towel in the wastepaper basket.

4. Completely wet your hands and wrists under the running water. Keep your fingertips pointed downward.

5. Apply soap or detergent.

6. Hold your hands lower than your elbows while washing.

7. Work up a good lather. Spread it over the entire area of your hands and up two inches above your wrists. Get soap under your nails and between your fingers.

8. Clean under your nails by rubbing your nails across the palms of your hand.

9. Use a rotating and rubbing (frictional) motion for one full minute:

   a) Rub vigorously.

   b) Rub one hand against the other hand and wrist.

   c) Rub between your fingers by interlacing them.

   d) Rub up and down to reach all skin surfaces on your hands, between your fingers, and two inches above your wrists.

   e) Rub the tips of your fingers against your palms to clean with friction around the nail beds.

10. Rinse well. Rinse from two inches above your wrists to hands. Hold your hands and fingertips down, under running water.

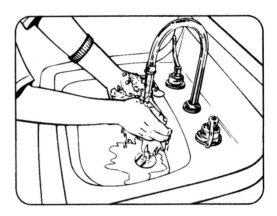

11. Dry thoroughly with paper towels.

12. Turn off the faucet. Use a paper towel between your hands and the faucet. Never touch the faucet with your hand, after washing.

13. Discard the paper towel into the wastebasket. Do not touch the basket.

FIGURE 4.6 Handwashing technique.

body fluids are considered potentially infectious. Well-fitting gloves should be easily accessible at all times. Gloves should be replaced as soon as practically necessary when they become contaminated, torn, or punctured. The hands must be washed after gloves are removed. Gloves must be disposed of in a biohazardous waste container that must be present nearby in your waste facility.

OSHA Bloodborne Pathogens Exposure Controls

The **Occupational Safety and Health Administration (OSHA)** has issued guidelines to control bloodborne pathogen exposure. With the advent of the AIDS epidemic and to protect health care workers from AIDS exposure, these guidelines have been put into effect in most facilities throughout the United States. As a medical clerical worker, you must be informed about AIDS, as well as the highly infectious hepatitis viruses that are also a danger to health care workers. Appendix A contains vital information that all medical clerical workers should be familiar with concerning AIDS and hepatitis viruses.

Universal blood and body fluid precautions, called **standard precautions,** are developed to prevent skin puncture and mucous membrane and nonintact skin exposures of health care workers to bloodborne pathogens and other potentially infectious materials. These controls include the following:

- Use of protective barriers such as clothing and shields for eyes.
- Correct selection and use of gloves.
- Use of biohazardous waste containers for contaminated materials; for example, containers (called *sharps containers*) for waste such as needles and scalpels.
- Classification of all body fluids as potentially infectious.

As a medical clerical worker, apply standard precautions wisely in your work environment. Be careful to always wear gloves when handling patient body fluids. Properly dispose of any contaminated materials in a biohazardous waste container. If your work surface becomes contaminated by a leaking specimen that a patient has just handed you (or a similar situation), be sure to immediately decontaminate the area with a bleach solution or Environmental Protection Agency–registered germicide. Many facilities will not allow the medical clerical worker to accept any specimen from a patient that is contaminated on the outside or leaking.

You are a part of the entire health care team and therefore share the responsibility for infection control. Infection control requires that you use common sense in situations that you may face, such as the following:

- A patient is in the waiting room, coughing and sneezing all over everyone near him or her. Make sure that the patient is seen as soon as possible or put into an examining room so that he is as isolated as possible.
- If a patient hands you a specimen, such as a urine specimen, which has obviously been collected carelessly, you may be instructed by your employer not to accept it. If your employer does tell you to accept a contaminated specimen, put on gloves and after removing wash your hands immediately, using techniques explained in Figure 4.6.
- You notice that an area has become contaminated with blood or other body fluid. You should immediately contact the person responsible for cleaning up such materials. If that falls under your job description, you are responsible for wiping up the contamination. Put on gloves and always use a disinfectant that will control the spread of infection effectively.

In addition, you should make every effort to stay healthy—by eating the right foods, getting plenty of sleep, and exercising. In this way you may reduce your chances of catching other people's infections or avoid the spread of your illness to patients, who may already be in a weakened condition.

*Q*UALITY OCCURRENCE REPORT

An *incident* is defined as any event that is not considered a part of the routine operation of the medical environment. It may involve an accident to a patient, health care worker, or a visitor, a theft, or any other unusual event occurring in the workplace. Some examples of such incidents are:

- A patient or visitor being injured inside the medical office or hospital, or within its property, such as on sidewalks, in parking lots, or in entrances.

I. **OCCURRENCE:**			(IF NO PLATE)	STATUS	
DATE	TIME	LOCATION	NAME	☐ INPT ☐ VISITOR	☐ OUT PT ☐ OTHER

AGE	SEX ☐ M ☐ F	Diagnosis or Procedure	Witness Yes ☐ No ☐
			Name _____
			Dept. _____

Condition Prior to Occurrence	Meds last 12 hrs (falls only)
☐ Alert ☐ Disoriented ☐ Asleep ☐ Anesthetized	

II. **MEDICATION** (all that apply)	**INTRAVENOUS** (Note all that apply)	**FALL (Complete** both sides)	
☐ Wrong medication ☐ Wrong amount ☐ Wrong ☐ Wrong pt date/time ☐ Wrong route ☐ Transcription error ☐ Allergic reaction ☐ Omission ☐ Incorrect narcotic count ☐ Other _____ Name of Med	☐ Wrong solution ☐ Wrong medication ☐ Wrong rate ☐ Wrong time ☐ Infiltration ☐ Transcription error ☐ PCA error ☐ Blood transfusion ☐ Hyperalimentation ☐ Other _____	☐ Ambulating ☐ In BR ☐ Out of bed ☐ To FRM B/R ☐ Other	☐ PT has fallen prev ☐ Restrained ☐ Side rails up ☐ Side rails down

Equipment (under Intravenous column)

Surgical — Please Comment

Consent:	☐ Not available ☐ Disconnected ☐ Procedure not followed ☐ Nonsterile ☐ Malfunction ☐ Other _____ ☐ Descript. of item _____	☐ Delay ☐ Consent mismatch ☐ Unplanned return ☐ Incorrect count ☐ Unplanned repair/removal ☐ Arrest ☐ Death ☐ Anesthesia related ☐ Other _____
☐ None written ☐ Mismatch ☐ Refused to sign ☐ Incomplete ☐ Other		

AMA	**Pressure Sore (complete both sides)**		**Other**	
☐ AMA signed ☐ Not signed ☐ AWOL ☐ Other	☐ On admission ☐ Hospital acquired ☐ Picture taken	☐ Stage I ☐ Stage II ☐ Stage III ☐ Stage IV	☐ Security ☐ Engineering ☐ Combative pt. ☐ Suicide attempt ☐ Fire ☐ Respiratory ☐ Pharmacy ☐ Code blue, expired ☐ Code blue, survived ☐ Complaint	☐ Self abuse ☐ Lost/damaged article ☐ Hazardous exposure ☐ Burn ☐ Lab ☐ X ray ☐ Food services ☐ Housekeeping ☐ Other (Comment)

III	**Severity of Outcome**
	☐ No Injury ☐ Inconsequential ☐ Consequential

IV	**Comments & Action**

V Follow up (Director to complete)

☐ Communicated with

_____

Name of MD notified	Date	Time	Seen by MD?	☐ Employee counseled ☐ Inservice ☐ Policy change / new ☐ Trend ☐ Other _____
			Yes ☐ No ☐	

X-ray / Lab / Tests ordered?	Equipment
Yes ☐ No ☐ State _____	Sent for repair ☐ Removed from service ☐

Reported by — Date — Dept	Persons Involved Dept	Department Director Sign — Date

Ballpoint Pen Only

QUALITY OCCURRENCE REPORT
- ● **Not Part of Medical Record** ●
- ● **DO NOT Photocopy**
- ● **Complete all Sections and forward to QRS Immediately**

FIGURE 4.7 Quality occurrence report.

- Any theft involving a patient, visitor, or employee.
- Abusive language or threats by patients or employees toward another person.
- Patients losing or misplacing property such as purses, hearing aids, or false teeth.

Whenever an incident occurs, a written report must be made. This is a very important part of your employer's safety program and can protect you against possible lawsuits.

Quality occurrence reports must be filled out completely and accurately (Figure 4.7). Please use a typewriter or your most legible handwriting. Reports should be checked over by your immediate supervisor and should be written on a standard form that your employer should keep available at all times. Try your best to describe the incident simply and clearly. Avoid lengthy, wordy descriptions. Failure to complete an employee incident report could result in workers' compensation being denied. There are many different forms, but most include the following information:

- Names of persons involved.
- Date of incident.
- Location of incident.
- Responsible person to whom the incident is reported and the time of reporting.
- Brief description of what happened.
- Names of any witnesses.
- Name of machines involved, if any.
- Action taken to prevent recurrence.
- Signature of person filling out report and the date.

$\mathcal{M}$EDICAL EMERGENCIES

A medical emergency is defined as any situation where an individual suddenly becomes ill, sustains an injury, or is in circumstances calling for immediate action. In a hospital setting, there is usually plenty of staff and equipment available immediately

---

Real-Life Scenario

You are a medical clerical worker at the offices of Dr. Laura Jackson, a dermatologist. You are looking out the window and you see a teenage girl named Sarah going up the office stairs. Suddenly you see Sarah trip on the stairs. You open the door and see her getting up. Her knee is skinned, and she winces in pain. You offer support, but Sarah assures you that she is fine and needs no help or treatment. Sarah is very introverted and does not want attention drawn to herself.

1. The accident didn't happen in the office. Do you fill out an incident report?
2. Sarah is at the dermatologist office for acne treatments. Dr. Jackson is not an orthopedist. Do you tell Dr. Jackson about Sarah's fall?

to handle respiratory and cardiac emergencies. If you work in a hospital as a medical clerical worker, you may be required to call for help, as every hospital has a team and/or facilities to deal with such emergencies. The **International Hospital Code System** is used to alert the staff of a hospital to four major emergency situations. This system is used internationally, with the four codes being:

- *Code Red* means that there is fire in the facility.
- *Code Blue* means that there is a **respiratory** or **cardiac arrest,** or both.
- *Code Yellow* means that there is an uncontrolled person or a threatening situation.
- *Code Green* means that a specially designated team in the hospital should report to a designated area to be used when a disaster occurs. Patients are sorted out for treatment according to the severity of their injury (**triage**).

Cardiac/Respiratory Arrest

Most health care facilities are equipped to handle cardiac arrest emergencies. A **crash cart** may be located in the health care facility where you work. A crash cart contains emergency supplies such as drugs, portable oxygen, resuscitation bags, and boards for external cardiac massage. This cart will be brought to the patient during such emergencies. Most employees working in a medical environment of any size are asked by their employer to take a course in **cardiopulmonary resuscitation (CPR),** offered by the American Heart Association and the American Red Cross. A CPR course teaches the student how to recognize when someone's heart and/or breathing stops. It also teaches how to maintain breathing and circulation. Certification must be renewed on a regular basis.

Medical Emergencies in the Medical Office

As a part of preparation for an emergency in the medical office, your employer should have a prepared emergency kit, available through most medical supply houses. This kit should include:

- Sterile dressings
- Bandage material and adhesive tape
- Hot and cold packs (easily activated)
- Disposable syringe and needle units
- Adrenaline and antihistamines
- Ipecac (to induce vomiting in a poisoning)
- Glucose for diabetics who have taken too much insulin
- Oxygen mask/oxygen tank

Every employee should be certified in first aid and CPR with certification current. The office must have written guidelines about what type of first aid care can be given by the medical clerical worker. A list of all necessary telephone numbers for police, fire, ambulance, hospitals, and poison control centers should be kept near your phone.

𝓕IRE SAFETY

The most common causes of fire include smoking and matches, heating and cooking equipment, electrical equipment and appliances, rubbish and trash, and flammable liquids (Figure 4.8). Each member of the health team has a responsibility to see that

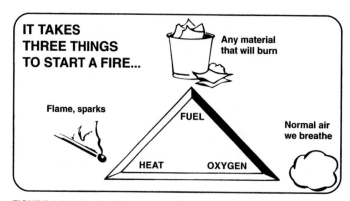

FIGURE 4.8 What it takes to start a fire.

proper care is taken to avoid fire. Fire safety means two things: (1) preventing fires and (2) knowing what to do if a fire breaks out.

It is important to understand the major causes of fire and ways to try to prevent each potential fire from happening.

- *Smoking and matches.* There are, in many areas of the country, strict regulations about smoking in hospitals, clinics, and doctors' offices. Some institutions forbid smoking completely, and others have designated smoking areas. You are responsible, along with the other members of the health care team, to see that smoking regulations are strictly enforced. Smoking must *never* be allowed where oxygen is in use. Never empty ashtrays into plastic bags, plastic wastebaskets, or containers of rubbish that burns (Figure 4.9).
- *Electrical problems.* Report any electrical equipment that does not seem to be functioning properly to the maintenance department or to your supervisor. A small spark, dimming or flickering lights, the smell of smoke or ozone, or the sense of extreme heat are all warning signals that should not go unheeded (Figure 4.10)
- *Flammable liquids.* Make sure that flammable liquids are stored in the proper place with all caps or lids on tight. Keep all combustibles away from a potential source of heat.

FIGURE 4.9 A small spark can start a large fire.

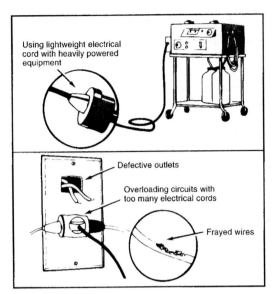

FIGURE 4.10 Misuses of electricity.

- *Rubbish and trash.* Make sure that all rubbish and trash are removed frequently. A small spark that lands on an accumulation of paper, rags, or other combustible trash can start a fire very quickly.
- *Heating system.* Report any problems with the heating system in the facility where you work. Defects in heating systems can cause serious fires.

Be sure that you are properly instructed in your institution's fire plan (Figure 4.11). Review the plan at least once a year and encourage your employer to conduct periodic fire drills. A fire starting in your workplace demands that you act immediately. You must know what to do and how to do it.

Alarm Boxes

At least one fire alarm box should be located near your workstation. There are many different kinds of alarms; learn to use your alarm box.

Extinguishers

Fire extinguishers are located at intervals throughout medical institutions. They vary in type in order to be effective against three basic types of fires (Figure 4.12):

- *Wood, paper,* and *cloth* fires, which can be extinguished by water.
- *Burning liquids,* which can be extinguished with dry chemicals or foam. The use of water will cause this type of fire to spread.
- *Electrical fires,* which can be extinguished only with dry chemicals. Water and foam will conduct electricity and may cause shock to the person using the extinguisher.

Fire Doors

Fire doors are constructed to separate one unit from another and one floor from another, in order to contain a fire and prevent its spread. They are designed to close automatically when a fire alarm is sounded, and they should never be wedged open. There are many fire doors in a large medical facility.

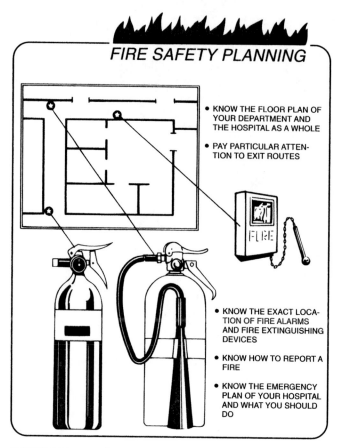

FIGURE 4.11 Fire safety essentials.

Exit Routes

There should be a plan in any facility where you work that indicates the safest exit route in case of fire. Learn this route thoroughly.

The most important thing to remember in a fire is *not to panic*. Lives could depend on your actions in an emergency. When you see a fire, follow these guidelines:

- Sound the fire alarm.
- Attend to the safety of the patients if the fire is immediately threatening to them.
- If possible, attempt to extinguish the fire with the appropriate extinguisher. Do not attempt firefighting if it would endanger you.
- Heed the instructions of your supervisor if the fire continues, following the fire emergency procedures outlined by your facility.
- If there is no risk to you, your employer may instruct you to make an effort to save medical records, ledger cards, or computer disks with financial records.

E ARTHQUAKE SAFETY

Earthquakes can occur in almost any area but are particularly likely to occur in coastal regions. There are some important rules to follow regarding earthquakes.

- Keep a portable radio (with extra batteries) and a flashlight (with extra batteries) at hand in case of an earthquake.

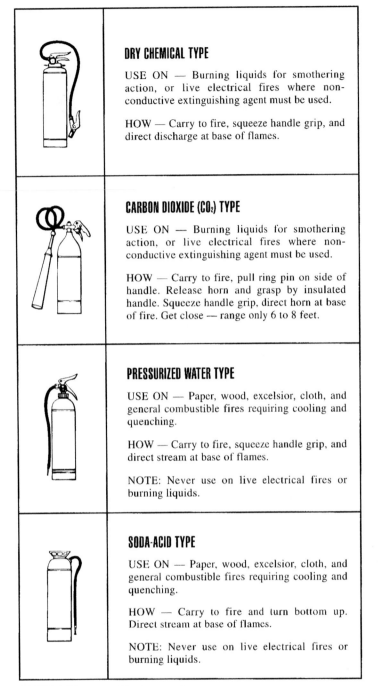

DRY CHEMICAL TYPE

USE ON — Burning liquids for smothering action, or live electrical fires where non-conductive extinguishing agent must be used.

HOW — Carry to fire, squeeze handle grip, and direct discharge at base of flames.

CARBON DIOXIDE (CO₂) TYPE

USE ON — Burning liquids for smothering action, or live electrical fires where non-conductive extinguishing agent must be used.

HOW — Carry to fire, pull ring pin on side of handle. Release horn and grasp by insulated handle. Squeeze handle grip, direct horn at base of fire. Get close — range only 6 to 8 feet.

PRESSURIZED WATER TYPE

USE ON — Paper, wood, excelsior, cloth, and general combustible fires requiring cooling and quenching.

HOW — Carry to fire, squeeze handle grip, and direct stream at base of flames.

NOTE: Never use on live electrical fires or burning liquids.

SODA-ACID TYPE

USE ON — Paper, wood, excelsior, cloth, and general combustible fires requiring cooling and quenching.

HOW — Carry to fire and turn bottom up. Direct stream at base of flames.

NOTE: Never use on live electrical fires or burning liquids.

FIGURE 4.12 Types of fire extinguishers.

- If an earthquake occurs, *keep calm*. Panic kills!
- If you are indoors, stay there. Help assemble patients under a desk, table, or in a doorway. Stay clear of windows. The greatest hazards from falling objects may be outdoors, so *stay inside*.
- After the earthquake, be alert for leaking gas. Gas may have to be shut off to avoid serious problems.
- Electricity may also have to be cut off.
- Cooperate with public safety efforts and do not use the telephone except to report fire or violent crime emergencies.

There are also other natural disasters that can occur in various regions of the country, such as tornadoes, hurricanes, floods, and tidal waves. Be sure that you are familiar with disaster plans for your region.

SUMMARY

The medical clerical worker has many medical environments to choose from when embarking on a career. Whether you work in a large medical institution or in a small physician's office, you are a part of a team that is responsible for the safety of the employees and the patients in your workplace. Be constantly aware of any safety hazards that might appear around your workspace and around the patient. Helping control the spread of infection means being vigilant about handwashing and wearing gloves when coming into contact with infectious materials. Quality occurrence reports should be filled out when there is any problem that is not considered a part of the routine operation of your medical environment. The medical clerical worker is also a responsible member of the medical team when dealing with medical emergencies and with unexpected physical disasters such as fire and earthquakes.

LEARNING ACTIVITIES

1. Tour a health facility, concentrating on the safety precautions taken by the facility to ensure the safety of patients and employees.

2. Carefully read the discussion in Appendix A concerning AIDS. Be prepared to discuss AIDS in your class. Make it a habit to look for articles in magazines and newspapers about AIDS issues. Be informed!

3. Call an infection control department of a hospital and ask about the most common hospital-acquired infections (nosocomial infections) in that facility. Report to your class.

4. Janice Jones is a medical clerical worker in the admissions department of City General Hospital. She works with Becky Fowler, a 25-year-old medical clerical employee who is five months' pregnant. Becky and Janice are filing reports. Janice notices that someone has piled up several large files on top of the file cabinet. Suddenly, the files slip off the file cabinet and land on Becky, who is knocked to the ground. Janice asks Becky if she is hurt and then calls the Emergency Room. The E.R. dispatches a transporter to the admitting office to take Becky in a wheelchair to be examined. It is found that Becky is fine, only suffering a bruise on the right forehead where the files hit her head. The accident occurred on August 17, at 4:30 P.M. Janice is asked to fill out an incident report. Fill out the quality occurrence report, found on page 47, for Janice.

5. Locate the nearest fire alarm and extinguisher in your classroom.

6. List six safety rules to follow in the medical environment.

7. What is infection control?

8. Define a *nosocomial infection*.

9. Name two situations when a medical clerical worker might be involved in infection control.

10. Indicate whether each statement below is true or false.

__ **(a)** You are not responsible for hazards caused by other members of your health team.

__ **(b)** When cleaning up broken glass, remove only the large pieces with your hands.

__ **(c)** Extension cords must be placed in an area where no one will trip over them.

__ **(d)** It is okay to put boxes and wheelchairs in the hallways.

__ **(e)** Always set the brake on a wheelchair when getting patients in and out of the chair.

11. List ways to avoid injury when *lifting*.

12. Describe the proper way to change the direction of movement when you are carrying something heavy.

13. State the two elements of fire safety.

14. List four major causes of fire.

15. Name three basic types of fires.

16. Explain why there are different types of fire extinguishers.

17. Identify what might be termed a *medical emergency*.

18. Explain what is meant by *ergonomics*.

19. How do *standard precautions* apply to the medical clerical worker?

20. Match each of the four International Hospital Codes with the proper description.

__ **(a)** Code Red	**(1)** Respiratory/cardiac arrest
__ **(b)** Code Blue	**(2)** Disaster occurring
__ **(c)** Code Yellow	**(3)** Fire in the hospital
__ **(d)** Code Green	**(4)** Uncontrolled person or threatening situation

The Human Body in Health and Disease

VOCABULARY

Anatomy	The study of the structure of the human body.
Anterior side	The front of a person.
Benign tumor	A tumor that grows slowly, never invading surrounding tissue, but occasionally encroaching on nearby tissue during expansion.
Cancer	Tumors that invade and spread to surrounding tissue, denying nutrition to healthy cells.
Cell membrane	The boundaries of a cell, which allow materials to pass in and out, and keep the living substances within the cell.
Chromosomes	Threadlike structures in the nucleus of the cell that control inheritance.
Coronal plane	Divides the front of the body from the back.
Cytoplasm	The area of the cell where the cellular activities take place.
Distal	Farthest from the point of attachment.
DNA	Deoxyribonucleic acid, the material that transfers genetic information in all life forms; also, the main component of chromosomes.
Dorsal	Referring to the back side of the body.
Dorsal cavity	Divided into the *cranial cavity* and the *spinal cavity*, containing the brain, its protecting membranes, large blood vessels, nerves, and the spinal cord.
Inferior	Referring to the areas of the body below the body's midline, closer to the feet.
Lateral	Away from the midline.
Malignant	Referring to a cancerous state.
Metastasis	Rapid growth and spreading of cancer throughout the body systems.
Midsagittal plane	Divides the right and left sides.
Neoplasm	New growth.
Nucleus	The part of a living cell that regulates the activity of the cell, playing an important part in reproduction.
Organs	A grouping together of tissues that perform similar functions.
Physiology	The study of bodily functions.
Posterior side	The back of a person.
Proximal	Nearest the point of attachment.
RNA	Ribonucleic acid, produced by DNA and sent to the cytoplasm to direct the formation of protein molecules necessary to maintain life.
Superior	Referring to the areas of the body above the transverse plane, closer to the head.
Systems	Organs that work together to perform a particular set of functions.
Tissues	Groups of cells of the same type, performing the same function.

Transverse plane	Divides the upper and lower parts of the body.
Ventral	Refers to the front of the body.
Ventral cavity	Divided into the *thoracic* and *abdominal cavities,* containing lungs, heart, major blood vessels, liver, spleen, stomach, pancreas, intestines, urinary bladder, part of the esophagus, and ovaries and uterus of the female.

OBJECTIVES

After completing this chapter, the student is responsible for performing the following objectives:

- Describe the relationship among cells, tissues, organs, and body systems.
- Identify the main body systems.
- Discuss the various medical specialties and specialists.
- Identify the various body areas, planes, and cavities.
- List and define several causes of disease.
- Recognize key terms referring to cancer.

I NTRODUCTION

Knowledge of the healthy human body as well as some common disease processes and terms is very valuable to the medical clerical worker. Your challenging job requires that you have a clear understanding of the human body's **anatomy** and **physiology.** Identifying certain common diseases will help you to perform your job more effectively and accurately.

T HE HUMAN CELL

To understand how the body functions, it is helpful to understand the foundation on which our bodies are built: the *cell.* You cannot see the individual cell—that requires a microscope. The human body is made up of millions of cells, with many different variations. Each cell is specialized, having a special place and function in the human body. All cells have many things in common:

- Cells have specialized functions, such as those of skin, muscle, and so on.
- Cells come from other cells.
- Cells require food (nutrients) to function.
- Cells use oxygen to break down their food.
- Cells need water to transport many substances (e.g., nutrients and waste products).
- Cells grow, repair themselves, and reproduce.

Cell Structure

Cells have similar structures, consisting of three main parts (Figure 5.1):

- The **nucleus,** which directs cellular activities
- The **cytoplasm,** where the cellular activities take place

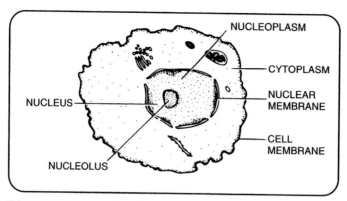

FIGURE 5.1 Diagram of a cell.

- The **cell membrane,** which surrounds the cell and keeps substances inside, allowing materials to pass in and out of the cell

The *nucleus* of the cell plays an important part in the process of heredity, growth, and cell division. The nucleus contains **chromosomes,** which control inheritance.

The *chromosomes* mainly contain **DNA** (deoxyribonucleic acid), the material that transfers genetic information in all life forms. DNA in turn makes **RNA** (ribonucleic acid), which is a partial copy of DNA. RNA acts as a messenger, passing into the cytoplasm of the cell and directing the formation of protein molecules necessary to maintain the life of the cell.

Cells reproduce by division. When a cell prepares for reproduction, the nucleus must duplicate its chromosomes exactly. Then, as the cell divides, the newly duplicated chromosomes pull apart and move to opposite sides of the nucleus. When division is complete, the new cell is identical to the old.

It is necessary for many reasons that the medical clerical worker have some understanding of the human body on the cellular level. Most current research to discover the causes of disease is focused on the cell and its environment. Patients may receive treatment aimed directly at destroying cells that have developed abnormally, such as cancer cells. It will be beneficial for the medical clerical worker to have an understanding of these terms and factors associated with their use.

$\mathcal{T}$ ISSUES

Cells cannot usually function alone. Groups of cells that do the same type of work are called **tissues** (Figure 5.2). Some of the primary types of tissues are as follows:

- *Blood and lymph tissue.* This tissue operates as single cells, traveling in fluid to every part of the body.
- *Cardiac muscle tissue.* This tissue is found only in the heart.
- *Connective tissue.* This tissue connects, supports, covers or lines, pads, and protects the body.
- *Epithelial tissue.* This tissue protects the skin, secretes hormones, aids in absorption, and receives sensations.
- *Muscle tissue.* This tissue ensures movement. *Striated* tissue is found in voluntary muscles, those you move consciously. *Smooth* tissue is found in the involuntary muscles, such as those that push food through the gastrointestinal tract.

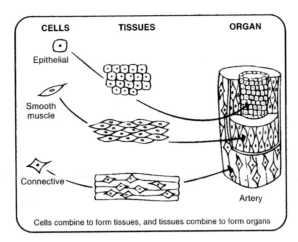

FIGURE 5.2 Cells, tissues, and organs.

■ *Nervous tissue.* This tissue carries nervous impulses from a portion of the brain or spinal cord to all parts of the body. This tissue cannot be renewed.

ORGANS AND SYSTEMS

Tissues are grouped together to form **organs** such as the heart, lungs, and liver. Each organ has a specific job. Organs, in turn, work together to form **systems**. The study of the human body most often is concentrated in a study of these systems. The body's systems are described in Table 5.1.

In addition to recognizing the function of each body system, the medical clerical worker should be aware of the specialties that are connected to each body system, as well as the physician who is involved in the specialty (Table 5.2). Many medical

TABLE 5.1	*B*ODY SYSTEMS	
System	**Functions**	**Organs**
Skeletal	Supports and protects the body	Bones; joints
Muscular	Gives movement to the body	Muscles, tendons; ligaments
Gastrointestinal (digestive)	Takes in and absorbs nutrients and eliminates wastes	Mouth; teeth; tongue; esophagus; salivary glands; stomach; duodenum; intestines; liver; gallbladder; ascending, transverse, and descending colon; rectum; anus; appendix
Nervous	Controls activities of the body	Brain; spinal cord; nerves
Excretory	Removes wastes from the blood, produces and eliminates urine	Kidneys; ureters; bladder; urethra
Reproductive	To reproduce, allows a new human being to be born; for sexual fulfillment and expression of sexuality	Male: testes, scrotum, penis, prostate glands; Female: ovaries, uterus, fallopian tubes, vagina, breasts
Respiratory	Gives the body air to supply oxygen to the cells through the blood and eliminates carbon dioxide	Nose; pharynx; larynx; trachea; bronchi; lungs
Circulatory	Carries food, oxygen, and water to the body cells and removes wastes	Heart; blood; arteries; veins; capillaries; spleen; lymph nodes; lymph vessels
Endocrine	Secretes hormones directly into the blood to regulate body function	Thyroid and parathyroid glands; pineal gland; adrenal glands; testes; ovaries; thymus; pancreas and pituitary gland
Integumentary	Provides first line of defense against infection, maintains body temperature, provides fluids, and gets rid of wastes	Skin; hair; nails; sweat and oil glands

TABLE 5.2	*M*EDICAL SPECIALTIES

Body System	Specialty	Specialist
Skeletal	Orthopedics	Orthopedist, orthopedic surgeon
Muscular	Physiatry	Physiatrist
Gastrointestinal	Gastroenterology	Gastroenterologist
Nervous	Neurology	Neurologist, neurosurgeon
Excretory	Urology	Urologist
Reproductive	Obstetrics, gynecology	Obstetrician, gynecologist
Respiratory	Pulmonary medicine	Pulmonary specialist
Circulatory	Cardiology, vascular medicine	Cardiologist, cardiac surgeon, vascular surgeon
Endocrine	Endocrinology	Endocrinologist
Integumentary	Dermatology	Dermatologist

TABLE 5.3	*D*EFINITIONS OF LATIN AND GREEK ROOT WORDS BY BODY SYSTEM

Word Element/ Combining Form	Refers to:	Word Element/ Combining Form	Refers to:
Integumentary system (skin)		esophago	esophagus, food pipe
dermo, dermato	skin	gastro	stomach
muco	mucous membrane	entero	small intestine
Musculoskeletal system		hepa, hepato	liver
myo	muscle	cholecysto	gallbladder
myocardia	heart muscle	chole	bile, gall
mycolpo	vaginal muscle	lipo	fat
myometro	uterine muscle	choledocho	common bile duct
osteo	bone	ileo	ileum
chondro	cartilage	colo	large intestine
fibro	connective tissue	append	appendix
arthro	joint	procto	rectum
costo	rib	ano	anus
cranio	skull	laparo	abdomen
ilio	hipbone, ilium	*Nervous system*	
sacro	tailbone, sacrum	encephalo	brain
myelo	bone marrow	myelo	spinal cord
Respiratory system		neuro	nerve
aero	air	oculo, ophthalmo	eye
naso, rhino	nose	oto	ear
pharyngo	throat	*Endocrine system*	
tracheo	windpipe	adeno	gland
thoraco	chest	thyro	thyroid
broncho	bronchus	glyco, gluco	sugar
pneumo	lung	*Urinary system*	
Circulatory system		nephro, renal	kidney
cardio	heart	pyelo	kidney, pelvis
hema, hemato	blood, chemo	hydro	water
vaso	blood vessel	uro	urine
arterio	artery	uretero	ureter
phlebo	vein	cysto	urinary bladder
lympho	lymphatic system	*Reproductive system*	
angio	blood and lymphatic vessels	andro	man
erythro	red	gyne	woman
leuko	white	orchi, orchido	testicles
cyano	blue	oophor	ovary
Digestive system		hyster, metro	uterus, womb
stomato	mouth	salpingo	oviduct
denti	teeth	colpo	vagina
glosso	tongue	mast	breasts
pharyngo	pharynx, throat	prostato	prostate

terms refer to anatomical structure or function. Learning the common terms connected to the various body systems will ensure more accurate work (Table 5.3).

Two important reference sources for the medical clerical worker to have near the workstation are a good *medical dictionary* and a clearly written *anatomy and physiology reference book*. You will find yourself often referring to both sources to make sure of correct spelling or perhaps to refresh your memory about the location in the body of a certain anatomical term.

Remember, when in doubt, always double-check! You may find yourself forgetting some of the many parts of the human body, but you will be required to transcribe orders and fill out insurance forms accurately using such terms. So you must remember how to find the correct answers when you need them.

If you work for a physician or a clinic with a specialty, you may be required to become familiar with very specific terms. For instance, if you work in a cardiologist's office, a valuable reference book would be one focusing on the heart. You may have to become very proficient with the terms related to your employer's specialty.

$\mathcal{B}$ODY AREAS, PLANES, AND CAVITIES

As well as studying the body systems, the medical clerical worker has to be familiar with the overall picture of the body and learn the names of areas, planes, and cavities (Figures 5.3 to 5.5). These words will also be used periodically in a doctor's orders, insurance forms, or medical history and physical reports.

In any demonstration or diagram of the human body, the body or body part shown is in the anatomical position. This position has the person standing up straight, facing you, palms out, and feet together. When you look at a person in the

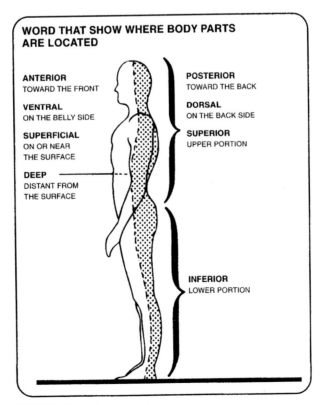

FIGURE 5.3 Body part locations.

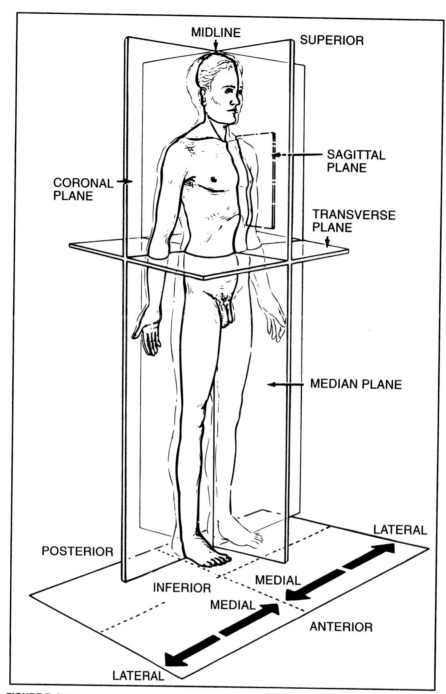

FIGURE 5.4 Directions and planes of the body.

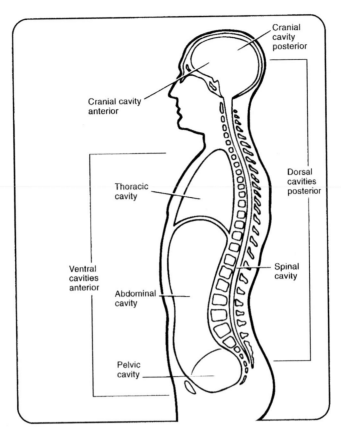

FIGURE 5.5 Body cavities.

anatomical position, remember that his or her left side is always on your right side. The front of a person is called the **anterior side,** also referred to as **dorsal.** The back, including the backbone, is called the **posterior side,** also called **ventral.** The areas of the body closer to the head are called **superior.** Those closer to the feet are called **inferior. Distal** indicates the farthest area from the point of attachment, while **proximal** refers to nearest the point of attachment. **Lateral** indicates a point away from the midline. You can describe the position of an organ of the body using these terms. For instance, the knee is superior to the thigh, or the collar bone is superior to the hip bone.

Often, the *planes* of the body are also used in doctor's reports as part of the description of a patient's condition. Examples of planes of the body include **midsagittal** (dividing the right and left sides), **coronal** (dividing the front of the body from the back), and **transverse** (dividing the upper and lower parts). In addition, *directions* in the body are used to specify regions of the body (Figure 5.4).

The body has two major cavities: the **dorsal cavity** and the **ventral cavity** (Figure 5.5). The dorsal cavity is divided into the cranial and spinal cavities. The *cranial cavity* is in the head and contains the brain, its protecting membranes, large blood vessels, and nerves. The *spinal cavity* contains the spinal cord.

The ventral cavity is divided by the diaphragm into the thoracic and abdominal cavities. The *thoracic cavity* is in the chest and contains the lungs, the heart, the major blood vessels, and a portion of the esophagus. It passes through the diaphragm and enters the stomach, which is in the *abdominal cavity.* Other organs in the abdominal cavity include the liver, spleen, stomach, pancreas, intestines, urinary bladder, and in the female, the ovaries and uterus.

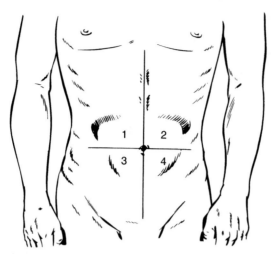

FIGURE 5.6 Quadrants of the abdomen.

In addition, the quadrants of the abdomen are divided into four quadrants: (1) the *right upper quadrant*, (2) the *left upper quadrant*, (3) the *right lower quadrant*, and (4) the *left lower quadrant* (Figure 5.6).

CLASSIFICATION OF DISEASE

Diseases, conditions, infections, and illnesses can all disrupt the normal function of the body. Classifications of disease can often overlap. Diseases are classified by the cause of the abnormality, the body system that has been affected, or the way in which a disease has been acquired (Table 5.4).

Many disease processes are caused by microorganisms. They are usually infectious conditions, causing inflammation, such as appendicitis. Sometimes there are abnormal conditions not related directly to microorganisms. These are described by terms that usually have -*osis* at the end, such as *nephrosis*.

Sometimes, cells grow at abnormal rates and patterns, causing tumors. A number of abnormal conditions can be caused by nutritional problems, chemical abuse,

TABLE 5.4	TYPES OF DISEASE/CONDITION CLASSIFIED BY CAUSE	
Type (Cause)	**Meaning**	**Disease/Condition (Examples)**
Aging	Degeneration of all the body systems	Hardening of the arteries; arteriosclerosis
Birth injury	Occurring at birth	Cerebral palsy
Chemical	Interference of foreign substance	Laënnec's cirrhosis of the liver
Congenital	Occurring during pregnancy	Cleft palate
Deficiency	Lacking the right foods or nutrients and/or hormones	Scurvy (lack of vitamin C)
Hereditary	Passed on through genes	Sickle-cell anemia
Infectious	Communicable; caused by microorganisms	Measles, chickenpox, mumps
Mechanical blocks	Formation of an obstruction of body wastes, fluids, or natural chemicals	Gallstones, kidney stones, blood clots
Metabolic	Failing to produce or break down substances needed for normal processes	Diabetes (lack of insulin)
Neoplastic	Abnormal growth of tissue—tumors (benign or malignant)	Fibroids (benign); cancer (malignant)
Occupational	Peculiar to a job	Lead poisoning (painter); black lung disease (miner)
Trauma	Injury, usually physical	Fracture, broken bone

or pollution. Injuries from accidents, as well as some illnesses, can result in long-term disabilities.

There are also numerous congenital conditions that have existed since birth. Some of these may be inherited and have a genetic cause, which has been passed on from the mother or father.

CANCER AND BENIGN TUMORS

Neoplasm refers to the condition when normal cells suddenly start to grow without control, organization, or purpose. Neoplastic growth can be slow or rapid, benign or **malignant.** The words *tumor* and *neoplasm* are interchangeable.

A **benign tumor** stays at its site of origin and does not usually regrow once removed. It never invades surrounding tissue; it grows slowly and looks like the tissue from which it grew.

Cancer refers to malignant neoplasms. *Malignant neoplasms* grow, spread, invade, and destroy organs. Cancer cells interfere with normal body function. If they are not controlled, they grow and spread between cells, invading tissues and sometimes causing death. Malignant neoplasms can sometimes recur after surgical removal. **Metastasis** refers to the rapid growth and spreading of cancer cells through the body's systems.

Medical clerical workers must be knowledgeable of cancer and its terms, as cancer affects all specialties and occurs in people of all ages. Some patients will not be very sick at all, and others will be facing terminal illness. Compassion and education will help the medical clerical worker deal with this very real health problem in our society.

SUMMARY

The very best reason of all to study human anatomy and physiology is that you can obtain an appreciation of the design of the healthy human body, and a grasp of diseases that can affect people. Accurate doctor's orders, histories, physical reports, surgical records, and insurance forms are crucial to safe, high-quality care of patients. You will learn many medical terms that relate to the body's structure, function, and abnormal conditions. Knowing what these terms represent will help you be more accurate and precise.

LEARNING ACTIVITIES

1. Look through the classified section of a local telephone book and write down all the medical specialties listed. Report to the class.

2. Select a disease/condition listed in Table 5.4 and locate an association in your area that is set up to disseminate information about the disease, such as the American Heart Association or the American Cancer Society. Give a report based on the information obtained.

3. With the aid of anatomical drawings, identify areas designated by the instructor.

4. Explain the difference between *physiology* and *anatomy.*

5. Name four things that living cells have in common.

6. Describe the three main parts of the cell.

7. Explain the difference between DNA and RNA.

8. Match each type of tissue with the correct primary function.
   ___ **(a)** epithelial   **(1)** Movement to all body parts
   ___ **(b)** muscle   **(2)** Carries impulses
   ___ **(c)** cardiac   **(3)** Supports bones
   ___ **(d)** connective   **(4)** Heart muscle
   ___ **(e)** blood and lymph   **(5)** Movement
   ___ **(f)** nerve   **(6)** Protects skin

9. Organize the following four terms from the most specific to the most general: organs, cells, systems, tissues.

10. Name the following medical specialties.
   (a) The work of a physician who deals with the nervous system.
   (b) A specialty dealing with the excretory system.
   (c) The specialty that deals with the skin.
   (d) The work of a physician who operates on the heart.
   (e) The specialty involved with the endocrine system.

11. Define the following terms referring to body areas.
   (a) Dorsal
   (b) Ventral
   (c) Anterior
   (d) Posterior
   (e) Superior

12. Name the four quadrants of the abdomen.

13. Name the two major body cavities.

14. List three types of diseases.

15. Define the following terms.
   (a) Benign
   (b) Malignant
   (c) Metastasis

Dealing Successfully with Patients and Co-workers

Active listening — A technique where the listener gives the communicator his or her full attention, responding to the words spoken and asking pertinent questions.

Constructive criticism — Criticism given in the spirit of cooperation, rather than being given with the purpose of insult.

Empathy — The quality of being able to put yourself in another person's place and appreciate what he or she may be feeling.

Maslow's hierarchy of needs — Five essential human needs as described by American psychologist Abraham Maslow.

Nonverbal communications — Communications accomplished by facial expressions, gestures, and touch.

Self-Esteem — Feeling good about yourself and your abilities.

OBJECTIVES

After completing this chapter, the student is responsible for performing the following objectives:

- Discuss how feeling good about yourself helps you to relate better to others.
- Identify Abraham Maslow's hierarchy of needs.
- List four methods to communicate effectively with patients.
- Discuss how to cooperate effectively with coworkers.
- Identify some ways to achieve a good employer–employee relationship.
- List three methods of nonverbal communication.
- Identify four barriers to effective communication.
- Discuss some special communication problems associated with special needs patients.

1 NTRODUCTION

Being able to get along with other people is one of the most important traits you can possess, both for personal success and for becoming a competent medical clerical worker. You will be exposed to an enormous range of people in your work, including patients and their families, office staff, your employer, and a wide range of medical professionals. Good human relations skills will help you become more successful in dealing compassionately and effectively with the people with whom you come into contact in your job.

*P*OSITIVE PERSONAL IDENTITY

Psychologists have found that people who do not feel good about themselves cannot relate well to others. If you are going to be successful at getting along with others, you must be able to get along with yourself.

There are many books, workshops, and seminars to build **self-esteem.** These programs all have in common one message: You have the ability to be a winner. If you accept yourself for what you are, you should be able to accept others for the way they are. Winners do not apologize for themselves.

Another key to a positive personal identity is to trust yourself. You must develop ways to believe in and rely upon yourself. You cannot always expect to succeed, but it is important to try your best. That is all you can ask from yourself. The real reward is often in the trying.

Winners seek new experiences to further their understanding of the world. Fear is something that can rule your life and interfere with your ability to relate to others. The more people you get to know, the more you will realize that no matter what race, color, or religion people are, they all have the same basic needs. Those needs are to be treated with respect and people are to be given a chance to make their contribution to the world.

The American psychologist Abraham Maslow (1908–1970) identified five categories of human needs, known as **Maslow's hierarchy of needs.** Through research and studies, Maslow identified the following needs, starting with the most important need:

1. *Physiological needs.* These include the physical, biological, or basic needs required by every human being. Examples include oxygen, food, water, and sleep.

2. *Safety and security.* These needs include the desire to feel secure in the environment and being free from anxiety and fear. Marital problems, financial struggles, and employment uncertainties may interfere drastically with this need.

3. *Affection and love.* These needs include the need for friendship, social acceptance, and love. People's need to belong, relate to others, and receive social acceptance are driving forces at this level. Sexual needs have been included at this level as well as at the physiological level.

4. *Esteem.* Receiving respect, approval, and appreciation from others enhances one's self-esteem. When self-esteem is high, the final level, self-actualization, can be possible.

5. *Self-actualization.* When a person achieves self-actualization, the individual is satisfied with the levels of growth and success he or she has achieved. Personal beliefs are strong, and ideas are expressed with confidence. This level can never be reached without needs met on all other levels.

As we identify a need, it is helpful to be motivated to act in a way that will attain that need. If the need is satisfied, the person will feel a sense of fulfillment. A positive sense of personality identity can result from setting realistic goals, hard work, and cooperation with others.

Winners do not separate themselves from the rest of the world. They are committed to improving the quality of their lives and the lives of others. Being a medical clerical worker gives you a great opportunity to help others with their problems, and in the process you will feel good about yourself.

Winners have the ability to live life to the fullest. Complainers, who worry about what could be happening instead of what really is, are not enjoying life. Winners understand that life is too short to waste time complaining about things over which they have no control. There is humor in most situations, and the winner can often find laughter in life.

COMMUNICATING EFFECTIVELY WITH PATIENTS

Possessing good human relations skills is as important as any other skill of a medical clerical worker. The first contact that a patient has with the medical community usually involves communication with a medical clerical worker. Listed below are some invaluable skills that should always be kept in mind when dealing with patients and coworkers.

Be a Good Listener

Both patients and co-workers appreciate someone who will listen and respond sympathetically to problems. When patients are explaining medical problems to you, you should give them your full attention. Looking out the window, shuffling papers, or glancing at your watch frequently are all actions that convey that you are not interested in their problems. **Active listening** requires that you respond continually to what the communicator is saying, making him or her aware that you are indeed listening and understanding what is being said. Your responses, however, should not interrupt the speaker's train of thought or lead the conversation. An active listener lets the speaker lead the conversation and gives responses that encourage further conversation and convey acceptance.

Have Patience

You are going to be dealing with sick people, who may not be acting normally. You are going to deal continually with people whose main emotion is fear. Will they be told that they have cancer? Are they going to die? Are they going to be told that they cannot go back to work? How will the bills get paid? Empathize with such fears, imagining what it would be like to be facing such obstacles. Sincere **empathy** is much appreciated by the patient.

Patients may have very little energy and may speak slowly. Their ability to communicate may be complicated by pain. Patients who are sick often dislike waiting in a crowded waiting room and may be very angry about not being seen immediately by the doctor. You must again put yourself in the patients' place and show consideration and patience when they display angry and rude behavior.

Patience is also required with co-workers. Medical environments are often stressful, and the hurry-up pace often makes medical personnel feel frustrated and difficult to work with. Try to improve the stressful situation by being calm.

Be Sensitive

A medical clerical worker must be sensitive to the emotional and physical concerns of patients. You will be asking questions about the patient's medical history that can be embarrassing. You must use a professional manner when asking such difficult

questions, and you need to make sure that other patients in the waiting area are not able to hear the patient's answers.

Most patients are very concerned about physical privacy while undressing or when they are on the examining table. When working in a doctor's office, clinic, or radiology department, the patient should be given clear directions about where and how to undress. Gowns and drapes should always be provided.

COMMUNICATING EFFECTIVELY WITH THE PATIENT'S FAMILY AND FRIENDS

Patients frequently are accompanied to a medical facility with one or more persons, usually family and/or friends. Often these people who come to support the patient will ask questions and possibly even have needs of their own.

In all cases, the needs of the patient must be primarily addressed. The medical clerical worker might ask the patient, "Mrs. Maxwell, do you wish to have your daughter accompany you to the examination room?" The issue of privacy for the patient must always be foremost in the medical clerical worker's mind. Very young children will usually have parents accompany them to the examination room. However, as children become young adults, it may be appropriate to allow the child privacy with the physician.

Friends and family of patients may get anxious in the waiting room when the patient has been with the physician for some time. One of the medical clerical worker's duties might be to acknowledge these people who seem nervous and explain any delays or assure them that the wait will not be much longer. These people may be a very significant part of the healing process for the patient, as they are lending their support and concern. However, the medical clerical worker must remember not to divulge any information about the patient considered confidential, such as diagnosis, treatment, and so on. Such questions must always be referred to the physician.

COMMUNICATING EFFECTIVELY WITH CO-WORKERS

You and your fellow members of the medical team have one clear purpose in your job—to help the patients get the best care possible. All activities should be performed with the patient in mind and in full cooperation with each of your fellow workers.

If you treat your co-workers in a professional manner, making them feel like people worthy of respect, you will probably have a good working relationship. The following are good rules for cooperation.

- Let your fellow workers know when you have to leave your workstation, even if it is for a short period. Always leave clear directions about where you are in your duties when you leave work. A co-worker who replaces you will appreciate your clear communications.

- Always ask questions if you feel you do not understand a procedure or duty. An honest question does not make you look foolish, but hours of work done improperly reflect very poorly on you.

- Try to leave personal problems at home when you come to the workplace. Continual discussion of personal problems gives co-workers and patients the impression that you cannot handle your life very well, and they may think that you will not be able to handle your professional duties well either.

- Accept **constructive criticism** from your co-workers with a spirit of cooperation. Try not to be defensive and *never* blame someone else when you are at fault.

- Show a willingness to learn new tasks and take on more responsibility when you feel you are ready to handle it.

- Make every effort to complete any task you are given. Try not to complain about assigned work.

- Use tact when dealing with patients and visitors.

Stress

Today's health care environment is a stressful one. Budgetary considerations may mean that your office is understaffed. Some days may occur where you do not have time to exchange two words with a co-worker. During these times, lunch and rest breaks are essential to your well-being. Just a little time away from the office pressure can give you a new outlook on a problem that seemed impossible minutes ago.

A great many communication problems among co-workers occur because of the high-pressure nature of the job itself. Exchanging common courtesies and being considerate can go far to alleviate such situations. You may be the target of patients' and co-workers' pent-up feelings from time to time. Your own feelings may need to be vented in difficult situations as well. It is critical that you handle such feelings in a constructive way. Promise yourself a vigorous exercise session right after work. Take a walk around the block twice instead of having a cup of coffee on your break. Realize the difference between the things you can and cannot control. Do not waste energy on situations over which you have no control.

If stress becomes unbearable for you, it is time to calmly discuss how you feel with your employer. Perhaps there is something that can be done immediately to relieve some stress. Try to correct a chronically stressful situation in the workplace as soon as possible. Working under constant stress can lead to several stress-related disorders, such as headaches, asthma, gastritis, peptic ulcers, and so on.

COMMUNICATING EFFECTIVELY WITH YOUR EMPLOYER

Successful communication with your employer is very important for a number of reasons. For example, it will enable you to understand what is expected of you in your specific employment situation. The atmosphere in which you work will be much more pleasant if you and your employer are clear about each other's needs and expectations.

An employer will expect you to:

- Have a good attitude.
- Deal honestly with every situation.
- Be dependable.
- Accept constructive criticism.
- Be loyal.
- Be willing to learn.
- Perform tasks according to instructions.
- Take initiative.

Conversely, you should have reasonable expectations regarding your employer. A happy work environment is a two-way street. You have every reason to expect that:

- You will receive the salary agreed to when you were hired.
- You will have adequate training before assuming your responsibilities.
- You will have the opportunity to advance.
- You may receive benefits if you work over 20 hours a week.
- You will be working in a safe environment.
- You will receive respect for a job well done.

The best working relationships are honest ones. If you really feel that you are not being treated fairly, you should not air your frustrations with your coworkers and patients, but should go directly to your supervisor. You should be prepared to state your frustrations clearly and be ready with suggestions as to how a negative situation might be changed. You also need to understand the chain of command in the organization, always going to your immediate supervisor first before directing a complaint to a person in a higher position. In many medical offices, there is an office manager whose job is to handle office relations.

Sexual Harassment

As discussed in Chapter 2, Title VII of the Civil Rights Act of 1964 defines sexual harassment as "unwelcome sexual advances, requests for sexual favors, and other verbal or physical conduct of a sexual nature when submission or rejection of this conduct explicitly or implicitly affects an individual's employment, unreasonably interferes with an individual's work performance, or creates an intimidating, hostile,

---

Real-Life Scenario

Jenny works for Dr. Winters, who has been a pleasant, fair employer for a year. However, lately Jenny has noticed that Dr. Winters is losing patience with employees often and has raised his voice at Jenny on more than one occasion in the last few weeks. Yesterday, Dr. Winters accused Jenny of not telling him about an important phone call, which was not the truth. Dr. Winters didn't believe her when she defended herself, and he swore at her.

Laura, the office manager, tells Jenny that she must be patient with Dr. Winters. His wife has left him, and he has to move out of his home. "Be patient with him," counsels Laura. "He'll calm down and return to normal soon."

1. Should Jenny heed Laura's advice and let Dr. Winters vent his emotions?
2. Should Jenny talk with Dr. Winters?
3. Should Jenny quit her job?

---

or offensive work environment." If you find that a co-worker or a supervisor at your workplace is making suggestive advances toward you or saying things of a sexual nature that make you uncomfortable, it is your responsibility to let the harasser know immediately that his or her conduct is unwelcome and must be terminated. You should report such actions to your supervisor immediately, or to a higher authority if the supervisor is the harasser.

*N*ONVERBAL COMMUNICATION

To interact successfully with patients, co-workers, and everyone else in your life, a general knowledge of communication is necessary. This will help you put to use the points made earlier in this chapter.

In addition to written and spoken communications, there are **nonverbal communications** including posture, facial expressions, gestures, and touch. It is essential

that you understand the elements of this type of communication. You may think that you are responding in a compassionate manner, but if you are not smiling and your body is stiff, you may convey a completely different message to a confused patient.

Facial expressions alone can convey much information to a patient. A smile when the patient enters the medical environment can mean a great deal, and so can a frown. You can say something very kind and have a message of disapproval in your eyes. When you are being sincere, your facial expressions will generally reflect your words.

Gestures are strong message givers. Turning your back to a co-worker while he or she is speaking to you is a very clear negative message. Walking away from a patient who is explaining something to you tells the patient that you are simply not interested in listening. Use of your hands and shoulders when you are speaking and listening conveys a message. You need to determine if you are sending the messages that you intend to send.

Touch can let the patient know that you really care, and it can also give a negative impression. If you roughly grab the arm of a patient who is having trouble walking, that is a clear message of impatience and lack of concern. But the gentle placement of a hand on the shoulder of an upset patient can convey caring.

Key nonverbal communications additionally include:

- The appropriate use of space (face-to-face positioning at the same eye level and not getting too close or too far away from the patient while communicating).
- Allowing time to converse so that you are not looking at the clock, shifting around in nervousness, and so on.
- Eliminating distracting body movements such as foot shaking and pencil tapping.
- Making sure to always maintain good eye contact while talking with the patient.

B ARRIERS TO COMMUNICATION

There are many barriers to good communication that you may not always notice. A good communicator will be aware of as many barriers as possible and try to ensure that these barriers can be effectively overcome.

Prejudice

Most of us have prejudices that we have formed as we have grown up. These prejudices can affect your ability to communicate with patients and co-workers. You need to be aware of these prejudices. Chances are that you will be able to overcome such ideas as you allow yourself to open up to people and realize how similar we all are.

Frustrations

You are irritated because your mother did not remember your birthday. Your child forgot his lunch for the tenth time. Your co-worker didn't do some filing, and you have to do his or her filing and your own as well. Unless you take the responsibility to control your behavior, these feelings of frustration will interfere with your ability to communicate effectively with others. The patient has not caused your problems and should not be punished for them.

Talking Too Fast

It is especially important when working with the elderly that you not talk too fast. You may deliver an important message so quickly that it is not understood. Slow down and take time to be an effective communicator. Remember also not to use complicated medical terminology when talking to nonmedical people.

Physical Disabilities

People who have significant physical disabilities can often present a communications challenge. A recent stroke victim may be very difficult to understand. Someone in pain may not be able to concentrate on important directions or explanations. In addition, someone who does not hear or see well may not understand what you have to say. All these situations plus the hundreds of others that you will see in the medical environment require common sense, patience, and some creativity on your part. Accept such disabilities as a challenge to be met and you will find many rewards.

Mental Confusion

Some patients will look very capable and may not have obvious disease processes. But due to drug usage, mental illness, or many other problems, patients may be mentally confused and unable to understand what you are saying. These people may require a relative or friend to be with them to help with communication. Much patience can be required in these circumstances.

Limited English Proficiency

You will encounter patients who do not speak English or have limited English skills. Most will be able to communicate on some level, but you may need an interpreter when giving important directions or obtaining complicated information. Many medical facilities have a list of people in the facility who can speak different languages and may be available to serve as an interpreter. Hopefully, patients will bring along a relative or friend who speaks both English and the patient's language. You must be

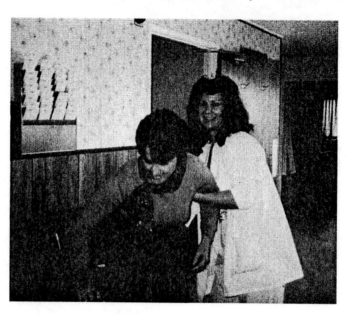

careful to watch for patients who want you to think they understand. In reality, they are not comprehending what you are saying.

Cultural Differences

Sometimes a patient may come from a culture that is uncomfortable with some of the ways you have been taught to communicate. Some cultures are uncomfortable with direct eye contact and look away. Your direct gaze might even give the impression of hostility. Some cultures look to the male in the family to make decisions, even though the female may be the patient. Overlooking the male's dominant role in favor of the patient may offend him. Some cultures are very uncomfortable with taking any clothes off at all in the examination room. Others may be offended by a stranger touching them, even shaking their hand.

Patients are to be treated as individuals. If certain cultures puzzle you and you feel you might have offended a patient, have your employer help you find materials that explain different customs so that you might better understand and make as comfortable as possible patients outside our culture.

The Elderly

With the advent of better nutrition and excellent health care, the elderly population is increasing by great numbers. The elderly tend to move at a slower pace and may require patience on the medical clerical worker's part. Words may be spoken slowly, and hearing may be impaired. Mental confusion and physical disabilities may affect many elderly patients. Remember to talk slowly and clearly if the patient is hearing impaired.

Children

Children require special communication skills. Many are afraid of the entire medical environment and may exhibit difficult behavior. Try to relate to the child as well as to the parent or adult with the child. Make the young patients feel like an important part of the whole process and speak to them so that they understand you. You can play a very important part in making fearful children feel more comfortable by treating them with directness and a calm, open manner.

*S*UMMARY

One of the most important aspects of a medical clerical worker's job is to be able to relate well to patients, patient family and friends, and fellow workers. Effective communication skills will help ensure a successful career as a medical clerical worker.

*L*EARNING ACTIVITIES

1. Choose a partner. Tell your partner ten things about yourself that you really like. Then use active listening while you hear your partner tell his or her ten most positive attributes. You both must list *all* ten attributes.

2. Using role playing, act out the following situations that various medical clerical workers might face.
   (a) Lorraine is a medical clerical worker employed in a hospital laboratory. She must reassure a frightened child who does not want to have her blood drawn.
   (b) Danielle is employed in a cardiologist's office as a medical receptionist. She encounters a patient who is very angry because he does not feel that the doctor has listened to his complaints.
   (c) John is working as an admissions clerk in a large hospital. He is taking information from a very sick patient who is facing serious, life-threatening surgery. Demonstrate how nonverbal communication can play an important role for John in dealing with the sick patient.
   (d) Jennifer works as a medical records clerk in a very busy health clinic. She is concerned about the poor working conditions in the medical records department. She wishes to approach her employer about the possibility of some changes taking place.

(e) Act out various scenarios where a medical clerical worker might feel uncomfortable with language and/or actions of a co-worker.

3. Make a list of some personal barriers to communication that you may possess.

4. Using body language alone, communicate various feelings to the class.

5. Research a different culture and find out a difference that a medical clerical worker should respect when performing his or her duties.

6. List four ways in which you can improve the way you feel about yourself.

7. Identify three methods that you can use to communicate effectively with patients.

8. Why is cooperation with coworkers so important?

9. Name five traits that most employers expect their employees to demonstrate.

10. Explain how to make patients comfortable when you initially greet them.

CHAPTER 7

Reception Techniques

Americans with Disabilities Act (ADA)	A Congressional act passed in 1990 to end discrimination against individuals with disabilities.
Answering service	A service hired to handle telephone calls when the office or facility is closed.
Appointment book	A book used to schedule patients' medical appointments.
Appointment reminder card	A card used to show the day, date, and time of a patient's appointment, serving as a reminder.
Cellular phone	Portable phone that communicates through radio signals.
Guarantor	Person responsible for payment of medical bills.
Multibutton key telephone	The most common telephone set used in the professional office.
Personal pager	Electronic device that can be activated to alert the carrier to phone a specific number.
Physician practice brochure	A brochure put together to give specific information about a physician's practice, such as office hours, staff names, fees, and other details.
Registration form	A form used by a medical office or facility to determine basic information about patients.
Speaker phone	A telephone with a microphone designed for hands-free communication.
Telephone log	A record of all incoming calls.
Tie line	A telephone service that permits a caller to bypass a switchboard and dial directly.

OBJECTIVES

After completing this chapter, the student is responsible for performing the following objectives:

- Discuss the importance of having a positive initial interaction with a patient.
- Define verbal and nonverbal communication.
- List six ways to improve the appearance of a medical reception room.
- Discuss the importance of the patient registration form.
- Identify four ways that you can improve your telephone communications.
- Discuss the difference between incoming and outgoing telephone calls.
- Identify incoming telephone calls that might be considered priority calls.
- Discuss the need for maintaining telephone logs.
- List various auxiliary telephone systems.
- Describe four appointment scheduling systems.
- Discuss referral appointment scheduling.

*I*NTRODUCTION

The most important element in the relationship between patient and medical staff is trust. The medical clerical worker when acting as a receptionist is often the first contact the patient has with the medical office, clinic, or hospital. The contact may be on the telephone or in person, and it is critical in setting the tone of the relationship to come.

It is crucial that the medical clerical worker assume the responsibility for making a patient feel safe and welcomed in the medical environment. Effective communication skills in person and on the phone, as well as efficient scheduling of appointments, help assure the patient of the best possible care.

*G*REETING THE PUBLIC

The patient's first impression of a medical environment is often the communication that he or she has with the medical receptionist. The tone of your voice and your general manner can establish the type of relationship that will develop between the patient and the medical staff.

When patients enter a medical office, clinic, or hospital, they should be greeted as soon as possible. The medical clerical worker should review the appointment sheet ahead of time and be aware which patients are expected. Greet the patient by name, making sure to pronounce the name correctly, which may involve recording a unique pronunciation on the patient's chart. For instance, if you have a patient named Mr. Zahnekahrian, you might write "Mr. Za-nee-car-i-an" on the chart. Learning a patient's name is a very good way to make the patient feel like he or she is not a part of an impersonal assembly line.

Children and young teenagers can be addressed by their first names, but adults should be addressed by Mrs., Miss, Ms., or Mr. In the interest of good manners, do not use an adult's first name until you have been given permission to do so. Patients should be recognized as soon as they enter the office, even if you are busy. It takes little time to give a cheerful greeting such as "Good morning, Mrs. Davis. Dr. Stephens will be with you in a few minutes."

When you get to know a patient, it is perfectly permissible to mention something personal: For example, "Hello, Mr. Jones. How's that lovely vegetable garden of yours?" A personal touch can make the patient feel he or she is an important part of the medical practice.

Remember, when you get behind in your work and your day is getting more and more frustrating, you may still be able to communicate a cheerful greeting to a patient. However, your nonverbal communications (gestures, facial expressions, tone of voice, appearance) may be giving a different message. Patients become confused when a medical clerical worker greets them with a friendly smile and an aloof manner. Be aware of both the verbal and the nonverbal communications that you express.

Patience is probably the most valuable trait that you can have when acting as a receptionist. People who are sick often act differently than when they are well. They may be very unpleasant, nervous, or completely withdrawn. They need your understanding. If a patient enters a crowded waiting room with children crying and people coughing, you may have to deal with a very annoyed patient who has to wait in this environment. Often you will hear such comments as: "I've been waiting at least thirty minutes. I'm going to be late for my next appointment!"

Your response should *not* be something like "Well, medical offices are busy places, and you'll just have to wait your turn." Instead, let the patient know that you understand his or her impatience. Apologize for the delay and explain briefly about emergencies that have come up. Reassure the patient that he or she is important, too, and will be seen as soon as possible. "I'm so sorry for the delay, Mrs. Allen. Dr. Peters knows you are here and will be with you shortly."

As discussed in Chapter 6, you will often have to deal with families and friends of the patient. They may routinely accompany their friend or loved one during appointments, and they may ask you questions or even make demands. Rules of courtesy and kindness apply to these people as well.

Confidentiality

You will find yourself in the position of being told confidences by patients and their worried loved ones. As discussed throughout this textbook, you must always respect the confidentiality of patients and visitors. Often, when people are frightened or medicated, they will tell you things they would not reveal under normal circumstances.

R ECEPTION AREA

A patient often spends more time in the reception area of the medical facility than with medical personnel. It is important to have that area be as pleasant as possible. It is easier to wait in attractive, welcoming surroundings than in a cluttered, unpleasant environment.

It may be part of the medical clerical worker's duty to check first thing in the morning to ensure that the reception room is neat and uncluttered. You will probably not be assigned janitorial tasks, but you may be called upon to make a comfortable place for patients to wait. The following list will help you create a pleasant environment in a reception room.

- Straighten the reception room several times a day, rearranging magazines, adjusting lighting, and making sure that furniture is arranged to make the reception room look as spacious as possible.
- Discourage smoking by placing a "Thank You for Not Smoking" sign in full view of the patients.
- Make sure that the temperature of the facility is a constant 70°F if you have control over the temperature setting.
- Magazines should have vinyl covers to avoid soiling or tearing. Outdated magazines should be discarded.
- If your facility has child patients, provide small chairs and a table with colorful books in good condition and toys that can be played with quietly. Avoid toys with several pieces or with very small pieces that could injure children. Choose toys that can be cleaned easily. Safety caps should be installed in electrical outlets.
- Music at a low volume can help calm patients. Avoid radio stations with advertisements. Music may not be possible in a large medical facility.
- Information pamphlets are readily available from various associations, such as the American Heart Association, American Cancer Society, Red Cross, and National Kidney Foundation. Patients appreciate being able to take home such information, and it can be displayed neatly and attractively in the medical reception area.

- Office furniture should be cleaned and replaced periodically, as needed.
- Care should be taken to see that walls are clean and free of marring. Subtle wallpaper is often an attractive addition. Colors that calm the patients (blues, warm browns) are preferred to loud colors that are not as soothing (oranges, reds, bright pinks). You may have no control over this in a large facility.
- Wall decor can include relaxing, pastoral scenes, or any pleasant pictures that make the patients feel welcome and relaxed. Many reception rooms have a well-kept aquarium and sometimes a television set.
- **The Americans with Disabilities Act** was passed by the federal government in 1990 to protect physically challenged persons. Barrier-free accommodations are required in public and commercial facilities. This law applies to businesses with at least fifteen employees, but some states are stricter in enforcing this act. People with disabilities must have access to your facility. Bathrooms in the facility should also have handrails, wide doorways, and other aids if your patient population contains disabled people.

$\mathcal{R}$ EGISTRATION FORMS

On or before a first visit, a patient should complete a **registration form** (Figure 7.1). This form is designed to gather minimum identifying information from the patient, including:

- Full name, address, and telephone number
- Date of birth
- Sex
- Social Security number
- Marital status
- Occupation
- Name, address, and telephone of employer
- Name of person responsible for payment (**guarantor**)
- Name and address of insurance company or companies that is/are providing medical coverage with health insurance policy numbers
- Name, address, and telephone of nearest relative or friend
- Referring physician

PATIENT INFORMATION FOR MEDICAL RECORDS *(Please Print)* DATE:

PATIENT MR. MRS. MISS — LAST NAME — FIRST NAME — MIDDLE

PATIENT ADDRESS — STREET — CITY — STATE — ZIP — HOME PHONE

SOCIAL SECURITY NUMBER — DATE OF BIRTH — AGE — DRIVER'S LICENSE NO.

PATIENT EMPLOYER — OCCUPATION

EMPLOYER'S ADDRESS — STREET — CITY — STATE — ZIP — BUS. PHONE

SPOUSE'S NAME — MARITAL STATUS M S D W SEP — REFERRED BY

SPOUSE'S EMPLOYER — STREET — CITY — STATE — ZIP — BUS. PHONE

IN CASE OF EMERGENCY CONTACT: — NAME — ADDRESS — CITY — STATE — ZIP TELEPHONE

MEDICAL INSURANCE INFORMATION

COMPANY — POLICY NUMBER

COMPANY — POLICY NUMBER

COMPANY — POLICY NUMBER

IF SOMEONE OTHER THAN PATIENT IS RESPONSIBLE FOR PAYMENT PLEASE COMPLETE THIS SECTION

RESPONSIBLE PARTY — LAST NAME — FIRST NAME — MIDDLE — RELATION

ADDRESS — STREET — CITY — STATE — ZIP — TELEPHONE

OCCUPATION — EMPLOYED BY

EMPLOYER'S ADDRESS — STREET — CITY — STATE — ZIP — BUS. PHONE

I hereby authorize Dr.____________________ to release any and all medical (including dental) information to the above-named insurance carrier (or to a designated attorney) for purposes of claims administration and evaluation, utilization review and financial audit. This authorization remains valid and effective from the date of signing until revoked in writing. I understand that I may request a copy of this authorization. I have read this authorization and understand it. I hereby assign Dr.____________________ all money to which I am entitled for medical and/or surgical expense relative to the service rendered by him, but not to exceed my indebtedness to said physician and/or surgeon. It is understood that any money received from the above named insurance company, over and above my indebtedness will be refunded to me when my bill is paid in full. I understand I am financially responsible to said doctor(s) for charges not covered by this assignment. I further agree in the event of non-payment, to bear the cost of collection, and/or Court cost and reasonable legal fees should this be required.

INSURED OR GUARDIAN'S SIGNATURE ____________________ PATIENT'S SIGNATURE ____________________

58-8409 © 1976 BIBBERO SYSTEMS, INC. PETALUMA, CA

FIGURE 7.1 Patient registration form.

In some situations, a registration form is mailed to the patient ahead of time, but in most offices the patient is handed the registration questionnaire at the time of the first visit. It is customary to hand the patient a pen with a form attached to a clipboard. This way, the patient can sit comfortably and write in private on a secure surface. When it is completed, check it over carefully for omissions and, if necessary, ask the patient for the missing information. Have a current telephone book available for patient use.

The registration form becomes a part of the patient's permanent record. It should be updated annually. Care must be taken to get *all* of the information necessary for the patient's type of health insurance. Throughout the year, make it a habit to ask patients if there have been any changes in this information. Has the patient moved? Is there a new telephone number? Has the patient changed employers or changed insurance coverage?

Physician Practice Brochure

Physicians today are improving communication with their patients by presenting each new patient with a printed **physician practice brochure.** This professionally produced brochure describes the basic policies and procedures of the physician's practice. The language of the brochure should be nontechnical and friendly in tone, perhaps addressing the patients as "you" and the staff as "we."

The brochure is designed for the patient's convenience as well as the convenience of the medical clerical worker. Information normally obtained by a call to the office is available in the brochure. Information might include:

Address and phone number of practice

Maps to locate physician/local health care facilities

Office hours

Listing of office personnel

After hours emergency procedures

Appointment scheduling

Procedures for canceling appointments

Billing, payment, and collection procedures

Participation in insurance programs, including managed care programs

Specialty information

Prescription information

*O*PENING AND CLOSING THE FACILITY

Often the medical clerical worker may be the first person to work in the morning and sometimes the last to leave the office. Opening and closing facilities is a responsibility to be taken very seriously.

Opening

When the first patient arrives in the morning, the facility should be completely ready. Alarm systems should be disarmed. Any equipment requiring warm-up that is used at the beginning of the day (such as copiers) should be turned on. It is recommended that whoever opens will arrive at least twenty minutes before the first patient. A visual check is made of each room to be certain preparations are made for the day. Patient comfort should be paramount. Answering services or machines should be checked for any telephone messages.

Closing

When your job is finished for the day, each room of the facility is checked to make sure all equipment is properly shut down with doors and windows secured. All *sensitive* materials should be locked away, including any drugs identified in the Controlled Substances Act list. Any cash should be locked in a safe container. Each room should be ready for opening on the next day.

If there is an answering service, the service should be notified as you leave and any alarms set. Your safety should be guaranteed if you leave the facility after dark. Lighting should be appropriate both inside and outside. If you have to walk a distance to your parking space after dark, you should be accompanied by a security guard.

$\mathcal{T}$ELEPHONE COMMUNICATIONS IN THE MEDICAL ENVIRONMENT

Anyone who has ever been in a medical environment can tell you that the telephone is an essential part of the medical world. Some experts feel that telephone technique can determine the success or failure of a practice. Developing good telephone communication skills is *absolutely essential* for a medical clerical worker.

Telephone Etiquette

When you communicate by phone, your voice should be cheerful and calm, and you should speak as you would in a face-to-face encounter. The patient should get the impression that you are glad to accept his or her call and that the needs of the patient are being listened to and will be addressed. If you are making the call, be brief and to the point. Excess conversation can confuse the issue you are addressing. The following are hints to improve your delivery over the telephone. Role-playing activities are particularly helpful toward developing a good telephone manner.

- Speak neither too loudly nor too softly; keep the mouthpiece about one inch from your lips.
- Speak distinctly and clearly. Your caller may be hard of hearing, on medication, or have difficulty with the English language.
- Concentrate on what is being said so that you will make the proper responses. Do not attempt to do a number of other things while you are on the phone.
- Avoid a monotone pattern in your voice. Be expressive in your speech, but avoid being overly dramatic, which might seem insincere. React appropriately. If you hear good news, sound happy. If it is bad news, communicate that you are sorry. Always be sincere.
- Be polite to your caller, never giving the caller the impression that the call is inconvenient for you or that you are rushed.
- Avoid being flippant and too familiar. You are a professional, and your speech should reflect your role as a medical clerical worker. Avoid slang phrases such as "O.K.," "you know," and "bye-bye."
- Give feedback. Repeat messages that are lengthy or confusing. Always repeat numbers, such as telephone numbers, laboratory reports, or amounts of bills.

Telephone Routines

Outgoing Calls

- Keep at your desk a list of frequently called outside numbers.
- Plan your conversation before you make your call. Know the points you want to cover. Have in front of you any orders, records, or other materials that you will need.
- Give the person or office you have called plenty of time to respond before you hang up—about ten rings.
- When the person answers, identify yourself. "Hello, Admitting Department, this is Mrs. Jackson."

- If the person who answers is not the person to whom you wish to speak, ask pleasantly: "May I speak to Dr. Jones, please? This is Mrs. Jackson from the Admitting Department of Valley Medical Clinic."

- Each office has its own procedures concerning calling pharmacies. The general rule is that the medical clerical worker does not call in a prescription or give out test information to patients without the specific direction of the physician.

- If you want to leave a message, be sure to state clearly who you are and what office you represent. Be sure to state the message clearly. Repeat any part of the message that is lengthy or might be confusing.

- Most medical facilities discourage employees from making personal calls that can tie up phone lines. Make calls from a pay phone during breaks and lunch.

Incoming Calls

- Answer all calls promptly, preferably by the second ring.

- Answer the telephone by giving the name of the business and your name: "Dr. Johnston's office, this is Kathy Leonard speaking." (You may get slightly different instructions from your employer as to how to answer the phone. Some employers may want you to answer with your title, and others may wish you to use your first name and the name of the facility or business.)

- *Always* have a pencil and pad ready to take down messages immediately, to avoid omissions and inaccuracies. You may be supplied with standard message pads. Messages may be transcribed onto a telephone log later (Figure 7.2).

- If the caller does not identify himself or herself, or you did not hear the name clearly, ask the caller to repeat the name. Then repeat it as soon as possible. "I'm sorry, I didn't hear your full name. Oh yes, Mrs. Peters, I can confirm that appointment for you."

- If you do not have the information that the patient requires, ask if the caller will hold. Try not to keep a caller on hold for more than *60 seconds* without checking to see if he or she wishes to continue to hold or to tell him or her how much longer it will be. Be sure to thank the caller for holding. If you

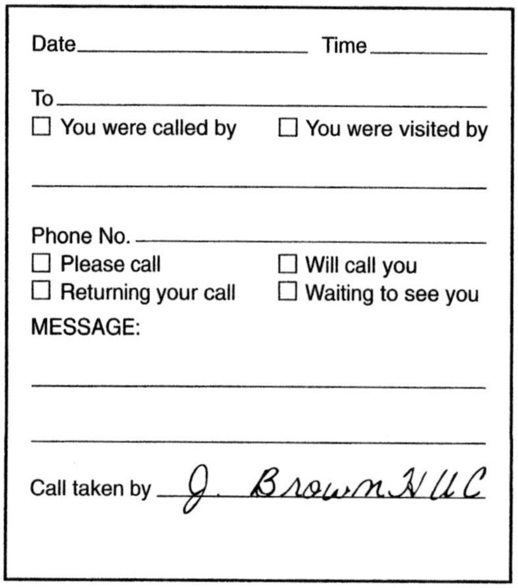

FIGURE 7.2 Telephone message pad.

find that you cannot get back to the caller quickly, ask the caller if you may call him or her right back. Nothing is more frustrating than being put on hold and left, making the patient feel unimportant.

■ If the call is for someone at your facility who cannot get to the phone immediately, ask the caller if he or she wants to:
   ■ Hold the line.
   ■ Call back.
   ■ Leave a message.
■ Never give out information about a patient. Never divulge medical orders to anyone other than an authorized party. Refer such calls to your supervisor or doctor, preferably taking a message and letting the supervisor or doctor screen such requests.
■ If you are given a lengthy message, write it down immediately; do not entrust it to memory. Be sure that your message is legible.
■ Calls from laboratories communicating results of laboratory tests must be carefully recorded. Offices have special laboratory result message pads to take down the information.

Prioritizing Calls

Some telephone calls should be put through immediately to the responsible person in your facility. Such calls include bona fide emergency calls (see Emergency Calls section), calls from other physicians that sound urgent, calls from the physician's family who insist on speaking to the doctor, calls from patients suffering from adverse medication reactions, and so on. Other calls, such as from patients wanting to talk about an overdue bill, or routine calls about a new symptom a patient might be experiencing, may be postponed until the physician or responsible party is free.

You need to receive complete instructions from your employer as to what kinds of calls he or she considers to have priority. You may not think a call from a tax accountant is a priority, but a physician might. You also might think that a call from the supervisor's child is a priority call, but the supervisor might not want his or her children calling unless it is an emergency.

The medical clerical worker handles as many telephone calls as possible to allow the physician to be free to treat patients without interruption. About two-thirds of the calls will be about appointments, health insurance problems, financial concerns, and requests for test results. A listing of how telephone calls should be handled (*triaging* phone calls) can be very helpful to the medical clerical worker. Some calls may need immediate response from a physician (emergencies), some may require a physician to return a call, some can be referred to another medical professional on the staff (for example, the registered nurse), and most should be able to be handled by the medical clerical worker. A reference sheet listing how to respond to calls should be near the telephone at all times.

Screening Calls

A medical clerical worker will be asked to screen incoming telephone calls. Screening calls is necessary in order to direct calls to their proper location and to see that the physician's time with calls is managed. For instance, a patient calls with problems with a bill. The patient asks to speak with Dr. Winters, who in this case has no knowledge of day-to-day billing. The patient needs to be directed to the office bookkeeper or whoever handles this area. A salesperson calls and immediately wants to talk with Dr. Winters. Bob the salesman wants to talk about selling the office a new

---

Real-Life Scenario

Dr. Maxwell is an excellent employer. She has a family, including three teenagers. You can depend on calls at the office from her children after school almost daily. Sometimes there are three or four calls, often disrupting your work during a very busy time of the day. The teenagers often are not interested in waiting on hold or having a message taken. A common mantra is "I need to talk with my mom NOW!"

How would you handle this situation?

---

copier. That call might go instead to the office manager, who handles the equipment decisions.

You must politely deal with the screening process. You must always ask for the caller's name when you are forwarding any call to another employee. If a caller refuses to give a name, ask to take a message and a phone number and have the physician or whomever the call is directed to return the call. Frequently, this type of call is a salesperson because physicians are on many lists to be contacted by salespeople. Let your employer decide what calls he or she wants to take and which calls are not to be returned.

Emergency Calls

The medical clerical worker must be aware of certain symptoms that a caller is experiencing constitute an emergency. The patient should not be given an appointment but should be connected to the physician immediately. If that is not possible, the medical clerical worker should tell the patient to call 911 (where available) or other appropriate assistance. If the patient is unable to make calls, the medical clerical worker should call for the patient. The patient's name, location, and telephone number should be obtained as soon as possible and the physician notified. A calm, reassuring voice is mandatory in this situation. Emergency symptoms include:

- *Severe chest or abdominal pain.* Be especially sensitive to chest pain, with or without shortness of breath and nausea. This pain can indicate a heart attack.
- *Severe difficulty with breathing.* The caller may be having a great deal of difficulty telling you what is wrong, telling you "Can't get my breath" or "Can't breathe."
- *Profuse bleeding.* Profuse bleeding is a continuous outpouring of blood, referred to as "hemorrhaging."
- *Loss of consciousness.* The caller might tell you that the patient cannot be awakened or has "passed out."
- *Severe vomiting or diarrhea.* Children and the elderly are particularly endangered by prolonged vomiting and/or diarrhea because of the possibility of dehydration.
- *Possible poisoning.* The patient should be seen by a physician as soon as possible, even if there is some question about whether the patient has been poisoned. The caller should also be told to bring the poison container with the patient if possible.

The physician must provide the medical clerical worker with careful, detailed instructions regarding the handling of emergencies such as those listed above. This is not by any means a complete list of potential emergencies.

Telephone Logs

To assure that no messages will be overlooked, a log of notes on all incoming calls assures that the telephone is utilized properly. A daily **telephone log** can be prepared by dividing a sheet of stenographic notepaper into columns with space to record the caller's name and telephone number, reason for the call, and action taken. Specialized phone logs can be purchased at a stationery store. Such log sheets should be saved for medicolegal reasons and as a reference of patient names and telephone numbers. You can also set up more than one log, perhaps restricting one log to prescription refill requests and one for all other calls. Your employer should check the logs at least twice a day, so it is necessary that the logs be legible. If you answer phones for more than one person, logs can be color coded to correspond to different doctors.

TELEPHONE TECHNOLOGY

Telephones and related equipment that are placed in medical facilities today are becoming more and more sophisticated. The choice of telephone systems depends on the type of medical practice, the size and complexity, and the type of call most frequently received and placed. Many facilities require the medical clerical worker to have some training on the specific system installed in the medical facility.

The typical small or medium-sized medical office uses a multiline telephone, such as a six- or ten-button telephone. Several telephone lines can come into the office, the office can have intercom capabilities throughout the office, and the caller can be placed on hold. In large office complexes, a small switchboard system may be appropriate. Complex systems can include built-in telephone directories, electronic memos, search and automatic speed dial, and other features.

Multibutton Key Phone

The **multibutton key telephone** allows the user to handle several incoming and outgoing calls simultaneously. Buttons may be placed on the bottom of the telephone, glowing intermittently. A steady light indicates that lines are in use, and a flashing light means that the line is on hold.

The *hold* button provides complete privacy by closing off all other extensions. This button should always be used when the caller is asked to wait so that the caller will not overhear other conversations. To operate the multibutton key telephone:

To Place a Call

- Choose a line not in use, a button not lit or flashing.
- Push down the button, pick up the receiver, and punch in the number to be called. In a larger facility, it may be necessary to punch in one or more numbers to receive an outside line (e.g., dial 9, then the number to be called).
- If you accidentally press a line that is on hold, depress the *hold* button to reestablish the hold.

To Answer a Call

- When the phone rings, determine the line to be answered by the lighting of the button on the bottom of the phone.
- Before removing the receiver, depress the key for the line to be answered. Remove the receiver and speak.

To Hold a Call

- Ask the caller if he or she will please hold the line. Wait for a reply. You may want to use the hold if two calls come in at once or if the caller has a question that requires you to be off the line for a short time.
- Depress the hold key for 2 to 3 seconds until you are sure that the line is holding. When a call is on hold, the light will flash on the holding line. To release the hold, simply push the button on the hold line and speak to the caller.

Answering Services

Most doctors' offices as well as many medical clinics use a telephone **answering service** to handle medical calls when the facility is closed. Unlike automatic answering machines used in private homes, the answering service can follow your employer's directions and help patients. These services can work during lunch hours, after the office closes on weekdays, and on weekends. It is important to select a competent answering service. Verification of the service's efficiency can be made by calling the facility office number periodically from a separate phone. Smaller facilities may use a simple answering machine with a recorded message. A number to call in an emergency must be included in the message.

Speaker Phone

A **speaker phone** is designed with a microphone and a loudspeaker. It does not require the use of hands, and it can be used for conference calls. Several persons at different locations can participate in one conversation. Most modern telephone systems in the medical office have this feature. A button on the telephone will activate this feature.

Tie Line

A **tie line** is like an office extension. It can be installed in a medical office, connecting the office with a nearby hospital so that all hospital extensions and other doctors' offices can be contacted by punching the last four digits of the number.

Mobile Communications

Physicians have increasingly found the use of **cellular phones** to be one of the best tools for maintaining constant contact with office staff, hospital, and patients. Physicians keep the portable phones with them when not in the office environment. The medical clerical worker has the cellular phone number in order to quickly get in touch with the physician. Because private conversations on cordless telephones can be overheard by others due to signal interference, conversations about patients must be handled with discretion to protect patient confidentiality.

Another mobile device is the **personal pager** (beeper). A physician can carry the electronic device comfortably in a pocket. If an emergency arises, the staff can dial a predetermined number that activates the pager. The physician can then go to a telephone and contact the office or hospital. Many pagers include a screen that displays a number for the paged person to call.

Facsimile (Fax) Machines

Fax machines are common equipment in the medical office. These machines are used to send reports, referrals, insurance business, and more informal communications. A fax is a transmission sent over telephone lines from one fax machine to another. These messages can also be sent from a modem to a fax machine as well. As a medical clerical worker, you may be responsible for seeing that the machine has paper and that the fax receiving tray is not blocked.

One challenge in using the fax machine is confidentiality. If you have a fax machine that is in the middle of the office, make sure you pick up the fax as soon as it arrives. If the message sent by fax is sensitive, not picking it up promptly could be a breach of confidentiality.

Electronic Mail

Electronic mail (e-mail) involves sending, receiving, storing, and forwarding messages in digital form, often over telephone lines. E-mail is a great money and time saver when there isn't time to make telephone or personal contact. Many offices use e-mail to inquire to insurances companies about the status of an insurance case. Memos can be sent through e-mail as well in the interoffice environment. Additionally, the Internet can be accessed through high-speed connections, allowing the physician access to fantastic amounts of medical information from all over the world.

APPOINTMENT SCHEDULING

The complexity of practicing medicine and the increased demand for expanded services has increased the need for flexible appointment scheduling practices. The traditional scheduling approach of plugging patients into an appointment book every half hour has been challenged by the development of medical centers where patients are seen without an appointment. Also, the appointment book has been replaced in many instances by computerized appointment scheduling. The radiology department, the clinical laboratory, and other therapeutic and diagnostic departments in hospitals also schedule patients.

Optimal use of resources and efficient management of hospital, physician, and the patient's time often require flexible scheduling where some appointments are longer than others. Many methods of scheduling have evolved to respond to the ever-changing needs of the patient and of specific medical specialties.

Appointment Scheduling Systems

Stream Method   This time-specified system is still the most widely used system for appointment scheduling. Patients are assigned to specific times, with accommodations for emergencies, staff availability, and unpredictable disruptions. The time interval between appointments is a matter of physician discretion. Appointment books are typically blocked in 15-minute time segments. Patients requiring more than 15 minutes would have an arrow extending from below their name and through the required number of segments. Figure 7.3 illustrates this type of scheduling.

Open Hours Scheduling   The main scheduling required in this method is the opening and closing hours of the office. This system is used in urgent care settings

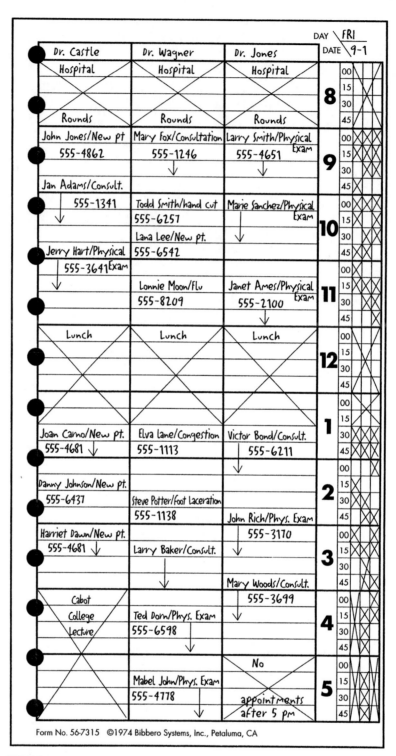

FIGURE 7.3 Typical appointment sheet.

where patients are seen on a first come–first served basis. These facilities have physicians available seven days a week and can be open long hours. Patients accept that they may have to wait to be seen. Flexibility is practiced, with patients with greater needs seen before patients with lesser needs.

Wave Scheduling   This system is more flexible than the blocking method. Several patients may be scheduled in a specific period (usually one hour). Patients are instructed to arrive on the hour and are seen in order of arrival. This schedule is used if the 15-minute interval seems too confining, and the assumption is made that some patients will be late and some will not show up. Patients should be advised ahead of time about this method. Confusion can arise when patients realize that others have been scheduled at the same time. Many patients prefer a time-specified approach.

Modified Wave   The modified wave schedule combines blocking methods and wave scheduling. Patients are instructed to arrive in planned intervals within the designated hour. Patients may be scheduled in a 30-minute period at 10-minute intervals. The second half of the hour might be used for catching up or for seeing only two patients.

Double Booking   Double booking is a system that allows more than one patient to have an appointment at the same time. Two patients that have minor complaints might be scheduled at the same time. Two other patients might be scheduled at the same time if one has a radiological procedure first and the other can be immediately seen by the physician.

Cluster Scheduling   Also known as categorization system, patients with similar procedures may be seen in certain time frames. All routine physical examinations might be seen during two mornings a week. All sick children in a pediatrician's office might be seen in the morning with routine well-baby visits scheduled for the afternoon.

S CHEDULING AIDS

Appointment Book

Today, computerized appointment systems are available from a number of different companies. Some offices, especially in large practices are fully computerized. Your employer will provide training for computerized appointment programs. However, the **appointment book** is still used in some private practices and hospitals.

There are many different styles and formats available for appointment scheduling books. Regardless of style or format, essential information must be recorded on all appointment sheets in the appointment book. The following information should be included (refer to Figure 7.3):

- Patient's name
- Purpose of the appointment
- Length of time for visit
- Patient's home and work (if relevant) telephone numbers in case of cancellation or change of schedule

A *daily list of appointments* is prepared and circulated to the medical facility staff. Some facilities use a computerized printout from an appointment program. Others copy the appointment book page for the day. Some facilities type up a separate list with the patient's name, time of appointment, and reason for visit.

Appointment books are considered legal documents. If entries are made in pencil for ease of scheduling, cancellations and no-shows should be documented in red on both the appointment sheet and the chart. The Internal Revenue Service can legally demand records from the beginning of a practice. Although they often are only called from three to five years previously, it is not difficult to save such records indefinitely. Taking time to carefully document all aspects of patient care reflects positively on the quality of patient care in your facility.

Appointment Abbreviations

There are several appointment abbreviations that are used in patient scheduling to save space. Examples of such abbreviations are found in Table 7.1.

Appointment Reminder Cards

One of the most successful ways of reminding patients of appointments and avoiding misunderstandings about times is the **appointment reminder card.** This card can be given to a patient after the appointment is made. A reminder card can also be mailed to people who have appointments scheduled periodically. Some offices make *reminder telephone calls* the day before the appointment to make sure the patient has not forgotten. Remember that a patient's visit to a medical facility is confidential. Reminders should not be left on answering machines at work or with family members unless permission to do so has been given by the patient.

A forgotten appointment means lost revenue for the medical facility. It also means another patient could have been given the appointment.

Canceled/Missed Appointments

Patients must be told when they come to a medical facility for the first time how to cancel appointments and what happens if an appointment is missed without cancellation. Most facilities require a 24-hour period for appointment cancellations, although some exceptions are made when the patient has a compelling reason why the appointment had to be canceled in less than 24 hours before the scheduled time. When a cancellation is made, a line is drawn through the patient's name on the schedule. Try to reschedule the appointment, working with the patient to find a new date as soon as possible. If an appointment is missed without notification, many practices send a reminder card to the patient, seen in Figure 7.4. Many practices charge the patient for missed appointments.

TABLE 7.1	SOME MEDICAL APPOINTMENT ABBREVIATIONS		
accident	accid	laceration	lac
annual physical exam	a PX	low back pain	LBP
blood pressure check	BP	new patient	N/P
breast check	breast ck	no future appt	NFA
cancel	canc	no-show	N/S
cast check	cast ck	office visit	OV
chest x-ray	PA chest	Pap smear	Pap
consultation	consult	physical exam	PX
didn't keep appt	DKA	postop check	PO
electrocardiogram	EKG, ECG	pregnancy confirm	PC
emergency	E	preop office visit	Pre-op
emergency room	ER	referral	R
follow-up visit	FU	return visit	RV
gynecological check	Gyn ck	suture removal	SR
headache	Hdak	weight control	WT
influenza syndrome	flu syn	work-in	W/I
injection	inj	x-ray	X

YOU WERE SCHEDULED FOR AN APPOINTMENT ON_____

at _____ a.m./p.m.

Your account has been charged. Please let us know if you wish to reschedule.

Doctor's Name, Address
Phone Number

FIGURE 7.4 Reminder of missed appointment.

Emergency Appointments

When a patient has a medical emergency as discussed earlier in this chapter, the patient must be seen at once. Appointments of noncritical patients must be arranged to accommodate the emergency. If the doctor is occupied for some time, patients may have to be sent home and rescheduled later in the day or another day. If the emergency will not take too long, the patients waiting must be told about the delay. Rescheduling patients takes a great deal of tact on the part of the medical clerical worker. Be clear about the problem and listen carefully with empathy to the patients' irritation about having to wait or change the appointment altogether.

$\mathcal{R}$ EFERRAL APPOINTMENT SCHEDULING

You may be asked to set up outside appointments for your patients. Such appointments may include:

- Laboratory tests
- Surgeries
- Hospital admissions
- X-rays and other special procedures

Work with the patient to make sure that the appointments you make are at a time that is convenient for the patient. Do not schedule a battery of time-consuming tests for a patient who tires easily.

You must have pertinent information available when making referral appointments. This is a valuable service that the patients will appreciate, and you must make sure that details are handled properly. The information listed below is generally required for each of the following procedures.

Admitting a Patient to the Hospital

Complete the following:

- Name of the patient to be admitted
- Patient age and date of birth
- Type of surgery (if necessary)
- Patient's address
- Preferred date of admission into the hospital

- Accommodations preferred by patient
- Prior admissions, hospital district residence
- Doctor's name
- All health insurance information

Scheduling a Patient for Diagnostic Testing

Diagnostic testing, especially blood tests and radiology procedures, often require that patients prepare themselves ahead of time, with a special diet, fasting, and so on. You must make every effort to communicate to the patient the importance of special preparations, or the test will not be able to be done.

When scheduling the patient, you must know:

- Patient statistics (name, address, phone, and so on)
- Procedure/testing to be performed
- Date, time, and location of procedure/test
- Any special requirements

Patients should be given the information obtained about the hospital admission or diagnostic procedure in written form. All arrangements should be posted in the appointment book.

Scheduling Consultations

Consultations are handled in the same manner as hospital admissions or procedures and tests. The consulting doctor's office receptionist is notified, and the information is given to the patient in written form.

SUMMARY

The medical clerical worker is often the first person that a patient sees in a medical facility. The medical clerical worker sets the tone for the facility, whether in person or communicating by phone. The same skills of flexibility and tact used to receive patients are also invaluable in scheduling appointments.

LEARNING ACTIVITIES

1. Using the form in Appendix B, fill out an appointment schedule for Dr. Castle's patients. You will need the following information. Your medical office is opened from 9 A.M. to 5:30 P.M., with a two-hour lunch period from 11:30 A.M. to 1:30 P.M. Dr. Castle works at a free clinic Friday afternoons from 1:30 to 5:30 P.M. and is not available. He takes Wednesdays off entirely and makes hospital visits from 9 to 10 A.M. daily. Dr. Castle also teaches a class at the local college at 4:30 P.M. on Tuesdays.
   (a) Schedule as many patients as you can for Dr. Castle, using the guidelines given in the "Appointment Scheduling" section of this chapter.
   (b) Discuss how you would schedule these patients using (1) the clustering system; (2) the wave system; (3) double booking.

3. In Appendix B you will find forms for taking telephone messages. Complete three telephone message forms. You might write down information on the calls acted out in Activity 2.

4. You are the medical clerical worker acting as a receptionist in a doctor's office. Write a response to the following patient remarks.
   (a) "I am sick of waiting in this reception room. If the doctor doesn't see me soon, I will leave!"
   (b) "I'm going to complain that you couldn't give me an appointment for three weeks. I was one of Dr. Moore's first patients. I should be treated better!"
   (c) "This reception room is filthy! I want it cleaned up."

5. List at least six ways you can improve the look of a reception room in a medical office.

6. What information should be included in a patient registration form?

7. List five things to remember when communicating on the phone.

8. Why is a telephone log important in a medical office?

9. Name three auxiliary telephone services.

10. What information should be put in an appointment book for a patient's scheduled appointment?

11. Name three scheduling systems.

12. When you are scheduling a patient for surgery, what information should be available to you when making the appointment?

Written Communications

Annotation	Practice of reading correspondence and underlining or highlighting important words or phrases.
Certified mail	A postal service that provides a receipt to the sender of first-class mail, for a fee.
Express mail	Quick delivery service offered by the U.S. Postal Service.
Full block	A style of letter writing where all lines of the letter begin at the left margin.
Memorandum	Also known as a *memo,* referring to interoffice correspondence.
Mixed punctuation	A punctuation style in a letter that calls for a colon after the salutation and a comma after the complimentary closing.
Modified block	A style of letter where all lines begin at the left margin except date, closing, and signature lines, which are placed at the center of the page.
Open punctuation	A punctuation style where no punctuation is used after the salutation and the complimentary closing.
Optical scanner	A device used by the post office to automatically read addresses.
Priority mail	"Second-day" service offered, but not guaranteed, by the U.S. Postal Service.
Proofread	To carefully read a document to check for accuracy as well as proper punctuation, spelling, grammar, and capitalization.
Registered mail	A first-class mail service that provides a record that mail has been sent and allows the mail to be insured in the event of a loss.
Word processor	A computer program that allows you to sort material in a memory and includes features such as spelling correction, a thesaurus, and mail merge.

After completing this chapter, the student is responsible for performing the following objectives:

- Discuss the elements of a professionally written letter.
- State the most common types of letter styles.
- List the parts of a letter.
- Discuss the different types of office equipment used in medical facilities for written communication.
- List the proper procedures for receiving and sorting incoming mail.
- Discuss equipment used to process the mail.
- Discuss the correct preparation of a mailing envelope.
- List the mail classifications and the special mail services.

*I*NTRODUCTION

Written communications provide your employer with an effective way to conduct much of the business of running a medical facility. Written correspondence also provides a means for obtaining a permanent record of many important matters in medical practice. The proper handling of written correspondence coming in and out of a medical facility is an extremely important task of the medical clerical worker. Written correspondence from your employer must be neat, with correct use of grammar and punctuation.

Correspondence coming into a facility must be cared for with speed and efficiency. These tasks, properly performed, will require sound judgment and excellent clerical skills, as well as knowledge of the operation of office equipment.

*W*RITTEN COMMUNICATION SKILLS

As a medical clerical worker, you may be asked to write letters independently as well as to transcribe letters from your employer. References useful for writing letters can include a book on English grammar, a medical dictionary, a standard English language dictionary, a secretarial manual, a thesaurus, and a drug reference book.

The first paragraph of a letter should be positive in tone and deal immediately with the subject matter. Sentences should average no more than twenty words. Another paragraph might deal with action being taken in the matter, and the final paragraph should include a positive note, with thanks expressed if relevant. Every letter should have at least two paragraphs; every paragraph should have at least two sentences.

All correspondence should be prompt, mailed within 24 hours if possible. If you find that you have to delay a letter, a tactful explanation should be included in the letter. Remember, the tone of the letter, as well as the spelling, punctuation, grammar, and appearance, reflect upon your employer and yourself. Letters should be:

- Clear and concise, free from excess wordiness
- Positive in tone
- Free from cliches
- Courteous and sincere
- Free from erasures
- Grammatically correct
- Free from misspellings or typographical errors

Proofreading

Prior to showing a correspondence to your employer and/or sending written documents, the correspondence must be **proofread.** Proofreading is the process of checking a document for accuracy as well as mistakes in spelling, punctuation, capitalization, and grammar. Table 8.1 gives some examples of proper writing styles.

Proofreading tips that can be useful include:

- Have someone else with writing skills read your document.
- Proofread yourself at least two times. Some people proofread on the computer screen and then print out a hard copy to look over again.
- Cut out excess words that do not add to the letter.
- Make sure the letter is not too negative. Add a positive note if necessary.

TABLE 8.1	*EXAMPLES OF CORRECT WRITING STYLES*

When a number is used at the beginning of a sentence, spell out the number.
  Example: Fifty workers went on strike.

Spell out a round number in the body of a sentence when it is the only number in the sentence.
  Example: It seemed like we traveled at least twenty miles.

Use numbers to express dimensions, weight, or temperature.
  Examples: 5 feet 4 inches, 135 pounds, 68 degrees Fahrenheit

Use numbers if several are used in a sentence.
  Example: She bought 3 dresses, 2 purses, and 3 belts.

If you only approximate an age, the age is typed as a word. If you know the age exactly, numbers are used.
  Examples: She appears to be about forty years old.
             She is 41 years old.

When the day of the month stands alone or when it comes before the month, use *d, st,* or *th.* You use just numbers when the day follows the month.
  Examples: The concert is on the 30th of November.
             The concert is November 30.

Spell out "cents." Use figures for amounts expressed in dollars and cents.
  Examples: She paid 45 cents for the card.
             The car cost $12,345.66.

When using the term "percent," spell it in full in a letter. The percent sign (%) is used in tabulated work and in naming interest. Do not put a space between the numbers and the percent sign.
  Examples: We lost 20 percent of our workers.
             Our new tax rate is 6 1/2%.

When using quotation marks, put periods and commas inside quotation marks.
  Example: The President said, "Call the Vice President."

If the word is singular, the possessive is achieved by adding *'s.* If a plural ends in *s,* add an *'* only. If the plural does not end in *s,* add *'s.*
  Examples: The girl's coat
             The girls' rest room
             The women's rest room

- Do not proofread when you are tired.
- Sometimes reading the document out loud will pick up mistakes you don't see when reading to yourself.
- Sometimes setting aside a document and reading it later after the initial proofread will allow a fresh look.

Real-Life Scenario

You are a well-trained medical clerical worker with excellent writing skills. You come to work for Dr. Churchfield, who prefers to write many of his correspondences by computer. He then asks you to print out the letters on proper stationery and mail them.

 The first time you handle a letter for Dr. Churchfield, you notice that the letter is excessively wordy, negative, and contains errors in punctuation. You tactfully ask Dr. Churchfield if you should proofread his work. He looks at you with displeasure and informs you that he already checked the letter with his spelling/grammar checker. He makes it clear that he does not want your help as he considers himself an excellent writer.

What do you do?

---

*V*ARIOUS CORRESPONDENCES

Letter Styles

There are many different formats that you can use in preparing a medical office letter. Four styles are most commonly used: block, modified block, modified block with indented paragraphs, and simplified style. These styles provide you with effective ways to make your correspondence look readable and attractive.

Full Block The **full block** style has all lines of the letter beginning at the left margin (Figure 8.1).

Modified Block The **modified block** style of letter is a form where all lines begin at the left margin except the date, complimentary close, and signature lines, which are located in the center of the page (Figure 8.2). The parts of a business letter are also noted in Figure 8.2. It is important for you to know all the various options that you can use in a medical letter. As you saw in Figure 8.1, the letter did not include an attention line or a reference line. Not all letters will include all of the following options, but you will be required to understand how to use all parts of a letter effectively.

Letterhead. Letterhead lines can be designed in many attractive formats, usually including the physician's or medical facility's name, title, address, and telephone number. They are generally engraved or printed on a bond paper. Continuation sheets are generally plain bond paper.

Date Line. The date line is typed thirteen to fifteen lines from the top of the page, or three lines below the letterhead. The traditional format for the date is generally used: April 14, 200_. Occasionally, in a medical facility, the military format is used: 14 April 200_.

Inside Address. The inside address includes the name and address of the person, firm, or medical facility receiving your letter, including the correspondent's title, department, or office name. It is typed four or more lines below the date line. This space can be adjusted to improve the letter's placement on the page. The first line is the name of the addressee, followed by title and firm, then address with the city spelled in full, the state, and the ZIP code.

William J. Harris, M.D.
Pediatric Practice

Lila D. Van Wyck, M.D.
Pediatric Practice

Riverview Medical Group, Inc.
1235 Broadmore Way
Daly City, CA 94775
(415) 555-9506

3 lines

April 5, 200—

Monica V. Smith
2254 Boundary Oaks Drive
San Francisco, CA 94719

2 lines

Dear Ms. Smith:

2 lines

Thank you so much for your kind words about our staff. We very much appreciated the time you took to let us know that you felt we were doing our job well.

2 lines

Your lovely letter has been posted on our employee bulletin board. Many staff members have mentioned how much they have appreciated your kind words.

2 lines

The Riverview Medical Group will continue to aspire to give the best service possible to all of our patients. Thank you again for your encouraging letter.

2 lines

Sincerely,

4-5 lines

Lila D. Van Wyck, M.D.

2 lines

LV: jm

FIGURE 8.1 Full block style letter.

Attention Line. The attention line is used when the letter is sent to an organization rather than to a person. If used, it is placed two lines below the inside address.

Bayview Convalescent Hospital
444 Merriview Way
Concord, CA 94520

Attention: Dr. Robert Allen, Director

Salutation. The salutation is placed two lines under the last line of the inside address, or two lines under the attention line. Ms. is used for women if you are unsure of marital status.

Dear Mr. Morris   Dear Ms. White

a. *letterhead*

Robert J. Brady, M.D.
Family Practice
2543 East Lansing Drive
Lansing, Michigan 54309
(609) 555-9675   **(a)**

3 lines

b. *date line*

April 14, 200_   **(b)**

c. *inside address*

4 lines

Morris Pharmaceutical Supply
198 Laney Street
Lansing, Michigan 54307   **(c)**

2 lines

d. *attention line*
ATTENTION: Robert L. Morris, President   **(d)**

2 lines

e. *salutation*
Dear Mr. Morris   **(e)**

2 lines

f. *reference line*
RE: Pharmaceutical order of 4/1/0_   **(f)**

2 lines

It has been brought to my attention that our pharmaceutical order of 4/1/0_ was not complete. Enclosed, please find a list of items not included in this order, as well as a copy of our original order.

2 lines

I also would like to let you know that this order represents the third order that was not delivered to our office on the date promised in our original agreement. It is very difficult for this office to function efficiently with disruption in our pharmaceutical supplies.

2 lines

We have been very happy with your company in the past and expect that these situations mentioned above will be rectified as soon as possible.

2 lines

g. *complimentary closing*

Sincerely   **(g)**

4-5 lines

h. *signature line*

Robert J. Brady, M.D.   **(h)**

2 lines

RB:kk   **(i)**

2 lines

Enclosure: Order form, order listing   **(j)**

2 lines

Copies: Douglas Shaw, Sales Representative   **(k)**

2 lines

i. *identification initials*
j. *enclosure notation*
k. *copy notation*

FIGURE 8.2 Modified block style letter.

Reference Line.   The reference line draws attention to a subject or, sometimes in medical correspondence, to a patient's name who is the subject of the letter. It usually comes two lines down from the salutation. In the modified block style, it may be centered, but in the block style, it is located at the left margin.

RE: Pharmaceutical order of 4/1/0_   SUBJECT: Drug order

Complimentary Closing.   At the end of a letter, one to three words are typed two lines after the last line of the body of the letter. Only the *first word* is capitalized.

Sincerely,   Very truly yours,   Yours truly,

Signature Line.   The signature line includes the first and last names of the person writing the letter, and it is typed four to five lines below the complimentary closing. The signature line is followed by the title of the person writing the letter, if applicable.

The decision about who signs a letter is based on the content of the letter. The physician will sign letters of a medical nature, to patients or other doctors, medical reports to a third-party payer, and personal letters. The medical clerical worker will write and sign letters regarding business matters and collection letters.

Sincerely,   Very truly yours,
Robert J. Brady, M.D.   Linda J. Franks, Administrative Assistant

Identification Initials.   Identification initials are typed two lines below the signature line to indicate the writer's initials and those of the person who has typed the letter. The trend is to omit the writer's initials if the name is used in the signature block and put only the initials of the person who has typed the letter.

RB: kk or kk

Enclosure Notation.   The enclosure notation reminds the person who receives the letter that there is additional material enclosed with the letter.

Enc: Order form, order listing

Copy Notation.   The copy notation tells the person receiving the letter that copies of the letter have been sent to other parties. The parties are named in this section.

cc: Douglas Shaw, Sales Representative   CC Bonnie Sharp, M.D.

Modified Block with Indented Paragraphs   This style is the same style as the modified block, but the beginning of each paragraph is indented five spaces. This style is not used as commonly as the nonindented format. The complimentary closing and the signature line are also indented (Figure 8.3).

Simplified Style   The simplified form for a business letter looks very much like a full block form. However, the complimentary closing line is eliminated. In addition, the subject line may replace the salutation. Instead of "Dear Ms. Castle," a subject

J. T. Maxwell, M.D.
General Practice
3412 Belmont Circle
Charlottesville, VA 22902
Telephone 804-555-0011

May 6, 200_

Ms. Jennifer Castle
2435 Lynn Avenue
Charlottesville, VA 22901

Dear Ms. Castle:

I am honored that you wish to include me in your book entitled *Progressive Physicians of Virginia.* I am particularly pleased with your choice of the prominent physicians that you will include in the book.

I am available for an interview on May 22 at 12:00 noon. I will bring the information that you requested during our telephone conversation of May 4.

I look forward to seeing you on May 22. Please confirm this date with my office manager as soon as possible.

Sincerely yours,

J. T. Maxwell, M.D.

JTM:lc

FIGURE 8.3 Modified block style with indented paragraphs.

line could be inserted referring to the subject of the letter, such as "Speaker for Lyons Club Breakfast."

Punctuation Styles   In business letter common styles, you have a further choice of punctuation styles used in medical facilities today. The most common is the **mixed punctuation** style, shown in Figure 8.1. Mixed punctuation requires a colon after the salutation and a comma after the complimentary closing. **Open punctuation,** shown in Figure 8.2, means that no punctuation is used after the salutation and the complimentary closing.

Other Forms of Written Office Communication

Memoranda   An interoffice written communication is called a **memorandum,** also called a *memo.* A memo format may be available on your computer. A typical memo would have the following headings: *Date, To, From,* and *Subject.* Memos are very brief but require proofreading to avoid errors.

E-mails   In many health care facilities today, memos have been replaced by e-mails, providing that all employees have access to a computer. Generally, all clerical staff members have their own computers and e-mail addresses. Be very careful what you write in e-mails—as even when erased, e-mails can be retrieved. Be brief, to the point, and aware of confidentiality issues.

Faxes   A fax format is generally included in any word processing package on your computer. Faxes should be neatly prepared with proper proofreading. Again, as mentioned in Chapter 7, faxes should not contain confidential material that can be retrieved by parties not addressed in the fax.

Meeting Agendas and Minutes   A meeting agenda lists the specific items that the attendees are going to discuss. If you are asked to make an agenda for a meeting in your facility, you must contact all attendees to ask what items they wish to place on the agenda. Then, after drawing up the agenda, you are required to distribute copies of the agenda to all who are going to attend the meeting.

You may also be asked to take minutes of a meeting. The minutes record what actions were taken at the meeting. The first paragraph of the minutes lists what kind of meeting, the group meeting, time, date and place for the meeting, who ran the meeting, and members present.

Each subject discussed at the meeting should merit a paragraph. Motions are recorded with exact wording of the motion, the name of the people making and seconding the motion, and if the motion passed or failed. The last paragraph mentions the next meeting date, time, and place, as well as the time the present meeting adjourned. A copy of all minutes are saved in a notebook specifically for the storage of minutes.

WRITTEN COMMUNICATION SUPPLIES

Paper

A medical clerical worker may compose a professional letter with no errors, but if the letter is not sent on paper of good quality, the entire professional effect may be lost. Paper should be at least 20 to 24 pound stock with a *watermark,* a mark that you can see when the paper is held to the light. Bright colored paper is not recommended. White, cream, or gray paper is preferred. Make sure the paper stock can be used with your printer.

Letterhead

Your employer will want to choose his or her own letterhead, perhaps with your help. The letterhead appears on the top of the office stationery, with the physician/practice name, street address (or post office box), city, state, and ZIP code. A telephone number appears below the city address, and some facilities might add a fax number and an e-mail address. Information can be centered at the top of the page, and some prefer to have the information at one of the margins (either left or right) at the top.

When letterhead is ordered, second sheets are ordered as well, additional plain paper (no letterhead writing) of the same type as the letterhead paper. This paper will be used for second page sheets. The quantity depends on how many lengthy documents you prepare for your employer. Most documents are probably no longer than a page.

Envelopes

The stock and quality of the envelopes should match the letterhead stationery. The envelopes should be addressed with the name, address and ZIP+4 codes. An example of a correctly addressed envelope would be:

Savannah Jones, MD
PO Box 1234
Bellevue, WA 98005-4321

The number 6¼ (6½" long by 3⅝" wide) envelope and the number 10 (9½" long by 4⅛" wide) are the most often used envelopes. A window envelope can also be used when mailing billing statements. The address on the bill will show through the window of the envelope to avoid duplicate addressing.

*C*OMMUNICATION TECHNOLOGY

You may use many different types of office equipment in handling medical office communications. Some of the most common are listed below.

Computers/Word Processors

Because of the rapid advancement of computer terminology, many medical facilities have completely replaced the typewriter with microcomputers with word processing capabilities or stand-alone (dedicated) **word processors.** An office computer has the advantage of providing many other programs for the facility besides word processing (programs for billing, making appointments, accounting, and so on). The stand-alone word processor is a fully equipped automatic typewriter with the capability to store information and correct spelling mistakes, along with many other editing features. The text may be displayed on a screen and can be changed any time before the letter is finally generated.

The training of all medical clerical workers should include computer science. Not only must the medical clerical worker today have excellent keyboard skills, but he or she must be able to understand the basic components of the computer and feel comfortable using a variety of programs, especially the word processing component.

Transcription Equipment

Transcription equipment varies with the size of the facility where you work, as well as the type of medical specialty. If your physician requires you to transcribe information he or she has dictated into a machine, you must be familiar with the basic operation of the transcription machine. This equipment can range from a small portable dictation unit to a combination dictation and transcription desktop unit. The physician may dictate information into the machine, recording the message. Then the medical clerical worker listens to the recording through headphones and simultaneously types the data onto paper. Your training should include practice sessions using the equipment.

Chapter 12 of this textbook further discusses the medical clerical worker's interaction with office equipment, including the fax machine and computers.

*P*ROCESSING THE MAIL

In addition to sending out written communications, your job as a medical clerical worker might include sorting and distributing incoming mail. You will also need to know how to choose the mail service that will be the best and most inexpensive method for the delivery of outgoing mail.

You might want to include in your office the U.S. Postal Service's *Postal Operations Manual* (POM), which provides current information on postage rates and services. You should also have available the *National ZIP Code Directory,* which identifies areas of the United States and its possessions by a five-digit number. Most facilities now have directories that confirm the "ZIP code plus four" system—a nine-number system designed to make deliveries to urban areas more efficient. If the ZIP code is not used on a letter, delivery can be delayed by several days.

The task of opening and preparing the daily mail is an important responsibility. You may receive the mail directly from the mail carrier at your desk or obtain the mail from the mailroom of your medical facility.

Opening the Mail

Before opening the mail, it is helpful to separate it into categories, such as business correspondence, publications, and advertising. Business correspondence should be opened first, using a letter opener to preserve the mailing envelopes. Anything marked *personal* or *confidential* (Figure 8.4) must not be opened and should be taken directly to the addressee as soon as possible.

As you open the mail, make sure that the listed enclosures in each letter are present. If they are missing, attach a small note. Then call the office that sent the letter to let it know that the enclosure is missing.

Before discarding an envelope, make sure that the return address is on the correspondence. If not, save the envelope as a record of the address. Some offices require that all envelopes be saved, for the date of the postmark in case of problems.

Annotation refers in the medical office to the practice of identifying and isolating key points of a letter. This can be done by the medical clerical worker underlining important words or phrases and writing notes in the margin. Some letters, such

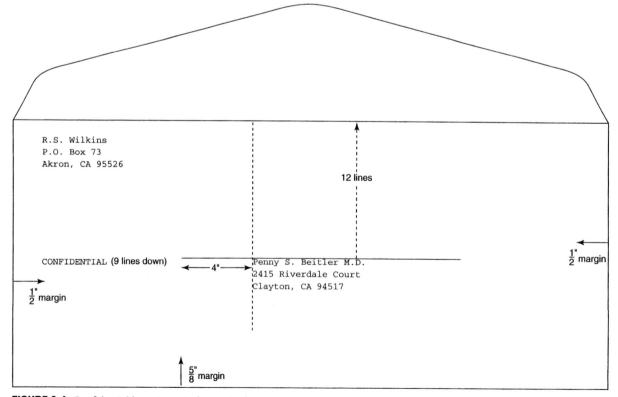

FIGURE 8.4 Confidential letter in optical scanning layout.

as those pertaining to the patient record and diagnosis and treatment, are not annotated. Examples of letters that can be annotated to save the physician time and assure that important points are not overlooked include notices of business meetings, convention times and places, and so on. Your employer will tell you if he or she wishes you to annotate certain types of correspondence.

Dating the Mail

Most facilities will require that you use a date stamp with the mail. The stamp may include office or department information and the time. It is important for your employer to know when the mail is received. Never stamp the date over any typed information.

Delivering the Mail

The mail should be opened, sorted, and delivered as soon as it is received. Ask your employer where to put the opened mail, and then consistently leave the mail at that location. Do not take mail to your employer when he or she is with a patient or is on the telephone. Some offices may use *mail logs,* maintained for registered or certified mail, insured mail, special delivery mail, or legal correspondence.

Equipment for Processing the Mail

The type of equipment used in a medical facility for processing mail depends on the volume of mail received. You may work in a facility where a letter opener, postal scale, and stamps are all the equipment that you will need. Other facilities may have *postage meters,* which are used to print prepaid postage directly on envelopes or on adhesive strips that are placed on envelopes or packages.

The meter is for every class of mail and for any amount of postage. Models vary in design and sophistication. Usage records are kept, and the meter can be locked at night. Rental fees for postage meters are paid based on the amount of postage used. When using the postage meter, you must remember to:

- Change the date every day.
- Check the amount of postage set on the meter before stamping the envelope, making sure that the postage is printed in the upper right-hand corner of the envelope.
- Put the meter back to zero each time you finish your metering tasks.
- Save all unused postage metered tapes and envelopes to get a refund.
- Be prepared to request a refund (up to 90 percent) if the machine is in error or the ink does not print correctly.

Large medical facilities may have *sorting machines* to help you process the mail. You will learn to operate such machines during your orientation and training.

PREPARING OUTGOING MAIL

When you begin to process outgoing mail, you must make sure, first, that the envelope is prepared correctly. Include the envelope with the letter before presenting the letter to the writer for signature. Each envelope should contain the return address of the writer and the complete address of the person or organization that is to receive the letter. Both the return address and the address to which the letter is mailed should include the two-letter state abbreviation and ZIP code. Refer to Appendix C for a complete listing of state abbreviations.

Preparing a Proper Mailing Envelope

The envelope is the first part of a letter that the receiver sees, and it can create a negative impression if not done neatly and properly. Mistakes on the envelope can also prevent the letter from reaching the destination. Parts of a properly addressed envelope are outlined in Figure 8.4.

Return Address. An envelope should have in its upper left-hand corner the name and address of your medical facility. You may have letterhead envelopes preprinted, or you may have to type this information. The return address should be typed two lines from the top edge and three to four spaces from the left edge.

Mailing Address. The mailing address should be typed five spaces to the left of the horizontal center, or on line 14. On a small envelope, type the address ten lines left of center, on line 12.

Envelope Notation. These notations can include PERSONAL, PLEASE FORWARD, HOLD FOR ARRIVAL, CONFIDENTIAL, and many more. These should be typed in capital letters three lines below the return address, on the ninth line, and three to four spaces from the left edge.

There are also mailing notations that are intended for the U.S. Postal Service, such as REGISTERED SPECIAL DELIVERY, and RETURN RECEIPT REQUESTED. These notations should be typed three lines below the postage stamp (or meter mark) in capital letters.

Computerized Mail Processing

All major cities in the United States now have computerized mail processing. Addresses on envelopes are read by a piece of electronic equipment that scans envelopes, called an **optical scanner.** The scanner reads only the last two lines of the envelope address. The last line must always contain the city, state, and ZIP code, and the next-to-last line must be the address of the delivery. Punctuation marks such as periods and commas will be eliminated, and all standard items will be abbreviated. Figure 8.4 illustrates the optical scanning layout.

A letter can be professionally prepared, but if it is then improperly folded and stuffed into an envelope, the professional look can be lost. When folding a 6¾-inch envelope, fold the paper almost in half, leaving a ¼-inch space at the top. Then the paper is again folded twice, leaving a ¼-inch gap at the right. A 10-inch envelope is folded up one-third of the way and then folded down approximately one-third before being put into the envelope.

𝓜AIL CLASSIFICATION

The medical clerical worker must be familiar with mail classification systems and special mail services in order to choose the least expensive and most efficient systems. Mailing costs vary today due to private competitors of the U.S. Postal Service, such as Federal Express (FedEx) and the United Parcel Service (UPS). Many cities have local companies that specialize in short-distance quick delivery. In an emergency, local courier companies and messenger services offer fast delivery to nearby destinations.

Postal Classes

Express Mail   This service is available seven days a week for mailing items up to 70 pounds and 108 inches in combined length and width. **Express mail** can be sent for delivery by noon the following day.

First-Class Mail   Correspondence and billing statements are usually sent first class. All single-piece letters weighing less than 11 ounces can be sent this way. Forwarding is included in this rate.

Priority Mail   Mail weighing more than 11 ounces and up to 70 pounds can be sent by **priority mail.** The cost of mailing depends on the weight and the destination.

Second-Class Mail   This service includes newspapers and periodicals that have been given second-class privileges.

Third-Class (Bulk) Mail   Circulars, books, catalogs, and other printed material and goods weighing less than 16 ounces can be mailed through bulk mail. A minimum of 200 pieces of mail is required to utilize the bulk rate, all sent from one post office.

Fourth-Class Mail   This mail must weigh more than 1 pound and not more than 70 pounds.

Certified Mail   This is used when it is necessary to prove that a piece of mail has been delivered. The sender is given a receipt, and the post office makes a record of delivery. Legal papers, income tax forms, and important letters are examples of mail often sent by **certified mail.**

Registered Mail   **Registered mail** is first-class mail with a declared value that may require added protection, such as mailing checks, money, or valuable merchandise. There is also insurance coverage available.

SUMMARY

The medical clerical worker must be able to be comfortable handling incoming and outgoing communications with ease and efficiency. This requires much skill and knowledge and, if properly done, will add greatly to the smooth running of a medical facility.

LEARNING ACTIVITIES

1. Beverly Altman is a medical clerical worker employed by Dr. Donald Castle, a dermatologist. Using the "stationery" in Appendix B, compose two letters to the following patient, using (a) full block style and (b) modified block style:

   Ms. Daphne Dupris
   2940 Yard Street
   Yuba City, CA 95948

   The letter should be a notification that Dr. Castle is having an open house in honor of his new associate, Dr. Jennifer Wagner.

2. Using the blank envelope form in Appendix B, practice preparing an envelope from Dr. Castle to Ms. Daphne Dupris, using the optical scanning layout described in this chapter.

3. Using Dr. Castle's stationery in Appendix B, compose a letter using a modified block style with indented paragraphs. Also make an envelope for this letter.

4. Which is correct when typing correspondence?
   (a) 1. Twenty men were present.
       2. 20 men were present.
   (b) 1. He ordered 3 chairs, 6 lamps, and 7 stools.
       2. He ordered three chairs, six lamps, and seven stools.
   (c) 1. Her age is about forty.
       2. Her age is about 40.
   (d) 1. The report is due June 10th.
       2. The report is due June 10.
   (e) 1. The report is due on the 10th of June.
       2. The report is due on the tenth of June.
   (f) 1. Janey said, "You are my friend".
       2. Janey said, "You are my friend."
   (g) 1. The girl's father treated her well.
       2. The girls' father treated her well.
   (h) 1. I took him to the men's rest room.
       2. I took him to the mens' rest room.
   (i) 1. The girls' P.E. program has been expanded.
       2. The girl's P.E. program has been expanded.

5. List the following parts of a letter in order of appearance.
   __ Identification initials   __ Salutation
   __ Letterhead   __ Attention line
   __ Signature line   __ Reference line
   __ Date line   __ Enclosure notation
   __ Complimentary closing   __ Copy notation
   __ Inside address

6. State the difference between open and mixed punctuation styles.

7. Name types of office equipment used for written communications in a medical facility.

8. Why is a postage meter generally used in a medical facility?

9. List the two-letter abbreviations for the following states and territories. (Refer to Appendix C.)

   (a) Virgin Islands
   (b) North Dakota
   (c) Wyoming
   (d) Georgia
   (e) Connecticut
   (f) Hawaii
   (g) Nebraska
   (h) Montana
   (i) Michigan
   (j) Iowa

10. State the elements of a properly addressed envelope.

11. Define the following terms:

 (a) Fourth class
 (b) Express mail
 (c) First class
 (d) Certified mail
 (e) Priority mail

12. What are the unique elements of the simplified style format of a business letter?

13. What is an optical scanning device used for in the post office?

The Patient's Record

Alphabetical filing	An arrangement of names in sequence in alphabetical order.
Alphanumerical filing	A filing system designed for alphabetical retrieval and numerical refiling.
Chart holder	A metal or vinyl cover to hold a patient's medical record while in the hospital (also called a *chart back*); manila folders can also be used.
Chart rack	Special racks to hold charts kept in each nursing unit.
Diagnosis	The determination of the nature of a disease or injury.
JCAHO	Joint Commission on Accreditation of Health Care Organizations.
Laboratory report	A record of the findings of physical and chemical analysis of specimens.
Medical record	Written account of a patient's illnesses, diagnoses, symptoms, treatment, and care.
Medical records department	A separate department in a medical facility that is responsible for maintaining hospital records.
Numerical filing	The filing of medical records in a number sequence.
Objective symptoms	Symptoms that are observable and measurable.
POMR	Problem-oriented medical record system; a form of record keeping.
Progress notes	Notations made by the physician after the initial and subsequent visits.
SOAP	An abbreviation for subjective complaints, objective findings, assessment of status, and plan (diagnosis); a method of structuring progress notes.
SOMR	Source-oriented medical record system, a conventional method for organizing medical records consisting of a chronological set of notes for each patient visit.
Subjective symptoms	Description of symptoms of a patient, perceivable only to the patient, not to the observer.
Transcription (medical)	Typing or word processing of dictated information such as history and physical examinations, operative reports, and consultations.
Transcription (order)	Act of rewriting doctor's orders onto requisitions and other forms or using a computer to obtain tests, medications, diet, and other services for the hospitalized patient.

After completing this chapter, the student is responsible for performing the following objectives:

- State the purposes of medical records.
- Identify standard chart forms on a hospital patient's medical chart.
- Explain the importance of maintaining the confidentiality of medical records.
- Explain how the medical record of a patient is also a legal document.
- Identify the medical clerical worker's responsibilities toward the patient's record.
- Describe three methods of filing medical records.
- Utilize the basic rules of correct alphabetical filing.

*I*NTRODUCTION

The **medical record** is a written account of a patient's illnesses, diagnoses, symptoms, treatment, and care. This document contains detailed observations of various members of the health care team. The patient's medical record, or medical chart, is also a vehicle of communication for the health care team in the proper treatment of a patient. The importance of the medical record requires that hospitals have a medical records department responsible for maintaining hospital records.

A patient's medical record is permanent and is considered a legal document. Medical records are used in courts of law as a record of a patient's medical treatment and care.

Efficient filing systems are critical in the medical environment to meet the needs of retrieval, security, and expansion. Patients have the right to expect that their medical records will remain confidential. Records also should be maintained in an efficient manner. Computerization plays an important role today in storing medical records.

*P*URPOSES OF MEDICAL RECORDS

The Joint Commission on Accreditation of Health Care Organizations, **JCAHO,** has established some reasons why all patients should have medical records.

- To serve as a basis for the planning of patient care.
- To provide a practical means of communication between physicians and other members of the health team.
- To furnish documentation of the course of a patient's illness and care.
- For legal purposes in a court of law.
- To provide data for use in research of diseases and injuries to benefit other patients.

Patient records are also used to complete various department forms required by law, such as communicable disease reports, child abuse, criminal injuries, and newborn diseases and illnesses. This information is also used to complete insurance claims for state and federal programs.

The patient record will include such information as:

- Patient's personal information such as full name, address, occupation, marital status, and complete information about the patient's medical insurance.
- Patient's personal as well as family medical history.
- Complete details of physical examinations, **laboratory reports,** x-ray findings, **diagnoses** of medical problems, and all treatments for such problems.
- Consent forms for procedures.
- Authorization forms for any release of medical information.
- Special instructions for organ donation if patient is terminally ill in the hospital (as well as instructions about the use/no use of life support systems in case of terminal illness).

Some medical records also contain a photograph of new patients (taken with a Polaroid camera) and/or a photocopy of the patient's driver's license or military identification.

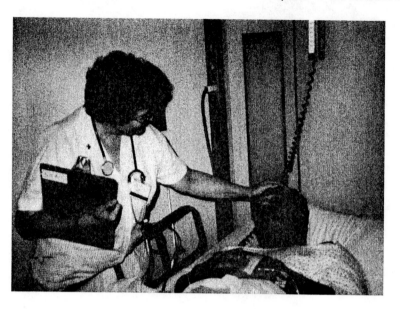

A physician always keeps a complete medical record for each patient. A hospital starts a medical (patient) record (often called a medical [patient] chart) when a patient enters the hospital. A patient can have a medical record at the office of his/her physician and can also have a medical record filed in the **medical records department** of a hospital after the patient is discharged. During a hospital stay, the hospital medical chart is located temporarily on the same floor and unit as the patient.

ℋOSPITAL MEDICAL RECORDS

A patient's hospital medical record is a detailed report on all phases of his or her medical progress. During the hospitalization, the medical record may be bound together in looseleaf fashion, with a metal or vinyl cover, called a *chart back* or a **chart holder.** When not in use, the charts are put in a device called a **chart rack,** with charts arranged in the same order as the patients' rooms on the nursing floor. Charts should always be put back in the chart rack when not in use.

Since the patient's chart is a legal record, all entries are made in ink. There is a prescribed method of dealing with error, discussed later in the chapter.

There are several chart forms that become a part of every patient's chart after hospital admission. Additional supplemental forms are used when required.

- *Doctor's order sheet* (Figure 9.1). This chart form is of primary importance. All medical procedures and treatments of the patient are recorded by the doctor on this form. He or she must sign and date the list of orders each time they are written. This becomes the "blueprint" of the care a patient is to receive, as these orders are then transferred to other records for use as patient care guidelines.
- *Graphic chart.* The main characteristic of this chart is a graph that gives a visual record of vital signs. The patient's temperature, pulse, respiration, and blood pressure are recorded on it as they are taken. Other information is often recorded as well, such as appetite, total fluid intake, output, weight, and height.
- *History and physical record.* When a patient is admitted to a hospital, a medical history is taken and a physical examination is given. Observations are

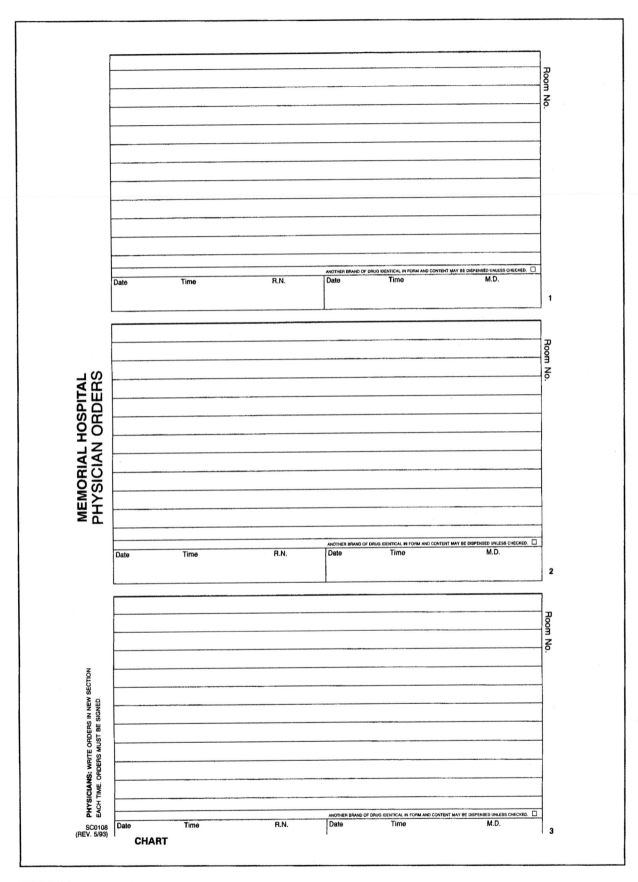

FIGURE 9.1 Doctor's order sheet.

recorded by the doctor on this record. This record may be handwritten or dictated for a transcriptionist to type. There are abbreviated forms for a short stay for such illnesses as dental extractions and tonsillectomies and longer forms for research and educational purposes.

■ *Progress notes.* **Progress notes** contain recorded observations, impressions, and recommendations of all physicians who examine the patient during hospitalization.

■ *Nurses' notes.* This is a form that provides space for nurses to record their observations of the patient's condition. This provides communication between nurse and doctor. Most treatments given are reported here.

■ *Summary or face sheet* (Figure 9.2). This record comes from the hospital admitting department, where certain basic identification information is recorded on the patient being hospitalized. There is detailed information about the patient's identification, and space is provided for the doctor to summarize the patient's status at the time of discharge. There can be a release of liability clause that patients are required to sign on admission. This protects the hospital in case emergency measures are necessary.

■ *Laboratory report.* All medical facilities require that certain laboratory tests be performed on every patient admitted, including a complete blood count and a urinalysis. In most modern medical facilities today, laboratory test results are reported on a computerized result list that is updated daily. In less modern facilities, individual laboratory tests may still be attached to a larger sheet. The single sheet of results is a much more efficient and compact method of including *laboratory reports* of a medical chart.

■ *Medication record (also known as MAR, medication administration record).* The medication record is included to keep track of each medicine prescribed for a patient throughout the day. (The nurse records in ink the medication and time that it was given.)

There are also many supplemental chart forms that hospitals may use in addition to the eight listed. Such additional forms may or may not be included on the patient's chart. Specific charting details vary from hospital to hospital, and you must learn the routine of your particular hospital when you are hired. Additional chart forms may include:

■ Surgical records
■ Special therapy records
■ Consultation forms

Medical facilities have a separate department called the *medical records department.* All medical records of any person who has been admitted to the facility both as an inpatient and as an outpatient are kept in this department. As medical record keeping has become more complicated over the years, a position known as the *medical records clerk* has evolved.

$\mathcal{M}$EDICAL RECORDS IN THE DOCTOR'S OFFICE

In a doctor's office or clinic atmosphere, the patient's medical record will look very much like the patient chart in a hospital. The *patient registration form* filled out at the time of the patient's first visit will be a part of the medical record, as well as a *medical history.* As a medical clerical worker in a medical office situation, you may be responsible for typing a patient's history from the doctor's notes.

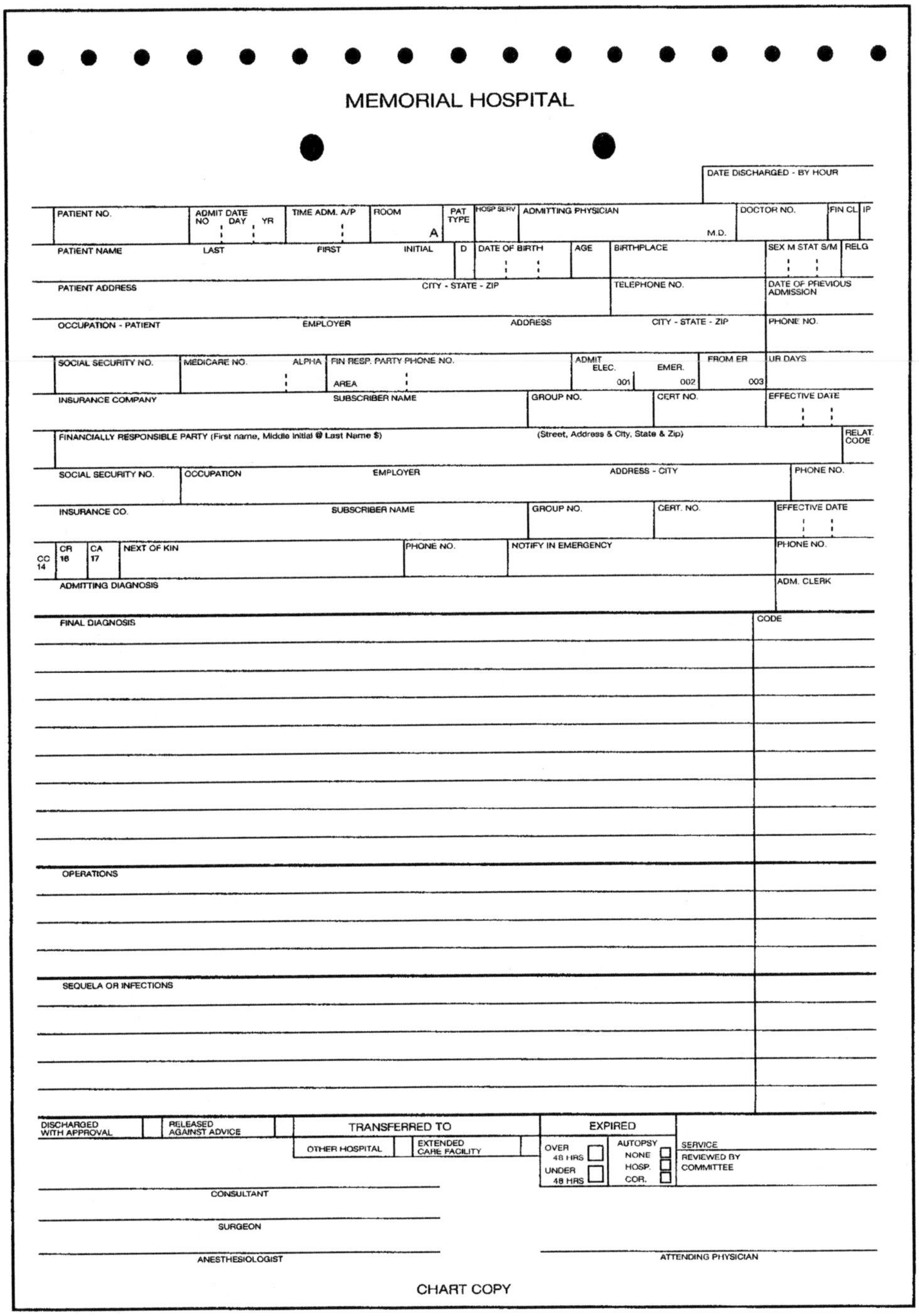
MEMORIAL HOSPITAL

DATE DISCHARGED - BY HOUR

PATIENT NO. | ADMIT DATE NO DAY YR | TIME ADM. A/P | ROOM | PAT TYPE A | HOSP SERV | ADMITTING PHYSICIAN M.D. | DOCTOR NO. | FIN CL | IP

PATIENT NAME LAST FIRST INITIAL | D | DATE OF BIRTH | AGE | BIRTHPLACE | SEX M STAT S/M | RELG

PATIENT ADDRESS CITY - STATE - ZIP | TELEPHONE NO. | DATE OF PREVIOUS ADMISSION

OCCUPATION - PATIENT | EMPLOYER | ADDRESS | CITY - STATE - ZIP | PHONE NO.

SOCIAL SECURITY NO. | MEDICARE NO. | ALPHA | FIN RESP. PARTY PHONE NO. AREA | ADMIT ELEC. 001 | EMER. 002 | FROM ER 003 | UR DAYS

INSURANCE COMPANY | SUBSCRIBER NAME | GROUP NO. | CERT NO. | EFFECTIVE DATE

FINANCIALLY RESPONSIBLE PARTY (First name, Middle Initial @ Last Name $) | (Street, Address & City, State & Zip) | RELAT CODE

SOCIAL SECURITY NO. | OCCUPATION | EMPLOYER | ADDRESS - CITY | PHONE NO.

INSURANCE CO. | SUBSCRIBER NAME | GROUP NO. | CERT. NO. | EFFECTIVE DATE

CC 14 | CR 16 | CA 17 | NEXT OF KIN | PHONE NO. | NOTIFY IN EMERGENCY | PHONE NO.

ADMITTING DIAGNOSIS | ADM. CLERK

FINAL DIAGNOSIS | CODE

OPERATIONS

SEQUELA OR INFECTIONS

DISCHARGED WITH APPROVAL | RELEASED AGAINST ADVICE | TRANSFERRED TO: OTHER HOSPITAL | EXTENDED CARE FACILITY | EXPIRED: OVER 48 HRS | UNDER 48 HRS | AUTOPSY: NONE | HOSP. | COR. | SERVICE | REVIEWED BY COMMITTEE

CONSULTANT

SURGEON

ANESTHESIOLOGIST

ATTENDING PHYSICIAN

CHART COPY

FIGURE 9.2 Summary sheet.

There are different styles of formatting of patient histories. Some doctors prefer short, succinct histories written on blank paper. Others prefer detailed histories written on printed forms. It is your responsibility to learn in your training how your specific employer wishes the histories to be made.

Medical history and physical examination may be put on the same document in the full block style.

Progress notes are included on a patient's medical record to document subsequent patient visits. Entries are made when the doctor has seen any patients in the hospital or has made house calls. Prescriptions refilled are noted here also.

Laboratory reports and other specialized medical reports, such as x-rays and EKGs, are included with a patient's medical record. If there are a great many such reports, a separate folder may be used.

All parts of the medical record may be seen by attorneys, other physicians, and insurance companies. They may be closely scrutinized during litigation. Therefore, the notes must be current, with no omissions, and dated and signed or initialed by the physician. All entries onto the record should be *neat, accurate,* and *complete.* Always remember that anything you enter on a record may someday be a part of a legal defense of your employer. You could be required to swear in a court of law that everything you put on a chart is to your knowledge truthful and accurate. The date and time should be recorded clearly each time the patient is seen. Avoid skipping lines. Chart to the margins. Also remember that *if it is not charted, it did not happen.*

*Y*OUR RESPONSIBILITY TOWARD MEDICAL RECORDS

The first responsibility that a medical clerical worker has toward the patient's medical records is to remember that patient records are *confidential.* You *must* remember that you will have access to information of a very personal nature. Do not discuss this information with patients or visitors, with friends, or even with fellow workers. An exception is made to this rule if you are discussing the patient's record with personnel who are involved directly with the care of the patient.

Such serious medical problems as HIV or AIDS make confidentiality even more crucial. Positive results on an AIDS test *must* be kept confidential. In some hospitals and doctors' offices, such records are sealed, with only a few people having permission to handle the records. Make sure that you know the details about how your employer handles such critical test results concerning HIV status, AIDS, or other communicable diseases.

Patient records are the *legal property* of a hospital or medical office. Information cannot be released to another doctor without written consent of the attending doctor. Charts can be inspected at any time by court order but can be removed from a hospital only if requested by court order. The American Medical Association can provide forms for disclosure of medical record information.

In a medical office, medical records are considered the property of the physician who is treating the patient. No record should be shown to a patient without the consent of the physician, as there may be some reason that the physician does not want the patient to see the entire record. For instance, some physicians will include personal opinion notes after an examination. Problems might occur if a patient sees a physician comment like "patient can be manipulative and dishonest, exaggerating symptoms for attention."

Each office should have a written policy regarding releasing medical record information. Local and state statutes may vary. In some states, the state legislature allows a patient the right to examine or copy the medical record. If a patient is allowed to review his or her record, a physician or other knowledgeable health professional should be nearby to interpret medical terms or abbreviations. The requirement for confidentiality may not apply when the patient initiates a malpractice claim against a physician.

It is the medical clerical worker's duty to assist the physician in keeping the records as current and as accurate as possible. Some doctors and hospitals require detailed records, and some keep more basic records.

Entries in the patient's medical record must be as legible as possible. If a doctor writes a medication order that can easily be misread, the doctor is held accountable if an error is made. Some basic rules of medical record keeping are:

- *Record information on medical records accurately.* Information recorded incorrectly can lead doctors to wrong conclusions about their patients. *Be accurate.*
- *Handwriting must be neat and legible.* Mistakes can be made if your messy handwriting is misinterpreted. Make sure to write neatly.
- *The patient's medical record is a legal document.* The patient's medical record can be admitted as evidence in a court of law in a lawsuit against a hospital or doctor. Any chart with erasures will not be admitted as legal evidence. *Do not erase or use white-out.*
- *Write all entries in ink. All* recording is to be done in ink on a medical record.

Despite all your best efforts, recording errors will be made. If you are charting by hand, one accepted way to make corrections is to draw a single line through the error, write in the correction, and date and initial the correction. An example would be:

2/12/0_ J.M.
Patient complains of ~~nasea~~ nausea.

If you are typing medical records, it is permissible to make corrections as you would normally, for example, with a correctable tape or self-correcting typewriter. However, *never* erase, obscure, or put self-adhesive strips over an original entry.

Outdated Files

When a patient has not visited a doctor for a certain period, his or her medical record is moved to *inactive files.* Most doctors consider inactive status to be after two to three years. *Closed files* contain the medical records of patients who have changed doctors, moved, or died.

Closed and inactive files are kept indefinitely because they are protection against medical malpractice suits. Lawsuits can be filed many years after the disputed treatment, depending on which state is involved. Knowing your state's regulations concerning how long a claim can be made after the treatment is given is essential for determining how long the inactive records should be kept.

Many medical facilities may use microfilm and microfiche technology to store records. Others may use computerized technology for storage. Medical records finally ready to discard should be destroyed in such a way as to obscure the identity of the patient and ensure confidentiality. With hard copies, records should be shredded and burned.

$\mathcal{M}$EDICAL TRANSCRIPTION

Order transcription is the act of rewriting doctor's orders onto requisitions and other forms or using a computer in order to obtain tests, medications, diet, and other services for the patient. General **medical transcription** involves typing or word processing of dictated information such as history and physical examinations, operative reports, and consultations.

You can have a very successful medical clerical career as a medical transcriptionist working for a medical facility or being a freelance transcriptionist.

MEDICAL RECORD SYSTEMS

With our knowledge of medicine doubling about every eight years, there is an increased need for more comprehensive, efficient medical record systems. There are three basic ways to store medical records:

- Source-oriented medical records
- Problem-oriented medical records
- Computer-generated records

Source-Oriented Medical Records

A conventional method of charting is called **source-oriented medical records (SOMR),** which includes a chronological set of notes for each visit. This is not a problem-oriented system, so it may be difficult to track a patient's ongoing problem. The physician must search through the record to find particulars about a particular problem.

Problem-Oriented Medical Records

A more efficient method for keeping medical records is called **problem-oriented medical record (POMR).** This method is a preferred method by many clinics and for medical practices where more than one physician attends to a patient. Each problem that the patient has is assigned a number. The problem or problems are identified by number throughout the record, making it easier for the physician to trace problems throughout various visits.

SOAP Method of Medical Records

Whether or not an office uses the SOMR or POMR techniques for assembling medical records, follow-up visits are charted efficiently by using **SOAP** (see the form in Figure 9.3), an acronym standing for a method to divide progress notes into four sections:

S *Subjective* statements about how the patient feels and what the symptoms are
O *Objective* details about diagnostic tests such as lab reports, x-rays, and physical examinations
A *Assessment,* referring to the doctor's analysis of the subjective and objective details of the subjective and objective details of a patient's problem
P *Plan,* including the doctor's diagnosis and therapeutic plans, including patient instructions

Computerized Records

There are many computer programs available for health care facilities that allow medical records to be generated by computer. Both POMR and SOMR methods can be used together to state the medical problem and have the record grow in chronological order. Past health challenges may be shown at the top of each entry.

Computerized records are especially helpful when computer terminals are tied into a network that is then connected to a main computer. Records are always available all hours of the day and night and can be accessed on a physician's personal computer.

As has been emphasized in former chapters, protecting patient confidentiality must be foremost in all health care workers' minds. Computerizing sensitive medical

OUTLINE FORMAT PROGRESS NOTES

Patient Name _____

Prob. No. or Letter	DATE	**S** Subjective	**O** Objective	**A** Assess	**P** Plans	Page_____

Start each Progress Note (Subjective, Objective, through the intervening columns to the right   Assessment and Plans) at the appropriate margin of the page.   shaded column to create an outline form. Write

ANDRUS/CLINI-RES ® PRIMARY CARE CHARTING SYSTEM, FORM NO. 26-7115-01, © 1976 BIBBERO SYSTEMS, INC., PETALUMA, CA.

FIGURE 9.3 SOAP form.

records can create a serious problem, and safeguards must be put in place to avoid unauthorized persons from getting such information.

FILING SYSTEMS

A good, flexible filing system is critical for the efficient operation of a hospital or other medical facilities. No single filing system is superior. But facilities adopt some form of filing system to assure retrieval, expansion of the system, and security for the medical records of the patients.

The medical clerical worker must understand that there are four areas of managing records that ensure the safekeeping and correct handling of medical records.

- An efficient system must be in place to manage the large volume of records to be kept for each patient. Some systems are manual, and others in larger facilities may be fully computerized.
- Any medical facility, whether large or small, needs a rapid and efficient method of recalling and replacing records.
- Records must have a classification system for documents designating which records are more important and how to file each classification.
- There must be a clear determination of how long which documents are to be stored, as well as when and how documents are purged from active files.

Alphabetical Filing System

The simplest filing method is by **alphabetical** name sequence. This system is the oldest and simplest system available. Many consultants recommend this simple system unless the number of patients exceeds 10,000. Patient records are filed by the first letter of the patient's last name. Care must be taken to spell names correctly. The section on basic rules of filing explains how to file charts of patients with the same name.

Numerical Filing System

Another system is called the **numerical filing** system. If privacy is a particular problem, this system may be effective. This system is also efficient in handling situations in which a medical system is rapidly expanding. It allows for unlimited expansion. This is called an "indirect" system.

Each patient is assigned a number and an alphabetical cross-index card prepared in order for the name of the patient to be identified. Assigned numbers are often a hospital number, Social Security number, telephone number, and so on. The problem with this system is having to go through two steps to get to the patient file. Computerized numerical systems can make this system more accessible.

Alphanumerical Filing System

The **alphanumerical filing** system is designed for alphabetical retrieval and numerical/color refiling. A number and color are provided to each alphabetical grouping to provide easy identification for presorting, filing, and finding. A misplaced color-coded folder will stand out, breaking the pattern of color, and avoiding gross misfiling. This system can be quite complex and difficult to learn.

Color-Coded Filing System

Color-coded filing systems usually have five different-colored file jackets (orange or red, yellow, green, blue, and purple). These file jackets are coded around the *second* letter in the patient's last name (78 percent of the second letters in names are vowels).

For example, a patient whose name is *Maxwell, Robin C.* would have a white tab for the last name and three colored tabs, which vary in color according to the manufacturer. A large red <u>M</u> would be affixed in the code color of this name. After the red <u>M</u>, there would be another color (e.g., green) for the <u>A</u> in the name Maxwell. When the file drawer is opened, the medical clerical worker sees many red *M*s. Some of these files then have green *A*s. This system calls filing errors to the attention of the medical clerical worker because the color coding immediately identifies misfiled records.

A file tab also contains a color-coded year tag (1997 might be blue, 1998 red, and so on). Each time a file is used, the proper year tag is affixed to the file. Old files can be systematically purged using color tab designations.

B ASIC RULES OF FILING

There are very important rules of filing that you as a medical clerical worker will need to master. The following list includes critical aspects of learning to file correctly.

Names

Names are alphabetized in the following order: last name (surname), first name, and middle name (if any). The last name is the primary filing unit. The first name and middle name are used only if the last names and first names are the same.

> William Elliot Marshall
> William Elton Marshall

Prefixes

Some last names have a prefix, such as a *D', Mac, St., Mc, Des,* and so on. This prefix is considered in combination with the rest of the last name. All apostrophes, spaces, and capitalizations are disregarded.

> McDuffey is considered Mcduffey.
> D'Angelo is considered Dangelo.

Remember: St. George as a last name is considered as Saint George, or for filing purposes, Saintgeorge. St. is always considered S-A-I-N-T. This is a difficult rule to remember and is the cause of frequent misfilings.

> St. George   Dennis
> Sargent   William

Abbreviations

Abbreviations are treated as though the words represented were written in full. For example, if a man calls himself Chas. Baker, he is listed as Charles Baker for filing purposes.

Hyphenated Names

Hyphenated names are considered to be one unit.

Ander	Peter
Ander-Jones	James
Anders	Kathleen

Degrees and Titles

Degrees, titles, and seniority following the names are not considered part of the name and are ignored in filing. These terms may be put on filing cards and folders, but should appear in parentheses. If names are totally identical, these are still not used; instead, the address is used.

Lexington	John
Lexington	Judy (Dr.)
Lexington	Keith S. (Jr.) 4115 Oak Street
Lexington	Keith S. (Sr.) 5453 Sea Street

Married Women

When a woman marries and takes her husband's name, she legally takes only his last name. Her own given first and middle names are also used for filing, or sometimes her first name and maiden name as her second name. Sometimes, women choose not to take their husband's name. On filing folders, (Mrs.) is placed after a married woman's name, and the husband's name is placed under her legal name in parentheses.

Wagner	Jennifer L. (Mrs.)
	(Donald A.)
Wagner	Robin C. (Mrs.)
	(Robert Lakewood)

Some women may wish to be referred to as Ms. rather than Mrs. or Miss.

Addresses

Sometimes a physician may see two patients with identical names. For instance, two patients may each be named Mary Sue Jones. In this case, their separate addresses are used when filing these records. The surname is indexed first, then the state, city, street, and finally by street number from the lowest to the highest.

Mary Sue Jones Austin, Texas	Jones	Mary	Texas	Austin
Mary Sue Jones Waco, Texas	Jones	Mary	Texas	Waco

If, by chance, Mary and Mary lived on the same street in the same town, the first record to be filed would be the lowest of the addresses. For instance 121 Wood Street would be filed before 124 Wood Street.

Businesses

The names of hospitals, medical supply companies, and other business facilities are filed in the same order as written unless the firm's name includes a complete name of a person. In that case, the surname would be used in filing. Numbers are filed as though they are written out, filed as one unit. Compass directions are filed as though they are separate units. Prepositions, conjunctions, and articles are not considered units except when *the* is the first word of a title. In this case, *the* is the last filing unit.

The Southwest Medical Center	*filed as*	Southwest Medical Center The
John Frank Medical Supply	*filed as*	Frank John Medical Supply
95th Street Linen Company	*filed as*	Ninety-Fifth Street Linen Company

Record Retention

There are many different kinds of records kept in a medical practice or a hospital setting. General guidelines for record retention include:

- Financial statements, active correspondence, inventory, and payroll records are kept for seven years.
- Applications for employment, expired or canceled insurance policies, petty cash vouchers, purchase orders, office reports, and general correspondence are kept for three to four years.
- Generally, patient files are kept active from one to three years; it is basic medical office policy to purge the files every three to five years.
- To protect the practice against malpractice claims and to provide information from patient histories, closed patient files are kept indefinitely unless a patient is deceased.
- Vital papers such as government tax records, financial papers, property records, employee information, and insurance policies are kept indefinitely.

SUMMARY

Accuracy and confidentiality are the two most important points to remember about a patient's medical record. As a medical clerical worker, you must strive always to make medical record entries that are accurate and legible. Medical records are to be considered confidential legal documents. You must do everything you can to ensure that no one has access to medical records except those people who are directly involved in patient care. As handling medical records becomes more complicated, medical clerical workers must remain flexible about learning new methods of handling records.

LEARNING ACTIVITIES

1. Interview a medical records clerk in a health facility's medical records department. Find out how AIDS has changed the way the health facility handles medical records. Also ask about the work environment and employment opportunities for the medical records clerk.

2. Take a field trip to an acute care and/or a long-term care setting to see the medical records department.

3. Interview a medical transcriptionist. Find out about employment opportunities and skills needed for this medical clerical specialty.

4. The class breaks up into teams. Each team researches and demonstrates how to file:
   - alphabetically
   - alphanumerically
   - by a color-coded filing system
   - numerically

5. Name some purposes of keeping a patient medical record.

6. List five standard hospital medical chart forms.

7. Define the following filing methods.
   (a) Numerical filing system
   (b) Alphabetical filing system
   (c) Alphanumerical filing system

8. Describe the POMR medical record system.

9. Describe the SOAP system.

10. Arrange the following names in correct order for proper alphabetical filing: Thomas Andrew Johnstone, Thomas Andrew Johnston, Thomas A. Johnson, Thomas Anthony Johnstone.

11. Put these names in proper alphabetical filing order: John P. Sarno, John Patrick St. George, John Joseph Sajak, John Patrick Sands-Thomas.

12. What is the rule for filing when two people have the same name but live in different towns?

13. What are the general rules for filing a married woman's medical records?

Understanding Medication Orders

VOCABULARY

Antimicrobial drugs	Drugs that destroy or render harmless microorganisms in the body that are causing disease.
Brand name	The copyrighted name (trade name) given to a drug by a manufacturer.
Chemical name	A long and usually complicated name for a drug that describes its chemical content.
Chemotherapeutic drugs	Drugs that have a selective effect on the invading cells or organisms of certain diseases, usually cancer.
Controlled Substances Act of 1970	Legislation enacted by Congress to regulate drugs with a high potential for abuse.
Diagnostic	A drug used in diagnostic testing such as during x-ray or laboratory testing.
Drug Enforcement Agency (DEA)	A federal agency that issues narcotic licenses to doctors.
Drug scheduling	Drugs that fall under the *Controlled Substances Act of 1970;* drugs that are considered potentially addictive and in need of categorizing according to addictive potential.
Generic name	The established, official name by which a drug is known, no matter who is the manufacturer of the drug.
PDR	The best known drug reference textbook; the full title is *Physicians' Desk Reference to Pharmaceutical Specialties and Biologicals.*
Pharmacist	Professional trained to prepare, preserve, compound, and dispense drugs.
Pharmacodynamic drugs	Drugs that either stimulate or depress normal body functions so that the nature or course of a disease is altered.
Pharmacology	The study of drugs.
Physicians' Desk Reference	Drug reference book containing valuable information about many drugs prescribed today.
Prescription	Medicine that has been prepared by a pharmacist (druggist) according to the directions written by a physician to the pharmacist.
Preventive	A drug such as a vaccine given to immunize and therefore protect a patient against certain diseases.
Therapeutic	A drug given to treat symptoms or the cause of the disease or to replace substances in the body that are depleted, such as vitamins or hormones.

OBJECTIVES

After completing this chapter, the student is responsible for performing the following objectives:

• Discuss the medical clerical worker's responsibilities concerning drugs and prescriptions.
• Explain the Controlled Substances Act of 1970 and its relevance to the medical clerical worker.
• Differentiate between the duties a medical clerical worker may and may *not* perform in relation to medications.
• State the four parts of a prescription.
• Identify the most common symbols, terms, and abbreviations related to drugs.
• Explain what is meant by the chemical name, brand name, and generic name of a medication.

*I*NTRODUCTION

The medical clerical worker must know about federal and state laws concerning medications, help patients with prescriptions, and transcribe drug information. However, it is important that as a medical clerical worker you *never* give advice about medications, nor should you dispense, administer, or prescribe drugs.

Since the medical clerical worker will be asked to call in prescriptions to **pharmacists** and record medication orders on patient charts, knowledge of names and categories of drugs is crucial for you to carry out your job effectively. As in all other duties of a medical clerical worker, working with medications requires great attention to detail and a commitment to accuracy. The medical clerical worker must also be aware that both the prescription pad and drugs kept in your facility can be a target for theft by the drug abuser.

*P*HARMACOLOGY

Pharmacology is the study of drugs. A drug is a substance that, when taken into the body, can change the functioning of the body. Three primary uses for drugs are:

■ **Diagnostic:** A drug used in diagnostic testing such as during x-ray or laboratory testing.
■ **Preventive:** A drug such as a vaccine given to immunize and therefore protect a patient against a certain disease.
■ **Therapeutic:** A drug given to treat symptoms or the cause of disease or to replace substances in the body that are depleted, such as vitamins or hormones.

Drugs come from many sources, such as plants, animals, and minerals. Drugs produced in laboratories of pharmaceutical companies are called *synthetic* drugs. Drugs can also be created through the process of genetic engineering.

Many factors affect the action of drugs upon the human system. Some factors include how rapidly the drug is absorbed into the body, how quickly it is transported throughout the system by the blood, how quickly the drug is broken down for elimination, and how quickly the body can eliminate the drug.

A *side effect* is an action of a drug other than what was intended. A patient taking antibiotics might feel queasy if a drug is not taken with a meal. An *adverse reaction* is an undesirable and harmful side affect. A patient who vomits repeatedly or gets a painful rash after taking a drug is considered to be having an adverse reaction to the drug. All staff must be alert to patients' complaints about symptoms that may be related to their medication.

There is much to learn about medications. New or different medications may be continually ordered for patients. Be inquisitive and listen and learn about medications whenever possible.

*Y*OUR ROLE IN HANDLING MEDICATIONS

The following responsibilities are commonly assigned to the medical clerical worker in relation to drugs and prescriptions.

- You must understand federal and state regulations concerning the dispensing and administration of medications.
- You may be asked to order, store, and keep track of medications. You may also be asked to destroy drugs when expired. No patient should ever receive a drug that has gone past its expiration date. Expired controlled drugs are handled differently. Find out how the DEA wishes such substances to be handled in your facility.
- You must know medication symbols and abbreviations, as well as names of drugs in common usage and drug categories.
- You will be asked to assist patients in filling or refilling a prescription by having the doctor call their pharmacist. You may be required to remind patients to bring in their medications in the original bottle when they see a physician or are entered into the hospital.
- If you work in a doctor's office, you may be responsible for assisting with record keeping of narcotic prescriptions for your employer, and possibly to arrange for the renewal of a narcotic license annually.

The following responsibilities are *not* to be assumed by any medical clerical worker under any circumstances:

- You cannot give advice about medications to any patient or patient's family at any time. Any questions about which medication a patient should use must be referred to a physician.
- You must not administer any medications to a patient. That is clearly not the role of the medical clerical worker and is the responsibility of a licensed nurse, physician, physician's assistant, or properly trained clinical medical assistant in some states.
- You are not allowed to dispense medications to a patient without the request of a physician. You may be asked to assemble medication for dispensing. You may have access to the drugs in the area where you work, but the physician is totally in charge of how drugs are dispensed.
- You are never allowed to prescribe any drugs to a patient, including writing out a prescription on your employer's prescription pad without permission or calling a pharmacist without direct orders from a physician.
- You are generally not allowed to take a telephone order or verbal order for drug dispensing or administration from a doctor. There are exceptions to this rule. If you are allowed to take a verbal order you must write "verbal

order" on the patient's record and sign your name. Be sure to follow your employer's *exact* instructions.

It is very important that you clearly understand your responsibilities toward medications at your work site. There are specific laws and regulations concerning this area of medicine, and you could be penalized for performing duties not legally assigned to you.

$\mathcal{L}$ AWS ABOUT DRUGS

The manufacture, distribution, and use of medications is the subject of a huge body of federal and state laws. The first law regulating drugs by the federal government was the *Food and Drug Act of 1906.*

In the last several decades, the government realized that there were many drugs with a high potential for abuse, such as morphine and cocaine. Therefore, the **Controlled Substances Act of 1970** was passed, containing laws regarding such abused drugs. Pharmacies are required by law to be registered with the Drug Enforcement Administration. Physicians and hospitals that keep controlled drugs in offices and on hospital units must keep careful licensed records.

Drugs that fall under the Controlled Substances Act of 1970 are put into five categories of *schedules* (**drug scheduling**). These schedules are labeled with Roman numerals I through V. Schedule I drugs are considered to have the highest possibility for addiction and are not recommended for medical use. Schedule V drugs are considered to have the least potential for abuse but are still scheduled. A complete list is available from the federal **Drug Enforcement Agency (DEA).** A partial list appears in Table 10.1.

Individual states may add drugs to schedules or change some drug classifications. Marijuana is an example of a drug that can effectively control nausea. There have been several state ballot measures to allow a controlled production of marijuana for such medical use.

The licensed staff must count the medications and sign the records, but you may be responsible for making sure that the records are maintained correctly. Learn what controlled drugs are located at your work site. There are periodic checks by the Drug Enforcement Administration to see how carefully records are kept, and fines and even imprisonment can result when irregularities are found. Scheduled drugs must be placed in a separate locked cabinet.

When scheduled drugs are dispersed, records of such administration should be kept for a minimum of two years and include the following information:

- Patient name and address
- Name of drug and date of administration
- Dosage and how drug is administered (route)
- Method of dispensing

This detailed record keeping is required only when a scheduled drug is administered or dispensed in a doctor's office. A completed prescription for the pharmacist to fill does not require this kind of detail.

TABLE 10.1	SCHEDULE OF DRUG CATEGORIES MANDATED BY THE CONTROLLED SUBSTANCES ACT OF 1970

Schedule I: This schedule lists drugs of high potential for abuse and that have no current accepted medical use. Schedule I drugs will be used by physicians only for purposes of research, approved by the Food and Drug Administration and the DEA, and only after a separate DEA registration as a researcher is obtained. The manufacture, importation, and sale of these drugs is prohibited. However, some states have enacted legislation to permit the use and possession of marijuana for certain medical patients.
Examples: heroin, marijuana, LSD, mescaline, peyote.

Schedule II: These drugs have current accepted medical use in the United States, but with severe restrictions. There is with these drugs a high potential of abuse that may lead to severe psychological or physical dependence.
Examples: *Narcotics:* morphine, codeine, Percodan.
Non-narcotics: amphetamines, Ritalin, Nembutal, and Quaalude.

When Schedule I and II drugs are ordered, the physician must use a special order form (DEA Form 222) that is preprinted with the physician's name and address. The form is issued in triplicate. One copy is kept in the physician's file while the remaining copies are forwarded to the supplier who, after filling the order, keeps a copy and forwards the third copy to the nearest DEA office.

Prescription orders for Schedule II drugs must be written and signed by the physician. Some states, by law, require special prescription blanks with more than one copy. The physician's registration number must appear on the blank. The order may not be telephoned in to the pharmacy except in an emergency, as defined by the DEA. A prescription for Schedule II drugs may not be refilled.

Schedule III: These drugs have less potential for abuse than substances in Schedule I and II. They have accepted medical use for treatment in the United States, but abuse may lead to moderate or low physical dependence or high psychological dependence.
Examples: *Narcotics:* various drug combinations containing codeine and paregoric.
Non-narcotics: amphetamine-like compounds and butabarbital.

Schedule IV: These drugs have a lower potential for abuse than those in Schedule III and have accepted medical use in the United States, but their abuse still may lead to limited physical or psychological dependence.
Examples: Chloral hydrate, meprobamate, Librium, Valium, and Darvon.

Schedule III and IV drugs require either a written or an oral prescription by the prescribing physician. If authorized by the physician on the initial prescription, the patient may have the prescription refilled up to the number of refills authorized, which may not exceed five times or beyond six months from the date that the prescription was issued.

Schedule V: These drugs have less potential for abuse than drugs in Schedule IV, and their abuse may be limited to physical or psychological dependence. Refills are the same as for drugs in Schedules III and IV.
Examples: This schedule includes cough medications containing codeine and antidiarrheals such as Lomotil.

According to the law, the only person authorized to issue prescriptions is the registrant. A prescription issued by the physician may be communicated to the pharmacist by the medical office employees. This regulation may be less restrictive for medications *not* in the Controlled Substances Act.

If your state requires triplicate prescription blanks, they will be used for prescribing drugs. These are not to be confused with the Form DEA 222 described earlier for the ordering of Schedule I and II drugs. The triplicate blanks will be furnished by the state, and the regulations should be followed.

All prescriptions for controlled substances must be dated and signed on the day issued, bearing full name and address of the patient and the name, address, and DEA registration number of the physician. The prescription must be written in ink or typewritten and must be signed by hand by the physician.

Physicians must know the laws of their state on controlled substances. The state regulations may be more strict than federal regulations and may require a separate state registration.

Narcotics laws should be studied carefully by any physician who opens an office. *The Code of Federal Regulations, Title 21* should be obtained from the nearest federal government bookstore and studied carefully before handling controlled substances in the medical office.

COMPONENTS OF A PRESCRIPTION

Since you will probably deal directly with transcribing **prescriptions,** you need to know many things about prescriptions. Generally, you will not be asked to write out a prescription, since it should be in the physician's handwriting. Remember, the prescription is a legal document.

You should know prescription terms and abbreviations, as you will have to use them when answering the telephone, taking dictation, and interpreting instructions on the administration of drugs.

All prescriptions follow a specific format. The prescriptions are usually written on sheets, often put in a pad, with the physician's name, address, and phone number printed on the top (Figure 10.1) Also, the DEA narcotic number is located on the prescription when prescribing controlled substances. There is traditionally a space for

```
                    THOMAS A. SCOTT, M.D.
                        General Practice

                        135 So. Elm St.
                      Sacramento, CA. 94106
                    Telephone: (916) 555-5550


    FOR _____  DATE _____

    ADDRESS _____

       Rx




                              SAMPLE
                            DO NOT FILL

    CAL. LIC. #G099914
    DEA #AK08888888


    REFILL _____ TIMES
      # 25-8294               Thomas A. Scott, M.D.
```

FIGURE 10.1 Prescription form.

the patient's name, address, and the date of the prescription. Triplicate forms are used for narcotics. The following items make up the rest of the prescription:

- *Superscription.* This is the first part of a prescription, represented by either the word *Recipe* or the familiar symbol "Rx" (meaning "take thou" from the Latin *recipe*).
- *Inscription.* This is the name of the drug or medication (generic or brand name), the quantities of ingredients, and the dose strength. You normally will see the amount in grams or milligrams when dealing with capsules, tablets, or suppositories. With ointments and creams, the strength is given in a percentage. If the drug is an oral liquid medication, it is given as grams or milligrams per milliliter.
- *Subscription.* These are directions given to the pharmacist on the size of the dose, the total quantity of the drug, and the form of the medication (whether it is a capsule, liquid, and so on).
- *Signature, or transcription.* These are instructions the pharmacist is to print on the label so that the patient will know how and when to take the medication (from the Latin *signetur* meaning "write on label").
- Physician's signature and registry number.
- Number of times a prescription can be refilled.

The most common abbreviations and symbols that you have to know to understand a prescription are listed in Appendix D.

$\mathcal{P}$ROBLEMS WITH PRESCRIPTIONS

Drug abuse is an extremely serious problem today. Some abusers target physicians to obtain illegal drugs. The medical clerical worker must be on the alert for such people. You should be suspicious if a patient states that he is a patient of another doctor, but that your employer occasionally prescribes drugs on the controlled drug list for him. Always verify this information with the other doctor if this is the case. When a patient is uneasy and avoids questions, you should be suspicious.

The prime target of the drug abuser is the prescription pad. You should avoid having the pad stolen by following these precautions:

- Use as few pads as possible. Try to limit pads in use to one. Avoid leaving any prescription pads unattended.
- Keep the pads in a locked drawer or cabinet so they cannot easily be taken.
- Make sure that the prescription pads are numbered consecutively. It is also recommended that pads be printed in an ink that cannot be copied.
- There are generally prescription pads for nonrestricted drugs and for controlled drugs. Some physicians have nonrestricted drug pads that have a phrase printed on them such as "not valid for narcotics, barbiturates, or amphetamines."
- Alterations can be prevented by having the physician write on the pads in ink.
- Physicians should never sign the prescription pads in advance.
- To avoid alteration of the prescription, numbers should be written out. For instance, "30 tablets" can easily be changed to "80 tablets."
- Tamperproof prescription pads are available that are tinted to easily detect erasures and white-out correction fluid.

If a pad is stolen, you should report the theft to authorities. You should be able to tell the police which numbers are missing. Some communities have a phone network that alerts pharmacists in the area about a stolen pad.

Real-Life Scenario

Jacob is a recent hire medical clerical worker at Dr. Fleming's office. One of Jacob's challenges as an employee is to keep his workspace neat. His supervisor Maria has reminded Jacob to tidy up his desk. However, Jacob is not a naturally organized person.

Dr. Fleming has asked Jacob to bring her a new prescription pad. On the way to Dr. Fleming's office, Jacob is asked to help a patient at the front desk. Jacob puts down the pad on the counter while talking with a patient. When finishing with the patient, Jacob picks up some patient papers but leaves the prescription pad on the counter. A few minutes later, Jacob remembers that he was supposed to give the pad to the doctor. When he remembers where he put it, he realizes that the pad has disappeared.

1. What does Jacob do right away?

2. Will his employer be angry?

3. What other problems could take place because of Jacob's disorganization?

COMMUNICATING WITH THE PHARMACIST

Frequently called telephone numbers should be placed near a telephone where the medical clerical worker makes most telephone calls. One of the most important numbers to have nearby is the pharmacy of the medical facility where you work. In the case of working in a doctor's office, your employer will designate a pharmacist or pharmacists (possibly in the same office building) who will fill prescriptions for your patients. Sometimes a patient may ask you to call the prescription into another pharmacy.

The most important thing to remember about communicating with the pharmacy is that you *must* give the pharmacist all the information that the prescription contains. To ensure accuracy, you should ask the pharmacist to repeat the information. This practice will help avoid dangerous misunderstandings. If you phone in a prescription to a recorder, you must speak slowly, give the recorder all information requested, and be sure to leave your name and position, as well as your employer's name and phone number in case there are questions.

NAMES OF DRUGS

As a medical clerical worker, you will probably become very familiar with the names of drugs frequently ordered by physicians. You may be confused at first about the names, and they may all sound the same to you. Each drug generally has three names, and some have more (Table 10.2).

- *Chemical name.* This name refers to the exact chemical content of the drug. The **chemical name** rarely appears in doctors' orders.
- *Generic name.* This name is licensed under this title by the manufacturer. The **generic name** is never changed. It is a name derived from the chemical name, but a much simpler form. It is never capitalized.
- *Trade or brand name.* This is a special name given to the drug by each company that manufactures it. These drugs are capitalized. The superscript ® to the right of the **brand name** indicates that the drug is registered with the U.S. Patent and Trademark office.

You are much less likely to make errors when trying to read your employer's handwriting if you know the meaning of the abbreviations and terms for medications.

TABLE 10.2	EXAMPLE OF DRUG NAMES FOR A SINGLE MEDICATION	
	Drug	Manufacturer
Chemical name	(±)-2-(*para*-isobutylphenyl) proprianic acid	
Generic name	ibuprofen	
Brand name	Nuprin®	Bristol-Myers
	Ibuprin®	Thompson Medical
	Motrin®	Upjohn

DRUG CATEGORIES

Drugs may be put into many different categories. Some general categories of drugs with which you will come into contact (Tables 10.3 to 10.5) include:

- *Antimicrobial drugs.* **Antimicrobial drugs** may destroy or disable microorganisms in the body that cause disease. Bacteria, fungi, protozoa, and other such microorganisms can be destroyed by such drugs as penicillin, sulfanamides, and keflex.
- *Pharmacodynamic drugs.* These drugs either stimulate or depress normal body functions so that the nature or course of a disease is changed. **Pharmacodynamic drugs** include stimulants, barbiturates, and tranquilizers.
- *Chemotherapeutic drugs.* These drugs are used to treat diseases with uncontrolled cell growth, such as cancer. **Chemotherapeutic drugs** have a selective effect on invading cells or organisms. Such drugs generally kill cancer cells or parasites invading the body.

MOST COMMONLY ORDERED DRUGS

Obviously, the drugs that you need to be most familiar with include the drugs most often prescribed. Some common drugs are listed in Table 10.6. The categories were defined in Tables 10.3 to 10.5.

ROUTING OF DRUG ADMINISTRATION

The same drug can often be prepared in a variety of ways and be given to patients by many different routes. Penicillin can be given orally, by an intravenous injection, or by injection in the muscle. Most routes of administration are abbreviated in a doctor's order. You should be familiar with the abbreviations listed in Table 10.7.

DRUG REFERENCES

You may or may not be required to commit to memory the categories and the names of all the drugs mentioned in this chapter. An easy familiarity, as mentioned before, will help you comfortably transcribe orders and make sense of the physician's handwriting. But you will always have available a reference text, which will contain valuable information about drugs, including correct spelling. Supplements are issued annually to update the medical profession continuously about the most dynamic changes in pharmacology.

TABLE 10.3   ANTIMICROBIAL DRUGS THAT AFFECT DISEASE-CAUSING ORGANISMS

Category	Description
Antiseptics	Chemicals that kill or inhibit the growth of micoorganisms and are used on living tissue
Disinfectants	Chemicals that kill or inhibit the growth of microorganisms and are applied to inanimate objects
Antibiotics	Drugs produced by bacteria that prevent the growth of, or destroy, other bacteria
Antifungals	Drugs that inhibit or stop the growth of fungus
Anti-infectives	Drugs that act on susceptible bacteria, rickettsiae, and spirochetes by inhibiting their growth and replication
Antivirals	Drugs that inhibit or stop the growth of viruses
Antituberculars	Drugs that inhibit or stop the growth of the bacteria that cause tuberculosis, the tubercle bacilli
Sulfonamides	Chemical substances that weaken susceptible bacteria; commonly called "sulfa drugs"

TABLE 10.4	*P*HARMACODYNAMIC DRUGS AND THE BODY SYSTEMS THEY AFFECT
Category	**Description**

NERVOUS SYSTEM

Category	Description
Stimulants	Drugs that produce increased functional activity; often used to counteract mental depression.
Analgesics	Medication given primarily for relief of pain without loss of consciousness.
Narcotic analgesics	Habit-forming analgesics that, when withdrawn from the addicted patient, produce certain uncontrollable physical symptoms.
Nonnarcotic analgesics	Differ from narcotics in not being habit-forming. In addition to their pain-relieving action, some drugs in this group reduce fever (antipyretics).
Hypnotics and sedatives	Compounds that exert a general depressant effect on the central nervous system and are defined based on the dose and degree of effect.
Barbiturates	A group of compounds structurally related to barbituric acid. The body may develop a strong dependence upon barbiturates.
Nonbarbiturate hypnotics	Drugs used as sleeping medications when the doctor chooses not to order barbiturates.
Tranquilizers	Drugs that reduce anxiety or tension; however, this group differs from the hypnotics in that they are not usually given to produce sleep.
Antidepressants	Drugs that elevate the mood and relieve depression.
Anesthetics	Drugs that produce loss of sensation and an inability to perceive pain.
General	Drugs that produce loss of sensation and muscle relaxation accompanied by loss of consciousness; administered by inhalation of a gas or by intravenous injection.
Local	Drugs that produce loss of sensation in a limited area of the body by "deadening" the nerves in that area and are usually administered by injection. Topical anesthetics are applied to the skin, usually to mucous membranes.
Anticonvulsants	Drugs that suppress convulsions or seizures.

ENDOCRINE SYSTEM

Category	Description
Insulin	Hormones that aid in the metabolism of sugars; used primarily in the treatment of diabetes.
Oral hypoglycemics	Chemicals taken by mouth to lower blood sugar in certain cases of diabetes.
Corticosteroids	Hormones produced by the adrenal glands; often used to treat inflammatory conditions.
Other hormones	Hormones such as estrogen and thyroid used for replacement when the individual gland is not producing enough of its hormone.

RESPIRATORY SYSTEM

Category	Description
Antitussives	Formulations given for the purpose of relieving coughs.
Expectorants	Drugs that increase or modify mucus secretions in the bronchi and aid the expulsion of sputum.
Bronchodilators	Drugs that widen the bronchial tubes.
Antihistamines	Drugs that help relieve allergic symptoms by counteracting the effect of histamine in the body. Also relieves allergic symptoms of the skin, such as hives and other reactions caused by allergy.

GASTROINTESTINAL SYSTEM

Category	Description
Antacids	Drugs that lower the acidity of the gastric secretions; commonly used to treat the symptoms of "indigestion."
Antiemetics	Drugs that stop vomiting and relieve nausea.
Antiflatulents	Formulations that decrease the amount of gas in the gastrointestinal tract.
Emetics	Drugs to produce vomiting.
Cathartics	Drugs that aid in causing bowel movements.
Antidiarrheals	Drugs used in the treatment of diarrhea.
Antispasmodics	Drugs used to relieve spasm of the digestive tract.

CIRCULATORY SYSTEM

Category	Description
Cardiotonics	Drugs that affect the heart, usually improving the quality of the heart's action.
Diuretics	Drugs that increase the flow of urine; used primarily to reduce the blood pressure by reducing fluid retention.
Vasoconstrictors	Drugs that cause blood vessels to constrict or narrow; often used in emergencies to counteract shock by raising the blood pressure.
Vasodilators	Drugs that cause the blood vessels to dilate or widen; may be used to treat hypertension and other diseases of circulatory impairment, where the blood vessels have narrowed.
Anticoagulants	Drugs that inhibit the clotting of blood. In disease, they are used most frequently on patients with abnormal clotting within blood vessels.
Hematinics	Iron supplements.

MUSCULOSKELETAL SYSTEM

Category	Description
Antiarthritics	Drugs used to treat symptoms of arthritis and related diseases.
Antigout medications	Formulations used to treat gout.
Muscle relaxants	Drugs that reduce painful spasms of the muscles.

TABLE 10.5	*C*HEMOTHERAPEUTIC DRUGS
Category	**Description**
Antineoplastics	Drugs used to kill cancerous body cells
Antiparasitics	Drugs used to treat diseases caused by such animal parasites as helminths (worms), amoeba, and protozoa

TABLE 10.6	*C*OMMONLY *O*RDERED *D*RUGS

ANALGESICS (Relieve pain)

Nonnarcotic
- Aspirin (acetylsalicylic acid)
- Bufferin
- Darvon (propoxyphene hydrochloride)
- Empirin

- Ibuprofen (Advil)
- Talwin (pentazocine)
- Tylenol (acetaminophen)

Narcotic
- Codeine
- Demerol (meperidine)
- Empirin or Tylenol with codeine
- Morphine (morphine sulfate)

- Percocet
- Percodan
- Vicodin

ANTACIDS (Neutralize stomach acid)
- Amphojel (aluminum hydroxide)
- Elusil
- Maalox

- Mylanta
- Riopan (magaldrate)

ANTIBIOTICS (Kill microorganisms)
- Amikacin
- Amoxicillin
- Ampicillin (principen, omnipen, polycillin)
- Cefoxitin (mefoxin)
- Cipro (ciprofloxacin)
- Erythromycin (ilosone)
- Gantrisin (sulfisoxazole)
- Garamycin (gentamicin)
- Kanamycin (kantrex)

- Keflin (cephalothin)
- Methicillin (staphcillin)
- Neomycin (mycifradin sulfate)
- Oxacillin (prostaphilin)
- Penicillin G (wycillin)
- Septra (trimethoprim; sulfamethoxazole)
- Streptomycin
- Vibramycin (doxycycline)

ANTICOAGULANTS (Inhibit blood clotting)
- Coumadin
- Dicoumaril

- Heparin

ANTICONVULSANTS (Prevent seizures)
- Dilantin (phenytsin)
- Luminal (phenobarbitol)

- Valium

ANTIDEPRESSANTS (mood elevators)
- Aventyl (nortriptyline)
- Elavil (amitriptyline)
- Nardil
- Norpramin (desipramine)
- Prozac

- Sinequan (doxepin)
- Tofranil (imipramine)
- Triavil
- Zoloft

ANTIDIABETICS OR HYPOGLYCEMICS (Reduce blood sugar)

Oral Hypoglycemics
- Actos
- Avandia
- Glucophage

- Glucotrol
- Micronase
- Precose

Injectable Hypoglycemics
- Humalin L: insulin, Lente
- Humalin N: insulin, NPH
- Humalin 70/30: insulin, NPH and regular

- Humalin U: Ultralente: insulin, ultralente
- Humalog: insulin, analog injection (lispro)
- Novolin R: insulin, regular

ANTIDIARRHEALS
- Donnagel
- Imodium
- Kaopectate

- Lomotil
- Pepto-Bismol

ANTIEMETICS/ANTINAUSEANTS (Prevent nausea, vertigo, motion sickness)
- Compazine
- Dramamine
- Phenergan

- Thorazine
- Tigan
- Vistaril

(Continued)

TABLE 10.6	*C*OMMONLY ORDERED DRUGS (CONT.)

ANTIFLATULENTS (Relief from gas)

- ilopan
- Mylicon

- simethicone

ANTIHISTAMINES (Counteract histamine production)

- Actifed
- Allegra
- Benadryl
- Claritin
- Dimetane

- Ornade
- Phenergan
- Teldrin
- Triaminic

ANTIHYPERTENSIVES (Reduce blood pressure)

- Aldomet
- Apresoline
- Capoten
- Lopressor

- Papaverine
- Vasotec
- Zestril

ANTI-INFLAMMATORY AGENTS (Diminish inflammation)

- aspirin
- Butazolidin
- clinoril

- ibuprofen
- Indocin
- Prednisone

ANTINEOPLASTICS (Treat cancer)

- adriamycin
- Cytoxan
- L-asparaginase
- Leviceran

- Platinol AQ (cisplatin)
- S-Fluorovracil
- Tamoxifen

ANTITUSSIVES/COUGH AND COLD PREPARATION

- Benylin DM
- Hycodan
- Sucrets (lozenges)

- Sudafed
- Tuss-Ornade

ANTIVIRALS

- Cytovene
- Epivir
- Famvir
- Flumadine
- Foscavir

- Invirase
- Retrovir
- Symadine
- Valtrex
- Zovirax

BRONCHODILATORS (Dilate bronchial tubes)

- Aminophyllin
- Atrovent
- Bronkotabs

- epinephrine
- Isuprel
- theophylline

CARDIOTONICS (Increase strength of heart contraction)

- Digitoxin
- Digoxin
- Inocor

- Lanoxin
- Primacor

CATHARTICS, LAXATIVES, AND STOOL SOFTENERS

- Cascara
- Colace
- Dulcolax
- Ex-lax
- Fleet enema

- Metamucil
- Milk of Magnesia
- mineral oil
- Senokot

DIURETICS (Increase urination)

- Aldactone
- Diuril
- Dyazine

- Lasix (furosemide)
- Midamor

EMETICS (Cause vomiting)

- Ipecac syrup

TABLE 10.6   **C**OMMONLY **O**RDERED **D**RUGS (CONT.)

HEMATINICS (Stimulate red blood cell production)

- Ferrous sulfate
- Imferon

- Ircon

HORMONES

- estradiol
- hydrocortisone
- Norplant
- prednisone
- Premarin

- Somatotropin
- synthroid
- Thyroxine
- Vasopressin

MUSCLE RELAXANTS

- Flexeril
- Robaxin

- Soma
- Valium

SEDATIVES–HYPNOTICS

- chloral hydrate
- Dalmane
- Doriden
- Nembutal (pentobarbital)

- phenobarbital
- Placidyl
- Seconal (secobarbital)

TRANQUILIZERS

- Compazine
- Equanil (meprobamate)
- Librium

- Thorazine
- Valium (diazepam)

The most common drug reference book, which most physicians and hospitals have in their libraries, is the ***Physicians' Desk Reference,*** better known as the **PDR.** The PDR is divided into nine color-coded, alphabetized sections. Those sections include:

- ■ *Alphabetical index by manufacturer*
- ■ *Alphabetical index of brand names*
- ■ *Product classification index.* Drugs are listed by their general classification, such as antihistamines.
- ■ *Generic and chemical name index*
- ■ *Product identification section.* This is a very useful section for the medical clerical worker, containing a color reproduction of the actual size of tablets and capsules for visual identification.

TABLE 10.7   **R**OUTES OF **D**RUG **A**DMINISTRATION

Route	Abbreviation
By mouth (orally)	p.o.
Subcutaneous	s.c., subcut.
Hypodermic	H.
Intramuscular	IM
Intravenous	IV
Intravenous push	IVP
In right eye	OD
In left eye	OS
In both eyes	QU
Sublingual (under the tongue)	subling

■ *Product information section.* This section contains detailed information on use, dosage, composition, action, and side effects of drugs.

■ *Diagnostic products information.* Another very useful section for the medical clerical worker, this section contains a list of injectable materials used in x-ray procedures and brand names of products used for laboratory and skin tests.

■ *Listings of poison control centers*

■ *Guide to management of drug overdose*

SUMMARY

You have a most important responsibility as a medical clerical worker in being part of a team that works to assure that patients receive correct pharmacological treatment. You must be careful to transcribe your employer's written orders correctly, paying attention to detail and accuracy. Do not hesitate to ask questions if you are not sure. A patient's well-being could depend on your accurate interpretation of orders!

You will be expected to use great care in seeing that the prescription pad does not get stolen or used illegally. Equally important is your understanding of the limitations of your position where medications are concerned. Remember, you are *never* allowed to give advice or administer, dispense, or prescribe drugs. Special attention must be given to the unique requirements when dealing with scheduled drugs.

LEARNING ACTIVITIES

1. Find out at a library or through a pharmacist what the ten most abused drugs are today (prescription or nonprescription). Would they all be available through a health facility? What are the ten most prescribed drugs today?

2. Besides the examples given in this chapter, what other suspicious behaviors might you expect from someone entering a health care facility in search of obtaining illegal drugs?

3. Transcribe doctor's orders given in the classroom.

4. Look up a list of drugs in a *Physicians' Desk Reference* and give pertinent information.

5. Although not listed in Table 10.6, make your own list of recent drugs developed to treat AIDS.

6. List at least five responsibilities that a medical clerical worker has in relation to medications.

7. What special treatment do scheduled drugs require?

8. List four responsibilities that are *not* the medical clerical worker's duties in relation to medications.

9. List and describe parts of a prescription.

10. What do the following prescription symbols and abbreviations mean?

    (a) ac   **(f)** s
    (b) qh   **(g)** tid
    (c) bid   **(h)** troc
    (d) ss   **(i)** sat
    (e) q4h   **(j)** hs

11. Describe three things you can do to help avoid having a prescription pad stolen from your work space.

12. Match each term with the correct definition.

    __ **(a)** anticoagulant   **(1)** Drug that increases urination
    __ **(b)** brand name   **(2)** Drug used to check bleeding
    __ **(c)** generic name   **(3)** Drug used to inhibit clotting of blood
    __ **(d)** hemostatic   **(4)** Drug whose distribution must be watched, due to potential abuse
    __ **(e)** sedative   **(5)** Name referring to components of drug
    __ **(f)** diuretic   **(6)** Drug name that varies with manufacturer
    __ **(g)** chemical name   **(7)** Drug reference book
    __ **(h)** PDR   **(8)** Official name of a drug (relatively simple)
    __ **(i)** antiemetic   **(9)** Drug that generally depresses the central nervous system of the body
    __ **(j)** controlled drug   **(10)** Drug that stops vomiting

13. Explain the differences in the following: *therapeutic, preventive,* and *diagnostic* drug administration.

Diagnostic Testing

VOCABULARY

Cardiology	Study of the heart.
Cerebrospinal fluid	Fluid that protects the brain and spinal cord; also called CSF.
Clinical laboratory	Area or separate department in a health care facility that analyzes body fluids, cells, and tissues in a precise, accurate, and rapid manner.
Complete blood count (CBC)	Automated blood test that determines the size, content, and numbers of red blood cells in a blood sample, as well as content of hemoglobin in a red blood cell; also counts the number of platelets and white blood cells present in a blood sample, estimating what kinds of white blood cells are present; also called a CBC.
Contrast medium	Special substances injected, swallowed, or inserted into a patient that are used to increase the contrast in an x-ray film when there is little difference in the density between some body parts; usually organic iodine or a barium preparation.
Critical values	Test results so far outside normal range that they pose a serious risk to the patient.
CT scan	Abbreviation for *computerized tomography;* special x-ray that produces three-dimensional pictures of a cross section of a part of the body; used to detect tumors, blood clots, abnormalities of brain structure, as well as for other uses.
Diagnostic imaging	Another term for x-rays; diagnostic imaging department refers to the radiology department.
Differential	Determination of the different types of white blood cells present in a sample of 100 white blood cells.
ECG	Abbreviation for *electrocardiogram;* a mechanical tracing of the heart's action made by an electrocardiograph.
EEG	Abbreviation for *electroencephalogram;* process of recording brain wave activity using electrodes attached to various places on the patient's head and recording the electrical activity of the brain.
Endoscopy	Examination of the body organs or cavities by the use of an instrument called an endoscope.
Enzymes	Biological catalysts present in body cells that help speed reaction rates.
Hematocrit	Percentage of the total blood volume of a sample occupied by the red blood cells.
Hemoglobin	Main content of the red blood cell; a molecule that transports oxygen from the lungs to the tissues and carbon dioxide in the reverse direction.
Histology	Division of laboratory that examines tissue samples.
Microbiology	Division of laboratory that analyzes specimens to identify pathogenic microorganisms.
MRI	Abbreviation for *magnetic resonance imaging;* procedure that uses a magnetic field to produce images of structures and tissues in the body.
Nuclear imaging	Use of radioactive materials and specialized equipment to help diagnose and treat certain diseases and injuries.
Pathogenic	Anything that is capable of producing disease.
Point-of-care testing	Simple laboratory tests done by health care professionals at the patient's bedside.

Radiology	Branch of medicine concerned with radioactive substances, including x-rays and radioactive isotopes, as well as the application of such information to the prevention, diagnosis, and treatment of disease.
Respiratory therapy	Treatment to preserve or improve lung function.
Sputum	Mucus that collects in the lungs; not to be confused with saliva from the mouth.
Ultrasound	Radiological procedure where the deflection of high-frequency sound waves directed at an organ or tissue is recorded.
Urinalysis	Testing the physical, chemical, and microscopic characteristics of urine that can indicate disease or damage to the urinary tract.

OBJECTIVES

After completing this chapter, the student is responsible for performing the following objectives:

- Discuss several commonly ordered clinical laboratory tests.
- List several radiology procedures, explaining their differences.
- Explain some common cardiology tests.
- Discuss why respiratory therapy might be necessary.
- Identify the difference between physical and occupational therapy.
- Explain why a patient might need an EEG.

*I*NTRODUCTION

As a medical clerical worker, you may often be required to fill out forms for various types of diagnostic testing. If you work in a hospital setting, one of your duties may be to fill out slips for various tests performed throughout the medical facility. In some facilities, you may automatically enter tests ordered by physicians directly into a computer. These orders are then immediately sent to departments that perform various tests, such as the Clinical Laboratory, Radiology, Cardiology, Respiratory Therapy, and other departments. In a medical office environment, you may be required to fill out forms and/or enter tests into a computer. You may also be required to direct the patients to various facilities where such testing is performed. Some private practices do some basic laboratory testing as well as simple x-rays, EKGs, and other procedures. Most expensive and complex procedures are performed in a specialty center.

It is important that you have knowledge of the names of various tests routinely ordered in the health care environment. You should also have a basic understanding of what the testing entails. This chapter will deal with general tests ordered in most health care facilities. Specific practices may order specialty tests that are not commonly ordered in most facilities. It is important for the medical clerical worker to be familiar with the specific tests requested by his or her employer.

*C*LINICAL LABORATORY TESTING

The physician continually relies on **clinical laboratory** testing as an invaluable diagnostic tool. Laboratory tests can be used to diagnose many different diseases. For example, a **complete blood count (CBC)** result can reveal a patient's *anemia* (deficiency of the red blood cells); an abnormal *glucose* (blood sugar) level can indicate *diabetes mellitus* (disorder of carbohydrate metabolism, resulting in excessive sugar in the blood and urine). When a physician performs a complete physical examination, a number of laboratory tests may be ordered to screen out major health problems.

You may also be responsible for accepting specimens from patients that will be transported to a clinical laboratory for testing. Such specimens can include (but are *not* limited to):

- Blood
- Sputum (coughed up from the lungs)
- Urine
- Throat and nose cultures
- Stool
- Various body fluids such as **cerebrospinal fluid** and knee fluid

The medical clerical worker *must* handle all specimens as if they are infectious. Gloves must be worn when accepting specimens from a patient. You should never accept a leaking, contaminated specimen. Ideally, you are handling specimens that are sealed in a leakproof bag. Hands must be carefully washed after gloves are removed.

Purpose of Laboratory Testing

In addition to aiding the physician in a diagnosis by facilitating early detection of a disease process, there are other important reasons for a physician to order a clinical laboratory test.

- *Establish normal baseline results on a patient.* Individual test results can vary, based on age, sex, race, and geographic location.
- *Evaluate the success of certain medications or other treatments.* An example would be when a physician tests for the blood level of a certain antibiotic in a patient's blood. The physician wants to make sure that the drug is present in a high enough level to treat an infection successfully.
- *Satisfy requirements of the law.* Many states require that a couple has premarital screening for syphilis. Many hospitals require a syphilis test for all patients entering the hospital. Pregnant women are also screened for syphilis and evidence of exposure to measles in many states. Mandatory AIDS testing continues to be a controversial issue and is not determined in many cases.

Ordering Laboratory Tests

Your employer may ask you to order clinical laboratory tests by giving you verbal or written orders to be put on a requisition form or entered into a computer. Your greatest concerns for ordering such tests should be:

- Recognizing test names, being sure not to misunderstand the orders.
- Knowing how to correctly spell test names.
- Understanding abbreviations commonly used for some tests.
- Possessing knowledge of using the correct laboratory slips when applicable (many facilities no longer use individual lab slips for different tests).

The primary concern of the medical clerical worker is to correctly order tests. Laboratory tests can be very expensive and inconvenient for the patient if it becomes necessary to come back to a laboratory and have more blood taken if a test is not ordered correctly.

Some tests require the patient to have some special preparation before a blood test. Many facilities have sheets of written instructions depending on the test ordered. The most common type of preparation is for the patient not to eat or drink for a designated amount of time before a test is performed.

Point-of-Care Testing

Point-of-care testing has become more popular in recent years with increased emphasis on getting laboratory results to the physician as soon as possible. POTC refers to near-patient testing or bedside testing. POCT uses small instruments that provide rapid, accurate results when used correctly. Some examples of tests that can be completed at bedside with sophisticated machinery are pregnancy, blood clotting, hemoglobin, and blood glucose testing. In hospitals, this testing is often performed by nurses or laboratory personnel.

Commonly Ordered Clinical Laboratory Tests

Most clinical laboratories in a health care facility have several different departments within the laboratory, with many instruments in each department (Figure 11.1). Laboratory order sheets may be divided into several parts corresponding to the following departments:

FIGURE 11.1 Laboratory components.

- *Hematology.* This department primarily concentrates on counting and assessing the formed elements in the blood, including white and red blood cells and platelets (cell fragments that aid in blood coagulation). Other coagulation testing may often be performed in the hematology department as well. A commonly ordered hematology test is the complete blood count.

- *Chemistry.* The chemistry department measures chemical changes in the body to obtain information about diagnosis, therapy, and prognosis of disease. Drug levels are tested in this department. Commonly ordered chemistry tests include *electrolytes* and *chemistry panels.*

- *Urinalysis.* Sometimes a part of the hematology department, this section is responsible for observing physical, chemical, and microscopic characteristics of urine that can indicate disease or damage to the urinary tract. The most common test in this department is the complete **urinalysis.**

- *Blood bank.* The blood bank in the clinical laboratory is the department responsible for storing, processing, and distributing blood and its components. *ABO and Rh blood typing* is a common test ordered for the blood bank department (Figure 11.2).

- *Serology.* This department concentrates on testing for *antigen/antibody reactions.* If the human body encounters an antigen (protein) that is foreign to the body, the body may respond by producing an antibody to defend the body against foreign substances. This department tests for the presence of antibodies to determine if the body has been exposed to particular types of antigens, including the *AIDS virus* and *syphilis.*

- *Microbiology.* This department encompasses the study of microorganisms that can be harmful to or cause disease in humans. These organisms are extremely small and cannot be seen with the naked eye. This department also identifies common human parasites, some of which can be seen individually with the naked eye. Common tests that are sent to this department include *throat cultures, stool cultures,* and *urine cultures.*

- *Histology Department.* The **histology** department of the clinical laboratory is submitted tissue samples from physicians and often from specimens taken directly during surgery. A *histology technician* prepares tissue samples for pathologists to examine for pathology.

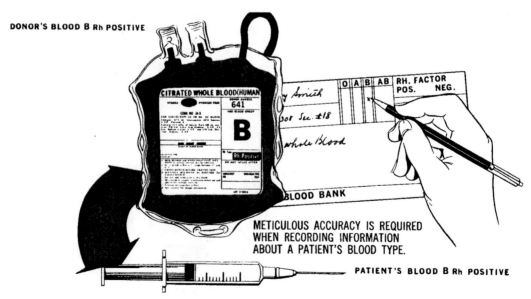

FIGURE 11.2 Blood typing.

Cytology is often located in or near the histology department. Cytology is the study of cells, and in this section trained *cytologists* and pathologists study cells obtained from body tissues. *Pap smears* are examined by this section, performed on various types of specimens to determine the presence of cancer. The most common Pap smear is taken from the cervix during a pelvic examination.

Table 11.1 summarizes commonly ordered clinical laboratory tests.

ℛ ADIOLOGY

Rapid advances are occurring in the field of **radiology,** also known as **diagnostic imaging.** Diagnostic imaging today refers to various x-ray techniques, such as noninvasive x-rays, x-rays using dyes, specifically controlled radiation, and radioactive isotopes. This department has a number of procedures that enable physicians to view organs at work and identify blockages and growths without the patient's having surgery. There can be many separate departments within radiology, making it neces-

TABLE 11.1	Commonly Ordered Clinical Laboratory Tests	
Name	**Department**	**Description**
Complete blood count	Hematology	Several tests including counting of red and white blood cells and platelets, **hemoglobin** and **hematocrit** determination, and estimating types of white blood cells (**differential**).
Reticulocyte count	Hematology	Counting immature red blood cells to see if new red blood cells are being produced (often ordered when patient is being treated for anemia).
Prothrombin time	Hematology	Measures clotting ability of blood. Ordered on a frequent basis to monitor patients on anticoagulant therapy.
Sedimentation rate	Hematology	Test to determine whether a patient has an inflammatory reaction in the body.
Chemistry panels (profiles)	Chemistry	Battery of chemistry tests ordered in a panel format; different laboratories offer different types of panels including general chemistries, liver panels, kidney panels, and so on.
Electrolytes	Chemistry	Panel including tests for sodium (Na), potassium (K), chloride (Cl), and carbon dioxide (CO_2).
Blood glucose	Chemistry	Test to determine glucose level of the blood. Sometimes ordered as fasting (no food for at least 8 hours before the test), random (anytime), 2 hours after a meal, and so on.
BUN, creatinine	Chemistry	Kidney function tests.
AST, ALT, LD	Chemistry	Liver **enzymes** that if elevated can indicate serious liver problems such as hepatitis and other liver diseases.
Urinalysis	Urinalysis	Testing of physical, chemical, and microscopic characteristics of urine that can indicate disease or damage to the urinary tract.
Blood typing	Blood Bank	Determination of a patient's ABO and Rh blood grouping.
Crossmatch	Blood Bank	Test performed in the blood bank to detect any reactions that might occur in a recipient during a blood transfusion; results in a unit or more of blood being set up for a patient for possible transfusion.
Antibody screen	Blood Bank	Testing of a patient's blood for antibodies that might interfere with a blood transfusion.
Rubella screening	Serology	Testing of possible antibodies in the patient's blood that can protect a person from getting rubella.
HIV testing	Serology	Initial testing for HIV can be done by determining if the antibody against HIV is present.
RPR, VDRL	Serology	Antigen/antibody testing for the presence of syphilis antibodies.
Mononucleosis testing	Serology	Antigen/antibody testing for the antibodies against the virus causing mononucleosis.
Rheumatoid arthritis test	Serology	Testing to determine antibodies to the rheumatoid factor, involved in rheumatoid arthritis.
Gram stain	Microbiology	Common stain used in microbiology to observe possible bacterial contamination of a specimen put on a slide and stained with special stain that targets bacteria.
Throat culture	Microbiology	A throat swab is used to inoculate various nutrient agar plates that are capable of growing bacteria that can cause disease, such as *streptococcus*.
Urine culture	Microbiology	A sample of *sterile* urine is put on nutrient agar plates to grow bacteria that could be causing urinary tract infection.
Sputum culture	Microbiology	A sample of **sputum** is placed on nutrient agar to grow bacteria that could be causing lung infection.
Stool culture	Microbiology	A sample of stool is placed on nutrient agar and observed for the growth of any **pathogenic** bacteria that could be causing infection.
Ova and parasites	Microbiology	A sample of stool is stained and observed for the presence of parasites (both eggs and organisms) in the sample.

sary for the medical clerical worker to make sure the proper type of x-ray is ordered and the patient sent to the proper place for the x-ray to be done.

X-rays (also called *radiographs*) can serve as a diagnostic aid to visualize internal structures and organs. X-rays are high-energy electromagnetic waves that are invisible. They are able to penetrate solid materials because of a very short wave length. They rely on differences in density or thickness of various body structures to produce shadows on the radiographic film. **Contrast medium,** which is swallowed or injected into a patient or inserted into the rectum, can be used when the densities of two structures or organs are similar and in the same proximity, making it hard to distinguish between the two structures. The simplest types of x-rays are those that do not require any patient preparation or use of a contrast medium (Figure 11.3). The following examples are x-rays that require no preparation of the patient.

- Chest x-ray
- Skull x-ray
- Flat plates (looking for bone problems, foreign bodies, and so on)

Contrast Media Radiographs

Many x-ray procedures may require the use of special substances to increase the contrast in the film to accentuate different areas. Contrast medium is generally barium sulfate powder for studies of the gastrointestinal tract and an iodine compound used for studies of arteries and veins, urinary system studies, and other areas. Patients are generally sent to a radiology department to obtain specific instructions for preparation for contrast media x-rays. Some examples of x-rays that use contrast media are listed on Table 11.2.

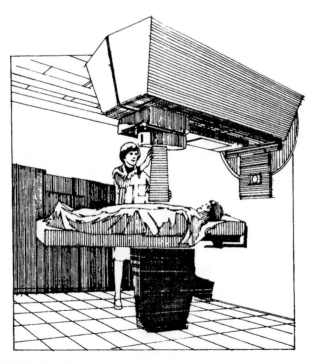

FIGURE 11.3 Taking an x-ray.

TABLE 11.2	X-Ray Contrast Media Studies	
Test	**Area**	**Contrast Media Information**
Intravenous pyelogram (IVP)	Kidney, ureters, bladder	Dye inserted into urinary tract; x-rays taken.
Cholecystogram	Gallbladder	Oral contrast media taken evening before exam.
Upper gastrointestinal series (Upper GI)	Esophagus, stomach, and sometimes small bowel	Patient drinks barium sulfate solutions.
Barium enema (BE)	Colon and sometimes ileum	Barium instilled into colon by enema; rectum and large intestine outlined on x-ray film.
Angiogram	Vascular structures	Contrast medium injected within body to visualize arteries and veins.
Arteriogram	Arteries	Contrast media injected into arteries for visualization of potential blockages, structural problems, and so on.
Cystogram	Bladder	Contrast medium inserted into bladder through a catheter.
Myelogram	Spinal cord	Contrast medium injected between the vertebrae into the spinal cord.

CT Scan

A **CT scan** (*computerized tomography*) is a specialized type of x-ray that produces three-dimensional pictures of a cross section of a body part. This procedure is a computerized analysis of the varying absorption by body tissues of a high-energy, pinpoint beam of x-ray that produces a precise, reconstructed image. Many new techniques are being continually developed to improve upon this procedure as well as many other procedures in radiology. These scans are used to detect tumors, blood clots, enlarged ventricles or openings in the brain, and other abnormalities of the brain structure and nerves or muscles of the eye. This procedure can be done with or without contrast medium, which may be given orally or by injection. Figure 11.4 illustrates this procedure.

Mammography

Mammography is a radiologic study of the breast used to help diagnose cancer. The most common form is film-screen mammography, which requires the patient to stand at a machine that compresses the breast to achieve the best x-ray possible. The patient is asked to wear no perfume, deodorant, or powder the morning of the examination, all of which can interfere with the film. Other forms of mammography are *thermography, diaphanography,* and *ultrasonography.* The medical clerical worker may be required to know the specifics of these three techniques if working in a facility where more than one type of mammogram is ordered.

Ultrasound

Ultrasound is not considered an x-ray, but is often performed in the radiology department. It is a procedure that uses sound waves at very high frequencies to produce images of internal body structures and organs. It is safe and painless, not involving the use of x-rays. Ultrasound is used widely in medicine, especially in diagnosis during pregnancy.

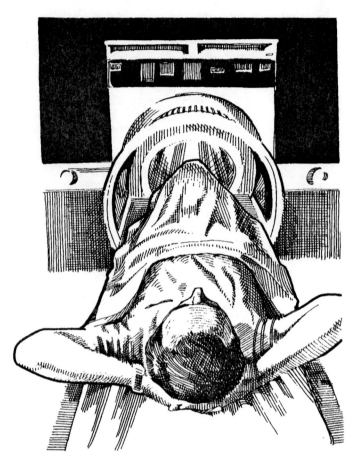

FIGURE 11.4 CT scan.

MRI

MRI (*magnetic resonance imaging*) is a diagnostic procedure that uses a magnetic field (instead of radiation) to produce images of structures and tissues of the bodies. The procedure results in high-resolution images without any risk to the patient.

The patient's head or body is placed in a strong magnetic field. The patient's hydrogen protons become aligned in the direction of the magnetic field. Then a pulse of radio-frequency energy is emitted from the MRI machine. That energy flips the hydrogen protons into a higher energy state. When the pulse ends, the protons relax. The energy they emit produces signals that the MRI machine translates into images. The MRI is especially effective in looking at tissues with high fat and water content that other procedures do not see well.

Nuclear Imaging

Nuclear imaging involves the use of radioactive materials and specialized equipment to aid in the diagnosis and treatment of certain diseases and injuries. Professionals trained in nuclear medicine administer radioactive substances to patients by routes such as oral, intravenous, intramuscular, or intracavitary (into a cavity). The material introduced travels to the organ to be x-rayed. Specialized equipment and material is then used to produce images from the gamma rays emitted from the radioactive material that was introduced into the patient. Patients who are allergic to contrast media can benefit from this type of procedure. Another advantage is that such procedures usually result in much lower doses of radiation than other radiographic techniques.

There are various other procedures that a radiology department may have under its umbrella. You are encouraged to become familiarized with all the procedures that might be ordered by your employer.

CARDIOLOGY

The **cardiology** or *cardiovascular* department is responsible for many important tests and procedures within the hospital. Most hospitals also provide cardiac rehabilitation on an outpatient basis. Your employer might refer patients often to cardiology laboratories for specific heart testing.

Some important cardiology tests include:

- **ECG** or *electrocardiogram.* An ECG (also referred to as an *EKG*) is a mechanical tracing of the heart's action made by an *electrocardiograph.* The ECG is an important aid in the diagnosis and treatment of patients with heart disease. Figure 11.5 illustrates the administering and recording of the ECG.
- *Echocardiogram.* This is a procedure where echoes are obtained by ultrasound that are recorded on paper and used to evaluate the inner structures of the heart.
- *Cardiac catheterization.* A catheter is inserted into a vein and passed into the heart. The catheter can be followed on a special screen. Dye may be injected for visualization of the vessels. This procedure is done to diagnose heart disease or defects. It is done in a cardiac catheterization laboratory and is closely observed for any complications.
- *Treadmill stress test.* This test records the patient's heart activity while the patient's blood pressure is being monitored. Electrodes attached to the patient's chest carry the electrical activity from the heart to a monitor in the form of a heart tracing. The angle of slant of the treadmill and the rate of walking is increased to the patient's tolerance. If certain changes in the tracing indicate danger, the treadmill is discontinued. This test helps the physician determine the patient's tolerance to activity and aids in planning an appropriate exercise regime.
- *Holter monitor.* This small device is worn by the patient on the nursing unit or can also be worn at home. Leads are attached to the chest and wires are connected to the pack worn by the patient via a shoulder strap. It provides a continuous ECG recording for a prescribed amount of time (often 12 to 24 hours) while the patient goes about normal activities. A diary is kept by the patient so that the physician can correlate changes in the ECG tracing with the patient's activities at the same time.

OTHER DIAGNOSTIC TESTING

There will be other diagnostic tests and procedures that a physician may ask a medical clerical worker to order for a patient during the workday. It is valuable for the medical clerical worker to be familiar with the names of tests and also with where the patient should be sent for testing.

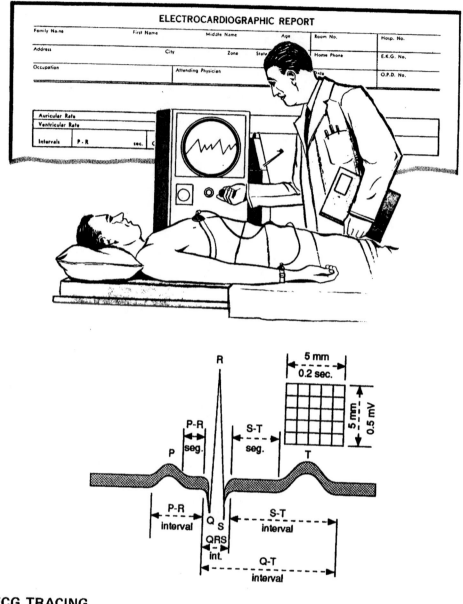

ECG TRACING

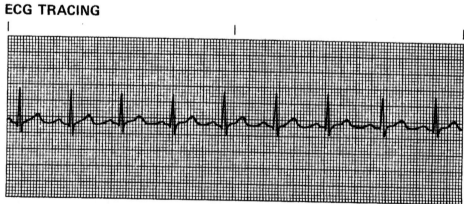

FIGURE 11.5 ECG.

Respiratory Therapy

Respiratory therapy is defined as therapy to preserve or improve lung (*pulmonary*) function. Many patients in the hospital may have compromised lung function as a result of an infection or chronic lung disease brought on by smoking, work-related hazards, or a history of chronic lung disease. Patients can also be susceptible to lung problems if immobilized for any period of time, especially in an elderly population.

Many hospitals have a separate respiratory therapy department, although some facilities have now combined this department with other departments such as nursing due to cutbacks in staffing. Patients may need supplementary oxygen, but oxygen given artificially may be harmful if used incorrectly. It must be given in proportion to need. Special monitoring is required to make sure how much oxygen is carried in the blood. Today these levels can be monitored by a *pulse oximeter,* a device that is attached to the fingertip. A more detailed, sophisticated testing for lung function is called the *arterial blood gas (ABG).* Respiratory therapists often perform this test (as well as laboratory personnel and nurses) where a heparinized needle with attached syringe is placed in an artery. The clearly labeled, iced specimen is then taken with an appropriate requisition if needed to the laboratory. In the laboratory, the blood is tested for oxygen content, carbon dioxide, pH, and other values.

Patients on continual oxygen may need to be assisted when coming in and out of the facility. They may also be referred to special respiratory therapy departments for breathing treatments and further diagnostic testing.

Physical Therapy

Patients with certain injuries may be referred to physical therapy centers if they need a qualified physical therapist to help with their rehabilitation. The medical clerical worker may be asked to fill out a physical therapy request form (Figure 11.6) or enter information into the computer. Because the patient may require a series of treatments, several appointments may have to be made with the physical therapist based on the frequency of the treatment ordered by the doctor.

Occupational therapy consists of directed activities, such as games and work projects. These activities aid in the treatment and rehabilitation of partially disabled patients. A program like this is adapted to suit the particular needs of each patient. For instance, stroke patients may often have to learn how to dress themselves again using only one side of the body. You may be required to make occupational therapy arrangements for patients.

Electroencephalogram (EEG)

The **EEG** (*electroencephalogram*) is the process of recording the brain wave activity. Electrodes are attached to various places on the patient's head, and a recording is made of the electrical activity within the brain (Figure 11.7).

During the procedure, the patient remains quiet with eyes closed. The procedure is used to help diagnose seizure disorders and other brain abnormalities and is diagnostic for brain death.

Endoscopy

An **endoscopy** is an examination of the body with the use of an instrument having a light source. Special plastic-coated endoscopes are often used that are easy to move around and provide excellent visualization. These tests are performed by a physician.

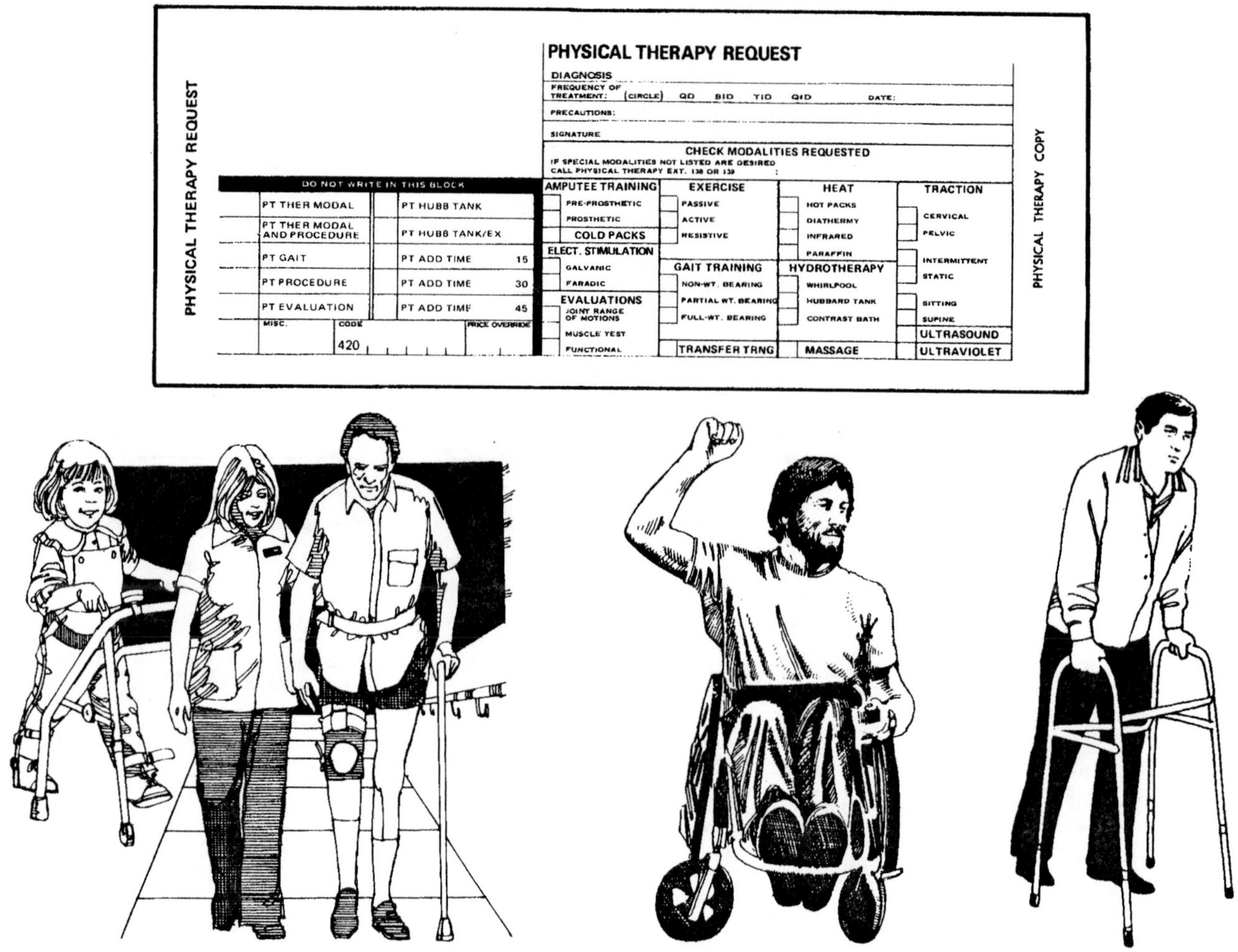

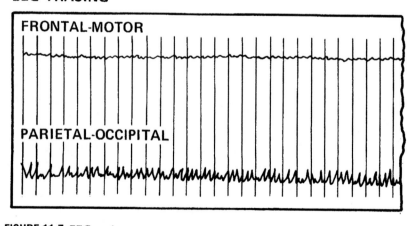

PHYSICAL THERAPY REQUEST

DO NOT WRITE IN THIS BLOCK		
PT THER MODAL	PT HUBB TANK	
PT THER MODAL AND PROCEDURE	PT HUBB TANK/EX	
PT GAIT	PT ADD TIME	15
PT PROCEDURE	PT ADD TIME	30
PT EVALUATION	PT ADD TIME	45
MISC.	CODE	PRICE OVERRIDE
	420	

FIGURE 11.6 Physical therapy.

EEG TRACING

FRONTAL-MOTOR

PARIETAL-OCCIPITAL

FIGURE 11.7 EEG tracing.

In large health care facilities, endoscopies may be performed in the endoscopy department. Some common endoscopies include:

- *Bronchoscopy:* Providing a visualization of the bronchi.
- *Esophagoscopy:* Looking into the esophagus.
- *Gastroscopy:* Visualization of the stomach.
- *Proctoscopy:* Viewing the rectum.
- *Sigmoidoscopy:* Visualization of the sigmoid portion of the large intestine (colon).
- *Colonoscopy:* Looking into the lower intesting as far as the cecum. As with many other endoscopic examinations, biopsies can be taken and polyps removed.
- *Cyctoscopy:* Visualization of the bladder.
- *Laparoscopy:* Looking into the inside of the abdomen or peritoneum through a small incision in the abdomen.
- *Arthroscopy:* Viewing the interior surface of a joint, most commonly the knee.

SUMMARY

The medical clerical worker may be asked to order several diagnostic procedures for patients every day. It is critical that the tests be ordered in an accurate, timely, and professional manner so that the patient has the test done as rapidly as possible. Errors in test ordering can result in delays in diagnosis, inconvenience to the patient, and unnecessary expenditures for the patient.

The medical clerical worker generally may be asked to order over the phone or through the computer tests for the clinical laboratory, radiology, cardiology, respiratory therapy, physical therapy, as well as other less frequently ordered tests.

LEARNING ACTIVITIES

1. Research the topic of mandatory AIDS testing. Are there now any laws in the country dictating mandatory AIDS testing? Why has this issue been such a controversial topic throughout our society?

2. Do a survey of several physicians' offices to find out what the five most commonly ordered laboratory tests are in each facility.

3. Obtain a list of radiology testing performed by your local medical center radiology department. Write a short explanation of each test. Obtain a fee schedule for each procedure if available.

4. Obtain some normal and abnormal ECG and EEG tracings to observe the differences in normal and abnormal results.

5. Research the education needed to become a physical therapy assistant, physical therapist, and occupational therapist.

6. Name four departments in the clinical laboratory.

7. What type of test might be ordered by law?

8. What is a complete blood count?

9. Explain the urinalysis procedure.

10. What is a chemistry panel?

11. What is the purpose of contrast medium in radiology testing?

12. What is a mammogram? An angiogram? An arteriogram?

13. Match each procedure with the correct description.

__ (a) ultrasound	(1) Magnetic field used to produce images
__ (b) mammogram	(2) X-ray specifically targeting the kidneys, ureter, and bladder
__ (c) CT scan	(3) X-ray procedure highlighting the arteries
__ (d) arteriogram	(4) X-ray of the breast
__ (e) IVP	(5) X-ray that provides a three-dimensional image of tissues or structures
__ (f) MRI	(6) recording high-frequency sound waves directed at an organ or into tissue

14. Indicate whether each statement below is true or false.
    __ (a) An ECG and an EKG are two different procedures.
    __ (b) An echocardiogram is basically a sonogram.
    __ (c) A cardiac catheterization can be done in a physician's office.
    __ (d) A Holter monitor can be worn by a patient at home.
    __ (e) A treadmill stress test records the patient's heart activity while the patient's blood pressure is monitored.

15. Name the process of recording brain wave activity.

16. What type of therapy involves directed activities, such as games and work projects?

17. What device measures the oxygen level of the blood through the fingertips?

18. What type of therapy preserves or improves pulmonary function?

19. Name a reason for chronic lung disease.

20. Name four types of endoscopic examinations.

CHAPTER 12

Medical Office Information Technology

VOCABULARY

CPU The abbreviation for *central processing unit,* referring to the working unit of the computer, consisting of many electronic components.

CRT Abbreviation for cathode ray tube (also called *video display terminal* and *computer readout terminal*), which shows information that is being put into the computer.

Fax machine Also known as a *facsimile machine,* a copy machine that sends and receives electronically typed pages, graphs, photos, and so on, over telephone lines.

Floppy disks A flexible magnetic storage device for computer programs and information.

Hard copy Information printed from a computer to paper.

Hardware Computer equipment that uses software to operate computer programs.

Input Computer term to describe information entered into the computer, provided through a keyboard, from another computer, or from storage.

Mainframe The largest computers, capable of performing multiple tasks at rapid speeds. Usually found only in the larger facilities, due to their expense.

MEDLARS A computerized retrieval service operated by the National Library of Medicine.

Microcomputer The smallest computer, also called a personal computer (PC), popular as a home computer and also used in business.

Minicomputer A medium-sized computer capable of stand-alone functions or used as an auxiliary to a mainframe.

Output The information processed by a computer, including any information on the computer screen, printed out, or stored.

Photocopier Equipment that produces copies directly from the original.

Software Programs that make the computer operate.

Transcriber Machine that allows a person to listen to and retrieve recorded information at varying speeds.

Word processing A system of producing typewritten documents by use of automated typewriters and electronic text-editing equipment.

OBJECTIVES

After completing this chapter, the student is responsible for performing the following objectives:

- Discuss the uses of transcribers, electric and electronic typewriters, word processors, computers, calculation devices, mailing machines, fax machines, and copiers in medical facilities.
- Describe the three types of computers.
- Identify selected computer terminology and the basic parts of a computer and their functions.
- Discuss the functions of computers in medical facilities.

*I*NTRODUCTION

Because of the huge amount of record keeping and accounting required in the health care industry, office automation is quickly becoming a necessity in medical facilities. Automation makes it possible to serve an increased patient load much more efficiently and effectively. Medical clerical workers are spared many time-consuming tasks that are now being done by the machines discussed in this chapter.

*T*RANSCRIBERS

As discussed briefly in Chapter 8 of this textbook, some physicians may require that the medical clerical worker retrieve information that he or she has dictated into a machine. This requires the use of a **transcriber** machine, where the medical clerical worker listens to recorded information and produces a hard copy of the information.

There are many different kinds of transcriber machines. Standard features on many models are listed below.

- *Volume, tone, and speed control.* The transcriptionist can adjust the volume and the different tones (increasing treble makes consonants easier to hear) and slow or increase speed.
- *Headphone.* Using a headphone excludes other office sounds, which may be distracting; also allows for confidentiality rather than playing the transcription for others to hear.
- *Foot pedal control.* The foot pedal control permits hands to remain on the keyboard.
- *Erase control.* This allows for a cleaner tape erasure.
- *Scanning.* This feature allows rapid identification and location of all dictation on a cassette.
- *Automatic backspace control.* This control allows the tape to rewind slightly when it is stopped. No words are missed when the tape is restarted.
- *Index counters.* Index counters measure the length of the dictation on a cassette. They are helpful when scanning the cassette to find a location of a specific dictation.

Digital dictation is a development that has made transcribing much easier today in many facilities. Dictation is recorded directly into computers and managed on the computer. Digital dictation can be transferred by telephone lines through modems. It can also be transcribed live and re-recorded at a later time.

*C*OMPUTERS IN THE MEDICAL ENVIRONMENT

Computers can be intimidating to those who have had no exposure to them and their uses. The health care field has become computerized in almost all areas, including the medical clerical field. With some knowledge and hands-on experience, you will quickly learn that computers are in your workplace to make your job much easier and more enjoyable.

This chapter is designed to help familiarize you with computers and to help you recognize their valuable place in your chosen profession. After being exposed to the medical environment, you will see how important computer literacy is for you.

The computer is indeed critical to health care. Visit a hospital, and you will see patients being admitted, cared for, and treated using computerized equipment. Many commercial computer systems are available today specifically designed for the health care environment.

Your job may be to enter personal data into the computer system, including name, address, phone number, medical notes, and insurance policy numbers. You may also play an active roll in preparing patient billing and submitting insurance claims.

Other valuable uses of the computer that you may encounter in your job include:

- *Correcting mistakes.* Deleting mistakes is very easy on a computer by using a delete key and the computer cursor or by pointing to the mistake with a *mouse.*
- *Verifying orders.* You can call up an order that has already been put into the computer by calling it up on the **CRT.** It is easy to correct information if there is an error.
- *Inquiring about orders.* You can call up a program that will give you a list of all orders on a certain day. You can also locate people by calling up names using a similar inquiry program.
- *Notification of other departments/doctors.* Many times an order request affects another hospital department or another physician. Computers can be designed to forward messages to departments or other offices that need this information. For example, when diagnostic tests will require fasting, the dietary department of a hospital may be notified that the patient should not have breakfast the morning of the test. Similarly, a physician may want to get a second opinion from another physician nearby and can immediately send information about the patient to the consulting physician.

Physicians use computers not only to keep track of patient information and charges, but for diagnostic purposes as well. Some programs for the computer tell the physician the probable effect of administering drugs to various kinds of patients.

When using a computer system, the medical clerical worker must remember the importance of ethics and confidentiality. The computer, like other medical records, contains privileged information that must be protected.

$\mathcal{T}$YPES OF COMPUTERS

You could think of computers as coming in three different sizes: small, medium, and large.

Mainframes

The largest computers are called **mainframes.** These computers, which are very expensive, are capable of performing many tasks at a very rapid speed. Most large facilities own their own mainframe system, which can access information from auxiliary storage devices as well as send information to other computers or terminals located in remote sites. Mainframes need a special environmentally controlled room and sophisticated electrical wiring.

Minicomputers

Minicomputers are capable of processing data like a large computer, but they do not need special environmental conditions or complicated wiring. Many facilities operate with a minicomputer as the main computer.

Microcomputers

Microcomputers, also known as personal computers, are very popular with individuals who enjoy **word processing** and setting up household accounting systems. Small businesses and schools rely extensively on the microcomputer. Such computers are self-contained and can do all of the things a larger computer can do, but on a more limited scale.

As a medical clerical worker in a hospital, you will probably be working on a minicomputer system that may or may not be connected to a mainframe system. All three systems have much in common and operate in much the same way. Computers can be linked together to communicate with each other and share information.

COMPUTER COMPONENTS

To have an understanding of computers, you should understand the basic computer components. All computers must have a means to *input* information, a means to *process* information, and a means to *output* information (Figure 12.1).

Input

The most common way to put information into a computer is by a *keyboard.* The keyboard looks like a typewriter keyboard, with a few extra keys. One key plays a very important function—the ENTER key. After you have put information into the computer, you press the ENTER key. Other **input** devices for computer systems include diskettes, magnetic tapes, and light pens.

Process

A computer processes information that is put in it and displays the information on the computer screen, or *cathode ray tube.* The computer processes information by means of the **CPU,** or *central processing unit,* which often consists of many electronic components and microchips. The computer performs in computer or machine language. You do not have to understand the particular language the computer uses, but you must understand how to get the computer to initiate its functions. Information

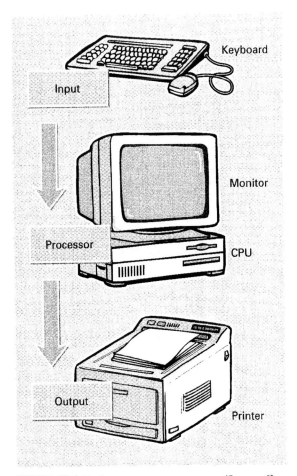

FIGURE 12.1 Basic computer components. (Source: Cox-Stevens, K., *Being a Health Unit Coordinator* (5th ed.). Prentice Hall, 2002).

input is accurate only if you put it in correctly. It is important to be very careful with input information. Computers depend on you to input information, which they process in a logical, rapid, and consistently accurate manner.

Output

There are several ways to get information out of a computer once you put it in for processing. The information obtained from a computer is called **output.** The most common way to obtain output is by a monitor, called the cathode ray tube (CRT). A CRT looks very much like a television set. Today, screens can be as thin as a magazine.

As you input information, it can be seen on the screen of the monitor. When it is processed, it returns to you and can be seen on the screen. Information that is stored can also be called to the screen. If you need a printed copy of the results of your work, a printer is used to type information on the paper. Information printed out on paper is called **hard copy.** Information can also be transferred to **floppy disks.**

The computer machinery—keyboard, CPU, CRT, and printer—is known as the **hardware. Software** includes the computer programs that tell the computer what to do and how to do it. Software can include *spreadsheets,* which are electronic worksheets containing numbers and formulas in columns and rows. Spreadsheets mainly produce budgets, profit and loss statements, and other cash flow reports. Word processing software manipulates, edits, writes, and prints text. *Database* software allows for collection of data, either numeric or text, to produce different types of reports.

Both hardware and software are being developed at an astonishing speed. A medical clerical worker may have just gotten used to one system in the medical facility, and a new training program will be set up for the next system to be introduced. Flexibility is incredibly important in dealing with the constant change of the computerized world.

Today's medical knowledge is more and more available due to several *computer-search* services. The National Library of Medicine offers a computerized retrieval service called **MEDLARS,** available at libraries in medical centers, hospitals, and universities. Other services are also available that allow physicians and other medical professionals the ability to request a search for all articles pertaining to a particular medical topic. The medical clerical worker may be asked to perform a search for an employer.

CONFIDENTIALITY AND COMPUTERS

In past chapters of this textbook, it has been continually stressed that confidentiality is extremely important for all health care workers. When using the computer, you must not let your identification code or password get in the hands of the wrong person. The consequences could be disastrous to patients. If you alter patient information, serious consequences can result, including disciplinary action or termination of employment.

A confidentiality statement should be signed for all caregivers who receive a computer access code. The employee will be asked to read and sign a confidentiality statement at the completion of the system training period (see Figure 12.2).

You will mainly be using computers in the health care environment. Additionally, you may be asked to use other pieces of equipment. Hopefully, all the machines you use will have clear, readable training manuals. When the manuals are confusing, your supervisor should be able to help you with any problems that you might encounter. Ample training time is often given on all such machines, as well as the occasional opportunity to attend seminars put on by factory representatives of the product you are using.

OTHER OFFICE EQUIPMENT

Calculators

Machines that perform calculations for you reduce the time needed to process numbers. Just as computers have software to perform word processing, they also have programs that develop spreadsheets for accounting and other calculations.

Your facility may have a calculator to process numbers. Such machines help you in the basic arithmetic processes of adding, subtracting, multiplying, and dividing. Some machines are also modified to include features that simplify many business computations. There may be an *automatic constant* for chain calculations. There may also be a *non-add key* that prints numbers that do not become part of your calculation. Remember, you must at least double check your work. The calculations are only as accurate as the person who enters the numbers!

MEMORIAL HOSPITAL
Computer User's Access Codes (Log-ins)
Confidentiality Statement

Obtaining access to the Hospital's computerized information system requires a clear understanding of your responsibilities regarding access and adequate training on the system. The following statements will provide an understanding of the significance of the User Access Code you receive following your training. Please, read them **carefully.**

1. **My User Access Code (password) is confidential. It identifies me in a *unique* manner. I am responsible for all data entered into Merlin under my code.**

2. **I will not disclose my User Access Code to anyone, nor will I attempt to learn another person's access code.**

3. **I will not use another person's access code to enter, update, or retrieve data on Merlin.**

4. **If I have reason to believe the confidentiality of my code has been compromised, I will notify Information Systems Services immediately so that my code can be deleted and a new code issued to me.**

5. **I understand that all patient data viewed, printed, or entered is confidential patient data and part of the medical-legal record. I will not access data on patients for whom I have no responsibilities and for whom I have no "need to know."**

6. **I understand that any misuse of my confidential User Access Code is a violation of Hospital policy, and will subject me to disciplinary action up to and including termination of employment.**

Your signature below acknowledges agreement with and understanding of these statements.

Signature _____ Name Printed _____

Department _____ Date _____

Trainer's Initials/ I.S. Issuer _____ Date _____

DISTRIBUTION: ORIGINAL - HUMAN RESOURCES, Employee File   PHOTOCOPY - DEPT. DIRECTOR

- -

Employee# _____   Access Code _____
　　　　　　(if known)　　　　　　　　　　　　　　　　　(PRINT password CLEARLY)

Please Note: If you have not received a certificate of class completion and/or access is not available within 4 days, please notify your director.

FIGURE 12.2 Example of a confidentiality statement.

It is very helpful to use a calculator that has a tape included in the machine. This way, you may review the tape after making calculations to check your work.

Mail Machines

As discussed in Chapter 8, offices with heavy mailings will provide their employees with scales and postage meters to use when preparing mail. Such equipment is very easy to use, requires little training, and cuts down on the time required to handle mailing.

Fax Machines

Fax machines (facsimile machines) are machines designed similarly to copiers, with important differences. A fax machine will send a document put into it for copying to an output terminal located elsewhere, over telephone lines. A medical clerical worker can send a patient's record instantly to a consulting physician far away. Sophisticated fax machines now send messages by microwave, using satellites. This allows messages to be sent in less than one second.

Photocopiers

Photocopiers, also called copying machines, reproduce copies directly from original copy. Most facilities in the health care field have some type of photocopying machine. Much activity in a medical facility will revolve around preparing, distributing, presenting, and storing copied materials. Special features that might be present in a photocopier include:

- An automatic sorting device
- The ability to copy instantly both sides of the paper
- A stapling capability
- Use of a wide range of paper stock
- The ability to make overhead transparencies
- High-speed operation
- The ability to receive, transmit, and store data
- Variations in print sizes, line justification, and the ability to number pages
- Direct connect to computers for instant copying

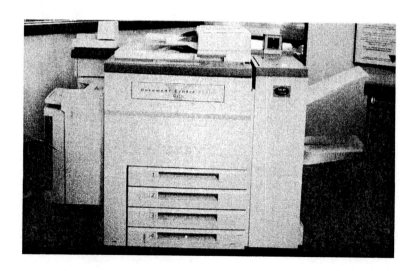

Unlike other machines in the medical office environment, copy machines are shared by many people and are used constantly. As a result, they often have operational problems and require troubleshooting from time to time. Often the problem is minor and does not require a service call. You should learn how to solve minor problems such as paper jams and reloading paper.

SUMMARY

Office automation has streamlined many tasks that once tied up most of a medical clerical worker's day. The opportunity is there to be more efficient in your role in the medical facility. Constant changes in automation allow you to grow on the job, to learn new skills, and to become more proficient on a piece of equipment you once thought would defeat you.

LEARNING ACTIVITIES

1. Peggy Johnson works as a medical clerical worker in a new sports medicine clinic. She has to add figures quickly for some new equipment that is being ordered for the clinic. Using a calculator, see how fast you can accurately add each of the following columns of figures. Record your times.

$149.55	$154.88	$233.56
233.45	444.56	344.00
900.89	466.89	950.77
33.44	11.22	99.88
998.77	345.66	123.45
23.44	77.88	98.76
245.66	1.56	1.66
776.88	4.56	8.76
567.89	23.45	23.55
678.99	1.23	3.45
678.99	5.67	6.78
990.33	3.44	23.56
876.99	5.66	5.66
123.45	23.45	67.88
987.65	1.67	1.56
555.77	34.99	34.55
999.66	21.33	1.45
234.55	7.65	1.34

2. If you have access to a personal computer, go through the machine's tutorial program. This program will give you a valuable overview of how a computer works.

3. There are many popular software programs written especially for the health care environment today. Make a brief report on a computerized medical software program.

4. Obtain the following information through a computer expert, computer store, or local library.
    (a) Define (1) hard disk; (2) floppy disk.
    (b) What is the most common size of floppy disk used in microcomputers today? Are there special handling instructions for these disks?
    (c) Define (1) modem; (2) random access memory (RAM); (3) read-only memory (ROM); (4) telecommunications; (5) laser printer.
    (d) Name as many different categories of software as you can find.
    (e) Report on how CD-ROM technology has changed the computer world.

5. As a class or an individual, observe the process of medical transcription.

6. Define each of the following terms.
    (a) Transcriber
    (b) Software
    (c) Hardware
    (d) Input
    (e) CRT
    (f) CPU
    (g) Hard copy

7. Briefly describe the three basic types of computers.

8. Name four functions that a modern photocopier might be able to perform.

9. What is a fax machine?

10. Why might a physician want to take advantage of computer-search services?

CHAPTER 13

Health Insurance

VOCABULARY

Assignment of benefits An agreement by which a patient assigns insurance benefits over to another party, usually a medical care provider.

CHAMPUS Government health insurance for dependents of active-duty and retired military personnel; stands for Civilian Health and Medical Program of the Uniformed Services.

CHAMPVA Government health insurance for spouses and dependent children of veterans who are totally disabled or who have died in service-related activities; stands for Civilian Health and Medical Program of the Veterans Administration.

COBRA Continuation of Benefits Reconciliation Act; provides temporary continuation of health care benefits to employees when employment ends and to employee spouses who become divorced.

Copayment Sharing of cost where the insured pays a prearranged amount and the insurer pays the rest.

CPT codes Known as Physicians' Current Procedural Terminology, a list of medical procedures and treatments published yearly by the American Medical Association.

Deductible Amount an insured person must pay before policy benefits begin.

Diagnosis-related groups (DRGs) Classification code system where patients are put into groups according to diagnosis.

HCPCS Health Care Financing Administration Common Procedures Coding System; a coding system used primarily for Medicare insurance billing; updated yearly.

Health insurance claim form Also known as the *Universal Health Insurance Claim Form (HCFA 1500),* a form that includes information about the patient, physician, and illness diagnosis; accepted by most insurers including Medicare, Medicaid, and CHAMPUS.

Health maintenance organizations Popularly known as HMOs, health organizations that offer prepaid medical services, with emphasis on disease prevention.

HIPAA An acronym for the *Health Insurance Portability and Accountability Act of 1996,* a complicated act that protects health insurance coverage for workers and their families when they change or lose jobs, among other provisions.

ICD-9-CM Short for *International Classification of Diseases, Adapted, Revision 9, Clinical Modification;* book containing a coded system for classifying diseases and diagnoses.

Individual practice associations Known as IPAs, networks of individual health care providers who have joined together to provide prepaid health care to individuals and groups who purchase the coverage.

Major medical Insurance policy that includes basic medical insurance and insurance that offsets heavy medical expenses resulting from prolonged illness.

Managed care Medical insurance plan designed to reduce the cost of health care by managing health care benefits by contracting with providers.

Medicaid Government health insurance for low-income persons who are medically needy but not disabled, those who receive aid to dependent children and blind and disabled persons.

Medicare Government health insurance covering people over 65 years old; also covers medical costs of end-stage kidney failure, organ donors, and patients with a total disability for over 29 months.

Preferred provider organizations	Known as PPOs; include networks of physicians and hospitals that have contracted together with insurance companies to provide care for a reduced fee.
Proof of eligibility	Also called *POE,* investigation that may be performed by a medical clerical worker to make sure that a patient meets all criteria for being covered under his or her insurance policy.
Provider	Person or institution providing medical care.
Release of information	Form that must be signed by a patient before information may be given to an insurance company, attorney, or another third party; also known as an authorization form or consent form.
Superbill	Combination of a charge slip, statement, and an insurance reporting form.
Workers' compensation	A program providing income and health care insurance, established by law in each state providing cash benefits to workers injured or disabled in the course of employment.

OBJECTIVES

After completing this chapter, the student is responsible for performing the following objectives:

- Explain important insurance terms.
- Discuss government-sponsored medical insurance programs.
- Explain differences between group-sponsored and individual medical insurance programs.
- Describe when unemployment compensation disability might be used.
- Discuss the steps in processing a Universal Health Insurance Claim Form (Form HCFA 1500).
- Explain the importance of correctly using health insurance codes.
- Identify situations where ethical and legal issues could arise for the medical clerical worker when processing insurance claims.

INTRODUCTION

The medical clerical worker plays a critical role in the financial health of the medical office by keeping up with all of the changes that go on constantly in the insurance world and filing claims properly and correctly. Much has changed in the last several years in the medical insurance environment. More patients choose HMOs and other managed care plans. Some of the traditional insurance companies such as Blue Cross have changed some of their plans to have aspects that resemble managed care plans.

Additionally, the medical clerical worker must understand the insurance policies of individual patients to help them understand the conditions of those policies. The increasing complexity of health insurance means that medical clerical workers must continually be updated as to the continual changes. This may mean attending classes either put on by individual employers or companies to understand the complexities that constantly come in front of the medical clerical worker.

B ASIC INSURANCE RESPONSIBILITIES

As a medical clerical worker, you will need to understand many areas involved in health insurance, including the following:

- Basic health insurance terminology
- Different types of insurance coverage
- Assignment of insurance benefits
- Handling claims and forms
- Translation of medical terminology into various health insurance codes

Processing insurance claims is time consuming and requires much attention to detail, as well as the ability to communicate well with the insured. Patients may be very anxious about their coverage and impatient to have their insurance companies respond immediately. The more knowledgeable you are about insurance matters, the more capable you will be to serve the patient as quickly and efficiently as possible.

B ASIC INSURANCE TERMS

There is a separate language that the medical clerical worker must understand in order to best serve the patient. Listed below are some terms that must be understood.

- *Beneficiary:* The person covered under the terms of an insurance policy.
- *Deductible:* The money the insured must pay for medical services before the policy pays.
- *Coinsurance:* The amount the insurance company pays after the deductible has been paid; the amount often varies from 50 to 100 percent.
- *Copayment:* Some companies, most often the HMOs, ask the patient to pay a specified amount at each visit, usually $5 to $10.
- *Pre-existing condition:* When a person has experienced a disease, illness, or injury prior to the beginning of a new health insurance plan, it is possible that the new insurance will not cover such pre-existing conditions.
- *Claims:* A patient, having received treatment, asks to receive reimbursement under insurance policy provisions.
- *Exclusions:* Some insurance policies state that certain procedures that are not medically necessary (such as cosmetic surgery) are not covered.
- *Preauthorization:* Often a medical clerical worker will have to contact an insurance company with a treatment plan for a patient before that patient can be seen by the doctor.
- *Assignment of benefits:* Insurance coverage payments may be sent directly to the physician or sometimes to the patient.
- *Coordination of benefits:* The medical clerical worker may often be involved in collecting benefits from more than one insurance company; a husband may have insurance and also be covered by his wife's policy.

$\mathcal{P}$ATIENT OPTIONS FOR MEDICAL INSURANCE

The medical clerical worker must have a clear understanding of the different types of medical insurance available today. As said before, new types of insurance are available continually. This is a very dynamic field! Options include traditional types of insurance (Blue Cross, Blue Shield), managed care organizations (HMOs are one type), national health care coverage (Medicare for example), as well as other types of coverage.

Traditional Insurance Policies

Coverage for these policies is on a fee-for-service basis. These policies generally have a **deductible** and a coinsurance fee. Physician bills are submitted to the insurance company.

These policies often pay only for diagnoses of disease, injury or illness. Only a few carriers provide coverage for preventive health care (physical examinations, and so on). Basic insurance policies in this category cover doctor bills, hospital care, surgery, and anesthesia. Additionally, there is usually **major medical insurance** built into the policy to take care of the costs of catastrophic expenses from illness or injury.

Blue Shield and *Blue Cross* are examples of traditional insurance companies.

Managed Care

Directly because of the high costs associated with medical care, **managed care** is used more and more in this country. The insurance carrier contracts with preferred providers who agree to change a set fee for services. The emphasis is on outpatient care instead of hospitalization. Emphasis is placed on health education and preventive care. There are many different forms of managed care, including HMOs, PPOs, and others.

Health maintenance organizations (HMOs) are a type of managed care facility. HMOs cover a large group for a monthly premium and a small **copayment** from the patient for each visit. Sometimes, physicians are available under one roof, such as the Kaiser Permanente System in the West. Others have an established network system not necessarily under one roof. Members generally cannot see a provider outside the system.

Preferred provider organizations (PPOs) include networks of physicians and hospitals that have contracted together with insurance companies to provide health care for a reduced fee. The premiums are usually higher for a PPO than for an HMO. Members can see nonplan providers for a greater out-of-pocket fee. Other similar organizations include an *exclusive provider organization (EPO)* that requires the health care provider to work exclusively for the EPO organization. Subscribers cannot go outside the EPO organization. *Physician-hospital organizations (PHOs)* result from certain physicians' contracting an organization with a specific hospital.

Medicare/Medicaid

Medicare is a federally funded health care program created in 1965 by the United States Congress under Title 18 of the Social Security Act. Medicare was originally designed to help senior citizens pay for medical care. However, today Medicare can also cover medical costs for people with end-stage kidney disease requiring treatment by kidney dialysis or transplant, organ donors, and for patients with a total disability lasting longer than 29 months. Figure 13.1 is an example of a Medicare card carried

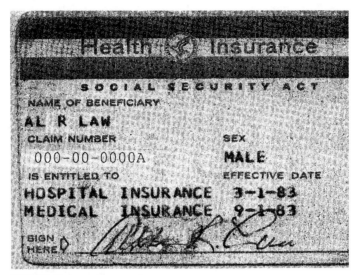

FIGURE 13.1 Medicare card.

by subscribers. Many Medicare patients buy extra insurance, called *Medigap policies,* to supplement any gaps in the Medicare insurance plan.

When a physician agrees to take a Medicare patient, Medicare pays 80 percent of the cost of service, and the patient pays 20 percent. Medicare has two parts, *Part A* and *Part B.* Part A covers hospitalization, home health care, and hospice care. There is a limit to the number of days per hospitalization and the number of hospitalizations per year. There is also a deductible payment.

Part B covers outpatient services, which include physicians' fees, occupational and physical therapy, lab tests, diagnostic tests, radiology, ambulance services, and charges for medical equipment (walkers, wheelchairs, and so on). Part B reimbursement was affected by a scale adopted by the government in 1992. Called the *resource-based relative value scale (RBRVS),* the scale dictates how much will be paid for fees for medical and surgical procedures.

Physicians can enter into a **provider** agreement with Medicare, or they can choose not to participate. Patients seen by Medicare-participating physicians pay only the annual deductible and 20 percent copayment for physician charges.

Eligibility for Medicare is determined by the Social Security Administration. Everyone on Social Security and age 65 is automatically enrolled in Part A. Part B can be gotten by paying a monthly premium. People who are not in the Social Security system but are over 65 years old can pay for both Part A and B.

Medicaid was also created in 1965 by Congress to provide funding for medical care for qualifying persons. This is a federally funded program but administered through each state's department of human services. Qualification for this program includes the following persons:

- Persons on Aid for Families with Dependent Children and Supplemental Security Income (SSI)
- Single pregnant women with an income at or below the national poverty level
- People with physical, emotional, and mental problems who cannot work

Billing to Medicaid is done only after all other insurance payments have been made. For instance, if a patient has both Medicare and Medicaid, Medicare would be billed first. Errors in such billing can be seen as fraud and may carry criminal penalties.

CHAMPUS/CHAMPVA

CHAMPUS is a federal government medical program covering the dependents of active-duty and retired military personnel. **CHAMPVA** is a federal program covering the surviving spouses and dependent children of persons who died as a result of military service and those veterans totally or permanently disabled as a result of military service.

All nonemergency inpatient care in a civilian hospital must be preapproved by CHAMPUS if the program is to be responsible for payment. This authorization form, called *Form DD 1251,* is obtained at a local military medical facility. A physician may elect to participate in CHAMPUS/CHAMPVA on a case-by-case basis. A physician participating in these programs must sign the claim form, submit it for billing, and absorb any amounts greater than those CHAMPUS allows.

Workers' Compensation

The U.S. Congress has set up minimum state requirements to cover the employer's cost of on-the-job injury or illness. The Congress felt the need for this program because regular medical insurance does not cover job-related illness or injury. The employer purchases this compensation insurance from an insurance carrier. Figure 13.2 is an example of a **workers' compensation** form.

Patients are required to report job-related illness or injury to the employer before seeking medical care. The medical clerical worker must ask the patient to make sure this has been done and also get the name and address of the employer's insurance carrier.

Physicians who accept workers' compensation cases agree to accept the compensation carrier's approved fees as payment in full for services. The patient is responsible for any bill rejected by the workers' compensation board. The patient can appeal any rejected bill.

General compensation benefits may include the following:

1. Medical treatment

2. Temporary weekly wage compensation

3. Permanent disability income

4. Death benefits for dependents of workers killed on the job

5. Rehabilitation benefits

Most medical offices require that the medical clerical worker keep separate records on a patient who is seen by the physician for a work-related problem as well as non-work-related visits. A separate workers' compensation chart and ledger card must be established. Current information should be available in the office for the address of the state and federal compensation boards or commissions, state deadlines for filing a *Doctor's First Report of Occupational Injury or Illness,* and current guidelines and fee schedule published by your state's workers' compensation carriers.

Individual Medical Insurance Plans

In order to be covered by health insurance, a person who is not eligible for medical coverage through the government, through an employer, or through some type of organization has to apply to one of the many commercial insurance companies that

DOCTOR'S FIRST REPORT
OF
OCCUPATIONAL INJURY OR ILLNESS

AGRICULTURE AND SERVICES AGENCY
DEPARTMENT OF INDUSTRIAL RELATIONS
DIVISION OF LABOR STATISTICS AND RESEARCH
P.O. Box 965, San Francisco, Calif. 94101

Immediately after first examination mail one copy directly to the Division of Labor Statistics and Research. Failure to tile a report with the Division is a misdemeanor. (Labor Code Section 6413.5) Answer all questions fully.

A. INSURANCE CARRIER ....

	Do not write in this space

1. **EMPLOYER** ....
2. Address (No., St. & City) ....
3. Business (manufacturing shoes, building construction, retailing men's clothes etc.) ······································

4. **EMPLOYEE** (First name, middle initial, last name) .... Soc. Sec. No. ....
5. Address (No., St. & City) ....
6. Occupation .... Age .... Sex ....
7. Date Injured .... Hour .... M.   Date last worked ....
8. Injured at (No., St. & City) .... County ....
9. Date of your first examination .... Hour .... M.   Who engaged your services? ....
10. Name other doctors who treated employee for this injury ....

11. **ACCIDENT OR EXPOSURE:** Did employee notify employer of this injury?   Employee's statement of cause of injury or illness:

12. **NATURE AND EXTENT OF INJURY OR DISEASE** (Include all objective findings, subjective complaints, and diagnoses. If occupational disease state date of onset, occupational history, and exposures.)

13. X-rays: By whom taken? (State if non) ....
    Findings:

14. Treatment:

15. Kind of case (Office, home or hospital) .... If hospitalized, date .... Estimated stay ....
    Name and address of hospital ....
16. Further treatment (Estimated frequency and duration) ....
17. Estimated period of disability for: Regular work .... Modified work ....
18. Describe any permanent disability or disfigurement expected (State if none) ....

19. If death ensued, give date
20. **REMARKS** (Note any pre-existing injuries or diseases, need for special examination or laboratory tests, other pertinent information.)

Name .... Degree .... (PERSONAL SIGNATURE OF DOCTOR) ....
     (Type or print)

Date of report .... Address (No., St. & City) ....

FORM 5021 (REV. 1)   *Use reverse side if more space is required*

FIGURE 13.2 Workers' compensation form.

provide individual medical insurance policies. These policies are usually the most expensive types of health insurance. When a person's employment is terminated or when employee spouses are left without insurance due to divorces and separations, group plans are required to provide health care continuation coverage temporarily. This extension is made possible by **COBRA,** the *Continuation of Benefits Reconciliation Act.* The person must pay both the employer's and the employee's contribution. The extension period extends from 18 to 36 months, depending on how the person qualifies for COBRA.

HIPAA

In August 1996, President Clinton signed into law the **Health Insurance Portability and Accountability Act (HIPAA).** This complicated legislation deals with a wide set of health policy issues ranging from health insurance access, to healthcare reimbursement fraud and abuse, as well as simplification of a variety of administrative tasks associated with healthcare services. Among the provisions of this bill is a protection of worker health insurance coverage for workers and their families when they change or lose their jobs. Your employer should be familiar with the various parts of this important act and how it affects your workplace.

Unemployment Compensation Disability

Several states and a territory (including California, Hawaii, New Jersey, New York, Puerto Rico, and Rhode Island) have a state disability insurance program. These programs are known as *UCD, TDI,* and *SDI.* Most of the states do not allow hospital benefits, and, generally, payment begins after seventy consecutive days of a disability. Filing deadlines vary, but most require filing within twenty days of the disability.

There is a restriction on the amount of compensation that one disability can bring, usually up to six months of compensation on the same illness or injury. *Remember,* there is much variation among states concerning this insurance.

$\mathcal{P}$ROCESSING THE INSURANCE CLAIM

When the first appointment is made with a patient, the medical clerical worker should ask the patient for all of his or her insurance information. This information includes general information obtained for the doctor's records (name, address, telephone, Social Security number, etc.). You must also obtain a copy of the information on the patient's insurance card or cards and the name of the primary subscriber to the policy. The names and addresses of the insurance companies involved must also be obtained.

The patient should be informed in writing as to the official policy of the medical facility in regard to health insurance. If your office does not accept direct payment from insurance providers, you *must* let the patient know immediately that he or she will be in charge of all insurance billing.

Assignment of Benefits

If a physician accepts insurance benefits for services, the medical clerical worker must have the patient complete an **assignment of benefits** form (Figure 13.3), or check a box within an insurance form assigning benefits. This is an authorization to the insurance company to make payment of benefits directly to the physician. The patient must pay any balance that is not paid by the insurance company. This should also be made perfectly clear to the patient.

ASSIGNMENT OF INSURANCE BENEFITS
FOR PATIENTS REQUIRING ANESTHESIA SERVICES

As a courtesy to our patients we will bill your insurance directly. Please sign the insurance assignment of benefits below.

ASSIGNMENT OF ANESTHESIOLOGY BENEFITS

I HEREBY AUTHORIZE THE _____
INSURANCE COMPANY TO PAY BENEFITS DIRECTLY TO MY ANESTHES-SIOLOGIST. I AGREE TO PAY ANY BALANCE OF THE ANESTHESIA FEE OVER AND ABOVE THE INSURANCE BENEFIT.

Date _____   _____

Signature

FIGURE 13.3 Assignment of benefits form.

Release of Information

The **release of information** form is a medicolegal form or an area set aside within an insurance form that must be signed by a patient before information may be released to an insurance company, attorney, or any other party. Some facilities may call this a consent or authorization form.

The Universal Health Insurance Claim Form (Form 1500)

Also called the HCFA 1500, the *universal health insurance claim form* (Figure 13.4) was developed by the American Medical Association. It has been adopted for use by most group and individual health insurance claim organizations and many government health insurance programs. The form may have differing headings, but the body of the document is usually the universal claim form.

Use of the universal form eliminates having to complete insurance forms brought by patients to the medical facility. The medical clerical worker simply completes the **health insurance claim form** and attaches it to the patient's form. You must make sure that the patient identification part of the private insurance form is complete and that the patient has signed the release of information box and/or assignment of benefits, if applicable.

The claim form is divided into two sections. The top section contains patient and insured information, and the lower section is for physician or supplier information. Some medical clerical workers may ask the patient to fill out the top, but the bottom is *always* filled out by the medical office. Exceptions to this occur when the patient pays the entire bill; then the entire copy of the transaction record is given to the patient. The form is filled out completely by the patient and mailed as well. Also, the office may complete the entire form for the patient. For optical scanning, the form must be done in all capital letters. No punctuation is included.

PATIENT FILLS OUT FIRST 13 ITEMS AND SIGNS THE FORM

PLEASE
DO NOT
STAPLE
IN THIS
AREA

APPROVED OMB-0938-0008

CARRIER →

| | PICA | **HEALTH INSURANCE CLAIM FORM** | PICA | |

| 1. MEDICARE   MEDICAID   CHAMPUS   CHAMPVA   GROUP HEALTH PLAN   FECA BLK LUNG   OTHER | 1a.INSURED'S ID NUMBER   (FOR PROGRAM IN ITEM 1) |

☐ (Medicare #) ☐ (Medicaid #) ☐ (Sponsor's SSN) ☐ (VA File #) ☐ (SSN or ID) ☐ (SSN) ☐ (ID)

2. PATIENT'S NAME (Last Name, First Name, Middle Name)

b. OTHER INSURED'S DATE OF BIRTH
MM ┃ DD ┃ YY   M ☐   F ☐

4. INSURED'S NAME (Last Name, First Name, Middle Name)

5. PATIENT'S ADDRESS (No., Street)

6. PATIENT RELATIONSHIP TO INSURED
Self ☐   Spouse ☐   Child ☐   Other ☐

7. INSURED'S ADDRESS (No., Street)

CITY   STATE

8. PATIENT STATUS
Single ☐   Married ☐   Other ☐

CITY   STATE

ZIP CODE   TELEPHONE (Including Area Code)
( )

Employed ☐   Full-Time Student ☐   Part-Time Student ☐

ZIP CODE   TELEPHONE (Including Area Code)
( )

9. OTHER INSURED'S NAME (Last Name, First Name, Middle Name)

10.IS PATIENT CONDITION RELATED TO:

11.INSURED'S POLICY GROUP OR FECA NUMBER

a. OTHER INSURED'S POLICY OR GROUP NUMBER

a. EMPLOYMENT? (CURRENT OR PREVIOUS)
☐ YES   ☐ NO

a. INSURED'S DATE OF BIRTH
MM ┃ DD ┃ YY   SEX   M ☐   F ☐

b. OTHER INSURED'S DATE OF BIRTH
MM ┃ DD ┃ YY   SEX   M ☐   F ☐

b. AUTO ACCIDENT?   PLACE (State)
☐ YES   ☐ NO

b. EMPLOYER'S NAME OR SCHOOL NAME

c. EMPLOYER'S NAME OR SCHOOL NAME

c. OTHER ACCIDENT?
☐ YES   ☐ NO

c. INSURANCE PLAN NAME OR PROGRAM NAME

d. INSURANCE PLAN NAME OR PROGRAM NAME

10d. RESERVED FOR LOCAL USE

d. IS THERE ANOTHER HEALTH BENEFIT PLAN?
☐ YES   ☐ NO   *If yes*, return to and complete item 9 a-d.

READ BACK OF FORM BEFORE COMPLETING & SIGNING THIS FORM.
12.PATIENT'S OR AUTHORIZED PERSON'S SIGNATURE I authorize the release of any medical or other information necessary to process this claim. I also request payment of government benefits either to myself or to the party who accepts assignment below.

SIGNED _____ DATE _____

13.INSURED'S OR AUTHORIZED PERSON'S SIGNATURE I authorize payment of medical benefits to the undersigned physician or supplier for services described below.

SIGNED _____

PATIENT AND INSURED INFORMATION →

MEDICAL CLERICAL WORKER COMPLETES RELEVANT ITEMS 14 THROUGH 33

14.DATE OF CURRENT:
MM ┃ DD ┃ YY   ◀ ILLNESS (First symptom) OR INJURY (Accident) OR PREGNANCY (LMP)

15. IF PATIENT HAS HAD SAME OR SIMILAR ILLNESS. GIVE FIRST DATE   MM ┃ DD ┃ YY

16. DATES PATIENT UNABLE TO WORK IN CURRENT OCCUPATION
MM ┃ DD ┃ YY   MM ┃ DD ┃ YY
FROM   TO

17.NAME OF REFERRING PHYSICIAN OR OTHER SOURCE

17a.I.D. NUMBER OF REFERRING PHYSICIAN

18. HOSPITALIZATION DATES RELATED TO CURRENT SERVICES
MM ┃ DD ┃ YY   MM ┃ DD ┃ YY
FROM   TO

19.RESERVED FOR LOCAL USE

20. OUTSIDE LAB? $ CHARGES
☐ YES   ☐ NO

21.DIAGNOSIS OR NATURE OF ILLNESS OR INJURY. (RELATE ITEMS 1,2,3, OR 4 TO ITEM 24E BY LINE)

1. └── . ──
2. └── . ──
3. └── . ──
4. └── . ──

22.MEDICAID RESUBMISSION CODE   ORIGINAL REF. NO

23.PRIOR AUTHORIZATION NUMBER

24. A DATE(S) OF SERVICE						B Place of Service	C Type of Service	D PROCEDURES, SERVICES, OR SUPPLIES (Explain Unusual Circumstances) CPT/HCPCS MODIFIER	E DIAGNOSIS CODE	F $ CHARGES	G DAYS OR UNITS	H EPSDT Family Plan	I EMG	J COB	K RESERVED FOR LOCAL USE
From MM ┃ DD ┃ YY			To MM ┃ DD ┃ YY												

24. FEDERAL TAX I.D. NUMBER   SSN EIN ☐ ☐

26.PATIENT'S ACCOUNT NO.

27.ACCEPT ASSIGNMENT? (For govt. claims, see back) ☐ YES   ☐ NO

28.TOTAL CHARGE $

29.AMOUNT PAID $

30. BALANCE DUE $

31. SIGNATURE OF PHYSICIAN OR SUPPLIER INCLUDING DEGREES OR CREDENTIALS (I certify that the statements on the reverse apply to this bill and are made a part thereof.)

SIGNED _____ DATE _____

32.NAME AND ADDRESS OF FACILITY WHERE SERVICES WERE RENDERED (If other than home or office)

33.PHYSICIAN'S, SUPPLIER'S BILLING NAME, ADDRESS, ZIP CODE & PHONE #

PIN#   GRP#

PHYSICIAN OR SUPPLIER INFORMATION →

(APPROVED BY AMA COUNCIL ON MEDICAL SERVICE 8/88)   ***PLEASE PRINT OR TYPE***   FORM HCFA-1500 (U2) (12-90)
FORM OWCP-1500   FORM RRB-1500

FIGURE 13.4 Universal health insurance claim form (revised 12/90).

Each numbered box on the form asks for specific information to be typed in that space. Each item must be carefully entered to avoid any mistaken information that could delay payment. All completed information should be carefully proofread to ensure accuracy.

Today, the most common and efficient way to submit claims is electronically. Only a few insurance carriers do not accept electronic billings. When they are not accepted, the HCFA 1500 form probably will be used, and also when additional information will be needed.

Other Health Insurance Forms

When a patient presents a special company form that does not follow the format of the HCFA 1500 form, there are several things that the medical clerical worker must do.

- All information is provided by the patient for the employee or insured portion of the special form.
- The patient must sign authorizations for release of information and assignment of benefits to the provider on both the special form and a copy of the HCFA 1500 form.
- Look for any questions not on the HCFA form. Answer them on the special form.
- Also fill out an HCFA form. Copy both forms for the patient records. Attach the HCFA form to the company form and forward to the insurance company.

HEALTH INSURANCE CODES

As health insurance has become more and more complex, it has been necessary to identify services and diagnoses by codes. Coding is changing the descriptions of diseases, injuries, and medical procedures into designations by number.

Coding lends itself well to computerization, and the computer is an integral part of claims processing. Without the use of a computer, claims centers would be much less efficient in processing up to 65,000 claims a day in an average claim center.

Today, coding is a part of government regulation for programs such as Medicare and Medicaid, as well as for many private insurance companies. Several types of codes are used in insurance processing:

- *Physicians' Current Procedural Terminology,* published yearly by the American Medical Association.
- *The Health Care Procedural Coding System (HCPCS),* mandated by the United States Congress for Medicare claims; updated yearly.
- *The International Classification of Diseases, Adapted, Revision 9, Clinical Modification* (**ICD-9-CM**), published by the World Health Organization, with an *Official Authorized Addendum to ICD-9* published each October.

Classes are available for the medical clerical worker to update one's knowledge of the yearly changes in CPT and ICD-9 codes. Medicare and a variety of insurance companies also publish newsletters and bulletins to explain their code changes.

Procedure Codes

There are medical insurance codes for procedures, numbers that have been established and assigned to describe precisely every procedure performed and every service given by physicians and their staff. **CPT codes** use five-digit codes and two-digit modifiers. Table 13.1 shows examples from CPT codes.

Modifiers to CPT codes are also used frequently. For instance, if a -78 is added to a code, it means that the patient returned to the surgery department for a related procedure during the postoperative period. The lists of modifiers are very important because they can increase the value of the service.

CPT codes are used for government insurance programs (federal and state) as well as private insurance companies. If these codes are not used, claims are not processed until further information is submitted.

Codes can allude not only to the level of care given but also to where it was given, whether in the office, hospital, emergency room, nursing facility, and so on. Codes can also give information as to whether a patient was new or an established patient. Codes can also be accompanied by a brief description of the visit.

Diagnostic Codes

Diagnostic codes have been precisely established to describe every disease, condition, problem, and diagnosis currently recognized in the medical world. *ICD-9* is currently recognized as the international standard for diagnostic coding. Table 13.2 lists examples of ICD-9 codes.

The ICD-9 uses three-digit codes, with a fourth digit added when more detail is required regarding cause, site, or manifestation of the disorder. Sometimes a fifth digit is added for greater specificity.

ICD-9 coding is used on all Medicare claims. Most private insurance companies also require ICD-9 diagnostic codes as well as CPT procedural codes. The complete set of ICD-9 codes are contained in three volumes. Volumes 1 and 2 are used to code diagnoses in the physician's practice. Volume 3 is used primarily in the hospital setting.

HCPCS Coding System

HCPCS stands for the *Health Care Financing Administration Common Procedures Coding System.* HCPCS is a procedure for coding materials, supplies, injections, and services performed by health care professionals.

TABLE 13.1 *C*PT CODE EXAMPLES	
Outpatient Surgeries and Procedures	
Appendectomy	44950
Breast biopsy	19120
Arthroscopy, knee, diagnostic	29870
Cardiovascular stress test	93017
Cholecystectomy	47600
CPR	92950
Professional Service	
Laboratory	
CBC with differential	85022
Occult blood	82270
Strep throat/kit	87082
Urinalysis without microscopy	81001

TABLE 13.2	*I*CD-9 CODE EXAMPLES	
Abnormal loss of weight	7832
Abscess of lung	513
Acne vulgaris	7061
Acute alcoholic intoxication	3030
Acute conjunctivitis	3720
Acute hysterical psychosis	2981
Acute myocardial infarction	410
Acute nephritis	580
Acute prostatitis	6010
Acute renal failure	584

The HCPCS book is divided into three levels. Level 1 is a more complete section of the CPT-4 codes. Level 2 comprises national codes divided into 18 sections. Level 3 contains local codes generally assigned by your local Medicare carrier. This level is used to identify new supplies, services, and materials. Every year, several changes are made to the HCPCS book, making it necessary to purchase a new code book for HCPCS yearly.

E THICAL AND LEGAL CONSIDERATIONS

When you as a medical clerical worker are given the responsibility of working with medical insurance claims, you must be aware of important ethical and legal issues in this field: breach of confidentiality and insurance fraud.

Confidentiality

Keeping patient information confidential has been emphasized throughout this textbook. *Breach of confidentiality* is defined as the unauthorized release of confidential patient information to a third party (person other than the patient, physician, or staff member). A written consent form to release medical information must be signed by a patient, parent, or legal guardian before a health insurance claim form can be completed (often the signature in Box 12 on the HCFA 1500 form is used). After the release is signed, a photocopy of the form should be placed in the patient's record, and another copy is attached each time the insurance is billed to the company.

When information is requested by phone, the medical clerical worker must verify that anyone calling the office is entitled to the information. If verification procedures are objected to by the calling party (the medical clerical worker can call the party back or request information on the original claim form), the information should not be given. The request should be submitted in writing on company stationery, specifying what information is needed.

Many insurance claims, including Medicare, are now submitted electronically. In a computerized system, everything concerning billing and reimbursement is computerized and transmitted electronically. HIPAA has a provision that regulates the security and privacy of transmitted health care information.

Fraud

Fraud is defined as the deliberate misrepresentation of facts. A patient might ask a medical clerical worker if he or she can change the date of a visit to ensure that coverage will be at the highest rate. A patient might also ask for a change of diagnosis in order to receive more compensation. A patient might also request that an insurance claim be eliminated from the patient's record. The medical clerical worker in all cases must politely tell the patient firmly that the records will not be altered in *any* way.

Real-Life Scenario

Steven Wood is a medical clerical worker who possesses a great deal of compassion for the patients he serves. Steven realizes how expensive health care costs are and often anguishes along with the patients about their difficulties in paying.

Mrs. Robertson is a 63-year-old client with multiple health problems. She has just lost her husband to cancer, and his insurance coverage for her has lapsed a few week ago. Mrs. Robertson has just been received a large bill from the physician for whom Steven works. In fact, her treatment took place only a few days after her late husband's insurance policy lapsed. Mrs. Robertson is desperate about the latest charges. With great shame, Mrs. Robertson asks if Steven can change the date on her service to a few days previous, in order to be covered by her late husband's policy.

1. Could it hurt anything if Steven just changed the date of service?

2. Shouldn't Steven be compassionate to this poor widow?

3. What other options does Steven have?

There have also been cases when physicians have requested that a medical clerical worker bill a patient for fees greater than the insurance company's allowable fee. Participating physicians in an insurance program have signed a contract to accept the insurance company's fee as the total fee to be billed for services. The medical clerical worker should not be asked to participate in any such fraud.

SUMMARY

Handling health insurance claims can be a very time-consuming job. You can perform an important service to patients by processing insurance claims quickly and efficiently. Patients are reassured when they have expert help when wading through the highly technical insurance forms. This takes knowledge, patience, and flexibility, as changes in this area occur frequently. You are also performing an extremely important service for your employer. Correctly filled out and sent insurance forms bring reimbursement in a timely manner.

LEARNING ACTIVITIES

1. Interview a medical clerical worker in a health facility who specializes in health insurance. Ask the following questions.
   (a) Is special education/certification needed to be a health insurance specialist?
   (b) Are jobs available in this field?
   (c) What salary and benefits are involved in this specialty?
   (d) Can you advance in this field?

2. Diana Stephens is a medical clerical worker who works for a physician with a general practice. She must complete a Health Insurance Claim Form for the following patients. Duplicate the form available in Appendix B and complete it for these patients.

Doctor seeing both patients: Laura A. Feldman, M.D.
600 Quail Court
Houston, TX 25173
Soc. Sec. No. 548-73-1549
Employer No. 11-2354891
Telephone (718) 555-4900

Patient 1: Thomas Oliver Burns lives with his parents, Ingrid and Bruce Burns, at 2424 Quincy Road, Houston, TX 25174. Thomas was born on 5/5/94. On 8/20/03, Thomas developed a high fever and cough. He was seen on 8/21/03 for the problem, having never been seen by the doctor before this visit. Dr. Feldman diagnosed the problem as an upper respiratory infection. The procedure code is 41640. The charge for the visit was $65, paid by Ingrid Burns at the time of the visit. The mother's Blue Cross number is 543-33-1192, Group A 11900.

Patient 2: Jonathan Allen Baxter lives at the Lenox Arms, 2960 Chapman Avenue, Apartment 62, Houston, TX 25174. DOB: 6/4/1905. Medicare No. 500-98-6785A. Mr. Baxter suffered angina previous to suffering sharp pains on 8/4/03. He was seen once for the same problem on 3/2/02. The diagnosis by Dr. Feldman was coronary artery disease, procedure code 60421. The patient paid $200 at the time of the visit. The patient has Medicare.

3. Contact an HMO in your area and report to the class on the benefits provided to subscribers by the HMO. Contrast the preventative medicine emphasis with a traditional group health insurance policy.

4. Do a coding exercise using both CPT and ICD-9 codes.

5. What are the three categories of medical insurance benefits?

6. What is the difference between Part A and Part B of Medicare?

7. Explain the difference between an HMO and traditional insurance.

8. Match each insurance term with the correct definition.

__ **(a)** CHAMPUS	**(1)** Covers occupational disease and work-related injuries
__ **(b)** Workers' compensation	**(2)** Provides senior citizen medical benefits
__ **(c)** HMO	**(3)** Covers low-income people who have medical needs
__ **(d)** CHAMPVA	**(4)** Covers dependents of the military service
__ **(e)** Medicare	**(5)** Emphasizes wellness instead of illness
__ **(f)** Medicaid	**(6)** Covers dependents of totally disabled vets

9. What is the purpose of workers' compensation?

10. What is the name of the Universal Health Claim form?

11. State the difference between CPT codes and ICD-9 codes.

12. What do the following letters stand for?
    (a) PPO
    (b) CPT
    (c) HMO
    (d) ICD-9 CM
    (e) HIPAA

13. Explain a situation where a medical clerical worker could aid a patient in perpetrating an insurance fraud.

CHAPTER 14

Daily Financial Responsibilities: Bookkeeping

VOCABULARY

Accounts payable	Commonly known as A/P, referring to amounts owed to creditors for regular business operating expenses.
Accounts receivable	Commonly known as A/R, referring to claims arising from services rendered.
Assets	Money and things of value in a business.
Bonding	An insurance policy protecting an employer against financial loss caused by acts of employees.
Bookkeeping	The analysis and recording of business transactions, in order to report the financial condition of a business at a later date.
Computerized bookkeeping	Software specifically written for bookkeeping that allows bookkeeping tasks to be fully computerized.
Daysheet	Also called the daily record, a record of daily business transactions.
Disbursement	A chronological listing of monthly and yearly business expenses.
Double-entry system	A bookkeeping method that maintains equality of debits and credits.
General ledger	A record containing all financial statement accounts.
Liability	Debt owed.
Pegboard system	A bookkeeping system used in some health care facilities, using a lightweight board with pegs and forms layered one on top of the other.
Petty cash	A small amount of cash available for small office expenses.
Net worth	Assets minus liabilities.
Single-entry system	A simple bookkeeping system, using a daysheet, checkbook, and an accounts receivable ledger.
Social Security	Also known as FICA (Federal Insurance Contributions Act).
Superbill	Also known as a transaction record, a comprehensive list of examinations, procedures, and treatments that a patient receives, plus a fee listing.
Transaction record	Also called a transaction slip, charge slip, and superbill, record used to record all information about services performed during a patient visit.
Withholding	Deductions made by an employer from an employee's paycheck.

After completing this chapter, the student is responsible for performing the following objectives:

- State the basic rules of bookkeeping.
- Discuss the four most common methods of bookkeeping used in health care facilities.
- Explain the difference between accounts receivable and accounts payable.
- Identify the uses for petty cash.
- Describe how payroll records are handled in a health care facility.

*I*NTRODUCTION

Any business, including a health care facility, cannot function effectively without well-kept financial records. The medical clerical worker will be expected to handle bookkeeping duties in a thoroughly professional and businesslike manner.

The most important personal traits you can possess as a medical clerical worker assigned to keep financial records are paying attention to detail, being well organized at all times, and maintaining consistency in work habits. These traits are essential for billing and collection procedures to be properly done, as well as accomplishing financial planning and accurate reporting of income taxes.

You may be responsible for a portion of the bookkeeping. In smaller facilities, you may be in charge of all bookkeeping duties. Computerization has made many of these tasks far easier.

*B*OOKKEEPING GUIDELINES

Bookkeeping requires a well-established routine, with the medical clerical worker constantly adhering to some important guidelines of bookkeeping. If these rules are followed, you should be able to perform the responsibilities of bookkeeping in an orderly, efficient manner.

- *Immediately* record all charges and receipts into the daily record. One of the most common mistakes made in bookkeeping is allowing charges and receipts to pile up without recording them immediately. As a result, receipts can get misplaced, forgotten, or even lost.
- Endorse all checks as soon as they are collected.
- Prepare receipts in duplicate for currency received. Your employer may ask you also to draw up receipts for checks, but some employers consider the check itself to be an adequate record.
- Be sure to pay all facility bills before their due dates. Record the date the bill was paid and the check number on the paid bill receipt.
- Post all charges and receipts to the general ledger daily (see the section on the general ledger).
- Promptly deposit in the bank all monies received, usually on a daily basis.

- Always check to make sure that the amount you have deposited in the bank plus the amount you have on hand in petty cash equals the amount you have recorded in the daily ledger (also called journal).
- A petty cash fund is available for small expenses (see the section on petty cash). Pay all other expenses by check, as you will have an immediate record of the expenditure that way.

In addition, you should make entries in ink, consistently using the same color of ink and the same type of pen. Check arithmetic continually, making sure that you keep columns of figures straight and carry decimals correctly. Do not rely totally on calculating devices. Use good penmanship

Errors should not be erased. A straight line should be drawn through the incorrect figure and the correct figure written above it.

It is recommended that the medical clerical worker set aside a certain time each day to attend to bookkeeping tasks. Try to find a section of time when you are not continually distracted or interrupted.

$\mathcal{B}$OOKKEEPING SYSTEMS

In a health care facility, there are four bookkeeping systems that are generally used. The choice of which to use is based on the kind of facility that will be using the system. The four systems are (1) **single-entry,** (2) **double-entry,** (3) **pegboard,** and (4) **computerized bookkeeping.**

All systems of bookkeeping record daily income and payments by patients, receipts and disbursements, patient ledger cards, and include a petty cash fund.

Single Entry

The single-entry system is easy to use and can be considered a basis for filing income tax returns. The parts of single-entry bookkeeping include:

The **general ledger,** in which charges to patients and payments received are recorded every day (also called *daybook*).

- An *accounts receivable ledger* showing the amounts owed by each patient (also called *ledger cards*).
- A *checkbook* showing expenses of the health care facility.
- *Payroll records* showing salaries and wages paid out, with deductions also noted.
- *Petty cash* records showing what cash is available for small expenditures and what cash has been spent.

Due to the entries that have to be transferred from one record to another, errors are common in this method. Some medical clerical workers may keep only part of these records, and an accountant may be hired to do the rest, such as keeping ledgers.

Double Entry

Balancing the books is the key to the double-entry system, which depends on the following accounting equation:

$$assets - liabilities = net\ worth$$

Assets are defined as the money and things of value in a business. **Liabilities** are debts owed. If one takes assets and subtracts liabilities, what is left is the owner's **net worth.** These terms are all an integral part of the double-entry bookkeeping system.

This system is an exact science and is usually set up by an accountant or a consultant who does most of the bookkeeping. The medical clerical worker usually maintains only a daily journal, from which an accountant takes figures once a month. The accountant then may work with numerous additional journals, always balancing each side of the accounting equation.

Double-entry systems give a more complex picture of a health care facility and the employer's net worth. The skill level required generally does not make this system popular with small health care practices.

Pegboard

Also called the *write-it-once system,* the pegboard system is a less-used system for the medical office today. The pegboard bookkeeping system gets its name from the lightweight board with pegs on the right- and/or left-hand side that is its basis. It also uses forms with holes for the pegs so that the forms may be layered on top of each other and held in place by the pegs (Figure 14.1).

The forms used in the pegboard method are usually printed on no-carbon-required paper, so that when an entry is made it is registered simultaneously on the first three forms listed below. This minimizes errors and saves clerical writing time. Some practices use a pegboard system in addition to computerized accounting systems if the computerized system does not have good safeguards against embezzlement.

Component parts of a pegboard bookkeeping system include:

1. *Daysheet.* To begin the day's bookkeeping transactions, a **daysheet** is placed on the pegboard. This sheet will record all transactions made by the medical clerical worker. Refer to both Figures 14.1 and 14.4.

2. *Transaction record* (superbill). A series of prenumbered, perforated transaction slips are aligned so that the posting line is directly over the first available line on the daysheet near the top. Each record acts as a receipt if payment is made. Figure 14.2 illustrates a properly filled out **transaction record (superbill)**.

3. *Patient ledger card.* Also known as the patient financial record, this card is placed below the transaction slip on the pegboard. This card lists all financial activity involving one patient's account over a certain period of time. An example of a patient statement that reflects such transactions is shown in Figure 14.3.

4. *Deposit slip.* Bank deposits are also recorded using overlapping forms in the same manner.

When an entry is placed on the pegboard system, it is registered simultaneously on all three items—the daysheet, the ledger card, and the transaction record. The patient receives a copy of the transaction record. This record serves as a charge slip, receipt for cash or check, statement of account showing prior and any new balances, and also an appointment reminder. It can also be used by the patient to bill insurance if a payment has been made. After each patient, the ledger card is removed, and the next patient's ledger card is inserted.

Embezzlement is prevented in this system because the transaction records are prenumbered and must be accounted for at the end of each day. If an error is made on any slip, the slip must be voided and kept.

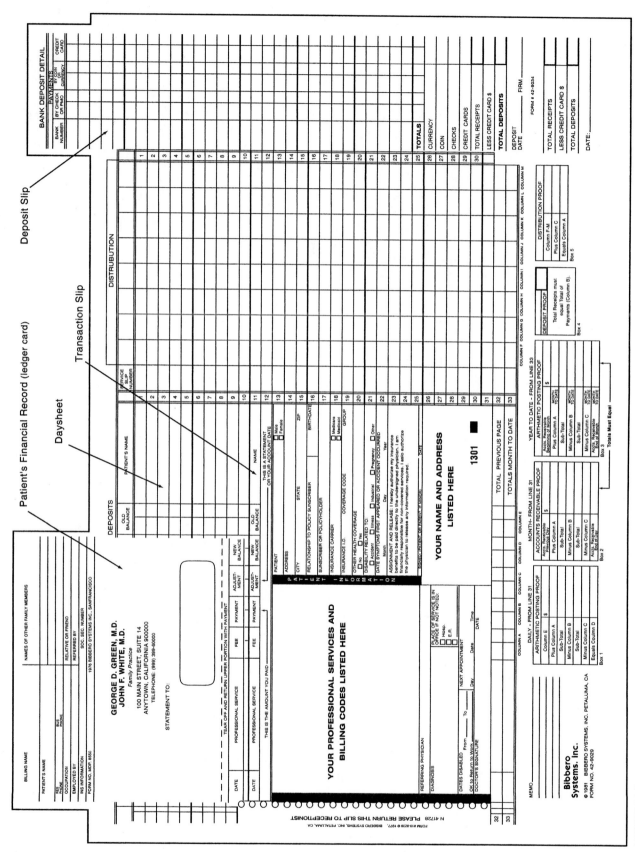

FIGURE 14.1 Setup for pegboard bookkeeping.

188

JOHN R. JOHNSON, M.D.
Family Practice
1000 MAINSTREET
SOME PLACE, USA 70000

TELEPHONE: (123) 555-5678

STATE LIC # 123456789
SOC. SEC # 000-11-0000

☐ PRIVATE ☒ BLUE CROSS ☐ BLUE SHIELD ☐ IND. ☐ MEDICARE ☐ GOV'T. ☐ MEDI-CAL OR MEDICAID

PATIENT'S LAST NAME	FIRST	INITIAL	BIRTHDATE	SEX	TODAY'S DATE
Smith	Mary	S.	4/14/41	☐ MALE ☒ FEMALE	8/16/--

ADDRESS: 21 Oak St. CITY: Anytown STATE: CT ZIP: 90006 RELATIONSHIP TO SUBSCRIBER: SPOUSE

SUBSCRIBER OR POLICYHOLDER: Smith John J. INSURANCE CARRIER: BLUECROSS

ADDRESS: same CITY STATE ZIP INS. ID: 465-52-6633 COVERAGE CODE: 0732 GROUP: 4-15407

OTHER HEALTH COVERAGE? ☒ NO ☐ YES INDENTIFY

DISABILITY RALTED TO: ☐ ACCIDENT ☒ ILLNESS ☐ OTHER ☐ IND.
DATE SYMPTOMS APPEARED, OR ACCIDENT OCCURRED: 8/14/--

ASSIGNMENT: I assign & request payment of major medical benefits to undersigned physician for services described below.
SIGNED (Patient. or Parent, if Minor) Mary Smith DATE: 8/16/--

RELEASE: I hereby authorize undersigned physician to furnish information to my insurnace carriers concerning this illness.
SIGNED (Patient. or Parent, if Minor) Mary Smith DATE: 8/16/--

√	DESCRIPTION	CPT/MD	FEE	√	DESCRIPTION		CPT/MD	FEE	√	DESCRIPTION	CPT/MD	FEE
	1. OFFICE VISIT	NEW	EST.		3. HOSP SERVICES	NEW	EST.			6. SURGERY		
	Minimal	90030			Interm (days)	90215	90260			Anoscopy	46600	
X	Brief	90000	90040	35.00	Extended		90270			Sigmoidoscopy	45355	
	Limited	90010	90050		Comprehensive	90220	90280					
	Intermediate	90015	90060		Discharge 30min. - 1hr		90292			Surgery		.80
	Extended	90017	90070		Detention Time 30min-1hr.		99150			7. MISCELLANEOUS		
	Comprehensive	90020	90080		Detention Time ___ Hrs.		99151			Booklets	99071	
										Special Reports	99080	
	2. INJECTIONS & IMMUNIZATIONS				4. SPECIAL SERVICES					Supplies, Ace Bandage	99070	
	Injections, Arthrocentesis	206 •			Called to ER - during ofc. hrs.		99065			Telephone Call	99013	
	DPT	90701			Night Call - before 10 pm		99050			X-Ray		
	DT	90702			Night Call - after 10 pm		99052			Dressing Tray Sm.	99070	
	Tetanus	90703			Sundays or Holidays		99054			Med.	99070	
	OPV	90712			5. LABORATORY - IN OFFICE					Large.	99070	
	NMR	90707			Urine		81000			8. EMERGENCY ROOM-ESTAB. PATIENT		
	IM inject. Therapeutic	90782			Occult Blood		82270			Brief	90540	
	IM inject. Antibiotic	90789			ECG		93000			Limited	90550	
	Drug			X	Hemoglobin		85018	10.00		Intermediate	90560	
	Dosage			X	Hematocrit		85014	10.00		Extended	90570	
	TB-PPD	86580		X	Routine Venipuncture		36415 •	10.00				

DIAGNOSIS	ICD-9					
☐ Abrasion-sup. Injury	919	☐ Diabetes Mellitus	250.	☐ Irratable Colon	564.1	☐ Pneumonitis 468.
☐ Amenorrhea	626.0	☐ Duodebal Ulcer	532.	☐ Laryngo-Tracjeitis	464.	☐ Prostatitis 601.
☒ Anemia	28	☐ Duodenitis	535.6	☐ Lipoma	214.	☐ Renal Stone .592.
☐ Anxiety-Stress-Depression	30	☐ Dysmenorrhea	625.3	☐ Lipid Cholesterol Ab	272.2	☐ Subaceous Cyst 706.2
☐ Arteriosclerosis	440	☐ Epicondylitis	726.32	☐ Low Back Pain	724.2	☐ Seizure Disorder 780.3
☐ Arthralgia	719.	☐ Epilepsy	345	☐ Lymphangitis	457.2	☐ Tinea Corpus-Pedis 110.4
☐ Asthma Hayfever	493.0	☐ Exogenous Obesity	278.0	☐ Memorrhagia	626.2	☐ URI-Viral Syndrome 460.
☐ Bleeding Post Men	627.	☐ Fatigue	780.	☐ Menopausal Syndrom	627.2	☐ UTI 599.0
☐ Boil-Carbuncle-Furuncle	680	☐ Gastroenteritis	558.9	☐ Myofascitis	729.	☐ Vaginitis 616.10
☐ Bronchitis-Acute Chronic	490	☐ Heart Failure	428	☐ Pain		☐ Weight Loss. Abnormal 783.2
☐ Bronchopneumonitis	485	☐ Hiatal Hernia	553.3	☐ Paroxysmal Atrial Tachy	427.0	
☐ Cervitis	616.0	☐ Homorroids	455.	☐ Pediculosis Pubis-Scabies	133.0	
☐ Chonyloma Accuminatum	078.1	☐ Influenza	487.	☐ Pelvic Congestion	625.5	
☐ Conjunctivitis	372	☐ Ingrown Toenail	703.0	☐ Pharyngitis. Tonsil.-Acute	462.	
		☐ Insomnia	780.52	☐ Pigmented Nevus	216.	

DIAGNOSIS
ANEMIA

SERVICES PERFORMED AT:
☒ OFFICE ☐ State Hospital
☐ E.R. ☐ 200 State Street ☐
 Some Place, USA 70000

ADMIT: / /
DISHARGE: / /

	DATE	SERV.	CQDE Mod	FEE

DATES DISABLED
FROM: / / TO: / /
OK TO RETURN TO WORK: 8/18/--

DOCTOR'S SIGNATURE DATE
John Johnson MD 8/16--

Accept Assignment ☒ YES ☐ No

RETURN APPOINTMENT INFORMATION:
5 • 10 • 15 • 20 • ③⓪ • 45 • 60 (DAYS) WKS. MOS.

NEXT APPOINTMENT:
M · T · W · ⓉⒽ · F · S
DATE: 9/16/-- TIME: 230 AM ⓅⓂ

INSTRUCTIONS TO PATIENT FOR FILING INSURANCE CLAIMS

1. COMPLETE THE UPPER PORTION OF THIS FORM; SIGN AND DATE.
2. MAIL THIS FROM DIRECTLY TO YOUR INSURNACE COMPANY. YOU MAY ATTACH YOUR OWN INSURANCE COMPANY'S FORM IF YOU WISH, ALTHOUGH IT IS NOT NECESSARY.
   PLEASE REMEMBER THAT PAYMENT IS YOUR OBLIGATION, REGARDLESS OF INSURANCE OR OTHER THIRD PARTY INVOLVEMENT.

REC'D. BY:
☐ CASH
☒ CHECK # 5133

TOTAL TODAY'S FEE	65.00
OLD BALANCE	-0-
TOTAL	65.00
AMT. REC'D TODAY	65.00
NEW BALANCE	-0-

INSUR - A - BILL ® • BIBBERO SYSTEMS. • PETALUMA, CA • © 5/86

Office Copy
(Canary) Insurance Copy
(Pink) Patient Copy
(Goldenrod) Control Copy

(sample only — Codes may not be current)

FIGURE 14.2 Properly filled-out transaction record (superbill).

BILLING NAME		NAMES OF OTHER FAMILY MEMBERS
PATIENT'S NAME		
RES. PHONE	BUS. PHONE	
OCCUPATION		RELATIVE OR FRIEND
EMPLOYED BY		REFERRED BY
INS. INFORMATION		SOC. SEC. NUMBER
FORM NO. MDP. 8550		1976 BIBBERO SYSTEMS, INC. SAN FRANSISCO

GEORGE D. GREEN, M.D.
JOHN F. WHITE, M.D.

Family Practice
100 MAIN STREET, SUITE 14
ANYTOWN, CALIFORNIA 90000
TELEPHONE: (999) 555-6000

STATEMENT TO:

- - - - TEAR OFF AND RETURN UPPER PORTION WITH PAYMENT - - - -

DATE	PROFESSIONAL SERVICE	FEE	PAYMENT	ADJUST-MENT	NEW BALANCE

PROFESSIONAL SERVICE CODES:

1. OFFICE VISIT
2. HOME VISIT
3. HOSPITAL VISIT
4. EMERGENCY ROOM
5. CONSULTATION
6. IMMUNIZATION
7. INJECTION
8. DRUGS/SUPPLIES/MATERIALS

9. COLLECTION OF LAB. SPEC.
10. SPECIAL REPORTS
11. OTHER SERVICES
12. SPEC. DIAGNOSTIC SERVICES
13. SPEC. THERAPEUTIC SERV.
14. EXTENDED CARE FACILITY
15. CUSTODIAL CARE
16. OBSTETRICAL CARE

17. SURGICAL
18. CASTS
19. LABORATORY
20. X-RAY
21. ALLERGY TEST.
22. NO CHARGE
23. ADJUSTMENTS OR CORRECTIONS
24. TOTAL CARE

GEORGE D. GREEN, M.D.
CAL. LIC. # 6-2856

JOHN F. WHITE, M.D.
CAL. LIC. # G-5281

FIGURE 14.3 Patient statement.

Computerized Bookkeeping

In many medical facilities, especially in large practices, computerized bookkeeping has replaced all types of accounting management. There are many different types of software available for this purpose. Software can also be modified to fit the needs of specific practices. Common components of such programs include:

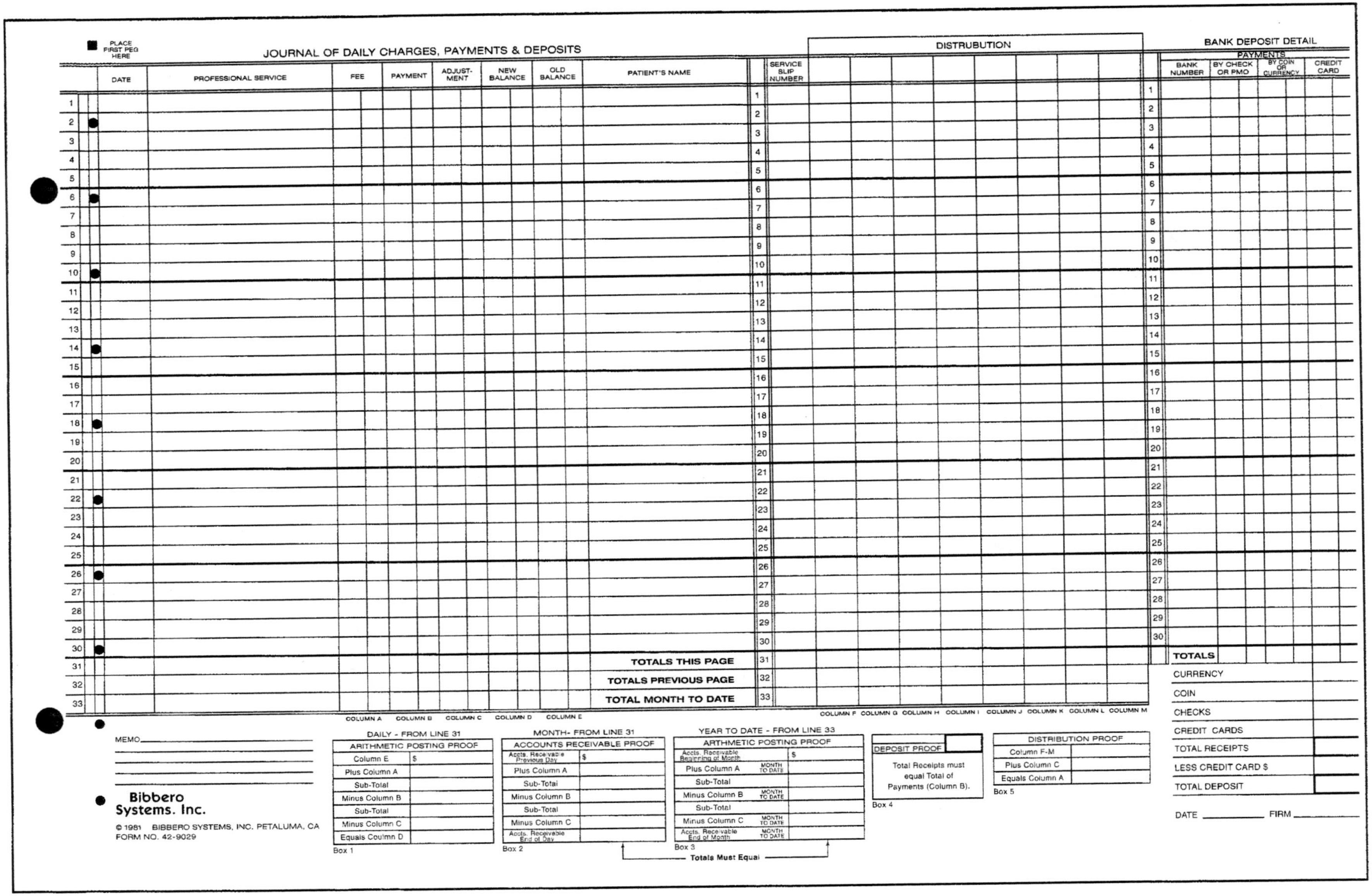

PLACE FIRST PEG HERE

JOURNAL OF DAILY CHARGES, PAYMENTS & DEPOSITS

	DATE	PROFESSIONAL SERVICE	FEE	PAYMENT	ADJUST-MENT	NEW BALANCE	OLD BALANCE	PATIENT'S NAME		SERVICE SLIP NUMBER	DISTRUBUTION		BANK DEPOSIT DETAIL: BANK NUMBER	PAYMENTS: BY CHECK OR PMO	PAYMENTS: BY COIN OR CURRENCY	CREDIT CARD
1									1			1				
2									2			2				
3									3			3				
4									4			4				
5									5			5				
6									6			6				
7									7			7				
8									8			8				
9									9			9				
10									10			10				
11									11			11				
12									12			12				
13									13			13				
14									14			14				
15									15			15				
16									16			16				
17									17			17				
18									18			18				
19									19			19				
20									20			20				
21									21			21				
22									22			22				
23									23			23				
24									24			24				
25									25			25				
26									26			26				
27									27			27				
28									28			28				
29									29			29				
30									30			30				
31								TOTALS THIS PAGE	31				TOTALS			
32								TOTALS PREVIOUS PAGE	32				CURRENCY			
33								TOTAL MONTH TO DATE	33				COIN			
			COLUMN A	COLUMN B	COLUMN C	COLUMN D	COLUMN E				COLUMN F COLUMN G COLUMN H COLUMN I COLUMN J COLUMN K COLUMN L COLUMN M					

CHECKS

CREDIT CARDS

TOTAL RECEIPTS

LESS CREDIT CARD $

TOTAL DEPOSIT

DATE ______ FIRM ______

MEMO______

Bibbero Systems. Inc.

© 1981 BIBBERO SYSTEMS, INC. PETALUMA, CA
FORM NO. 42-9029

DAILY - FROM LINE 31

ARITHMETIC POSTING PROOF	
Column E	$
Plus Column A	
Sub-Total	
Minus Column B	
Sub-Total	
Minus Column C	
Equals Coulmn D	

Box 1

MONTH- FROM LINE 31

ACCOUNTS RECEIVABLE PROOF	
Accts. Receivable Previous Day	$
Plus Column A	
Sub-Total	
Minus Column B	
Sub-Total	
Minus Column C	
Accts. Receivable End of Day	

Box 2

YEAR TO DATE - FROM LINE 33

ARTHMETIC POSTING PROOF		
Accts. Receivable Beginning of Month		$
Plus Column A	MONTH TO DATE	
Sub-Total		
Minus Column B	MONTH TO DATE	
Sub-Total		
Minus Column C	MONTH TO DATE	
Accts. Receivable End of Month	MONTH TO DATE	

Box 3

Totals Must Equal

DEPOSIT PROOF

Total Receipts must equal Total of Payments (Column B).

Box 4

DISTRIBUTION PROOF	
Column F-M	
Plus Column C	
Equals Column A	

Box 5

FIGURE 14.4 Daysheet.

Real-Life Scenario

Jeanette went back to school after her children were almost grown. She took a medical clerical course and had an internship in a small medical practice. Jeanette had learned basic computer skills, but she was happy to be in a small practice with minimal computerization. Recently, Jeanette's employer, Dr. Beitler, has taken on a new young assistant into her practice. The practice is expanding rapidly, and many functions Jeanette has learned as manual procedures are now computerized, especially bookkeeping.

Jeanette feels like her job has changed drastically. Instead of the bookkeeping she really enjoyed doing by hand, she has new complicated programs to learn on the computer. The training she was given was hurried and brief. It seems to be much more work for her than before. Jeanette goes home lately completely stressed and contemplates quitting her job.

1. Should Jeanette look for other work?

2. Should Jeanette talk to Dr. Beitler about this?

3. What could Jeanette do to make her job easier?

- *Computer database* entry for each new family seen by a physician, containing all patient information including insurance and billing information.
- *Computerized patient accounts* are used for recording all information about services performed during a patient's visit. Insurance information, account number, name, and date of visit are put on this record, which is then slipped into the medical chart. The physician then checks boxes on the record for services, fees, and diagnoses. The record is returned to the person in charge of bookkeeping for the practice. The computer then generates an itemized billing statement and a completed insurance form from information obtained by this record, which can also be used with the pegboard system.
- *Computerized patient ledger (statement)* listing all previous office visits with names of procedures, procedure codes, charges, and payments. This ledger can be printed up at any time an inquiry is to be made about the patient.
- *Daily log* generated from the information posted to accounts each day. At the end of the day, this log is printed out to show check and cash payments, charges, and adjustments by patient name and account number.

There are any number of possibilities for programs generated by computer software. However, time must be taken to learn the complexities of each program. A well-designed bookkeeping program can save a practice many hours of labor that the old manual systems required.

ACCOUNTS RECEIVABLE

The term **accounts receivable** refers to how much money is owed to the medical facility for services rendered. Statements are sent out every month to patients showing balances on each account. There needs to be a way to ensure that statements are sent

---

ACCOUNTS RECEIVABLE CONTROL

Total Outstanding A/R Balance
(from previous month) $ 55,000

Current Monthly Charges for Services   35,000

                                              Subtotal $ 90,000

Subtract Current Monthly Payments
Received and Adjustments   30,000

Balance Outstanding $ 60,000

FIGURE 14.5 Daily accounts receivable summary.

to all patients who owe money. To accomplish this, the medical clerical worker would take the following steps:

1. Total all balances due for each patient account record.

2. Total all amounts on all statements to be sent out. The totals of both step 1 and step 2 should agree.

3. If these two amounts do not agree, all records and figures must be checked.

Figure 14.5 is an example of a calculation of the monthly total of accounts receivable. The process is as follows:

■ The previous monthly accounts receivable figure is obtained ($55,000).
■ The current month's accounts receivable figure is added to the previous month's figure ($35,000) to equal $90,000.
■ The total payments received for the current month of $30,000 is subtracted from the $90,000 figure to come up with a new accounts receivable figure of $60,000.

Commonly made errors are made by carrying the wrong total forward from day to day. Often a digit of a number is put in the wrong column, such as writing 500 for 50, or 20 instead of 200. Zeros can often be misread as other numbers. Some bookkeepers will use a line instead of writing two zeros when even dollars are involved; for example, $50— instead of $50.00.

$\mathcal{A}$ CCOUNTS PAYABLE

Whatever is spent in a health care facility should be recorded on a **disbursement** record, referred to as **accounts payable** (A/P). This record usually has columns for the date, name of supplier or vendor, amount of the charge, amount of the check and check number, deposits, and bank balance. There are also columns for putting in a category for every business expense. Some categories might include:

■ Rent
■ Taxes and licenses
■ Dues and meetings
■ Medical supplies

- Employee payroll
- Office expenses
- Utilities
- Insurance
- Travel and entertainment

It is recommended that an employer keep a separate checking account for personal expenses. For income tax purposes, this is the best method.

PETTY CASH

Health care facilities have a need for a **petty cash** fund in case small payments are required. Typical petty cash expenditures include postage-due fees, parking expenses while on an errand for an employer, small amounts of office supplies, and so on. Remember, major expenses should always be paid by check.

A *petty cash voucher* is the form used to control petty cash expenditures. The voucher provides space to record the expenditure date, the amount paid, the purpose, and the name of the person to whom the payment is made. Vouchers should be numbered. A petty cash record of amounts received and spent can be kept in a standard cash book or on a voucher sheet. Petty cash may be reconciled daily.

Employees handling cash receipts should be bonded. In **bonding** an employee, an insurance or bonding company guarantees payment of a specified amount to an employer in the event of financial loss caused by an employee. Some policies automatically bond certain employee titles, and some automatically bond all employees in an office. If an employee handles very large sums of money, an extensive investigation into the employee's background may be made.

PAYROLL

Payroll is handled in a variety of ways in health care facilities. Some facilities are set up for a bank to handle all payroll, and others may hire an accountant to handle the task.

Today, payroll is often handled entirely by computer. Checks are issued and all withholding (deductions made by an employer from an employee's paycheck) is calculated automatically.

In many facilities, the medical clerical worker may have responsibility for the entire payroll, including explaining payroll policies to new employees, processing checks, and collecting payroll information. If you are to be responsible for payroll, you must also understand Social Security (also known as FICA: Federal Insurance Contributions Act), income tax laws, and unemployment regulations.

Complete records must be kept for every employee, according to government regulations. This is called the *employee's earnings record*. Such records include:

- Social Security number
- Exemptions claimed
- Amount of gross salary
- All deductions for Social Security, as well as federal, state, and local taxes, state disability insurance, and state unemployment tax, where applicable

Fair Labor Standards Act

The *Fair Labor Standards Act* regulates the number of hours employees may work, establishes a federal minimum wage, and dictates requirements concerning overtime pay. An employer must record the number of hours worked by each employee. A time book or time card is the most common recording format. Overtime premiums are generally paid when employees work on the sixth and seventh days in a scheduled work week. Some employees are exempt from such regulations.

Employer Identification Number

Each employer must have an *employer identification number* used for federal tax purposes. Form SS-4 from the Internal Revenue Service is used to receive this number. The employees use their Social Security number as their identifying number. If an employee has no Social Security number, he or she must apply for a number immediately. Applications are available at post offices and Social Security offices.

Withholding Allowance Certificate

Each new employee must complete an *Employee's **Withholding** Allowance Certificate,* known as a Form W-4 (Figure 14.6). This form states the number of exemptions claimed. Employees should be asked by December 1 of each year whether there has been a change in the number of exemptions since the last form filed the previous year.

FICA

The Federal Insurance Contributions Act, or **Social Security**, has three programs financed from one payroll tax in which employers and employees contribute at a rate as specified by the law. *Old Age Survivors Insurance* (OASI) provides the elderly and their surviving dependents with retirement benefits. *Medicare* (see Chapter 13) provides hospitalization insurance for the elderly. The *Disability Insurance* program (SDI) provides workers with insurance due to disability during working years.

Income Tax Deductions

Employers must withhold from employee salaries an advance payment on income taxes. This money is remitted periodically to a regional Internal Revenue Service office.

Unemployment Compensation Disability Deductions

This deduction is mandatory in many states. This is an insurance policy providing temporary cash benefits for employees suffering a wage loss due to a nonindustrial injury or illness. About 1 percent of an employee's gross pay is deducted each month.

Unemployment Tax

Under the *Federal Unemployment Tax Act* (FUTA), most employers pay a federal tax that is used to pay for administrative costs of state unemployment programs. Employers may also be required to pay for a state unemployment tax program.

Cut here and give Form W-4 to your employer. Keep the top part for your records.

Form **W-4**

Department of the Treasury
Internal Revenue Service

Employee's Withholding Allowance Certificate

▶ **For Privacy Act and Paperwork Reduction Act Notice, see instructions.**

OMB No. 1545-0010

2002

1 Type or Print Your First Name and Middle Initial   Last Name

2 Your Social Security Number

Home Address (number and street or rural route)   Apt

3 ☐ Single   ☐ Married   ☐ Married, but withhold at higher Single rate.

City or Town   State   ZIP Code

Note: *If married, but legally separated, or spouse is a nonres alien, check the 'Single' box.*

4 **If your last name differs from that on your social security card,
check here. You must call 1-800-772-1213 for a new card** ..... ▶ ☐

5 Total number of allowances you are claiming (from line **H** above **or** from the applicable worksheet on page 2) .... | 5

6 Additional amount, if any, you want withheld from each paycheck .... | 6 $

7 I claim exemption from withholding for 2002, and I certify that I meet **both** of the following conditions for exemption:
  • Last year I had a right to a refund of **all** federal income tax withheld because I had **no** tax liability **and**
  • This year I expect a refund of **all** federal income tax withheld because I expect to have **no** tax liability.
  If you meet both conditions, enter 'Exempt' here .... ▶ | 7

Under penalties of perjury, I certify that I am entitled to the number of withholding allowances claimed on this certificate, or I am entitled to claim exempt status.

Employee's Signature
(Form is not valid
unless you sign it.) ▶   Date ▶

8 Employer's Name and Address (Employer: Complete lines 8 and 10 only if sending to the IRS.) | 9 Office Code (optional) | 10 Employer Identification Number

FDIA8201   01/03/02

BAA

FIGURE 14.6 Form W-4.

| Form **W-2** | **Wage and Tax Statement** ► Keep for your records | **2001** |

Name | Social Security Number

Check if for spouse .... ☐

a Control number ....
b Employer's ID number
c Employer's name, address, and ZIP code

Street
City
State ____ ZIP Code
Check box if foreign address (see Help) ... ☐

**Check box to transfer items d and e below
from Federal Information Worksheet** .... ☐
d Employee's social security number
e Employee's name, address, and ZIP code
First _____ M.I. __
Last _____
Street _____
City _____
State ____ ZIP Code ____
Check box if foreign address (see Help) ... ☐

1 Wages, tips, other compensation
2 Federal income tax withheld
3 Social security wages
4 Social security tax withheld
5 Medicare wages and tips
6 Medicare tax withheld
7 Social security tips
8 Allocated tips
9 Advance EIC payment
10 Dependent care benefits
11 Nonqualified plans

Distributions from sect. 457 and nonqualified plans *(Important, see Help)*

Code .... ►___
12 Enter box 12 below

13 Statutory employee .... ☐
Retirement plan .... ☐
Third-party sick pay .... ☐

14 If you have entries in box 14, click . ► HERE then select Help before making any entries for box 14.

Box 12 Code	**Box 12** Amount	If Box 12 code is:
___	___	A: Enter amount attributable to RRTA Tier 2 tax .. ____
___	___	M: Enter amount attributable to RRTA Tier 2 tax .. ____
___	___	P: Double click to link to Form 3903, line 4 ...... ____
		R: Enter MSA contribution for Taxpayer .... ____
		Spouse .... ____

Box 15 State	Employer's state I.D. no.	**Box 16** State wages, tips, etc.	**Box 17** State income tax
___	___	___	___
___	___	___	___
___	___	___	___

Box 20 Locality name	**Box 18** Local wages, tips, etc.	**Box 19** Local income tax	Associated State
___	___	___	__
___	___	___	__
___	___	___	__

Box 14 Description	Amount	Type	TurboTax description of Type
___	___	_	___
___	___	_	___
___	___	_	___
___	___	_	___

NOTE: The box 14 "Type" is specific to TurboTax and may not be the same as one letter descriptions on your Form W-2.

FIGURE 14.7 Form W-2.

Form **W-2**	**Additional Wage and Tax Information** ► Keep for your records	**2001**

Name
_____

Employer's Name _____   Page **2**

ADDITIONAL INFORMATION

Foreign Income

1   Check this box if the income reported on this W-2 is from a foreign source **and**
     is eligible to be excluded on Form 2555 .... ☐

Electronic Filing

Complete if you are filing this return electronically.

2   Check this box if this W-2 is 'non-standard' (handwritten, typewritten, or altered in any way) .... ☐

Statutory Employees

Complete if box 13 Statutory employee box is checked.

3   Will you be deducting any expenses in connection with this income? .... Yes ☐   No ☐
4   If so, select the copy of Schedule C you want to report
     this income on (double-click) .... _____

Dependent Care Benefits

Complete if box 10 of this W-2 has an entry.

5   Did this employer hire an on-staff care provider or furnish dependent care at
     your workplace? .... Yes ☐   No ☐
6   Enter any amounts forfeited from a flexible spending account .... _____

Clergy, Church Employees, Members of Recognized Religious Sects

Complete if this W-2 is for clergy, church employment, or for a member of a recognized religious sect.
Clergy only:

7 a Enter your housing or parsonage allowance .... _____
  b Enter your unused (taxable) portion of your housing or parsonage allowance ... _____
     If no FICA was withheld, check box c, d, e, or f below as appropriate
  c Check box if you need to pay self-employment tax on housing or parsonage allowance only .... ☐
  d Check box if you need to pay self-employment tax on W-2 income only .... ☐
  e Check box if you need to pay self-employment tax on W-2 income & housing allowance .... ☐
  f If exempt from SE tax, check this box if you have an approved exemption Form 4361 .... ☐
Non-clergy:
     If no FICA was withheld, check box a or b below as appropriate
8 a Check this box if you need to pay self-employment tax on this W-2 income .... ☐
  b If exempt from SE tax, check this box if you have an approved exemption Form 4029 .... ☐

FIGURE 14.7 Continued.

Tax Reports

All health care facilities are required to prepare and file payroll records of employees.
The *Employer's Quarterly Federal Tax Return* must be filed quarterly. This document
must show:

- Number of employees
- Names of employees/Social Security numbers

- Total wages paid
- Withholding tax amount
- Wage amount subject to FICA; FICA taxes paid
- Total periodic tax deposits
- Undeposited taxes due

Annual reports should be given to employees by January 31. This includes Form W-2, which is called the *Wage and Tax Statement* (Figure 14.7).

Form W-2 must show:

- Employer identification number
- Employee's Social Security number
- Total wages and other compensation
- Total income tax and Social Security tax paid

Payroll Register

Some health care facilities require that a payroll register be maintained with information taken from employee time cards. The register contains hours worked, hourly rate, gross pay, FICA, federal and state taxes, disability insurance, net pay, and so on.

SUMMARY

Bookkeeping responsibilities are some of the most complicated tasks required of a medical clerical worker. There is wide variation among health care facilities as to what will be expected of you in this area.

Computerization increasingly has taken over more and more of the time-consuming bookkeeping responsibilities. Most computer software programs are easy to learn and will cut down the bookkeeping time for the medical clerical worker.

LEARNING ACTIVITIES

1. Duplicate eight copies of the patient statement form in Appendix B. Type the following information onto the statement, using one statement for each patient. Put the statements in alphabetical order and hand in to your instructor.

Name:	Ms. Annie Mae Bellsword (Single)
Address:	2940 Ralph Court
	Birdseye, USA 00009
Tel:	(213) 555-0987
Ins:	Aetna Casualty Company
	Policy No. 4536-7
	Previous Balance: $34.00
Name:	Miss Tiffanie Bellsworth
Address:	45 Tinkerbell Drive
	Altuna, USA 00008
Tel:	(213) 555-3425
Ins:	Blue Shield Group No. S12986754A

Name:	Alan C. Torrance (Single)
Address:	45 Buster Drive
	Birdseye, USA 00008
Tel:	(213) 555-8765
Ins:	Medicare ID No. 565-76-9087 A
Name:	Mrs. Geneva Torres (Married)
Address:	2314 Jetset Blvd.
	Altuna, USA 00009
Tel:	(213) 555-5567
Ins:	Insurance Company of Altuna
	Policy No. 7765-09
Name:	Jeremy Gilden (Divorced)
Address:	3265 Quail Drive
	Birdseye, USA 00007
Tel:	(213) 555-8796
Ins:	Hartford Insurance Group
	Policy No. 12349876
Name:	Mrs. Agnes Gilch (Widow)
Address:	3219 Ancient Lane, No. 43
	Birdseye, USA 00007
Tel:	(213) 555-3908
Ins:	Medicare ID No. 344-66-5533 B
Name:	Jonathan St. John (Single)
Address:	3241 North Oak Crossing
	Altuna, USA 00007
Tel:	(213) 555-2398
Ins:	Medicare ID No. 433-22-9876 A
Name:	Jason Starborn (Single)
Address:	321 Cherokee Lane
	Altuna, USA 00008
Tel:	(213) 555-8796
Ins:	Z. Z. Partridge and Co.
	Policy No. 332-33-09A

2. If your instructor has pegboard supplies available, perform the following bookkeeping exercise. As illustrated in Figure 14.1, the *pegboard bookkeeping system* consists of a transaction record (*superbill*), a *patient ledger card* (patient financial record), and a *daysheet* (daily financial log), which comes with an attached deposit slip. This system is also called the *write-it-once* method, because you can post charges and credits on several different records in one operation. Using the pegboard equipment provided by your instructor, follow these steps, using the patient information listed at the end of the exercise.

Beginning activities:
(a) Attach a daysheet (daily financial log) to the pegboard.
(b) Place the writing line of the transaction record for patient 1 over the first blank line of the daysheet.
(c) Write today's date, the name of the patient, the patient's identification number, and any previous balance from the patient's ledger card (none here). When there is no previous balance, draw a line in the Previous Balance column.

(d) The transaction record is then put in the front of the patient's medical record, where the physician and/or nurse will note procedures and charges.

(e) Follow the same procedure for Patient 2.

Ending activities: You will proceed as if a nurse or the patient has returned the transaction record after the medical examination. You will have to fill in the information that is usually provided by the physician or nurse, including codes for procedures. Proceed as if patients 1 and 2 had routine office visits and a CBC (complete blood count) under laboratory services.

(f) Place each patient's ledger card (one at a time) in the correct position on the daysheet. Align the first blank line of the card with the patient's name, which was transferred to the daysheet from the transaction record when you registered the patient. Line up the columns of the ledger card with the columns of the daysheet.

(g) Put the transaction record over the ledger card, lining up the columns of the transaction record with the columns of the ledger card.

(h) You will have to write in the fees beside the procedures that have been checked. The cost of an office visit is $40.00, and the CBC is $15.00. Add all charges to calculate the final bill.

(i) Write the charges in the *charges* column of the transaction record.

(j) If the patients pay total or partial payment, or if there are any adjustments from previous charges, place payments in the *amount received today* space, and old balances go in the *old balance* column.

(k) You are to give the transaction record to the patient. The transaction record serves as a statement and as documentation for insurance claims.

(l) File the ledger card in the office files.

(m) The deposit slip often attached to the pegboard system can also be filled out at this time, if payment is made.

Patient 1	Patient 2
Mrs. Judith Ann Spencer	Mr. Alan Spencer
34 Oak Street	34 Oak Street
Anytown, CA 90000	Anytown, CA 90000
Birthdate: 9/4/50	Birthdate: 8/30/46
Insurance carrier: Blue Cross	Insurance carrier: Blue Cross
Relationship to subscriber: Self	Relationship to subscriber: Spouse
Insurance ID: 545-66-7777	Insurance ID: 567-89-0876
Other health coverage: No	Other health coverage: No
Disability: Illness	Disability: Illness
Date: 8/9/03	Date: 8/9/03
Charges: Office visit (brief),	Charges: Office visit (brief),
CBC (laboratory in office)	CBC (laboratory in office)
Diagnosis: Influenza	Diagnosis: Influenza
No return visit	No return visit
Paid in full: Check No. 4355	Paid in full by wife, Judith Ann Spencer: Check No. 4355

3. Complete the following petty cash exercise. Dr. Andrea Doria is a pediatrician for whom Clarisse Hill works as a front-office medical clerical worker. Dr. Doria believes that Clarisse should have an ample amount of cash in the petty cash fund. She has asked Clarisse to be sure that $75.00 is always in the fund at the end of the week, on Friday afternoon. On the Friday before Christmas, Clarisse must total her petty cash expenditures for the past week. Please add up all of Clarisse's expenses for the week of December 19

through December 23. Calculate the amount of the check Clarisse needs to write to replenish the petty cash fund ($75.00).

EXPENDITURES DURING THE WEEK OF 12/19–12/23

Christmas decorations for office	$23.44
Stamps	$12.50
Tape/wrapping paper for employee presents from Dr. Doria	$6.50
Ink pad for "Confidential" stamp	$4.50
Box of 12 ballpoint pens	$8.23
Parking fee/Bob's Parking Lot/errand for Dr. Doria	$2.25
Paper glue/liquid correction fluid	$3.45
Band-Aids	$3.20
Replacement lamp shade for reception area	$10.92
Total amount of check to be written:	$_____

4. Using the petty cash form in Appendix B, fill out a petty cash voucher for the expenditures in Exercise 3.

5. State four guidelines for bookkeeping that will help you do a good job.

6. What are the four most common bookkeeping systems used in health care facilities today?

7. What is the difference between single- and double-entry bookkeeping?

8. Match each term with the correct definition.
   ___ (a) net worth   (1) Debt
   ___ (b) assets   (2) Assets − liabilities
   ___ (c) liability   (3) Things of value possessed by a business
   ___ (d) capital   (4) That which is owned

9. Where does the pegboard bookkeeping system get its name?

10. What are four forms used in the pegboard bookkeeping system?

11. What is the difference between accounts receivable and accounts payable?

12. State the accounting equation for double-entry bookkeeping.

13. What is a *disbursement record?*

14. Why would an employee be bonded?

15. Name three expenditures that might be made with petty cash.

16. What does FICA stand for? By what other name is it known?

17. What is (a) Form W-4; (b) Form W-2?

18. What is the significance of the Fair Labor Standards Act to an employee?

CHAPTER 15

Daily Financial Responsibilities: Billing and Collection

Bankruptcy A petition to a court by an individual who is stating that he or she cannot pay any debt incurred.

Credit laws Laws that govern the ways fees are collected.

Cycle billing The billing procedure where itemized statements are sent according to alphabetical breakdown.

Dun message A message to remind a person about a past-due payment.

Fee for service Collection of a fee at the time the service is performed.

Fee schedule A list of common procedures performed by a medical facility, along with their fees.

Garnishment Garnishment refers to a health care facility procuring a court order to obtain money directly from a patient who has a very delinquent account by attaching property and wages of the patient.

Ledger card A daily record, showing payments, charges, and balances due.

Professional courtesy A discount or no-charge policy extended to certain people by a medical facility or physician.

Skip A patient who has an outstanding bill and who disappears, leaving no forwarding address.

Small claims court A court set up for the purpose of settling cases, where the amount of the settlement has a limit on it. Varying from state to state, the average is from $2,000 to $2,500. This is a last resort option for a health care facility trying to collect a past-due account.

Truth-in-Lending Act An act by Congress established in 1968 to protect consumers by requiring that providers of credit state the charges clearly in writing and the interest charged as an annual rate.

OBJECTIVES

After completing this chapter, the student is responsible for performing the following objectives:

- Differentiate between *external* and *internal* billing.
- Discuss the need for full disclosure of fee schedules to patients.
- List several different methods for billing patients for services rendered.
- State the importance of understanding credit laws when billing patients.
- Identify ways to collect delinquent accounts from patients.

*I*NTRODUCTION

One of the most important responsibilities of a medical clerical worker in many health care facilities is the billing and collection of patient fees. Hospitals often have special personnel and departments to handle billing. Insurance payments are the main source of income for most hospitals and medical offices (health maintenance organizations are an exception). Prompt payment for the patient's portion of a bill is essential for the proper functioning of these facilities. As a medical clerical worker, you must be prepared to ask for payment for services rendered.

Effective interpersonal skills are essential in handling billing and collection. You must utilize tact and a businesslike approach when dealing with billing issues, sincerely attempting to help the patient with financial difficulties. Having an honest concern for the client with financial difficulties, and assisting him or her to explore options and determine a payment schedule, can help avoid collection problems and unnecessary conflict.

*I*NTERNAL VERSUS EXTERNAL BILLING

There are two main ways to handle billing in a health care facility. *Internal billing* refers to having the billing procedure handled in the health care facility where the patient is seen and/or treated. Internal billing can be very simple, as in a small medical office. It can also be very complex, as in large hospitals, with a fully computerized system for statement preparation and record keeping. An internal billing system should reflect the size of the medical practice. If an old-fashioned system is used for a practice that has expanded rapidly, new systems should be explored. Medical clerical workers should remain flexible, always prepared to upgrade and update such systems as medical practice changes.

External billing refers to hiring an outside service to handle patient accounts. The medical clerical worker acts as a go-between with the billing service and the medical facility, being responsible for good communication between the two. An external service cuts out much of the time-consuming tasks of billing. However, certain records must be maintained and accurate information given to the billing agency.

*O*BTAINING BILLING INFORMATION

A complete and accurate registration form at the time of a patient's first visit will secure the needed information from the patient about insurance coverage. Such a form should also contain a place for financial history relevant to billing and, if necessary, should state the collection procedures for overdue accounts. (See Figure 7.1 for an example of a registration form.) If a patient feels that the information required on a registration form is an invasion of his or her privacy, he or she may be given the option of paying for medical services at the time of each office visit.

It is a good idea to tell the patient when he or she calls for an appointment that fees are due at the time of service. Although patients are requested by most practices to pay immediately, there are many instances when partial or no payment is made. The physician may agree to honor the patient's insurance plan and will be paid usually 70 to 100 percent of the fee by the insurance company (Medicare pays 80 percent).

In other cases, the physician may not participate in an insurance plan, and the patient must take responsibility for processing and sending in the insurance form. In this case, the patient is required to pay at the time of service. For patients covered by health maintenance organization (HMO) copayment plans, only the patient portion of the fee (usually $5 to $10) is to be collected. In some insurance contracts, nothing is collected from the patient until the insurance has been billed and has paid the doctor or hospital.

𝓕EE DISCLOSURE

Fees for medical services should be clearly explained to the patient. A typed list of the most common services that the physician or hospital offers should be readily available to the patient. This list can include procedure code numbers, with a description of the services provided. By law, a **fee schedule** such as this must be posted in the facility and made available to patients.

Many physicians and medical facilities give the patient a written estimate of the services to be performed. This is often done in a physician's office after an examination or upon admission to the hospital. In other cases, the medical clerical worker is asked to discuss the fees with the patient. This discussion should be done privately in a professional manner, with a positive tone, being careful not to cause the patient embarrassment. If there is concern or confusion about the bill, refer the client to the department head or the physician.

In some cases, the patient may have difficulty understanding the fee schedule or be incapable of making decisions about treatment. In this case, the fee discussion should take place with the patient and the person responsible for paying the bill present.

Sometimes extra fees are requested of a patient that were not explained in the initial discussion about costs. Such fees might include telephone calls, no-show appointments, special medical reports, interest charges, special supplies and equipment, and so on. Medical clerical workers should inform the patient of the extra charges by phone or in writing before the billing process. If this procedure is not followed, patients can become very upset. A patient information brochure given to new patients can be very helpful in this regard.

𝓕EE COLLECTION METHODS

There are many ways for a medical office or hospital to collect fees. Factors that influence which billing method is chosen include the size of the practice, the type of specialty, the size of the bill, and so on.

Medical clerical workers should be familiar with the following methods of fee collection.

Payment at Time of Service

It is wise to require patients to pay their bill at the time of receiving medical services, called **fee for service**. This may not be practical for most hospital costs, but partial payment may be collected. This is very important for a patient who does not have medical insurance. Billing and bookkeeping expenses for bill collecting from patients who do not pay their bills or who are slow in making payment are avoided by payment at the time of service.

After a service has been performed and the patient stops at the reception desk, you should say to the patient, "Your total for today is $_____, Mrs. Jones. Will you be paying by check, cash, or credit card?" Your approach should be as if the patient will pay at the time of service, and let the patient bill his or her insurance carrier whenever possible.

Patients sometimes can be uncomfortable about paying fees. Some patients might be confused and need someone in the family or a friend to be responsible for such discussions. Some patients have appointed someone else to be responsible for all medical fees. If this is the case, the fee discussion should take place with both the patient and the responsible party present.

A medical practice might come into contact with a patient known as a "deadbeat," a person who has no intention of paying for services. Some signs to watch for this type of patient include:

- No telephone numbers where the patient can be reached
- Multiple addresses in the past several years
- Motel address
- No referral
- No insurance
- No medical records or a history of seeing many doctors
- Nonexistent or sparse employment record

In hospitals, many departments, such as a clinical laboratory and radiology, perform minor procedures. Such departments are often in charge of their own collections. You may obtain employment in one of these departments, where you might be responsible for bill collections for the entire department.

Extension of Credit

When a patient faces large fees for a service such as surgery or multiple visits to the medical facility, the facility may have a system that extends credit. This *credit policy* should be put into writing and given to the patient at the beginning of the relationship. Insurance coverage often insures credit until payment can be made by the insurance company.

Some offices and facilities do not have a formal policy and may evaluate each case individually. Regardless of how credit is extended, patients should be told when payments are due, what is done about past-due accounts, how the insurance payments will be handled, who will fill out the insurance forms, and other details.

Credit Card Billing

Many medical facilities allow patients to pay their bills by using a credit card (e.g., Visa, MasterCard, American Express), especially those practices where the patient has major expenses. Credit card companies charge a minimum monthly fee per location as well as a percentage that is calculated on the charges submitted. The patient pays the credit card company, reducing the possibility of collection costs by the practice. However, under some conditions a credit card company may hold participating professionals liable for the collection of credit card accounts. This can happen when a medical practice does not consult a list that is circulated by a credit card company listing credit card numbers not to be honored. If the card is then honored, the practice may be liable for the full amount of the charge.

Employers will require you to check carefully the expiration date on the credit card, as well as the name of the person listed on the card. Many facilities have a machine where you punch in the card number. An electronic check is performed automatically to see if the card is accepted. Some people abuse credit cards, running up bills far beyond the credit card limit. When this happens, the credit card is no longer recognized by the credit card company, and you will get a rejection code from the machine. You must then tell the patient that you cannot accept the card and that he or she should contact the credit card company to correct the problem.

Be prepared for the patient to become defensive if a credit card is rejected. The patient may become insistent that you accept the card because "there has been some mistake." You are *not* responsible for ironing out any problems between the patient and the credit card company. Be polite and nonjudgmental with the patient.

If the facility where you work does not have a machine to check credit cards, you may have to refer to a published bulletin that contains card numbers that are no longer acceptable. Some facilities require you to call a telephone number where a person will check to see if the credit card is valid.

Transaction Record

The transaction record (superbill) system has been adopted in many states. As discussed in Chapter 13, the superbill combines a bill and an insurance claim in one statement. The statement is given to the patient at the time of the office visit. The transaction record, seen in Figure 14.2, includes the patient's name, date, services received, treatment codes, diagnostic information according to the ICD-9-CM coding, insurance requirements, assignment of benefits, and physician's identification.

The transaction record eliminates much insurance paperwork and is designed to encourage payment immediately after services are received. The patient is then responsible for submitting the transaction record directly to the insurance company, where benefits can either be assigned to the patient or to the health care facility, if credit has been granted.

Monthly Itemized Statement

The patient may be sent a monthly itemized statement as a bill for services. This method increases collection costs and delays payment significantly. However, it is often used in larger facilities that are billing for multiple services and extended hospital stays.

Cycle Billing

In **cycle billing**, patients are billed according to alphabetical breakdown. With this method, billing goes on throughout the month and supposedly allows for continuous cash flow during the month.

Ledger Card Billing

A very simple method of billing is by use of a **ledger card.** Ledger cards for each patient are copied and mailed directly to the patient. Ledger cards show all charges, credits, and any adjustments that might be necessary (Figure 15.1). Unpaid bills often are flagged by use of a color strip on top of the ledger cards. When the bill is paid, the color strip is removed.

Computerized Statement

Some facilities have a sophisticated method of billing using billing software for the computer. During a billing cycle, the medical clerical worker asks the computer to search through the patient files and print out statements for patients who have outstanding balances. Some software allows the medical clerical worker to call up a prewritten collection letter for overdue accounts, reminding the patient of the delinquent bill.

BILLING NAME				NAMES OF OTHER FAMILY MEMBERS			
MAXWELL, JOHN, JR				MARY, JANE, PETER			
PATIENT'S NAME							
MAXWELL, PETER							
RES. PHONE 555-7766		BUS. PHONE None					
OCCUPATION	Student			RELATIVE OR FRIEND Dr. John Maxwell, Sr.			
EMPLOYED BY Father-Dow Chemical				REFERRED BY Same as above			
INS. INFORMATION Etna Casualty				557-76-8989		SOC. SEC. NUMBER	
THE BIBBERO SYSTEMS FORM NO. MDP. 8510				© 1965 BIBBERO SYSTEMS, INC. SAN FRANSISCO			

GEORGE D. GREEN, M.D.
JOHN F. WHITE, M.D.

Family Practice
100 MAIN STREET, SUITE 14
ANYTOWN, CALIFORNIA 90000
TELEPHONE: (999) 555-6000

STATEMENT TO:

> Mr. John Maxwell
>
> 40 Ash Lane
>
> Anytown, CA 90000

- - - - - - - - - - TEAR OFF AND RETURN UPPER PORTION WITH PAYMENT - - - - - - - - - -

DATE	PAYMENTS				PROFESSIONAL SERVICE		FEE		LAST AMOUNT IN THIS COLUMN IS BALANCE DUE	
	BANK NUMBER	BY CHECK OR P.M.O.		BY COIN OR CURRENCY						
8-7-					1	Office Visit	35	00	35	00
8-7-					19	Laboratory	20	00	55	00
9-1	11-24	55	00						0̶	

PROFESSIONAL SERVICE CODES:

OFFICE VISIT	9. COLLECTION OF LAB. SPEC.	17. SURGICAL
HOME VISIT	10. SPECIAL REPORTS	18. CASTS
HOSPITAL VISIT	11. OTHER SERVICES	19. LABORATORY
EMERGENCY ROOM	12. SPEC. DIAGNOSTIC SERVICES	20. X-RAY
CONSULTATION	13. SPEC. THERAPEUTIC SERV.	21. ALLERGY TEST.
IMMUNIZATION	14. EXTENDED CARE FACILITY	22. NO CHARGE
INJECTION	15. CUSTODIAL CARE	23. ADJUSTMENTS OR CORRECTIONS
DRUGS/SUPPLIES/MATERIALS	16. OBSTETRICAL CARE	24. TOTAL CARE

GEORGE D. GREEN, M.D.   JOHN F. WHITE, M.D.
CAL. LIC. # 6-2856   CAL. LIC. # G-5281

FIGURE 15.1 Ledger card statement.

Professional Courtesy

The term **professional courtesy** refers either to a discount or to a no-charge policy extended to certain people by a physician or facility. The medical clerical worker must be clear about the professional courtesy policy.

Professional courtesy is disappearing in some areas, with many hospitals and surgeons no longer offering professional courtesy policies. But many medical facilities still have a professional courtesy policy. People considered as eligible to receive professional courtesy benefits might be:

- Doctors and their immediate families
- Dentists
- Parents of doctors
- Nurses
- Pharmacists
- Hospital employees
- Medical clerical workers and their immediate families
- Clergy

CREDIT LAWS

Federal and state laws have been enacted over the last several years to govern the way businesses collect fees. State laws vary among states. The medical clerical worker must be aware of such **credit laws** before attempting to collect fees.

Federal Truth in Lending Act

The **Federal Truth-in-Lending Act,** passed in 1969, is focused on any business that charges interest or agrees to more than four payments for a given service. A *Regulation Z* form must be filled out and signed by the patient. The form includes full information about how the patient has agreed to pay a bill (down payment, installments and dates due, finance charge, and percentage of interest rate, if any). A physician is not required to charge interest.

This act does not apply to a patient who volunteers on his or her own to pay in installments. No disclosures are required. In discussing an installment plan with a patient, the medical clerical worker covers the amount of the debt, the down payment, the date of final payment, and the amount and date of each payment.

Equal Credit Opportunity Act

This act, enacted in 1975, was passed under the *Equal Credit Opportunity Act.* If a physician extends credit to one patient, he or she must extend credit to all patients who request it. Refusal is allowed only on ability or inability to pay. The physician must tell the patient the reason for a credit refusal or give the patient notice that credit is not going to be granted. The patient has 60 days to request the reason in writing why the request for credit was denied. If a physician chooses to charge interest, this practice may be governed by state laws. Many physicians accept credit cards to avoid being in the business of extending credit. The physician is also allowed by law to offer a 5 percent discount to patients who pay cash.

Fair Credit Reporting Act

This act provides guidelines for reporting and collecting credit background information and updates. Consumers under this act are allowed to learn about the information collected about them by credit reporting agencies, and to correct and update incorrect information.

Guide against Debt Collection Deception

Enacted by the Federal Trade Commission, this law provides collection guidelines to creditors and provides the patient with protection from fraudulent and deceptive tactics during the collection process.

Notice on Use of Telephone for Debt Collecting

Enacted by the Federal Communications Commission, the Fair Debt Collection Practices Act law outlines specific times when calls can be made to patients, prohibiting calls at odd hours (after 8 P.M., for example), threatening phone calls, and other harassment. State and local governments may have additional statutes concerning the telephone and debt collection.

If you as a medical clerical worker violate any credit law, the patient involved can sue the physician or facility. It is mandatory that you understand these laws.

COLLECTING OVERDUE ACCOUNTS

Patients should receive a billing notice at the end of the month in which charges for medical services occurred. Many patients at this time pay their bill (or most of the bill) immediately upon receipt of their statement. Studies have shown that enclosing a preaddressed envelope (a colored envelope is preferred by many practices) helps the collection process.

However, some clients are not always prompt about payments of bills. Every facility has a firm policy for collecting late payments. There is a statute of limitations, varying from state to state, setting a maximum time for collection of a debt by legal means.

Aging Accounts

This is a way to identify accounts according to the length of time the accounts have been delinquent. Sometimes colors are used to identify the length of time an account has been left unpaid. For instance, a red code could signify an account that is one month overdue, a blue code could stand for two months overdue, and so on.

In a computerized billing system, accounts are aged automatically. The first notation might be a record of a transaction record given at the time of visit. A statement would be sent after one month, and after two months a statement with an overdue

---

Real-Life Scenario

Darryl is a medical clerical worker for a geriatric practice. He is particularly fond of a patient named Agnes, who often brings the office edible treats because she appreciates the compassionate care received at the office. Agnes has a history of mental illness, as well as physical problems for which she is treated at Darryl's facility.

As time goes on, Agnes shows signs of increasing mental illness. Agnes has no family, and eventually she is placed in an institution. For the last several months, Agnes has not been paying her sizable bills at the geriatric practice.

Now that she is institutionalized, how does Darryl go about trying to collect from Agnes?

notice might be sent. Letters would be sent after three and four months, reminding the patient of the overdue account.

Collection Letter

Collection letters can be very useful in attempting to collect overdue bills from patients. After 90 days of delinquency for an account, you may begin to write collection letters. The goal of these letters is to encourage the patient to pay the balance due, which keeps the medical facility from having to pay a collection agency.

Times may vary according to the amount due, but after five and six months, the patient is told by letter that the account will be turned over to collections. During the seventh month, the collection agency attempts to collect. Usually by the eighth month, a lawsuit is begun if the amount is worth the effort. If the amount is too small, your employer may just have to write off the balance due. Figures 15.2 and 15.3 show samples of two collection letters relevant to an account that is approximately three months delinquent and six months delinquent, respectively.

If a patient has moved, the post office will forward the letter and will supply a card indicating the new address for a small fee if *Forwarding and Address Correction Requested* is printed on the envelope. A person who is not paying his or her bills will

---

Donald E. Castle, M.D.
7998 Berlin Avenue
Newburg, CA 94519
(415) 555-8574

February 28, 20--

Mr. Herbert Allen
2435 Eastwick Road
Newburg, CA 94500

Dear Mr. Allen:

Your account balance of $174.50 remains overdue after three months. We had expected that you would pay this balance within a reasonable amount of time after receiving treatment from Dr. Castle.

A reasonable amount of time has passed, and we will not be able to continue to keep your unpaid account on our books indefinitely.

Please send payment immediately, or call me with an explanation of why you are not able to pay this bill. I will be glad to discuss a realistic payment schedule with you.

Sincerely,

Janet Brooks
Office Manager

FIGURE 15.2 Collection letter: three-month delinquent account.

Donald E. Castle, M.D.
7998 Berlin Avenue
Newburg, CA 94519
(415) 555-8574

May 28, 20--

Mr. Herbert Allen
2435 Eastwick Road
Newburg, CA 94500

Dear Mr. Allen:

Please contact me within fourteen days of receipt of this letter concerning your past due account with a balance of $174.50. If you do not respond, your account will be turned over to the Newburg Collection Agency for collection.

I will be glad to arrange a payment plan suitable to both of us if you contact me immediately.

Sincerely,

Janet Brooks
Office Manager

FIGURE 15.3 Collection letter: six-month delinquent account.

more likely open a letter if it is not obviously a bill. Your facility might want to also include a self-addressed, stamped envelope to help prompt the payment. Sometimes better results are also achieved if the physician's signature is on the letter rather than that of the medical clerical worker.

Dun Messages

Collection agencies, **credit bureaus,** strongly worded letters, and lawsuits are aggressive efforts to collect a past-due bill from a client. There are other measures, such as the **dun message,** to remind a patient gently of the status of a delinquent account. Hopefully, by such methods, the health care facility will not have to resort to more drastic measures.

A dun message is a phrase put on a statement to remind a patient about a delinquent account. If a patient does not pay a bill immediately after receiving medical treatment, a bill is sent every thirty days. A dun message, which can be in the form of a brightly colored label, should say something like "The balance of your bill is due and payable now. Please send payment immediately."

Telephone Collections

Standard medical facility collection procedures usually call for a telephone contact after an account is sixty days overdue. If a patient with an overdue bill is about to come in for another appointment, you might take that opportunity to call the patient with an appointment reminder call and at the same time mention the overdue status of the patient's account.

When speaking over the phone to a patient about an overdue account, it is important to prepare thoroughly for the call. You must respect the patient's privacy, so be sure that patients nearby cannot hear your calls.

Threats are not considered ethical and may violate credit laws. The medical clerical worker should be courteous, but firm. The patient should realize that the medical office wishes to have the payment sent immediately. Listen carefully to any reasons why the payment has not been made. An agreement based on a short-term deadline may be made, making sure that the patient clearly understands the agreement.

The medical clerical worker should routinely make notations on the patient's ledger record indicating the date when any telephone calls and contacts were made concerning debt collection. This is ultimately very important when the debt remains uncollected and the case is taken to court. Be sure to document clearly all agreements and contacts that are made during collection procedures. Also be sure to call the patient during reasonable hours, as dictated by law.

Collection Agencies

Many facilities do their own collections. *Collection agencies* are a costly service to the physician. They are generally used if a bill is more than six months overdue. The collection agency can charge as much as 50 percent of the bill owed for its services.

Involving a collection agency is a delicate decision and must be made by your employer. Physicians must be careful in choosing a collection agency as the agency will represent the physician to the public. If a patient is threatened with a collection agency, you are then required to begin proceedings. Once you have turned over an account to a collection agency, the patient's financial record is removed from the regular file. Note on the record the name of the agency and the date. It is then illegal to send a bill to the patient after the collection agency takes over. The physician then receives a monthly statement from the agency.

If the collection agency efforts or the facility attempts to collect an overdue payment are unsuccessful, a lawsuit is the last resort.

Small Claims Court

Many health care agencies, facilities, and physicians will go to **small claims court** only when letters, telephone calls, and collection agencies have not been able to make a patient pay a long-overdue account. Others may file a claim in small claims court rather than turning it over to a collection agency. States vary as to how much money can be collected in small claims court. Most states have set an amount somewhere between $2,000 and $2,500.

Records must be shown to the judge proving that the account in question is indeed delinquent. Basic information must be submitted, including the facility or doctor's name, address, and telephone, the patient's name and address, and the sum of the delinquent amount, as well as services rendered. The court also requires a summary of the claim, including the actual bill and the activities surrounding the attempts to collect the bill. This, of course, requires accurate, organized record keeping, the responsibility of the medical clerical worker!

A representative of the medical facility, either the physician or the medical clerical worker, may have to appear during the trial. Failure of the health care representative to attend means that the case is dismissed.

If a judge finds in favor of the medical facility, the facility has the right to put a lien on the patient's wages, car, bank assets, or real estate holdings.

Garnishment of Wages

Garnishment refers to attachment of a patient's wages and property in order to pay a debt. Certain earnings, including tips, commissions, retirement programs, pensions, and so on, are exempt from garnishment. Federal government employees, court-ordered support payments, court orders concerning bankruptcy, and federal state tax levies are exempt also from garnishment. Garnishment is generally limited to 25 percent of disposable earnings in any workweek.

State laws and federal laws that apply to garnishment may not be consistent. Be sure that you know the law well if your employer uses garnishment of wages as a method of bill collecting.

Bankruptcy

Bankruptcy laws are federal in nature, organized into sections called *chapters*. A patient who files for bankruptcy becomes a ward of the federal court and is protected by the court. If a facility has been informed that a patient who has not paid a bill has filed bankruptcy, the medical clerical worker may not call or send bills to the patient. A medical practice can be fined for contempt of court for failing to recognize the bankruptcy.

A physician can file a proof-of-claim form available from an attorney, county clerk's office, or a local stationery store. Copies of the patient's unpaid bill are attached to the form and mailed to the bankruptcy court. Physician debts often go unpaid in such cases.

The Vanishing Patient

Sometimes, patients who have a balance due on their bill can no longer be reached at the address that is given on the patient record sheet. When they have not left a forwarding address, this is called a **skip.**

When a letter is sent out by the office to the patient about an overdue bill, a skip problem is evident when the letter is returned with a notation of "Address Correction Requested" or "Address Unknown." Some offices have preprinted envelopes with the notation "Address Correction Requested." This allows the post office to forward the mail to a new address. Of course, if a payment is returned in an envelope with the new address, it should immediately be noted on the patient's record.

As soon as a skip is realized, the medical clerical worker should begin the task of locating the patient. There are a number of ways that this can be accomplished.

- You may call the employer of the patient, being careful not to disclose any reasons for your search.
- You may call the person listed on the patient's registration form as nearest relative. You can also check references if they appear on a registration form. Again, you must not let these people know the nature of your search and may only communicate once with a third party.
- You may locate a landlord or a neighbor of the person to see if he or she has a forwarding address (your city's directory can be used to locate people living in the patient's neighborhood).
- Check the phone book for last names similar to the patient's, especially if the person has an unusual last name. You may be able to locate a relative.
- Ask the Department of Motor Vehicles if it has a change of address.

- Call the patient's bank, if you have that information, and ask for a transfer address, if given.
- If the patient had been hospitalized recently, check with the other facilities, agencies, and physicians to see if they have a forwarding address.
- Check with utility companies such as the phone company or the gas and electric company to see if they have a forwarding address.
- Check the patient's record to see if other physicians and laboratories are listed and call them.
- Other sources might include tax records, voter registration records, court records, death and probate records, and credit bureau records.

Estates

When a patient dies, collection of fees is directed to the executor of the estate or the one responsible for overseeing the deceased person's finances. Show courtesy by not sending a statement immediately (within days) of the death. Address the statement to "The Estate of Jane Doe" at the last known address. If you are unsure how to do this type of collection, refer the matter to your office's attorney.

SUMMARY

The success of a medical facility may depend on accurate, effective billing and collection practices. Communication skills are called upon, as well as tact and patience, when listening to the problems of a client with a delinquent payment.

Always remember that your facility may operate solely on the revenue gained from patient payments. You play a very important role in seeing that the medical facility continues to operate successfully. This cannot happen if bills are not paid and collection methods are not effective. This is an important responsibility that the medical clerical worker must take very seriously.

LEARNING ACTIVITIES

1. Jeanine Fogerty works as a medical clerical worker in Dr. Castle's outpatient surgery clinic. She must write two collection letters. Using the "stationery" in Appendix B, write two collection letters to two different patients whose accounts are at least ninety days overdue.

2. Using the following information, fill out the patient statement in Appendix B.

List of services for: PAMELA MATHEWS
2965 Shasta Way
Santa Clara, CA 95062

7/29	Outpatient surgery	$555.00
8/15	Paid on account	55.00
8/15	Office visit	35.00
9/1	Paid on account	100.00
9/15	Laboratory	35.00
10/1	Paid on account	155.00
10/15	Office visit	35.00
11/1	Physical exam	100.00
11/1	Paid on account	100.00

3. Fill out a transaction record on Ms. Mathews, using the form in Appendix B. The class should make up all pertinent information needed on the superbill for Ms. Mathews.

4. What is the difference between internal billing and external billing in the medical office?

5. Name four methods of bill collection.

6. What is a transaction record?

7. A patient pays you for an office visit at the time the treatment is given. Name this bill collection method.

8. In the medical field, who might be a recipient of *professional courtesy?*

9. Name four methods frequently used to obtain a payment from a patient who has not paid his or her bill.

10. If you call a patient about a bill after 9 P.M., what federal law are you violating?

11. If your medical office decides to take a patient to small claims court, what is the maximum amount your office can collect?

12. What might be a medical clerical worker's role in a courtroom situation if a physician takes a patient to small claims court?

13. If a patient informs your office that he or she has declared bankruptcy, what can you do to recover any overdue monies from the patient?

14. Name three laws that are considered credit laws.

15. Name six signs you might observe in a patient that may suggest that the physician will not receive payment.

CHAPTER 16

Daily Financial Responsibilities: Banking Procedures

VOCABULARY

Automated teller machine (ATM) A machine installed on the outside of a bank or many other facilities that allows depositors to automatically deposit and withdraw funds 24 hours a day.

Bank statement A periodic list of transactions of a checking account.

Check An order for a bank to pay against an existing checking account.

Checking account An account against which checks can be written, often with no interest being paid.

Deposit slip A form used to itemize deposits made to a bank.

Endorsement A signature on the back of a check, indicating that all rights in the check are transferred to another party.

Money market account A savings account that requires a minimum balance, can have check writing privileges, and draws interest at money market rates.

Passbook account A savings account accumulating interest at the lowest prevailing rate.

Payee A person or institution named on a check who will receive the amount shown on the check, also known as the bearer.

Payor The person who signs a check, ordering a bank to pay funds from an account; also called *maker*.

Postdated check A check dated in the future, not valid until the date notated on the check.

Power of attorney A legal document allowing a medical clerical worker to have limited check-signing authorization.

Safe deposit box A box available at many financial institutions, used for the storage of legal documents and securities.

Savings account Money placed in a financial institution for future use, gaining interest.

Service charge A charge by the bank for maintaining accounts and processing transactions.

Third party A check made out to a patient from an unknown party.

OBJECTIVES

After completing this chapter, the student is responsible for performing the following objectives:

- Discuss the most common types of bank accounts that a medical clerical worker may use.
- List different types of checks that you may use and receive in a health care facility.
- Explain how to fill out a check properly.
- Identify ways to help ensure that a check you receive from a patient is valid.
- Discuss how to make a bank deposit.
- Reconcile a bank statement.
- List items that might be put in a safe deposit box.

*I*NTRODUCTION

The medical clerical worker's job often includes involvement with large volumes of financial transactions, such as cash, checks, and credit cards. You must understand the fundamentals of banking procedures and terms associated with banking.

Banks receive deposits for checking and saving accounts, handle trust funds, loan money, and provide many other services. Many banking services are duplicated by credit unions, savings and loan associations, and similar institutions. Your employer may use the financial services of these institutions as well.

Banking involves confidential information that you must not reveal. You are also in a position of trust, handling large sums of money. This is a very important and responsible role for the medical clerical worker.

*B*ANK ACCOUNTS

The most common types of bank accounts are the **checking account** and the **savings account.** You may be responsible for placing monies in both types of accounts.

Checking Accounts

A checking account is a bank account against which checks can be written. A majority of payments that you will receive as a medical clerical worker are by **check.**

Today, there are many varieties of checking accounts, including some that pay interest as in a savings account. It may be your responsibility to determine which kind of checking account offered in your community will best suit your medical facility.

Savings Accounts

When money is not needed to pay expenses, it can be deposited into a savings account. Savings accounts earn interest on the amount deposited.

Like checking accounts, there are many different kinds of savings accounts. The simple **passbook account** draws interest at the lowest rate offered by the financial institution, usually requires no minimum balance to maintain, and has no check-writing options.

Other savings accounts include **money market accounts,** which require a minimum balance, usually over $1,000. These accounts give the depositor the option of writing a prearranged amount of checks per month, usually three. Interest is paid at money market rates.

In most types of accounts, the bank may charge a **service charge,** which is a fee for bookkeeping services. In some accounts, the service charge is based on how many services are used.

Cecks

A check is defined as a draft that a bank must pay to a person named, or to the bearer of the check. In addition to personal checks, there are many different types of checks that you may encounter as a medical clerical worker.

Types of Checks

You should be familiar with the following types of checks:

- *Cashier's check.* This is a bank's check drawn against itself and signed by a bank official. A cashier's check is obtained by giving a bank cashier cash or a check for the amount of the cashier's check. Some banks charge a fee for this type of service. Some customers use this type of check when they have a savings account but not a checking account.
- *Certified check.* This is a customer's own check, with CERTIFIED or ACCEPTED written across the face of the check. The date of the transaction and a bank official's signature are also on the check. The bank will guarantee that this certified check is good, as the amount of the check is deducted from the customer's account at the time the certified check is issued.
- *Money order.* Money orders are sold by banks, certain stores, money order companies, and the United States Postal Service. Domestic and international money orders are available.
- *Bank draft.* This is a check that is a written order to pay funds drawn by a bank on its account at another bank.
- *Traveler's check.* This is a check designed for travelers, for situations where personal checks would not be accepted. They usually come in denominations of $10, $20, $50, and $100, and occasionally in larger amounts. Two signatures are required on a traveler's check, one at the time of purchase and the other when the check is used. Banks as well as some travel agencies handle these checks.
- *Limited check.* This is a check that may be limited as to the amount of the check as well as the time during which it can be cashed. This kind of check is often used for payroll or insurance checks.
- *Voucher check.* A voucher check has a detachable form that is used to notate the purpose for which the check is written. The form is taken off before using the check, providing a record for the customer.

■ *Warrant.* This is a check that cannot be cashed but is evidence of a debt due. Governmental agencies will issue such warrants, as do some insurance companies, authorizing the insurance company to pay the claim.

Writing a Checks

Writing checks requires knowledge of proper procedure and attention to detail. You must know the parts of a check in order to always fill in a check completely. Many medical clerical workers type checks, giving the check a professional look. You may also handwrite checks using legible writing and a ballpoint pen.

Before filling out a check, be sure to complete a corresponding *check stub* or *check register,* verifying that both the check and the stub or register have the same number. A stub is connected directly to the check, whereas a register may be separate from the check itself.

Complete the stub or register, noting the date when you write the check, the payee's name, the check amount, and the purpose for which payment is being made. The new balance should then be carried to the next stub (Figure 16.1).

There are many different parts of a check (refer to Figure 16.2).

1. *Personalization.* Most checks contain the name of the company or individual, along with an address and a telephone number. Additionally, people sometimes include their driver's license number or Social Security number in this section of a check. Be careful about taking checks that are not preprinted with a name and address. Check with your employer to see if he or she will allow you to accept such checks.

2. *Check number.* This number serves as a method to keep a record of a check, for both the bearer and the maker of the check.

3. *ABA number.* This is a part of a coding system, originated by the American Bankers Association. It always appears in the upper right area of a check.

$$\frac{52\text{-}44}{124}$$

The code number is a fraction. The top part of the fraction contains the numbers 1 to 49, a code for cities in which a Federal Reserve bank is located. The numbers from 50 to 99 refer to states or territories. After the hyphen, the number corresponds to the bank from which the check originates. The bottom part of the fraction includes the number of the Federal Reserve District where the bank is located.

4. *Date.* The check is dated on the day it is written. Do not **postdate checks.**

5. *Payee.* This space is preceded by the words PAY TO THE ORDER OF and is where the name of the **payee** is placed. Always make the effort to enter

FIGURE 16.1 Check with attached check stub.

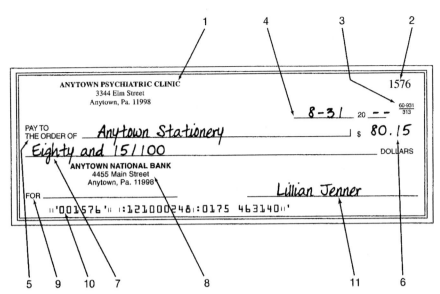

FIGURE 16.2 Check with parts labeled.

the name of the payee correctly. Do not use abbreviations unless instructed. Begin writing at the extreme left edge of the space, following the name with dashes if there is space left. Omit personal titles from the payee space. If the payee is receiving a check on behalf of an organization, enter the payee's name and then the office held in the organization. Example:

Grace Jones, President

6. *Amount in figures.* This space is used to put the amount of the check in numbers. Be sure to double-check the amount before entering it in this space.

7. *Amount spelled out.* Start writing in the extreme left of the space, making sure that there is no chance for the amount to be criminally altered. The dollar amount is written out, and the cents are notated in a fraction amount close to the dollars figure. Examples: Fifty-Five and 66/100, One Hundred Twenty-Five and No Cents, Twenty-Five Dollars Only (with no cents), Sixty Cents Only (when amounts are less than $1.00).

8. *Drawee.* This is located in the lower lefthand corner of a check, giving the name and address of the bank where the account is located.

9. *Memo.* This often appears on checks to allow the payor to notate the nature of the check expenditure.

10. *MICR* (magnetic ink character recognition). This includes numbers and characters printed in magnetic ink representing a machine language. A high-speed machine reads the characters, sorts the checks, and performs bookkeeping procedures. The amount of the check can also be added in magnetic ink just below the signature on the check.

11. *Payor.* The **payor** is also called the *maker.* The payor's signature should be written carefully in a legible form. As a medical clerical worker, you may be able to fill out all parts of the check but this area. When writing checks, you can prepare the checks with everything but a signature, and then take them to your employer for signing. In some facilities, you may be able to sign checks. This is accomplished by filing a **power of attorney** at your employer's bank. This legal document gives you limited ability to sign checks for your employer.

Correcting Mistakes on Checks

Do not cross out, erase, or change parts of a check. The bank can refuse such a check, and you should not accept an altered check from a patient. If a mistake is made, write the word VOID on the check, and file it with canceled checks. Do not throw it away, as it must be available for auditing procedures.

"Cash" Checks

It is not a good idea to write a check payable to "CASH" unless the check will be cashed at the time it is written. These checks are easily cashed without identification.

Overdrawn Accounts

Banks will not honor checks when there is not enough money in an account to cover the check. The bank will return the check with "Unpaid—Lack of Sufficient Funds" written on it. If a depositor is known at the bank, the bank may honor the check and tell the depositor the problem. Many depositors have accounts connected to a credit card, and any overdraws are charged automatically to the depositor's credit card.

Stop Payment

A depositor may wish to stop payment of a check recently written. This is usually done with lost checks or if there is a disagreement about a payment or a purchase. If you as a medical clerical worker write a check that is lost in the mail, a stop payment order should be made, making sure the check has not been presented for payment. The amount of the check is then added to the checkbook balance.

ACCEPTING PAYMENT FROM PATIENTS

Accepting checks requires good judgment on the part of the medical clerical worker. There are special precautions to be taken to make sure that the check you are receiving is good. It can be very awkward to explain to your employer that you accepted an incomplete or incorrectly filled out check. The following list summarizes precautions for the medical clerical worker to take.

- Make sure that a check has the correct information, including the date, amount, payor, and payee.
- If a check has been corrected, do *not* accept it.
- Ask for identification from the person presenting the check if you are not familiar with the patient. Compare signatures on the identification and on the offered check. Many employers consider a driver's license, a check guarantee card, and a major credit card to be acceptable identification. Some employers require that you ask for one, and some may want at least two identifications shown.
- Unless your employer authorizes it, do not accept **third-party** checks; for example, if a patient presents you with a check made out to the patient by an unknown party.
- It is not a good idea to accept out-of-town, payroll, or government checks unless you know the presenter well.
- *Do not* accept a check that has written on it PAYMENT IN FULL unless the check does pay the amount due in full.

■ Try not to accept checks made out for more than the amount of the service. If the check is bad, your office will suffer losses greater than the account balance due.

Endorsement of Checks

An **endorsement** is put on the back of a check or money order. An endorsement means that all rights in the check are transferred to another party. Endorsements must be made in ink, pen, or rubber stamp. The endorsement should be on the left, or perforated, end.

Endorsements are needed to make sure that the payee receives payment. The payee must endorse the back of a check exactly as stated in the PAY TO THE ORDER OF space (Figure 16.3). If a check is written incorrectly, the check is to be endorsed twice, once as the incorrect way appearing on the check, and then with the correct name. Checks written out to CASH require no endorsement.

There are different types of endorsements that the medical clerical worker may encounter.

■ *Blank.* The payee signs only his or her name. This should be used only when the check will be cashed immediately.

■ *Restrictive.* An example of a restrictive endorsement is found in Figure 16.4. The medical clerical worker may very well use this endorsement when preparing checks for deposit to an employer's checking account.

■ *Special.* This endorsement is used when the payee signs a check over to another party. Example: Kathy Marshall receives a check and endorses it to a physician. The endorsement reads:

PAY TO THE ORDER OF
DONALD E. CASTLE, M.D.
Kathy Marshall

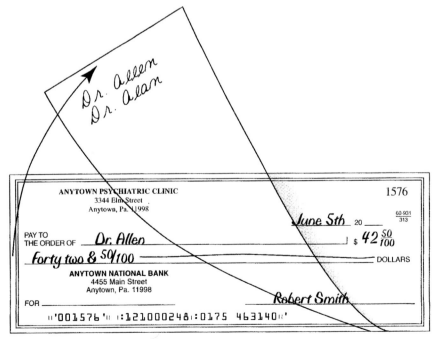

FIGURE 16.3 Corrected endorsement

FIGURE 16.4 Restrictive endorsement.

Credit Cards

Accepting credit card payment requires you, as a medical clerical worker, to be very careful to check several things:

- Check the signature on the credit card against the credit signature on the card slip.
- Be sure the name on the credit card is the same as the bearer's name.
- Check the expiration date of the card.
- If your employer has an automatic credit card machine, you may be required to enter the number of the credit card to make sure that the card is not over the patient's limit of expenditure.
- If your employer does not have a verification machine, you may be required to look up the credit card number in a listing of bad credit card numbers. Many employers ask you not to check credit cards of established customers.
- Make sure that the information is clear on the credit card charge slip and that you give the patient the proper receipt. There are often three parts to a charge slip, with the individual copies clearly marked as to where they should go.
- Some banks provide employers with machines that automatically draw funds from a patient's account by the use of a credit card.

Real-Life Scenario

Janice is a new medical clerical worker at an orthopedic clinic. She is not familiar with the patients. On her second day, a patient named Ben (37 years old) gives Janice a credit card to pay for his visit. Ben seems nervous and will not look at Janice directly. The name on the credit card has the same last name as Ben but a different first name. Ben's signature does not look like the signature on the credit card as well. Janice starts to question Ben about the name and signature on the card. Ben becomes angry immediately.

What does Janice do?

$\mathcal{B}$ANK DEPOSITS

A very important duty of a medical clerical worker includes the daily depositing of checks for your health care facility. Deposits should be made *immediately* to avoid losing checks or having them stolen. Delays may cause the checks to be returned for insufficient funds, or the check may eventually have a stop payment on it. It is also a courtesy to the patient to cash checks promptly, and insurance checks often have a restricted period for cashing.

Deposit Slips

A **deposit slip** is prepared by listing the cash and all checks involved in the deposit. The slip contains the name and address of your employer and the date of the deposit, as well as the checking account number. You should make a copy of the deposit slip for your place of business.

Figure 16.5 shows the proper form for filling out deposit slips. Notice that the listing of checks has the top fraction of the ABA numbers written next to the names of the check payors. The checks are arranged on the slip in alphabetical order, with all checks properly endorsed.

DEPOSIT TICKET

PLEASE BE SURE THAT ALL ITEMS ARE PROPERLY ENDORSED. LIST EACH CHECK SEPARATELY.

	DOLLARS	CENTS
CURRENCY	65	00
COIN	4	50
CHECKS (PROPERLY ENDORSED) LIST EACH SEPARATELY		
1 Clark 90-125	100	00
2 Davies 90-121	300	00
3 Fowler 90-125	52	00
4 Mann 90-422	61	00
5 Scott 90-4117	100	00
6		
7		
8		
9		
10		
11		
12		
13		
14		
15		
16		
17		
18		
19		
20		
21		
22		
23		
24		
25		
26		
27		
28		
TOTAL	682	50

PLEASE ENTER THE TOTAL AMOUNT OF DEPOSIT ON THE OTHER SIDE OF THIS TICKET

CASH COUNT — FOR OFFICE USE ONLY		
X 100		
X 50		
X 20		
X 10		
X 5		
X 2		
X 1		
TOTAL	$	

FIGURE 16.5 Completed deposit slip.

The total of the deposit is immediately entered into the checkbook, and the checks are clipped together or put in bank wrappers. Coins, currency, and checks are put in a large bank envelope or bag.

There are various ways to make deposits:

- *Banking by mail.* Banks provide special mail deposit slips and envelopes. Cash should never be sent in the mail, unless by registered mail. The bank will send a deposit receipt in the mail.
- *After-hours deposit.* A depositor may use the after-hours deposit service at the bank. There is a slot available on the outside of the bank. The bank processes all deposits through the after-hours deposit the following morning.
- *ATM.* The **automated teller machine (ATM)** is accessible at all times. It is installed in the outer wall of the bank for deposits and withdrawals as well. Additional terminals are placed in airports, shopping centers, grocery stores, and other areas. Depositors are given special access codes and a special banking card to use with the ATM.

*B*ANK STATEMENTS

At prearranged intervals, usually monthly, **bank statements** are sent to depositors showing the status of the depositor's account on a given date (Figures 16.6a and b).

The bank statement lists the date and amount of deposits and withdrawals made from the account. The date is the time the check is presented for payment, not when it is written. The statement should be reconciled with the checkbook stubs or register immediately. You may receive canceled checks, or you may have an account where checks are available upon demand.

Reconciling the bank statement should be done as soon as possible after its arrival in the mail. The balances in the checkbook and the bank statement will be different, because some checks have not yet appeared on the bank statement. The reconciliation is therefore necessary. Generally, the procedure format is as shown in Figure 16.7.

If the balances agree, you are finished. If they disagree, determine the amount of the disagreement. This is a clue to locating the error. The most common mistakes are as follows:

- Forgetting to include an outstanding check
- Incorrect math
- Failure to record deposits, or recording twice
- Figures carried forward incorrectly
- Failure to write down a check
- Transposition of a figure

*C*OMPUTERIZED BANKING

Banking in the medical facility includes making deposits, transferring funds between accounts, writing checks, and reconciling bank statements. Most if not all of these tasks can be done through computerized banking on the Internet. Many banks (especially the larger ones) provide extensive support to offices of all sizes.

As an example, funds can be transferred between accounts by logging on to your bank's Internet site. After first providing a proper password to ensure security, you then follow simple on-screen procedures to transfer money or make online pay-

```
PHYSICIAN'S BANK
STATEMENT


Dr. Darryl A. Marshall
1000 First Street
Any Town, USA 09090
```

Page 1 of 1	This statement covers 8-1-0- through 8-31-0-

Account Number
0166-466166

Summary

Previous Balance	2,504.29
Deposits	7,682.78
Withdrawals	8,351.14
New Balance	**2,013.54**

Checks and Withdrawals

CHECK	PAID	AMOUNT	CHECK	PAID	AMOUNT
253	8/1	56.50	273	8/15	643.33
254	8/1	9.97	274	8/16	351.54
255	8/2	275.96	275	8/16	27.80
256	8/3	12.00	276	8/16	229.20
260*	8/3	325.00	277	8/17	25.00
262*	8/4	128.95	278	8/18	39.45
263	8/5	50.00	279	8/18	399.70
264	8/6	50.00	280	8/18	399.70
265	8/7	250.00	281	8/18	9.00
266	8/8	200.00	282	8/18	275.96
267	8/9	76.99	283	8/19	2030.07
268	8/10	11.00	284	8/20	300.00
269	8/11	29.73	285	8/22	193.56
270	8/11	15.00	286	8/22	19.04
271	8/14	176.73	287	8/28	24.27
272	8/15	18.14	288	8/30	55.89

		PAID	AMOUNT
Transfer to checking	1175262955	8/1	325.00
Installment Loan Pmt	3062242623	8/1	618.67
Transmatic to S&L	5655420261	8/15	1084.00
Service Fee		8/30	7.50

Deposits

	PAID	AMOUNT
Customer Deposit	8/4	2151.13
Customer Deposit	8/11	1413.40
Customer Deposit	8/19	2230.58
Customer Deposit	8/28	2067.67

FIGURE 16.6a Front of a bank statement.

ments. Making an online payment means that you do not have to write a check for a service. Your bank will automatically take money from your account and transfer it electronically (or by check) to the person or company you wish to pay.

Reconciling bank statements can also be done at any time through your bank's Internet site. Again, following simple on-screen directions, you can access your account with up-to-date information on all activity of your account.

Modern security techniques make this process quite safe. However, some employers may be initially resistant to computerized banking because of security fears.

SAFE DEPOSIT BOXES

Most banks and savings and loan institutions have **safe deposit boxes** available to their customers. These boxes are used to store valuable papers and personal property. Many sizes are often available.

THIS WORKSHEET IS PROVIDED TO HELP YOU BALANCE YOUR ACCOUNT

1. Go through your register and mark each check, withdrawal, Express Stop® transaction, payment, deposit or other credit listed on this statement. Be sure that your register shows any interest paid into your account, and any service charges, automatic payments or Express Transfers withdrawn from your account during this statement period.
2. Using the chart below, list any outstanding checks, Express Stop withdrawals, payments or any other withdrawals (including any from previous months) which are listed in your register but are not shown on this statement.
3. Balance your account by filling in the spaces below.

ITEMS OUTSTANDING	
NUMBER	AMOUNT

ENTER
The NEW BALANCE shown on this statement........................... $_____

ADD
Any deposits listed in your $_____
register or transfers into your $_____
account which are not shown on $_____
this statement.   + $_____

TOTAL .... + $_____

CALCULATE THE SUBTOTAL..................... $_____

SUBTRACT
The total outstanding checks and withdrawals from the chart at left................................. - $_____

CALCULATE THE ENDING BALANCE
This amount should be the same as the current balance shown in your check register .... $_____

FIGURE 16.6b Back of a bank statement.

Bank Statement Balance $_____
    Less oustanding checks   _____
    Plus deposits not shown   _____
Corrected bank statement balance _____
Checkbook balance   _____
    Less bank charges   _____
Corrected Checkbook Balance_____

FIGURE 16.7 Account reconciliation format.

The safe deposit box is protected by a two-key system. The depositor has one key and the bank has the other key. Access is available only to a person or persons listed on a signature card when the box is procured. A bank attendant opens one lock and the depositor opens the other lock on the box.

Specific items to put in a health facility's safe deposit box might include deeds of trust, inventories, special contracts, and updated computer disks with patient information in case of theft or disaster in the office.

SUMMARY

Performing banking duties will require many of the attributes listed in earlier chapters for other medical clerical tasks. You must have a conscientious attitude and pay special attention to detail.

Financial responsibilities put the medical clerical worker in a position of a great deal of trust. You must perform your duties with professionalism, letting your employer know that he or she has reason to trust you with such important tasks.

LEARNING ACTIVITIES

1. Lillian Jenner works in a small psychiatric hospital as a medical clerical worker in the billing department. One of her duties involves paying some bills that the department has incurred. Lillian has a power of attorney that allows her to sign checks that she writes on the job. Utilizing the blank forms in Appendix B, write three checks, using the following information.
   (a) To Beitler Stationery Company, $45.87 for hospital letterhead stationery.
   (b) To Anders Computer Supply Corporation, $105.03 for computer supplies, including continuous-form paper and printer ribbons.
   (c) To Capitol City Office Equipment, $144.55 for a Sharp calculator, model 4455.

2. Lillian has collected ten checks and some currency throughout the day. She must fill out a deposit slip for a bank deposit. A sample deposit slip is given in Appendix B. Fill out a deposit slip using the following information:

John Hammond	90–144	$500.00
Larry Bowman	90–324	233.65
Bonnie Jacobs	90–454	444.50
Diane Chavez	90–234	190.00
Dixie Chambers	90–234	233.45
Bill Gilbert	90–214	320.00
Lillian Silvers	90–144	432.88
John Chew	90–324	500.00
Harriet Bonner	90–011	789.00
Louis Beitler	90–123	49.50
Currency		351.00
Coin		15.45

3. What is the difference between a savings account and a checking account?

4. Define the following terms:
   (a) Money market account
   (b) Passbook account
   (c) Service charge

5. List five types of checks that you may encounter as a medical clerical worker.

6. Identify the following terms:
   (a) ABA number
   (b) Postdated check
   (c) Payee
   (d) Maker
   (e) Power of attorney

7. Name five things to check when you accept a check from a patient.

8. Why is a check endorsement necessary?

9. What is the difference between a blank endorsement and a restricted endorsement?

10. List three items in a health facility that might be placed in a safe deposit box.

CHAPTER 17

Office Maintenance and Management

Environmental Protection Agency	In the medical field, a governmental agency that outlines procedures and products that help avoid accidents and hazardous conditions to both the patient and the medical staff.
Inventory	A list of all supplies and equipment on hand in a medical facility, usually updated once a year.
Office procedure manual	A written guide to office procedures and routines.
Physicians' Desk Reference (PDR)	A guide to pharmaceutical drugs.
Preventive maintenance	A maintenance contract purchased on equipment, where a service person comes into the facility on a regular basis to check the equipment, making minor adjustments and repairs. This should prevent most major breakdowns.

OBJECTIVES

After completing this chapter, the student is responsible for performing the following objectives:

- Identify factors in a general office environment that can detract from or add to making the facility a pleasant environment.
- Discuss why all areas of a medical facility should be well maintained.
- State why proper disposal of hazardous waste is so important.
- Identify the need for an equipment maintenance program in the medical office or facility.
- Discuss why supply inventory and ordering systems are necessary.
- Explain security measures that can help prevent theft.
- List duties a medical clerical worker might have in relation to drug storage.
- Identify several qualities of a successful office manager, as well as various duties of management personnel in a medical facility.
- Discuss the importance of an office procedure manual.

*I*NTRODUCTION

Care for the physical environment of the health care facility is a very important job of the medical clerical worker. A facility that is well supplied, with adequate lighting, and at a pleasing constant temperature is a much nicer place for the employees to work. The patients also respond positively to a pleasing, well-organized environment (see Chapter 7).

As you progress in your career as a medical clerical worker, you may be given an opportunity to manage a department in a health care facility or perhaps a medical office. If you show leadership qualities in your work and a commitment to increasing productivity, you may find yourself in a management position early in your career. There are many qualities that are essential for becoming an efficient manager who can handle such duties successfully.

A PLEASING FACILITY ENVIRONMENT

Maintaining a comfortable environment in a medical facility is another task often delegated to the medical clerical worker. You should be sensitive not only to the specific housekeeping details of the medical facility but also to other factors that contribute to making staff and clients feel comfortable in the facility.

Lighting

You will require excellent lighting by which to perform your medical clerical tasks. Additionally, other health care workers require effective lighting when dealing directly with patients. Lighting is usually uniform when achieved with fluorescent lights, which do not give off heat. Lamps need to be positioned properly in the reception room. Remember to place them at reading level, where the light will not shine into the eyes of the reader or other clients.

Sound

Part of an effective program to ensure patient privacy is adequate soundproofing of walls to prevent confidences between patient and medical staff from being overheard. If you can hear conversations through walls, please let your employer know. Perhaps the walls can be made more soundproof. Be sensitive to keeping your voice at a lower pitch when discussing private matters with patients.

Flooring

Usually, carpeting is the floor covering used in reception room and office areas. In treatment and examining rooms, washable flooring is used for hygiene. Be careful not to have a slippery wax coating on the washable flooring so that patients do not slip. In addition, rugs that are not tacked down are not recommended because of the possibility of patients' tripping.

Temperature

Seventy degrees is the optimum temperature at which to keep the reception room. If you have a number of elderly patients, you may want to keep the temperature a little higher. Some offices allow you to keep the staff working rooms at 68 degrees, where many people feel more comfortable.

Air should be kept circulating, either by an air-conditioning system or by open windows. Be careful about drafts, as many patients are very intolerant of drafts.

F ACILITY CLEANING AND MAINTENANCE

You will not be responsible for the heavy-duty cleaning and maintenance of the different parts of the medical office, which include the reception area, administrative area (office), clinical areas (laboratory, examination and treatment rooms, and consultation room), bathrooms, and storage areas. Most facilities use a janitorial service that might clean on weekends or evenings when patients are not present. However, you may be responsible for the day-to-day attention to maintaining a neat environment free of hazards to patients.

The **Environmental Protection Agency** recommends certain products, such as floor wax that does not create a slippery surface, for use in the medical care facility.

Reception Areas

As discussed thoroughly in Chapter 7, you may be responsible for picking up toys, magazines, and other minor housekeeping duties that keep the reception area tidy and pleasant.

Administration or Office Areas

You may be responsible for your reception desk, telephone, various business machines as discussed in Chapter 12, and records storage. Care should be to keep desks neat, making sure that cords are not stretched across a traffic area. Personal items should be kept in a drawer or in a personal locker provided by your employer. Records should be kept out of sight to assure privacy. An organized office area gives the client the immediate impression that you are in control and will be efficient about taking care of his or her needs.

Treatment and Examination Rooms

Nothing is more upsetting to a nervous patient than to be ushered into a treatment room that is in disarray from the last patient. Specimens collected from a previous patient should have been properly labeled and taken to a separate collection area, avoiding any mix-up with the next patient's specimens.

"Spotless" should be the description of the treatment rooms, with cabinets and drawers amply supplied with necessary equipment. All countertops and any sinks should be clean. All soiled linen, towels, and tissues should be out of sight, and fresh linens should be ready for the patient. The examining table should have fresh paper or linen on it.

It is recommended that treatment and examining rooms be kept at a temperature of 74 degrees, due to the fact that patients generally disrobe and put on a gown.

Laboratory

Of course, not all facilities have their own laboratory, but many clinics and doctors' offices do. The size of this area as well as the services offered vary dramatically in facilities. Generally, the laboratory space will be small and will need to be kept well organized and neat. Asepsis is very important here, and care must be taken to dispose of all specimens properly, with the idea of prevention of infection (especially hepatitis and AIDS) constantly on your mind. Ventilation is very important, and all surfaces should be cleaned frequently.

Specimens brought to the laboratory should always be labeled properly according to your employer's standards. Specimens usually include the patient's name, account or hospital number, date of the specimen drawn, and the patient's sex and age. This information may vary from facility to facility.

Bathrooms

Most medical facilities provide separate bathrooms for patients and staff. Every member of the staff should be instructed to leave the staff bathroom clean. The medical clerical worker may be asked to check the patient bathroom frequently to make sure that it is clean and that all supplies are in order.

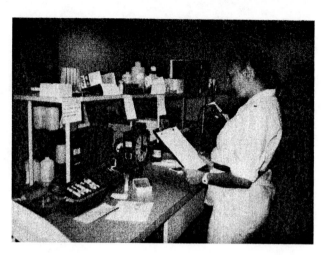

Storage Rooms

Because medical facilities are sometimes short on space, storage rooms are often not as large as they could be. Organization is absolutely essential for the storing of office supplies, medical supplies, cleaning equipment, staff lockers, and so on. You may be asked to obtain supplies quickly, and this is greatly facilitated by an organized system of storing items.

Periodic Maintenance

Maintenance services may carry out certain cleaning tasks that must be performed periodically. These include replacing light bulbs, cleaning out refrigerators, reorganizing cabinets and drawers, and watering plants. The facility staff generally has a plan for assigning such infrequent tasks. Be sure that you are clear on what is assigned to you, following through when the task is assigned.

$\mathcal{H}$AZARDOUS WASTE MANAGEMENT

In 1984, the *Occupational Safety and Health Administration* (OSHA—see Chapter 4 of this textbook) issued safety standards to handle sterilization in the medical office. More recently, emphasis has been placed not only on safety in the office but also in disposing of hazardous waste materials. Many states have laws to treat and dispose of waste from medical facilities.

Although the medical clerical worker may be less involved in handling medical wastes than the back office medical assistant, it is important that the medical clerical worker know the routine for disposing of hazardous medical wastes in the facility. Examples of hazardous waste products that need special attention when discarding are:

- Needles and scalpel blades
- Glass products
- Blood products
- Patient specimens such as urine, sputum, body fluids, and stool

There are many waste items generated as a result of routine examinations and procedures. The first step in handling such items is to wear personal protective clothing when dealing with these materials. Latex gloves, gowns, goggles, mouth guards, and other protective clothing are often used when handling such items. If a health care worker or patient is allergic to latex, other types of gloves are available. It is also *mandatory* to use heavy-duty bags and sharps containers that are leakproof, sturdy, and clearly marked as *biohazardous* items. None of these items should ever appear in a wastebasket used primarily for paper. Waste should also never be stored in the front office for pickup.

Some facilities may treat their waste on-site. More frequently, waste is hauled away and handled by a registered hauler. This requires careful attention to preparing the waste for the hauler to take off the premises. The medical clerical worker should be sensitive to the special waste handling needs of a particular employer and follow all precautions to keep the environment safe for all who work and visit the facilities.

$\mathscr{M}$AINTENANCE OF EQUIPMENT

In a small facility, it may be your job to keep a service file folder for every piece of equipment in the facility, whether it be office equipment or medical equipment. These files should include maintenance instructions for such equipment, as well as operating instructions, service agreements, and invoices for repairs.

Experienced and qualified repair persons will probably handle repairs on expensive equipment. Periodic servicing agreements are purchased by many offices to avoid costly breakdowns by adhering to a **preventive maintenance** schedule. The medical clerical worker may be responsible for renewing service contracts on a yearly basis. Records should be kept in a central location, with each service contract coded as to when it is due to expire.

You should expect prompt and efficient service. If a piece of equipment is not fixed promptly, the office can lose revenue. The medical clerical worker should be ready to recommend another repair service if delays are frequent. The medical clerical worker should also keep a list of all equipment and their repair costs. From such information it may become apparent that a piece of equipment should be replaced.

Real-Life Scenario

One of your responsibilities as a medical clerical worker in Dr. Jacob's office is to help Jessica, the clinical medical assistant in the office, to check the facilities at night before closing the office. You have been told to keep an eye out for any waste products that might be considered hazardous, such as materials with blood or other body fluids on them, used needles, gauze, wipes, aprons, and anything else that might been contaminated with body fluids. These types of products must be put in hazardous waste containers.

You have noticed in the past that Jessica likes to leave right on time and is often rather careless in her cleanup at night. You have seen her throw used gauze into the regular wastebasket a number of times. You mention it to her, and she says that it's only a tiny square. Besides, she then covers it up with paper so no one will see it.

What should you do? You want to keep a good working relationship with Jessica.

An organized approach to the maintenance of costly equipment prevents the medical office from losing excessive revenue from the temporary loss of critical equipment.

SUPPLY AND EQUIPMENT INVENTORY

A medical facility has a variety of supplies that need to be on a yearly **inventory** record. Inventories contain valuable information for preparing income taxes. Inventories are also valuable when the medical facility has a burglary or suffers loss from other causes, such as fire, earthquake, or water damage.

Once a year, an inventory should be taken. An inventory is a listing of all equipment and supplies found in the medical facility. All *capital purchases* should be listed, such as furniture, medical equipment and instruments, laboratory equipment, office machinery, and large decor items such as wall paintings. An inventory also includes smaller, less costly items that are considered to have a short life: such items as syringes and thermometers. Also on an inventory are lists of drugs (see the Drug Storage section) and office supplies.

ORDERING SUPPLIES

An established method to keep a medical facility from running out of supplies is mandatory. As a medical clerical worker, you will be responsible for ordering office supplies, and sometimes medical supplies as well.

Ordering System

There should be an established routine for ordering supplies. There are basically three types of supplies for a medical facility:

- *Office supplies.* These include stationery, accounting supplies, desk items, and appointment cards and books.
- *Medical supplies.* These include gowns, drapes, towels, lubricants, tongue blades, syringes and needles, and bandages. Also included here are drugs.
- *General items.* These include soap and towels for the bathrooms, tissue, cleaning supplies, and coffee for employees.

Forms should be kept for every category of supplies, noting diminishing supplies so that you can decide when to reorder. Salespersons come by offices quite often and will make your ordering much easier. Mail-order houses also allow you to make orders over the phone.

You may be responsible for all decisions about ordering, and you will have to pay attention to detail in order to make an economical decision for your employer. You will have to be aware of cost breaks for ordering in large quantities and know the supplies that will provide quality as well as low prices. If your employer or other staff members do not like a product that you have ordered, you must note that in your records to avoid reordering that item. You may be held accountable for your yearly expenditures and should keep detailed records of your ordering costs.

You should establish credit with several suppliers with good reputations. Change suppliers only with good reason, as you may find that you are rewarded by suppliers that view your office as a loyal customer. Supplies may arrive in a more timely fashion, and price breaks may be extended more often to frequent customers.

ANYTOWN URGENT CARE CLINIC
234 SUNVALLEY MALL ROAD
ANYTOWN, CA 90000

DATE SUBMITTED: ___8-8-0___

REQUISITION

DATE NEEDED: ____ASAP____

	VENDOR		SHIP TO
COMPANY:	THOMAS OLIVER STATIONERY	SITE/LOCATION:	ANYTOWN URGENT CARE CLINIC
ADDRESS:	4120 First Street	ADDRESS:	234 Sunvalley Mall Road
CITY:	Sarasota	CITY:	Anytown
STATE/ZIP:	Florida 32491	STATE/ZIP:	California 90000
ATTN:	Steve Bell, Factory Rep.	ATTN:	Jan Adam, Office Manager

***** **FOR OFFICE USE ONLY** *****

ASN # ___438___   APPROVED BY _Julia Kravetz, M.D_

PLEASE RETAIN COPY FOR OFFICE RECORDS

QUANTITY ORDERED	DESCRIPTION	UNIT PRICE	PER	TOTAL COST
3 PK.	Letterhead Stationery	$51.92		$155.76
4 PK.	Inventory Forms	5.20		20.80
2	Desk Blotters	10.50		21.00
		SUN TOTAL		$197.56
		TAX		
		SHIPPING		15.50
		TOTAL		$213.06

FIGURE 17.1 Filled-out requisition form.

When you order, pay attention to detail when filling out a requisition (Figure 17.1). Make sure that you are clear on what size, color, or type of item is being ordered. Often, there is seemingly very little difference in the items to you, but the health care workers or physician may care very much whether a needle received is a 19-gauge needle rather than the 22-gauge needle he or she ordered.

Purchase Orders

Many businesses have *purchase orders* to track what supplies have been ordered and from what vendors. Purchase order forms are available from office supply companies that are customized for your office. Forms can vary greatly. Some are very simple and have a number, your logo at the top, the vendor's name and address, your shipping address, as well as:

- Quantity ordered
- Item number (especially important for catalog ordering)
- Units
- Description of product
- Unit price
- Total price

Using a purchase order helps to keep track of your order. When a shipment arrives at the office, you can check off the items against your original purchase order form.

Before ordering huge quantities, be sure your storage area can safely handle your order. If an order has to be refrigerated, as is the case with some drugs, do you have the room to handle a large order?

When you receive an order, do not store it until you have checked the contents of the package against your order form. Check for the correct items, as well as sizes and styles. Make sure that the amounts are correct, and note on the requisition that the order is complete. Check the prices on the requisitions and compare them to your order to be sure that you are being charged the proper amount.

Computer Ordering

Many vendors are now set up to have customers order over the Internet. This way of ordering often cuts the time of processing order forms. You might want to explore such possibilities with your office manager and/or employer.

OFFICE SECURITY

The expensive equipment and drugs that are stored in a medical facility can be the target of theft. There are several steps that should be taken by the entire staff of a facility to prevent theft. Some steps include:

- Keep valuables such as purses, beepers, prescription pads, and cash locked in cabinets while working.
- Always put controlled substances in locked cabinets. This is mandated by law.
- Make sure all windows and doors are locked before leaving the facility. Keep a few lights on in the facility and close all window coverings tightly.
- Make sure the outside of your facility is adequately lit.
- Make sure keys to the facility are distributed carefully. Employees whose employment is terminated must hand in keys before departing.
- A burglar alarm should be installed in the facility and used when the office is closed. The local police department can offer valuable suggestions about installing security systems.
- If the neighborhood is unsafe, employees should leave in groups at night.

Drug Storage

The medical clerical worker, especially in clinics or doctors' offices, may be in charge of setting up and/or maintaining an orderly system for the storage of drugs. Inventories must be kept, especially making sure that all drugs are accounted for and that supplies do not run out. Sometimes the medical clerical worker is in charge of contacting a pharmacy or drug salesperson to place an order.

Some small medical offices keep a low inventory and rely on free samples from drug companies. Other offices, such as those not very accessible to a drug supplier, may keep huge inventories. Drug supplies in hospitals may be kept in a locked drug cart.

Different drug suppliers may provide you with their own ordering systems. These salespersons, also called pharmaceutical representatives or detail representatives, can be given access to the drug storage area and stock the drugs themselves. If not, you may be responsible for restocking and checking expiration dates to make sure that your office is not giving out expired medications. If a patient has a drug reaction and notices that the drug has expired, there are potential legal complications.

In addition, the medical clerical worker may be responsible to see that only certain staff members have access to the drug storage area (review Chapter 10 concerning controlled drugs and the need for rigid security). The medical clerical worker must also understand that there are different storage requirements for many drugs. For instance, some drugs must be refrigerated, and others must be kept in a dark, dry cabinet.

There are a number of different ways that drugs can be organized in the storage area. They can be organized by name in an alphabetical system. They can be organized according to the system listed in the **Physicians' Desk Reference** (see Chapter 10) as to their classifications. Categories include antacids, antibiotics, analgesics, and so on.

If, during storage, a label is removed accidentally, the drug in the package should be discarded immediately. Most can be poured down a drain or flushed down the toilet. Drugs should never be left in the trash where unauthorized people can take them. Of course, when drugs are discarded, careful records should be kept of their disposition.

QUALITIES OF AN OFFICE MANAGER

The medical clerical field is growing rapidly, and competent workers with effective leadership skills are in great demand. Studies show that the most satisfied employees are those who see opportunities for advancement in their field. If you cultivate some of the following traits in your work as a medical clerical worker, you may very well be recognized as "manager material."

- Leadership ability
- Organizational skills
- Common sense
- Commitment to fairness
- Eagerness to improve and learn new tasks
- Original ideas
- Flexibility, but firmness in commitment to office policy
- Excellent people skills
- Communication skills
- Sense of humor
- Challenge seeking
- Teaching ability
- Patience
- Interest in detail
- Marketing skills

Office managers and supervisors may be selected from office employees or brought in from the outside. Some employees do not want the extra stress of such a job, but others welcome the challenge of advancement.

There are various workshops designed to help medical clerical workers develop their management skills. The American Association of Medical Assistants or other local health care worker associations and societies have listings of such seminars and workshops.

*D*UTIES OF AN OFFICE MANAGER

It is important for you to have not only a clear idea of your talents in the area of managing personnel, but also an understanding of the scope of managing an office. Some medical clerical workers take on the responsibility without realizing the complexity and scope of the job. This can lead to failure if the new manager later realizes that he or she is not able to perform all the responsibilities assigned.

Personnel Management

Many managers may be very efficient at handling supplies and other physical aspects of management, but may have a great deal of difficulty in handling personnel. Personnel management can include:

- Recruiting new employees
- Hiring
- Firing
- Orientation and training
- Evaluation of performance and salary determination
- Disciplinary action

Recruitment and *hiring* are tasks that require careful study and good judgment. You may not be alone in your assessment, but you are often asked to make the final decision. It may be up to you to screen applicants, ruling out before the interview any applicant who does not have the correct qualifications, demands a salary that the office cannot afford, or cannot work the hours you will require. You must be familiar with the methods of advertising for personnel, as well as schools and agencies in the area that can help you locate good-quality personnel.

When interviewing prospective employees, you must be familiar with federal, state, and local fair employment practice laws. You may cause the medical facility to be sued if you discriminate in the hiring of minorities, women, handicapped persons, older people, and so on. It is important to be aware of the laws that govern fair employment practices.

As will be discussed in Chapter 18, the list of possible questions that a prospective employer might ask are among the questions you must be prepared to ask in an interview. Be sure to be clear and honest in your questions. Stay away from questions that might be illegal under fair employment laws. Such questions might include questioning a woman about her marital status and the ages of her children.

Make a careful note of whether the applicant seems to be a "people person," can listen, can follow directions, is interested in your facility, and is eager to work for you. Also note personal appearance and grooming.

After you finish interviewing the person, you should make notes about the interview, in case you are going to be interviewing several candidates. Don't trust your memory. However, it is best not to take notes during the interview.

Training is a very important part of a manager's job. It is critical for a person who manages people to be able to train personnel using patience and effective communication skills. Never assume that the trainee knows the procedure. Explain slowly, and allow time for questions. Do not get impatient with questions. Consider no question stupid when first asked. Be free with compliments and encouraging words.

Performance evaluation requires the office manager to be able to evaluate an employee fairly. Traditionally, a new employee is on probation for up to three months. A performance review should be given after the probationary period. This review will include a judgment of quality and quantity of work, team spirit, motivation, attendance, and other qualities necessary to be a good medical clerical worker in your facility. It is important that employees know from the start what behavior and performance is expected of them. The employee should be given a job description with expectations for job performance before an employer can give a performance evaluation.

Such evaluations should usually be done on a six-month basis. This is a time for clear communication, including compliments and suggestions for improvement. Being a good listener is important here, as the employee may give you suggestions on how to improve the medical facility environment.

Firing and *disciplinary action* are the most distasteful part of management to many people. It is very important that you document every step of disciplining or firing an employee. Employees must be given fair warning of a problem in their work habits, and that warning must be documented. Some reasons for firing are compelling, such as embezzlement, violation of confidentiality, and breaking laws. But other reasons for dismissal are harder to pinpoint, such as demonstrating a poor attitude, and must be carefully considered, communicated, and documented before the dismissal is completed.

When an employee is chronically late, does not follow directions repeatedly, or has similar common discipline problems, you have the option of suspending the employee for a few days. The employee knows that you mean business, and may change the behavior that causes trouble. Training expenses are significant, and you want to keep trained employees, if possible.

Once an employee clearly understands what is expected, validate and praise good performance and behaviors. If there continues to be a problem, discuss your observations with the employee. Offer your assistance, and make a mutual agreement to correct the problem. Establish a time frame for reevaluation. Document the results, bad or good.

This type of management offers employees an environment in which to improve and do their best. Let them know when they do well. However, if there is no improvement, document the facts and take the action agreed upon when you first discussed the problem.

It is important that employees understand that when they do well or fail to meet the expectations, it is their responsibility.

Office Procedure Manual

An **office procedure manual** kept up to date is the responsibility of the office manager and his or her staff. This manual contains job descriptions to guide each staff member in performing tasks. A well-put-together manual makes clear to the employees exactly what is expected of them. It is also an invaluable document for training new employees and is a guide for a substitute employee.

Updating the manual, including job descriptions, is mandatory in our rapidly changing medical environments. A good office manager asks each staff member to update his or her work assignment listings. Suggestions from the entire staff should be used to create the most current manual possible.

Office Management

For the work of the medical office to flow freely and the patients to be served as well as possible, there has to be effective management. Lack of communication is the most common complaint from office personnel when asked why tasks have not been accomplished.

A good office manager holds weekly or bimonthly staff meetings. These should be held at a time that least disrupts the office and when most staff members can attend. Meetings should begin and end on time.

These meetings can just be brainstorming, or they could be work sessions for updating a manual. They may be training sessions for a new piece of equipment, or they might be problem solving in nature. A specific agenda should be drawn up and followed, and allowing a meeting to dissolve into a gripe session should be avoided. Some meetings are combined with breakfast or lunch. Interruptions should be avoided, and everyone should have a chance to contribute.

Much accountability is demanded of an office manager concerning financial matters of the office. A good office manager will have his or her hand on the pulse of the finances constantly. This may include supervising banking, billing, and collection; preparing periodic profit and loss statements; and overseeing insurance problems, payroll, income tax statements, and employee benefits. This is indeed a large part of a medical office manager's role, and this should be an area where the office manager feels particularly confident and involved. There are training programs available to sharpen these skills as needed.

Marketing

In today's extremely competitive environment, patients can have the opportunity to choose among many medical practitioners. Good marketing techniques to attract patients become more and more critical for today's medical practice. Of course, the best marketing strategy involves a professional and friendly staff providing the best service possible for the patient.

Many facilities now produce eye-catching brochures to describe the scope of the practice for which the medical clerical works. These brochures often require updating on a regular basis. The medical clerical worker may have an important role in creating and distributing such marketing tools.

The office manager must keep an eye on ideas to attract and keep patients. Changes might have to be made in office hours. Advertising may become more important. Physicians and health care workers should be encouraged to speak to community groups. Patient newsletters might be sent to patients, letting them know that their physicians and health care facilities staff are familiar with the latest medical advances and are available to help with any medical problems.

Updating Computers and Skills

As more and more computerization appears in the everyday running of a medical office, the office manager must be on top of all changes and challenges the computer brings to the profession. As mentioned in previous chapters, many of the operations that were once performed manually are now fully computerized in larger offices, including payroll, billing, ordering supplies, banking, medical records, and so much more. The office manager will be expected to help update all employee computer skills and troubleshoot any problems. Continuing education will help the office manager be able to keep up with these changes.

SUMMARY

Not only is the medical clerical worker responsible for the day-to-day details of technical office work, but he or she must be aware of the physical environment at all times. Although professional maintenance services generally handle the facility cleaning, the medical clerical worker should see to it that the patient's environment is kept neat and pleasing.

As you consider your future as a medical clerical worker, you need to assess whether or not you have the traits and attributes to become an effective office manager. If you decide that this is eventually what you want to strive for, you should develop and display the qualities that make a good manager. At the same time, you should observe your office manager and make sure that the duties that he or she must perform are tasks that you can and want to handle someday as part of your job.

LEARNING ACTIVITIES

1. Make a list of the ten attributes that you think are the most effective traits that a supervisor can possess. List the five traits of a supervisor that you think are the most ineffective.

2. Design a system to take inventory of your class equipment and supplies.

3. In front of the class, interview a fellow student for a medical clerical job. You are an office manager, and you want to be able to determine if the person being interviewed has the necessary qualifications to be a responsible medical clerical worker.

4. Ask your instructor to have a medical professional come to your class and conduct mock interviews.

5. At what temperature should a medical facility be kept?

6. Why is it important to pay attention to a medical office's *lighting, sound, temperature,* and *flooring* in achieving a pleasant office atmosphere?

7. Name two hazards that can cause accidents in a medical facility.

8. What steps might a medical clerical worker take to make sure that an examining and treatment room is comfortable for the patient?

9. In a medical office, what is meant by *preventive maintenance*?

10. What duties might a medical clerical worker have in regard to drug storage? Be specific.

11. Name six qualities that might be recognized by an employer as indicating that a person is "managerial material."

12. Name five important duties of an office manager.

13. Why is it important to have formal performance appraisals and documentation of employee conferences?

14. List the three most important qualities that you think an office manager should possess.

15. Why is an office procedure manual important?

16. List five security measures that could prevent theft in the workplace.

17. Name five items that are considered "hazardous medical waste."

CHAPTER 18

Finding the Right Job

Civil service examination	An examination given to all persons applying for governmental positions.
Cover letter	A document prepared for a potential employer that is submitted with a resume.
Curriculum vitae	A summary of a person's education and work experience, also known as a resume.
Employment agency	A business that connects job seekers with potential employers.
Personnel department	A department in most health facilities that deals with finding qualified employees to fill the facility's job requirements.
Pocket resume	A list (to carry with you) of important details that are usually asked on job applications, such as Social Security number and names and addresses of schools you have attended.
Portfolio	Materials carried by a prospective employee during an interview; might include certificates, references, letters of recommendation, commendations and so on.
Resume	A summary of educational background and work experience, usually prepared for a potential employer.

OBJECTIVES

After completing this chapter, the student will be responsible for performing the following objectives:

- Identify at least six places where you can get information about a potential job.
- Create an effective cover letter and resume.
- Be prepared to fill out a job application.
- Recognize that some employers give employment tests.
- Prepare yourself for a successful job interview.
- Write an effective thank-you letter after a job interview.

1 NTRODUCTION

In today's competitive job market, medical clerical workers must possess skills not only to *do* a job, but to *get* a job as well. To be successful in a job search, it is helpful to know how to develop a plan to obtain the best job for you and your talents. The job hunt should begin before your graduation from medical clerical training and after you have an idea of the type of job that best coincides with your ability, interest, and employment goals.

IDENTIFYING POTENTIAL EMPLOYERS

The adventure of finding a job that fits your needs as well as your particular personality begins with identification of potential employers. Many job seekers have no idea of the many employment opportunities available and the services that are available to help you gain employment. The more resources you can identify, the greater chance you have to find the best job for your needs.

Teachers and Guidance Counselors

An excellent place to begin your job search is through the site where you have been trained. Your teachers have information on the job market for your particular skills. Often, employers call instructors directly if they have had good luck with former students. Your training site should also have a guidance counseling department. Counselors often help students find jobs and can give you valuable information on how to have a successful job search experience.

Professional Meetings

A job seeker in the medical clerical field might attend medical assistant association meetings and workshops open to the public. Such events could be a chance to hear from fellow professionals about hiring opportunities, excellent employers, and so on. Such meetings are usually announced in local newspapers.

Family and Friends

Many jobs are never advertised, hiring being done through a network of contacts called the "hidden job market." They are filled by relatives or friends of employees. An employer would often rather accept the judgment of a trusted employee than rely on references of people whom he or she does not know. Be sure to tell family and friends that you are looking for a job. Many good job leads can come from this source, as many as 75 percent of job opportunities.

Posted and Advertised Positions

There are many places that post or advertise medical clerical positions (Figure 18.1)

- The classified section of the newspaper
- Bulletin boards in health facilities
- "Job lines" in health care facilities
- School bulletin boards
- Professional magazines and fliers
- Government listings through the U.S. Civil Service

Personnel Departments of Health Facilities

Most health facilities have a **personnel department** that concentrates on filling jobs within the organization. Personnel officers are always looking for people with good potential. If there are facilities you especially like, contact the person in charge of personnel. Then send him or her a letter, indicating that you are interested in an interview. Even if there is no opening in your field at the present time, ask for an interview anyway. The personnel officer will get to know you, and your application will go on file for future reference.

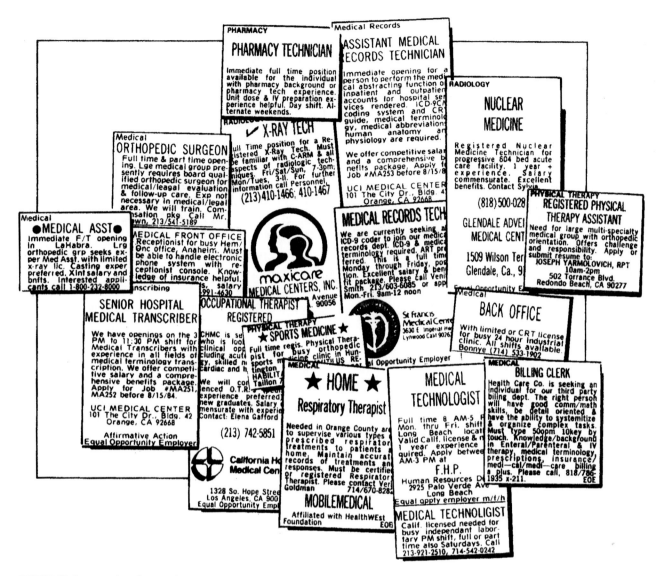

FIGURE 18.1 Examples of want ads.

Employment Agencies

Employment agencies are in business to match people to jobs. There are many kinds of employment agencies, including agencies in larger areas that deal strictly with medical employment. *Public employment agencies* are nonprofit agencies operated by state governments. Each state has such agencies, with branches in most larger cities and towns. These services are free. *Private employment agencies* are profit-making, charging either you or the employer a fee for their services. You may have to sign a contract with this type of agency. Read the contract very carefully, and always find out exactly how the fee will be handled. Shop around if you have more than one private employment agency available. Some may have more favorable rates than others.

Job Search by Computer

More frequently, schools and employers are using electronic job hunt methods to bring together employee and employer, bypassing the mail. Online services can be accessed by a personal computer with a modem and a standard communications program. Users can apply for specific positions by responding to a series of questions about a position. The applicant then has a profile that is sent to prospective employers.

Computerized employment services may register job seekers into their data bank by asking the applicant to fill out an extensive profile questionnaire covering experience, skills, and job-related factors such as availability for all shifts and desired physical location. Such services serve as a liaison between employers and applicants.

$\mathcal{T}$HE COVER LETTER

Once you have identified several job possibilities, the next step is to make a personal visit to the potential employer. You may choose to write a job inquiry letter, known as a **cover letter** (Figure 18.2) when sent with a **resume.** Many employers request a cover letter with the resume. This letter may be the first impression employers have of you.

The cover letter should be brief. You must clearly state the job for which you are applying, as sometimes employers advertise many jobs at once. The letter should be sent on white or cream-colored paper. There should be no strikeovers in the text,

---

424 Maple Street
Chicago, IL 80402

July 1, 20--

Mr. Peter Andrews
Personnel Director
Good Hope Hospital
4106 Good Hope Lane
Chicago, IL 80409

Dear Mr. Andrews:

In response to your advertisement of June 28, 20--, in the Chicago Times, I am applying for your position as a full-time medical admissions clerk. My résumé is enclosed.

I have recently completed my medical admissions clerk training at the Valley Adult School, where I was second in my class. As part of my course work, I completed a 100-hour internship at your facility, Good Hope Hospital, where I was very impressed with the quality of care.

I am available for an interview any weekday and can start work immediately. My telephone number is (801) 555-3245. I look forward to hearing from you.

Sincerely,

JANE BENNETT

Enclosure

FIGURE 18.2 Sample cover letter.

and all corrections should be neatly made. Spelling, punctuation, and grammar should be error-free.

If you have experience in the job field, mention it briefly. If you have just completed your training, mention your training site and your community classroom experience. If you did well in your class, include that in your letter. The letter should be short and to the point.

CREATING A RESUME

A resume is a *brief* summary of your work experience, your education, and other qualifications that might help you secure a job (Figure 18.3). Some employers might ask for a personal data sheet, a personal profile, or a **curriculum vitae.** All of these terms refer to the resume.

JANE BENNETT
424 MAPLE STREET
CHICAGO, IL 80402
(801) 555-3245

JOB OBJECTIVE   To obtain responsible employment as a Medical Admissions Clerk.

EDUCATION
9/01 - 6/02   VALLEY ADULT SCHOOL, Chicago, IL
Certificate of Completion, Medical Admissions Clerk Course.
Graduated 2nd in class of 25.

9/97 - 6/01   JOHN F. KENNEDY HIGH SCHOOL, Chicago, IL
High School Diploma, with business course emphasis.

WORK EXPERIENCE
6/01 - Present   GRAYSON'S DEPARTMENT STORE, Chicago, IL
Part-time salesperson on weekends, Christmas vacation, and summer. Work in many areas of the store, with opening and closing responsibilities. Often train new salespersons in the College Shop and have supervised other employees.

6/99 - 6/00   TACO BELL, Chicago, IL
Part-time cashier/cook. Heavy customer contact.

HONORS AND ACTIVITIES

6/01   BANK OF AMERICA AWARD, J.F.K. High School
Bank of America Award for Excellent Achievement in Business Courses.

9/00 - 6/01   CANDY STRIPER, GOOD HOPE HOSPITAL

SKILLS   Typing: 70 WPM
Experience on: Word processors, transcription equipment, copy and fax machines, calculators. Fluent in Spanish.

FIGURE 18.3 Sample resume.

Type your resume neatly, as it reflects on you directly. You should use the same color of paper as your cover letter, preferably white or cream. As in the cover letter, the resume must contain no strikeovers, and a correction should not be noticeable. Spelling must again be perfect.

A resume is your introduction to the employer and is a way for the employer to remember you after you leave the interview. Therefore, the resume must be prepared with care. It must be neat, well organized, and above all, accurate.

The resume should ideally be one typewritten page in length. On that page, the following information should be listed:

- Name, address, and phone number
- Job objective
- Education
- Work experience
- Honors and activities
- Skills

In a resume, be sure to include anything that sets you apart, such as a high rating in your class and responsibilities you held in past jobs. Remember, list all jobs that you have held, even if they are not in the medical field. Potential employers are as interested in your ability to be a punctual, hard worker as they are in your specific professional skills. They will be impressed if a past employer describes you as serious and reliable.

Remember, a resume is a brief description. Details belong on the job application, discussed below. References do not belong on a resume, as they are requested on the application form. Long, wordy resumes will not help your chances to get a job.

The Internet is an excellent resource for finding a variety of formats for creating resumes. Just by entering the word "resume" in your search engine, many resources become available in helping you make an excellent resume. There are also software programs that do the same as well as various manuals.

When you finish your resume, you can make photocopies. Do not use a photocopy machine that makes poor copies. Professional print shops will have machines that make duplicates that are identical to the master resume as cheaply as a machine can in a local drugstore.

FILLING OUT JOB APPLICATIONS

Many health facilities and employment agencies ask you to fill out an *application form*, a standard form that all potential employees are asked to fill out. Job applications ask for much more detailed information than is contained in a resume. These forms are used to screen job seekers, so take care to prepare a neat application. Read the application before you begin, to avoid errors in filling out the form. Have a black pen with you for the application. Take special note of such instructions as "please print." Following such instructions indicates an ability to follow directions.

Application forms may ask you information that you might not have available. Before you begin your job search, you might want to put together a **pocket resume**, a sheet of paper carried with you listing certain facts about yourself that you will probably be asked on an application or in an interview. Some applicants carry a completed application with them. Here are some types of data needed for filling out applications and answering interviewer questions:

- Your Social Security number
- Names and addresses of your elementary school, junior high school, and high school, as well as dates attended
- Exact names, addresses, and telephone numbers of former employers and the dates you worked for them
- Names, addresses, and telephone numbers of people who have agreed to give you a reference

On the application form, you may be asked to give a salary that you are seeking. The best thing to do here is say "Open" in the space for specific salary requirement. You might disqualify yourself by asking too much or undersell yourself by asking too little.

You must always tell the truth when filling out applications. When an application asks "reason for leaving" after each of your jobs, word your answers carefully. If the reason is negative, never say anything unpleasant about yourself or a previous employer.

When a part of the application does not pertain to you, such as military service, write "N/A" or "Not applicable" in the space provided. This shows the potential employer that you did not forget to fill out part of the application. See Appendix B for a sample of a health care application.

E MPLOYMENT TESTS

Many health employers give prospective employees some kind of pre-employment test. If you apply to a governmental agency, your chances are very good that you will receive some kind of testing.

Skills Tests

You may be given a written skills test, determining how well you spell, punctuate, and so on. Elementary math skills may also be tested by a written test. Other skills tests may be hands-on exams, such as a typing test.

Psychological Tests

Some facilities ask prospective employees to take a psychological test, evaluating such traits as leadership abilities, the ability to work with others, loyalty, and so on. These tests require no preparation.

Civil Service Examinations

Government jobs require a **civil service examination.** They are designed to select the best workers without discriminating because of race, sex, religion, or political leanings. Your score will be compared with those of other applicants applying for the same position. The classified section of the telephone directory lists civil service testing under "United States Government."

Medical Tests

You may be asked to undergo a complete physical examination. If you have a serious health problem, this could keep you from doing an adequate job for the employer. When you work in the medical world, your employer wants to be sure that you do not have a disease that you could pass on to others or that could keep you from being able to do your job.

*T*HE JOB INTERVIEW

The personal interview is the most critical part of your job search. You may have a wonderful cover letter and resume, a neat application, and impressive references. However, if your interview with your prospective boss goes poorly, you will probably not get the job. Remember, the interviewer will be assessing many things at once: your attitudes, personality, appearance, energy level, and your ability to communicate your ideas.

Prepare Ahead of Time

Before you interview with an employer, find out all you can about the facility. It is very impressive to the interviewer to hear that you have chosen to seek a job in that facility for concrete reasons. Such reasons might include "I have read about your exciting expansion plans" or "I understand that your facility has just been cited as one of the ten best facilities in the state."

Know ahead of time what skills are required for the job and that you are adequately trained. There is no sense in wasting your time and that of the employer if you are not qualified. Also find out about salary ranges and benefits before you go into the interview.

Prepare questions ahead of time to ask the employer. He or she will give you an opportunity to ask questions. You want to appear prepared, instead of tongue-tied when you are questioned. Some questions that you might ask are:

- Will there be a training period for my job?
- What are the biggest challenges I might face on the job?
- If I do well, are there possibilities for advancement?

Save specific questions about salary and benefits; they should be asked only after you are offered the job. You should have an idea ahead of time about these matters.

Practice answering questions that an employer might ask you. There are some questions that are standard for most interviews, such as:

- Why did you choose to interview at our facility?
- Why do you think you might be the best person for the job?
- What are your strengths? What are your weaknesses?
- Do you enjoy working with people?

You must always be truthful in answering. However, do not volunteer negative information about yourself if it is not necessary. Your weaknesses can be assets if you admit to working too hard sometimes and not taking breaks. Always try to answer negative questions in a positive way.

Personal Appearance

The clothes you wear to an interview should be nicer than the clothes you would wear on the job, unless your position will require that you "dress up" every day. Men should wear a jacket and tie or a shirt and sweater. A woman should wear an appropriate dress or skirt (no plunging necklines and tight skirts). Shoes should be polished. You should be conservative with cologne, makeup, and jewelry. Be conscious of accessories such as purse and hair ornaments.

Pay special attention to personal hygiene. Bathe, wash your hair, and put on clean, well-pressed clothes. Make sure that your hair is neatly combed.

Be on Time

Plan to get to the interview at least 10 to 15 minutes early. Allow for the worst traffic conditions and be prepared to have a difficult time finding parking near a health facility. Bring no one with you. Know ahead of time where you are going, even if you have to make a trial run the day before. Hospital layouts seem to be designed to confuse the newcomer, so be prepared. Try not to interview on late Monday or Friday afternoons. Monday is often a hectic day for your prospective employer and Friday is often a get-away day.

Body Language

When you meet your interviewer, introduce yourself clearly, shake hands, and look directly into the interviewer's eyes. The handshake should be firm, grasping the entire hand, not just the fingers. Practice your handshake with several people, men and women. Stand until you are invited to sit down by the potential employer.

Frequent direct eye contact will relay a message to the employer that you have nothing to hide and that you are confident. Your posture will also communicate a certain message about your attitude. Do not slouch or fidget in your seat. Appear as calm as you can, and avoid nervous habits. It is best to decline offers of coffee, as it is easy to spill when nervous! Allow the interviewer to lead the discussion. You should be prepared to answer questions, and to ask a few on your own, but taking the employer's lead. Avoid "yes" and "no" answers. Back up your response with an illustration.

Portfolio

A **portfolio** of pertinent information brought by the applicant to the job interview suggests that the applicant is serious about the position and is well-organized. Materials can be carried in a neat black folder or something similar. Portfolio items might include:

- Social Security card
- Diplomas, certificates, degrees
- Letters of recommendation
- Any honors, commendations
- Transcripts of courses
- Names and addresses of references
- Extra copies of your resume
- Timed typing sample certified by an instructor

Illegal Questions

Some questions may be asked in the interview that legally do not have to be answered if not relevant to the job. Jobs are to be offered on the basis of qualifications. You are not required to answer questions about the following topics:

- Age
- Marital status

- Dependents
- Pregnancy
- Family planning
- Child care arrangements
- Religion
- Height, weight
- Credit rating
- Home and car ownership

If you are asked one or more illegal questions, you might choose to answer anyway. You might also choose to answer with "I don't believe that question is relevant to the requirements for the position I am seeking." You can also refuse to answer and contact the nearest Equal Employment Opportunity Commission office. If a potential employer does ask illegal questions, it may be wise not to work in a facility where such questions are asked.

Ending the Interview

You should be able to tell when the interview is over. The interviewer will probably get out of his or her seat, start to look a bit distracted, or you will be told the interview is over. Do not take up the interviewer's time when it appears that the interview is over.

At the end of the interview, this is the opportunity to indicate your interest in the job. In most cases, you will be told nothing initially, as the employer will want time to consider all applicants. Be sure you are clear what steps are to happen next. Ask the interviewer a question, such as "Will I be notified about the job?" if you are not told what will happen next.

$\mathcal{T}$HE FOLLOW-UP LETTER

An employer is usually impressed if you take the time and effort to write a follow-up letter (Figure 18.4). Not only will the letter let the employer know that you are a courteous person, but he or she will be reminded of your interview and your qualifications. This is especially important when many people are interviewed for one position.

Thank the employer for the time taken to talk with you. Mention something that you learned during the interview. Follow up with a mention of your particular skills. This is also a chance to bring up something that you might have forgotten to mention in the interview. A well-done follow-up letter can give you an important edge in getting the job. Remember to keep the letter *brief* and proofread it well.

$\mathcal{K}$EEPING YOUR JOB

When you do obtain a job, the greatest challenge is ahead. You must now prove to your employer that his or her faith in you was well deserved.

There are a number of ways for you to assure that you will be successful in your new job.

424 Maple Street
Chicago, IL 80402

July 12, 20--

Mr. Peter Andrews
Personnel Director
Good Hope Hospital
4106 Good Hope Lane
Chicago, IL 80409

Dear Mr. Andrews:

Thank you so much for taking time out of your busy schedule last Wednesday
to meet with me. Your description of the job was quite comprehensive and very
informative.

I am very interested in working in the organization you have described. I am
confident I have the skills and enthusiasm to contribute to your department, and
I would appreciate the opportunity to work for you. I can be contacted at 555-
7196 after 4 p.m. on weekdays.

Sincerely,

JANE BENNETT

FIGURE 18.4 Sample follow-up letter.

- *Get off to a good start.* Get plenty of sleep, be punctual, and respond to your training with enthusiasm and a positive attitude. Read the employee handbook carefully. Be sure to ask questions if you are unclear about your duties. Follow instructions completely. Save any suggestions for change until you are more experienced.
- *Decide how to get along with your fellow employees.* Make a pact with yourself to work well with the other members of the team. Expect them to be cooperative and respond cheerfully when they ask for your cooperation. Proceed with optimism. You will encounter difficult people, but if you remain positive, it will be hard for people not to be positive to you.
- *Display a strong character.* Act in an ethical fashion, being honest, loyal, and courageous when necessary. Admit mistakes and avoid "passing the buck."
- *Do not gossip.* Health care facilities are not different from any other place of work—gossip will be circulating continually. Respect the right of privacy of patients and your co-workers. If you cannot say something nice, say nothing. You will save yourself much embarrassment by not participating in hurtful activities.
- *Be a good communicator.* Practice effective communication skills. Speak slowly and clearly. Take down all communications legibly. Accept criticism with grace and resist the urge to be bossy and argumentative. Be tactful with your fellow employees.

■ *Create a positive, businesslike image.* Paying attention to proper hygiene reflects pride in your new job. Proper clothing shows that you care about yourself as well as your job.

■ *Accept challenges.* Be ready to accept new assignments and opportunities to learn new procedures. You want your employer to know that you are enthusiastic about your job and are eager to improve your skills.

SUMMARY

You may find the world of work to be a very competitive place when you have finished your training. To get the job that you really want, the job that is suited to your skills and personality, you must be prepared to plan the best possible job search. You must be able to sell yourself and your skills successfully to a prospective employer.

LEARNING ACTIVITIES

1. Prepare your resume and a cover letter on white or off-white paper. Keep it brief (one page only).

2. Prepare a pocket resume for easy reference.

3. Prepare a portfolio to carry with you to an interview.

4. Fill out the practice application in Appendix B. Be as neat as you can.

5. Write a thank-you note to a fictitious employer, thanking her for an interview.

6. List six places where you can get information about obtaining a job.

7. Why is a cover letter important in the job search?

8. Identify the key elements of the resume.

9. Name four types of employment tests you could be given when applying for a job.

10. List and prepare to answer four questions that a prospective employer might ask you in an interview.

11. Give four examples of questions that a potential employer cannot ask legally.

12. Why is a follow-up letter important after a job interview?

Information about AIDS

The following material is reproduced with permission from the Centers for Disease Control and Prevention (CDC).

Research has revealed a great deal of valuable medical, scientific, and public health information about the human immunodeficiency virus (HIV) and acquired immunodeficiency syndrome (AIDS). The ways in which HIV can be transmitted have been clearly identified. Unfortunately, false information or statements that are not supported by scientific findings continue to be shared widely through the Internet or popular press. Therefore, the Centers for Disease Control and Prevention (CDC) has prepared this fact sheet to correct a few misperceptions about HIV.

*H*OW HIV IS TRANSMITTED

HIV is spread by sexual contact with an infected person, by sharing needles and/or syringes (primarily for drug injection) with someone who is infected, or, less commonly (and now very rarely in countries where blood is screened for HIV antibodies), through transfusions of infected blood or blood clotting factors. Babies born to HIV-infected women may become infected before or during birth or through breast-feeding after birth.

In the health care setting, workers have been infected with HIV after being stuck with needles containing HIV-infected blood or, less frequently, after infected blood gets into a worker's open cut or a mucous membrane (for example, the eyes or inside of the nose). There has been only one instance of patients being infected by a health care worker in the United States; this involved HIV transmission from one infected dentist to six patients. Investigations have been completed involving more than 22,000 patients of 63 HIV-infected physicians, surgeons, and dentists, and no other cases of this type of transmission have been identified in the United States.

Some people fear that HIV might be transmitted in other ways; however, no scientific evidence to support any of these fears has been found. If HIV were being transmitted through other routes (such as through air, water, or insects), the pattern of reported AIDS cases would be much different from what has been observed. For example, if mosquitoes could transmit HIV infection, many more young children and preadolescents would have been diagnosed with AIDS.

All reported cases suggesting new or potentially unknown routes of transmission are thoroughly investigated by state and local health departments with the assistance, guidance, and laboratory support from CDC. *No additional routes of transmission have been recorded,* despite a national sentinel system designed to detect just such an occurrence.

The following paragraphs specifically address some of the common misperceptions about HIV transmission.

HIV in the Environment

Scientists and medical authorities agree that HIV does not survive well in the environment, making the possibility of environmental transmission remote. HIV is found in varying concentrations or amounts in blood, semen, vaginal fluid, breast milk, saliva, and tears. (See section entitled *Saliva, Tears, and Sweat.*) To obtain data on the survival of HIV, laboratory studies have required the use of artificially high concentrations of laboratory-grown virus. Although these unnatural concentrations of HIV can be kept alive for days or even weeks under precisely controlled and limited laboratory conditions, CDC studies have shown that drying of even these high concentrations of HIV reduces the amount of infectious virus by 90 to 99 percent within several hours. Since the HIV concentrations used in laboratory studies are much higher than those actually found in blood or other specimens, drying of HIV-infected human blood or other body fluids reduces the theoretical risk of environmental transmission to that which has been observed—essentially zero. Incorrect interpretation of conclusions drawn from laboratory studies have unnecessarily alarmed some people.

Results from laboratory studies should not be used to assess specific personal risk of infection because (1) the amount of virus studied is not found in human specimens or elsewhere in nature, and (2) no one has been identified as infected with HIV due to contact with an environmental surface. Additionally, HIV is unable to reproduce outside its living host (unlike many bacteria or fungi, which may do so under suitable conditions), except under laboratory conditions, therefore, it does not spread or maintain infectiousness outside its host.

Households

Although HIV has been transmitted between family members in a household setting, this type of transmission is very rare. These transmissions are believed to have resulted from contact between skin or mucous membranes and infected blood. To prevent even such rare occurrences, precautions, as described in previously published guidelines, should be taken in all settings—including the home—to prevent exposures to the blood of persons who are HIV infected, at risk for HIV infection, or whose infection and risk status are unknown. For example,

- Gloves should be worn during contact with blood or other body fluids that could possibly contain visible blood, such as urine, feces, or vomit.
- Cuts, sores, or breaks on both the caregiver's and patient's exposed skin should be covered with bandages.
- Hands and other parts of the body should be washed immediately after contact with blood or other body fluids, and surfaces soiled with blood should be disinfected appropriately.
- Practices that increase the likelihood of blood contact, such as sharing of razors and toothbrushes, should be avoided.
- Needles and other sharp instruments should be used only when medically necessary and handled according to recommendations for health care settings. (Do not put caps back on needles by hand or remove needles from syringes. Dispose of needles in puncture-proof containers out of the reach of children and visitors.)

Businesses and Other Settings

There is no known risk of HIV transmission to co-workers, clients, or consumers from contact in industries such as food-service establishments (see information on survival of HIV in the environment). Food-service workers known to be infected with HIV need not be restricted from work unless they have other infections or illnesses (such as diarrhea or hepatitis A) for which any food-service worker, regardless of HIV infection status, should be restricted. CDC recommends that all food-service workers follow recommended standards and practices of good personal hygiene and food sanitation.

In 1985, CDC issued routine precautions that all personal-service workers (such as hairdressers, barbers, cosmetologists, and massage therapists) should follow, even though there is no evidence of transmission from a personal-service worker to a client or vice versa. Instruments that are intended to penetrate the skin (such as tattooing and acupuncture needles, ear piercing devices) should be used once and disposed of or thoroughly cleaned and sterilized. Instruments not intended to penetrate the skin but which may become contaminated with blood (for example, razors) should be used for only one client and disposed of or thoroughly cleaned and disinfected after each use. Personal-service workers can use the same cleaning procedures that are recommended for health care institutions.

CDC knows of no instances of HIV transmission through tattooing or body piercing, although hepatitis B virus has been transmitted during some of these practices. One case of HIV transmission from acupuncture has been documented. Body piercing (other than ear piercing) is relatively new in the United States, and the medical complications for body piercing appear to be greater than for tattoos. Healing of piercings generally will take weeks, and sometimes even months, and the pierced tissue could conceivably be abraded (torn or cut) or inflamed even after healing. Therefore, a theoretical HIV transmission risk does exist if the unhealed or abraded tissues come into contact with an infected person's blood or other infectious body fluid. Additionally, HIV could be transmitted if instruments contaminated with blood are not sterilized or disinfected between clients.

Kissing

Casual contact through closed-mouth or "social" kissing is not a risk for transmission of HIV. Because of the potential for contact with blood during "French" or open-mouth kissing, CDC recommends against engaging in this activity with a person known to be infected. However, the risk of acquiring HIV during open-mouth kissing is believed to be very low. CDC has investigated only one case of HIV infection that may be attributed to contact with blood during open-mouth kissing.

Biting

In 1997, CDC published findings from a state health department investigation of an incident that suggested blood-to-blood transmission of HIV by a human bite. There have been other reports in the medical literature in which HIV appeared to have been transmitted by a bite. Severe trauma with extensive tissue tearing and damage and presence of blood were reported in each of these instances. Biting is not a common way of transmitting HIV. In fact, there are numerous reports of bites that did *not* result in HIV infection.

Saliva, Tears, and Sweat

HIV has been found in saliva and tears in very low quantities from some AIDS patients. It is important to understand that finding a small amount of HIV in a body fluid does not necessarily mean that HIV can be *transmitted* by that body fluid. HIV has *not* been recovered from the sweat of HIV-infected persons. Contact with saliva, tears, or sweat has never been shown to result in transmission of HIV.

Insects

From the onset of the HIV epidemic, there has been concern about transmission of the virus by biting and bloodsucking insects. However, studies conducted by researchers at CDC and elsewhere have shown no evidence of HIV transmission through insects—even in areas where there are many cases of AIDS and large populations of insects such as mosquitoes. Lack of such outbreaks, despite intense efforts to detect them, supports the conclusion that HIV is not transmitted by insects.

The results of experiments and observations of insect biting behavior indicate that when an insect bites a person, it does not inject its own or a previously bitten person's or animal's blood into the next person bitten. Rather, it injects saliva, which acts as a lubricant or anticoagulant so the insect can feed efficiently. Such diseases as yellow fever and malaria are transmitted through the saliva of specific species of mosquitoes. However, HIV lives for only a short time inside an insect and, unlike organisms that are transmitted via insect bites, HIV does not reproduce (and does not survive) in insects. Thus, even if the virus enters a mosquito or another sucking or biting insect, the insect does not become infected and cannot transmit HIV to the next human it feeds on or bites. HIV is not found in insect feces.

There is also no reason to fear that a biting or bloodsucking insect, such as a mosquito, could transmit HIV from one person to another through HIV-infected blood left on its mouth parts. Two factors serve to explain why this is so—first, infected people do not have constant, high levels of HIV in their bloodstreams and, second, insect mouth parts do not retain large amounts of blood on their surfaces. Further, scientists who study insects have determined that biting insects normally do not travel from one person to the next immediately after ingesting blood. Rather, they fly to a resting place to digest this blood meal.

Effectiveness of Condoms

Condoms are classified as medical devices and are regulated by the Food and Drug Administration (FDA). Condom manufacturers in the United States test each latex condom for defects, including holes, before it is packaged. The proper and consistent use of latex or polyurethane (a type of plastic) condoms when engaging in sexual intercourse—vaginal, anal, or oral—can greatly reduce a person's risk of acquiring or transmitting sexually transmitted diseases, including HIV infection.

There are many different types and brands of condoms available—however, only latex or polyurethane condoms provide a highly effective mechanical barrier to HIV. In laboratories, viruses occasionally have been shown to pass through natural membrane ("skin" or lambskin) condoms, which may contain natural pores and are therefore not recommended for disease prevention (they are documented to be effective for contraception). Women may wish to consider using the female condom when a male condom cannot be used.

For condoms to provide maximum protection, they must be used *consistently* (every time) and *correctly.* Several studies of correct and consistent condom use clearly show that latex condom breakage rates in this country are less than 2 percent. Even when condoms do break, one study showed that more than half of such breaks occurred prior to ejaculation.

When condoms are used reliably, they have been shown to prevent pregnancy up to 98 percent of the time among couples using them as their only method of contraception. Similarly, numerous studies among sexually active people have demonstrated that a properly used latex condom provides a high degree of protection against a variety of sexually transmitted diseases, including HIV infection.

For more detailed information about condoms, see the CDC publication "*Facts about Condoms and Their Use in Preventing HIV Infection and Other STDs.*"

CDC's Response

CDC is committed to providing the scientific community and the public with accurate and objective information about HIV infection and AIDS. It is vital that clear information on HIV infection and AIDS be readily available to help prevent further transmission of the virus and to allay fears and prejudices caused by misinformation. For a complete description of CDC's HIV/AIDS prevention programs, see "*Facts about CDC's Role in HIV and AIDS Prevention.*"

*F*OR MORE INFORMATION

CDC National AIDS Hotline
1-800-342-AIDS (2437)
Spanish: 1-800-344-SIDA (7432) (HIV and STDs)
Deaf: 1-800-243-7889

CDC National Prevention Information Network
P.O. Box 6003
Rockville, Maryland 20849-6003
1-800-458-5231

*I*NTERNET RESOURCES

DHAP: http://www.cdc.gov/hiv
NCHSTP: http://www.cdc.gov/nchstp/od/nchstp.html
NPIN: http://www.cdcnpin.org

Samples of Forms

SUPERVISOR'S REPORT OF ACCIDENT #78

Name of Injured Employee _____

Job Title _____ Department/Floor _____

Date of Accident _____ Hour _____ A.M.
P.M.

Nature of Injury _____

Was injured acting in a regular line of duty? _____

Who gave first aid, if any? _____

Did injured go to E.R.? _____ If not, why not? _____

Did injured leave work? _____ Date _____ Hour _____ A.M.
P.M.

Did injured return to work? _____ Date _____ Hour _____ A.M.
P.M.

Name of Witnesses _____

Where and how did the accident occur? _____

_____

_____

What in your opinion, caused the accident? _____

_____

What has been done to prevent a similar accident? _____

_____

Had the specific hazard causing the injury been reported by telephone/writing? _____

_____

_____   _____
         DATE   EMPLOYEE'S SIGNATURE

_____   _____
         DATE   SUPERVISOR'S SIGNATURE

Supervisor's signature only indicates that the employee has reported an on-the-job injury.

IF TREATMENT IS NEEDED, TAKE ORIGINAL AND DUPLICATE
TO THE EMERGENCY ROOM

- -

FOR EMPLOYEE HEALTH OFFICE USE ONLY

Investigated? _____ YES _____ NO

Comments on reverse side

Original - Employee Health Office   Duplicate - Supervisor's Copy

FM 70505 (5/85)

APPOINTMENT SHEET

1	2	3	4	5	6	DAY	1 2 3 4 5 6
						8	00 15 30 45
						9	00 15 30 45
						10	00 15 30 45
						11	00 15 30 45
						12	00 15 30 45
						1	00 15 30 45
						2	00 15 30 45
						3	00 15 30 45
						4	00 15 30 45
						5	00 15 30 45

FORM # 56-7318   © 1976 BIBBERO SYSTEMS, INC., PETALUMA, CA

264

Appendix B

TELEPHONE MESSAGE FORMS

PRIORITY ☐   **TELEPHONE RECORD** ☎

PATIENT   AGE

CALLER

TELEPHONE

REFERRED TO

CHART #

CHART ATTACHED ☐ YES ☐ NO

DATE / /   TIME   REC'D BY

Copyright © 1978 Bibbero Systems, Inc.
Printed in the U.S.A.

MESSAGE

TEMP   ALLERGIES

RESPONSE

PHY/RN INITIALS   DATE / /   TIME   HANDLED BY

PRIORITY ☐   **TELEPHONE RECORD** ☎

PATIENT   AGE

CALLER

TELEPHONE

REFERRED TO

CHART #

CHART ATTACHED ☐ YES ☐ NO

DATE / /   TIME   REC'D BY

Copyright © 1978 Bibbero Systems, Inc.
Printed in the U.S.A.

MESSAGE

TEMP   ALLERGIES

RESPONSE

PHY/RN INITIALS   DATE / /   TIME   HANDLED BY

PRIORITY ☐   **TELEPHONE RECORD** ☎

PATIENT   AGE

CALLER

TELEPHONE

REFERRED TO

CHART #

CHART ATTACHED ☐ YES ☐ NO

DATE / /   TIME   REC'D BY

Copyright © 1978 Bibbero Systems, Inc.
Printed in the U.S.A.

MESSAGE

TEMP   ALLERGIES

RESPONSE

PHY/RN INITIALS   DATE / /   TIME   HANDLED BY

DONALD E. CASTLE, M.D.
7998 Berlin Avenue
Newburg, CA 94519
(415) 555-8574

BUSINESS ENVELOPE

HEALTH INSURANCE CLAIM FORM (FORM HCFA-1500)

PLEASE
DO NOT
STAPLE
IN THIS
AREA

APPROVED OMB-0938-0008

CARRIER

| PICA | | **HEALTH INSURANCE CLAIM FORM** | PICA |

1. MEDICARE MEDICAID CHAMPUS CHAMPVA GROUP HEALTH PLAN FECA BLK LUNG OTHER	1a.INSURED'S ID NUMBER (FOR PROGRAM IN ITEM 1)

(Medicare #)   (Medicaid #)   (Sponsor's SSN)   (VA File #)   (SSN or ID)   (SSN)   (ID)

2. PATIENT'S NAME (Last Name, First Name, Middle Name)

b. OTHER INSURED'S DATE OF BIRTH
MM   DD   YY   M   F

4. INSURED'S NAME (Last Name, First Name, Middle Name)

5. PATIENT'S ADDRESS (No., Street)

6. PATIENT RELATIONSHIP TO INSURED
Self   Spouse   Child   Other

7. INSURED'S ADDRESS (No., Street)

CITY   STATE

8. PATIENT STATUS
Single   Married   Other

CITY   STATE

ZIP CODE   TELEPHONE (Including Area Code)
(   )

Employed   Full-Time Student   Part-Time Student

ZIP CODE   TELEPHONE (Including Area Code)
(   )

9. OTHER INSURED'S NAME (Last Name, First Name, Middle Name)

10.IS PATIENT CONDITION RELATED TO:

11. INSURED'S POLICY GROUP OR FECA NUMBER

a. OTHER INSURED'S POLICY OR GROUP NUMBER

a. EMPLOYMENT? (CURRENT OR PREVIOUS)
YES   NO

a. INSURED'S DATE OF BIRTH
MM   DD   YY   SEX   M   F

b. OTHER INSURED'S DATE OF BIRTH
MM   DD   YY   SEX   M   F

b. AUTO ACCIDENT?   PLACE (State)
YES   NO

b. EMPLOYER'S NAME OR SCHOOL NAME

c. EMPLOYER'S NAME OR SCHOOL NAME

c. OTHER ACCIDENT?
YES   NO

c. INSURANCE PLAN NAME OR PROGRAM NAME

d. INSURANCE PLAN NAME OR PROGRAM NAME

10d. RESERVED FOR LOCAL USE

d. IS THERE ANOTHER HEALTH BENEFIT PLAN?
YES   NO   *If yes*, return to and complete item 9 a-d.

READ BACK OF FORM BEFORE COMPLETING & SIGNING THIS FORM.
12.PATIENT'S OR AUTHORIZED PERSON'S SIGNATURE I authorize the release of any medical or other information necessary to process this claim. I also request payment of government benefits either to myself or to the party who accepts assignment below.

SIGNED _____   DATE _____

13.INSURED'S OR AUTHORIZED PERSON'S SIGNATURE i authorize payment of medical benefits to the undersigned physician or supplier for services described below.

SIGNED _____

CARRIER / PATIENT AND INSURED INFORMATION

14.DATE OF CURRENT:
MM   DD   YY   ILLNESS (First symptom) OR INJURY (Accident) OR PREGNANCY (LMP)

15. IF PATIENT HAS HAD SAME OR SIMILAR ILLNESS. GIVE FIRST DATE   MM   DD   YY

16. DATES PATIENT UNABLE TO WORK IN CURRENT OCCUPATION
MM   DD   YY   MM   DD   YY
FROM   TO

17.NAME OF REFERRING PHYSICIAN OR OTHER SOURCE

17a.I.D. NUMBER OF REFERRING PHYSICIAN

18. HOSPITALIZATION DATES RELATED TO CURRENT SERVICES
MM   DD   YY   MM   DD   YY
FROM   TO

19.RESERVED FOR LOCAL USE

20. OUTSIDE LAB? $ CHARGES
YES   NO

21.DIAGNOSIS OR NATURE OF ILLNESS OR INJURY. (RELATE ITEMS 1,2,3, OR 4 TO ITEM 24E BY LINE)
1. L___ . ___   3. L___ . ___
2. L___ . ___   4. L___ . ___

22.MEDICAID RESUBMISSION CODE   ORIGINAL REF. NO

23.PRIOR AUTHORIZATION NUMBER

24.	A					B	C	D		E	F	G	H	I	J	K
	DATE(S) OF SERVICE					Place of Service	Type of Service	PROCEDURES, SERVICES, OR SUPPLIES (Explain Unusual Circumstances)		DIAGNOSIS CODE	$ CHARGES	DAYS OR UNITS	EPSDT Family Plan	EMG	COB	RESERVED FOR LOCAL USE
	From			To				CPT/HCPCS	MODIFIER							
	MM	DD	YY	MM	DD	YY											

24. FEDERAL TAX I.D. NUMBER   SSN   EIN

26.PATIENT'S ACCOUNT NO.

27.ACCEPT ASSIGNMENT?
(For govt. claims, see back)   YES   NO

28.TOTAL CHARGE $

29.AMOUNT PAID $

30. BALANCE DUE $

31. SIGNATURE OF PHYSICIAN OR SUPPLIER INCLUDING DEGREES OR CREDENTIALS
(I certify that the statements on the reverse apply to this bill and are made a part thereof.)

SIGNED _____   DATE _____

32.NAME AND ADDRESS OF FACILITY WHERE SERVICES WERE RENDERED (If other than home or office)

33.PHYSICIAN'S, SUPPLIER'S BILLING NAME, ADDRESS, ZIP CODE & PHONE #

PIN#   GRP#

PHYSICIAN OR SUPPLIER INFORMATION

(APPROVED BY AMA COUNCIL ON MEDICAL SERVICE 8/88)   ***PLEASE PRINT OR TYPE***   FORM HCFA-1500 (U2) (12-90)
FORM OWCP-1500   FORM RRB-1500

PATIENT STATEMENT

BILLING NAME		NAMES OF OTHER FAMILY MEMBERS	
PATIENT'S NAME			
RES. PHONE	BUS. PHONE		
OCCUPATION		RELATIVE OR FRIEND	
EMPLOYED BY		REFERRED BY	
INS. INFORMATION			SOC. SEC. NUMBER
FORM NO. MDP. 8550		1976 BIBBERO SYSTEMS, INC. SAN FRANSISCO	

GEORGE D. GREEN, M.D.
JOHN F. WHITE, M.D.

Family Practice
100 MAIN STREET, SUITE 14
ANYTOWN, CALIFORNIA 90000
TELEPHONE: (999) 555-6000

STATEMENT TO:

- - - - - - - - - - TEAR OFF AND RETURN UPPER PORTION WITH PAYMENT - - - - - - - - - -

DATE	PROFESSIONAL SERVICE	FEE	PAYMENT	ADJUST-MENT	NEW BALANCE

PROFESSIONAL SERVICE CODES:

1. OFFICE VISIT
2. HOME VISIT
3. HOSPITAL VISIT
4. EMERGENCY ROOM
5. CONSULTATION
6. IMMUNIZATION
7. INJECTION
8. DRUGS/SUPPLIES/MATERIALS

9. COLLECTION OF LAB. SPEC.
10. SPECIAL REPORTS
11. OTHER SERVICES
12. SPEC. DIAGNOSTIC SERVICES
13. SPEC. THERAPEUTIC SERV.
14. EXTENDED CARE FACILITY
15. CUSTODIAL CARE
16. OBSTETRICAL CARE

17. SURGICAL
18. CASTS
19. LABORATORY
20. X-RAY
21. ALLERGY TEST.
22. NO CHARGE
23. ADJUSTMENTS OR
    CORRECTIONS
24. TOTAL CARE

GEORGE D. GREEN, M.D.
CAL. LIC. # 6-2856

JOHN F. WHITE, M.D.
CAL. LIC. # G-5281

PETTY CASH VOUCHER

RECEIPT FOR EXPENDITURES

No. _____

PAY TO: _____

DATE _____

DESCRIPTION OF ITEMS	ACCOUNT NUMBER	AMOUNT

APPROVED	ENTERED	RECEIVED PAYMENT

JOHN R. JOHNSON, M.D.
Family Practice
1000 MAINSTREET
SOME PLACE, USA 70000

STATE LIC # 123456789
SOC. SEC # 000-11-0000

TELEPHONE: (123) 555-5678

Top Section

☐ PRIVATE   ☐ BLUE CROSS   ☐ BLUE SHIELD   ☐ IND.   ☐ MEDICARE   ☐ GOV'T.   ☐ MEDI-CAL OR MEDICAID

PATIEN'S LAST NAME	FIRST	INITIAL	BIRTHDATE	SEX	TODAY'S DATE
			/ /	☐ MALE ☐ FEMALE	/ /

ADDRESS	CITY	STATE	ZIP	EALTIONSHIP TO SUBSCRIBER

SUBSCRIBER OR POLICYHOLDER	INSURANCE CARRIER

ADDRESS	CITY	STATE	ZIP	INS. ID	COVERAGE CODE	GROUP

OTHER HEALTH COVERAGE?
☐ NO   ☐ YES INDENTIFY

DISABILITY RALTED TO: ☐ IND.
☐ ACCIDENT   ☐ ILLNESS
☐ OTHER

DATE SYMPTOMS APPEARED,
OR ACCIDENT OCCURRED:

ASSIGNMENT: I assign & request payment of major medical benefits to under-signed physician for services described below.
SIGNED (Patient.
or Parent, if Minor)   DATE: /   /

RELEASE: I hereby authorize undersigned physician to furnish information to my insurnace carriers concerning this illness.
SIGNED (Patient.
or Parent, if Minor)   DATE: /   /

Center Section

√ DESCRIPTION	CPT/MD		FEE	√ DESCRIPTION		CPT/MD	FEE	√ DESCRIPTION	CPT/MD	FEE
1. OFFICE VISIT	NEW	EST.		3. HOSP SERVICES	NEW	EST.		6. SURGERY		
Minimal	90030			Interm (days)	90215	90260		Anoscopy	46600	
Brief	90000	90040		Extended		90270		Sigmoidoscopy	45355	
Limited	90010	90050		Comprehensive	90220	90280				
Intermediate	90015	90060		Discharge 30min. - 1hr		90292				
Extended	90017	90070		Detention Time 30min-1hr.		99150		Surgery		.80
Comprehensive	90020	90080		Detention Time ___ Hrs.		99151		7. MISCELLANEOUS		
								Booklets	99071	
				4. SPECIAL SERVICES				Special Reports	99080	
2. INJECTIONS & IMMUNIZATIONS				Called to ER - during ofc. hrs.	99065			Supplies, Ace Bandage	99070	
Injections, Arthrocentesis	206 •			Night Call - before 10 pm	99050			Telephone Call	99013	
DPT	90701			Night Call - after 10 pm	99052			X-Ray		
DT	90702			Sundays or Holidays	99054			Dressing Tray Sm.	99070	
Tetanus	90703			5. LABORATORY - IN OFFICE				Med.	99070	
OPV	90712			Urine	81000			Large.	99070	
NMR	90707			Occult Blood	82270			8. EMERGENCY ROOM-ESTAB. PATIENT		
IM inject. Therapeutic	90782			ECG	93000			Brief	90540	
IM inject. Antibiotic	90789			Hemoglobin	85018			Limited	90550	
Drug				Hematocrit	85014			Intermediate	90560	
Dosage				Routine Venipuncture	36415 •			Extended	90570	
TB-PPD	86580									

DIAGNOSIS   ICD-9

☐ Abrasion-sup. Injury 919
☐ Amenorrhea 626.0
☐ Anemia 28
☐ Anxiety-Stress-Depression . . . 30
☐ Arteriosclerosis 440
☐ Arthralgia 719.4
☐ Asthma Hayfever 493.6
☐ Bleeding Post Men 627.1
☐ Boil-Carbuncle-Furuncle 680
☐ Bronchitis-Acute Chronic 490
☐ Bronchopneumonitis 485
☐ Cervitis 616.0
☐ Chonyloma Accurninatum . . . 078.1
☐ Conjunctivitis 372

☐ Diabetes Mellitus . . . . .250.
☐ Duodebal Ulcer . . . . .532.
☐ Duodenitis 535.6
☐ Dysmenorrhea 625.3
☐ Epicondylitis 726.32
☐ Epilepsy 345
☐ Exogenous Obesity 278.0
☐ Fatigue 780.7
☐ Gastroenteritis 558.9
☐ Heart Failure 428
☐ Hiatal Hernia 553.3
☐ Homorroids . . . . .455.
☐ Influenza . . . . .487.
☐ Ingrown Toenail 703.0
☐ Insomnia 780.52

☐ Irratable Colon 564.1
☐ Laryngo-Tracjeitis 464
☐ Lipoma . . . . .214.
☐ Lipid Cholestorol Ab . . . . . 272.
☐ Low Back Pain 724.2
☐ Lymphangitis . . . . 457.
☐ Memorrhagia 626.2
☐ Menopausal Syndrom 627.1
☐ Myofascitis . . . . .729.
☐ Pain . . . .
☐ Paroxysmal Atrial Tachy . . . 427.6
☐ Pediculosis Pubis-Scabies . . . 133.6
☐ Pelvic Congestion 625.6
☐ Pharyngitis. Tonsil.-Acute . . . 462.
☐ Pigmented Nevus . . . . .216.

☐ Pneumonitis . . . . 468.
☐ Prostatitis . . . . 601.
☐ Renal Stone . . . . .592.
☐ Subaceous Cyst 706.2
☐ Seizure Disorder 780.3
☐ Tinea Corpus-Pedis 110.4
☐ URI-Viral Syndrome . . . . . . .460.
☐ UTI 599.0
☐ Vaginitis 616.10
☐ Weight Loss. Abnormal 783.2

DIAGNOSIS

Bottom Section

SERVICES PERFORMED AT:
☐ OFFICE   ☐ State Hospital
☐ E.R.   ☐ 200 State Street
☐   Some Place, USA 70000   ☐

ADMIT: /   /
DISHARGE: /   /

DATE	SERV.	CODE Mod	FEE

DATES DISABLED
FROM: /   /   TO: /   /
OK TO RETURN TO WORK: /   /

DOCTOR'S SIGNATURE   DATE

Accept Assignment
☐ YES ☐ No

RETURN APPOINTMENT INFORMATION:
5 • 10 • 15 • 20 • 30 • 45 • 60
DAYS   WKS.   MOS.

NEXT APPOINTMENT:
M • T • W • TH • F • S
DATE: /   /   TIME: AM / PM

INSTRUCTIONS TO PATIENT FOR FILING INSURANCE CLAIMS

1. COMPLETE THE UPPER PORTION OF THIS FORM; SIGN AND DATE.
2. MAIL THIS FROM DIRECTLY TO YOUR INSURNACE COMPANY. YOU MAY ATTACH YOUR OWN INSURANCE COMPANY'S FORM IF YOU WISH, ALTHOUGH IT IS NOT NECESSARY.
   PLEASE REMEMBER THAT PAYMENT IS YOUR OBLIGATION, REGARDLESS OF INSURANCE OR OTHER THIRD PARTY INVOLVEMENT.

REC'D. BY:
☐ CASH
☐ CHECK
_____

TOTAL TODAY'S FEE	
OLD BALANCE	
TOTAL	
AMT. REC'D TODAY	
NEW BALANCE	

INSUR - A - BILL ® • BIBBERO SYSTEMS.   • PETALUMA, CA • © 5/86

Office Copy

(Canary) Insurance Copy

(Pink) Patient Copy

(Goldenrod) Control Copy

(sample only — Codes may not be current)

ANYTOWN PSYCHIATRIC CLINIC
3344 Elm Street
Anytown, Pa. 11998

1576

$\frac{60\text{-}931}{313}$

_____ 19 _____

PAY TO
THE ORDER OF _____ | $

_____ DOLLARS

ANYTOWN NATIONAL BANK
4455 Main Street
Anytown, Pa. 11998

FOR _____

⑈"001576"⑈ ⑊:121000248⑊:0175 463140⑈'

ANYTOWN PSYCHIATRIC CLINIC
3344 Elm Street
Anytown, Pa. 11998

1577

$\frac{60\text{-}931}{313}$

_____ 19 _____

PAY TO
THE ORDER OF _____ | $

_____ DOLLARS

ANYTOWN NATIONAL BANK
4455 Main Street
Anytown, Pa. 11998

FOR _____

⑈"001576"⑈ ⑊:121000248⑊:0175 463140⑈'

ANYTOWN PSYCHIATRIC CLINIC
3344 Elm Street
Anytown, Pa. 11998

1578

$\frac{60\text{-}931}{313}$

_____ 19 _____

PAY TO
THE ORDER OF _____ | $

_____ DOLLARS

ANYTOWN NATIONAL BANK
4455 Main Street
Anytown, Pa. 11998

FOR _____

⑈"001576"⑈ ⑊:121000248⑊:0175 463140⑈'

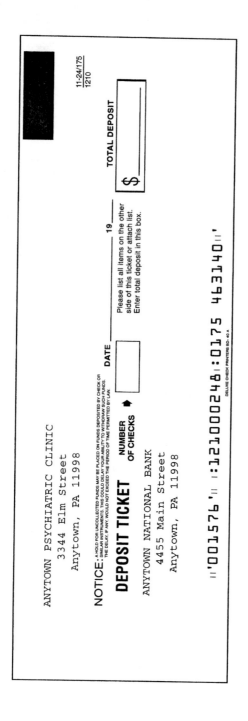

ANYTOWN PSYCHIATRIC CLINIC
3344 Elm Street
Anytown, PA 11998

NOTICE: A HOLD FOR UNCOLLECTED FUNDS MAY BE PLACED ON FUNDS DEPOSITED BY CHECK OR SIMILAR INSTRUMENTS. THIS COULD DELAY YOUR ABILITY TO WITHDRAW SUCH FUNDS. THE DELAY, IF ANY, WOULD NOT EXCEED THE PERIOD OF TIME PERMITTED BY LAW.

DEPOSIT TICKET

NUMBER
OF CHECKS

ANYTOWN NATIONAL BANK
4455 Main Street
Anytown, PA 11998

DATE _____ 19 ___

Please list all items on the other
side of this ticket or attach list.
Enter total deposit in this box.

TOTAL DEPOSIT

$

11-24/175
1210

||'001576'|| |:121000248|:0175 463140||'

DELUXE CHECK PRINTERS BD-40 A

DEPOSIT TICKET

PLEASE BE SURE THAT ALL ITEMS ARE PROPERLY
ENDORSED. LIST EACH CHECK SEPARATELY.

	DOLLARS	CENTS
CURRENCY		
COIN		
CHECKS (PROPERLY ENDORSED) LIST EACH SEPARATELY		
1		
2		
3		
4		
5		
6		
7		
8		
9		
10		
11		
12		
13		
14		
15		
16		
17		
18		
19		
20		
21		
22		
23		
24		
25		
26		
27		
28		
TOTAL		

PLEASE ENTER THE TOTAL AMOUNT OF DEPOSIT
ON THE OTHER SIDE OF THIS TICKET

CASH COUNT — FOR OFFICE USE ONLY		
	X 100	
	X 50	
	X 20	
	X 10	
	X 5	
	X 2	
	X 1	
TOTAL	$	

ACCOUNT RECONCILIATION FORMATS

THIS WORKSHEET IS PROVIDED TO HELP YOU BALANCE YOUR ACCOUNT

1. Go through your register and mark each check, withdrawal, Express Stop® transaction, payment, deposit or other credit listed on this statement. Be sure that your register shows any interest paid into your account, and any service charges, automatic payments or Express Transfers withdrawn from your account during this statement period.

2. Using the chart below, list any outstanding checks, Express Stop withdrawals, payments or any other withdrawals (including any from previous months) which are listed in your register but are not shown on this statement.

3. Balance your account by filling in the spaces below.

ITEMS OUTSTANDING		
NUMBER	**AMOUNT**	
TOTAL	$	

ENTER
The NEW BALANCE shown on
this statement . . . . $_____

ADD
Any deposits listed in your $_____
register or transfers into your $_____
account which are not shown on $_____
this statement.   + $_____

TOTAL . . . .   + $_____

CALCULATE THE SUBTOTAL . . . . $_____

SUBTRACT
The total outstanding checks
and withdrawals from the chart
at left . . . .   - $_____

CALCULATE THE ENDING BALANCE
This amount should be the same
as the current balance shown in
your check register . . . . $_____

Bank Statement Balance $ _____

    Less oustanding checks   _____

    Plus deposits not shown   _____

Corrected bank statement balance _____

Checkbook balance   _____

    Less bank charges   _____

Corrected Checkbook Balance _____

PHYSICIAN'S HOSPITAL
1000 FIRST STREET
ANYTOWN, USA 09009

APPLICATION FOR EMPLOYMENT

DATE _____

PERSONAL INFORMATION

LAST NAME   FIRST   MIDDLE

ADDRESS   STREET   CITY   STATE   ZIP

PHONE NUMBER   SOCIAL SECURITY NO.   HAVE YOU EVER WORKED FOR THIS HOSPITAL?
YES ☐   NO ☐   IF SO, WHEN:

IN CASE OF EMERGENCY NOTIFY:

NAME   ADDRESS   PHONE

DO YOU HAVE THE LEGAL RIGHT TO WORK IN THE U.S.?   HAVE YOU EVER BEEN CONVICTED OF A FELONY OR, WITHIN 5 YEARS
☐ YES ☐ NO IF YOU ARE OFFERED EMPLOYMENT, PROOF   A MISDEMEANOR WHICH RESULTED IN IMPRISONMENT? IF SO, GIVE
OF YOUR RIGHT TO WORK IN THE U.S. WILL BE REQUIRED   DETAILS. (A YES ANSWER WILL NOT NECESSARILY DISQUALIFY YOU
                                                     FROM THE POSITION APPLIED FOR.)   ☐ YES   ☐ NO

DO YOU HAVE RELATIVES IN OUR EMPLOY?

☐ YES   ☐ NO   NAME:

DO YOU HAVE TRANSPORTATION TO WORK?

☐ YES   ☐ NO

DO YOU HAVE ANY PHYSICAL CONDITION OR HANDICAP WHICH MAY LIMIT YOUR ABILITIES TO PERFORM THE JOB APPLIED
FOR?   ☐ YES   ☐ NO IF YES, WHAT CAN BE DONE TO ACCOMMODATE YOUR LIMITATIONS?

POSITION APPLYING FOR

FOR WHAT POSITION OR TYPE OF WORK ARE YOU APPLYING?   DATE AVAILABLE FOR WORK?

1. _____

2. _____

WHAT SHIFT DO YOU PREFER WORKING?   AVAILABLE TO WORK WEEKENDS?

☐ DAY   ☐ EVENING   ☐ NIGHT   ☐ ANY   ☐ YES   ☐ NO

WILL YOU WORK ROTATING SHIFTS?   STATUS OF WORK SEEKING:

☐ YES   ☐ NO   ☐ FULL TIME   ☐ PART TIME   ☐ ON CALL   ☐ TEMPORARY

ARE YOU PRESENTLY EMPLOYED?   WHY ARE YOU CHANGING JOBS?

☐ YES   ☐ NO

CAN WE CONTACT YOUR PRESENT EMPLOYER?   ADDITIONAL COMMENTS REGARDING WORK PREFERENCES

☐ YES   ☐ NO

Form 78035 (4/82 Rev.)

AN EQUAL OPPORTUNITY EMPLOYER

EDUCATION AND TRAINING	CIRCLE HIGHEST GRADE COMPLETED 1 2 3 4 5 6 7 8 9 10 11 12 COLLEGE 1 2 3 4 5 6		SUBJECT OR MAJOR	DID YOU FINISH? (GRADUATE)
	NAME OF SCHOOL	CITY AND STATE		
LAST HIGH SCHOOL				
COLLEGE OR UNIVERSITY				DEGREE
OTHER SPECIAL SCHOOLS OR TRAINING				

IF PROFESSIONALLY LICENSED OR REGISTERED: (STATE)   (NUMBER)   (DATE EXPIRES)

EDUCATION, TRAINING AND SKILLS

SPECIAL SKILLS AND/OR TRAINING

TYPING SPEED:_____ wpm

SHORTHAND SPEED:_____ wpm

CHECK IF YOU HAVE THE FOLLOWING SKILLS OR EXPERIENCE:

☐ MED. TERMINOLOGY   ☐ KEY PUNCH

☐ PBX   ☐ BOOKKEEPING

☐ ACCOUNTING   ☐ CREDIT & COLLECTIONS

☐ COMPUTER   ☐ CASHIERING

☐ CALCULATOR   ☐ ADMITTING

☐ TRANSCRIPTION

PLEASE STATE AMOUNT OF TIME YOU HAVE SPENT IN EACH OF THE FOLLOWING:

ADMINISTRATIVE _____
TEACHING_____
ICU _____
CCU _____
CPU _____
ER _____
MEDICAL/SURGICAL _____
ORTHOPEDICS_____
O.R. _____
RECOVERY ROOM_____
PEDIATRICS _____
OB _____
IV THERAPY _____
ONCOLOGY _____
HEMODIALYSIS_____
PUBLIC HEALTH _____
OTHER _____

MILITARY SERVICE

BRANCH: _____

SPECIAL TRAINING OR SKILLS ACQUIRED DURING U.S. MILITARY SERVICE THAT YOU FEEL ARE RELEVANT TO POSITION APPLIED FOR:

ADDITIONAL SKILLS OR TRAINING WHICH YOU BELIEVE ARE RELEVANT TO THE POSITION YOU ARE SEEKING:

LANGUAGES WHICH YOU CAN READ, SPEAK OR WRITE:

SOURCE OF REFERRAL: For Statistical Use Only. Not Used For Hiring Purposes.

☐ SELF   ☐ EMPLOYEE   ☐ NEWSPAPER   ☐ OTHER (SPECIFY)

EMPLOYMENT HISTORY

LIST LAST EMPLOYER FIRST

DATES OF EMPLOYMENT (MONTH, YEAR) From: To:	EXACT TITLE OF YOUR POSITION
NAME OF FIRM OR ORGANIZATION	ADDRESS AND PHONE OF EMPLOYER
TYPE OF BUSINESS OR ORGANIZATION	NAME AND TITLE OF IMMEDIATE SUPERVISOR
SALARY Starting $ Per Final $ Per	REASON FOR LEAVING

DATES OF EMPLOYMENT (MONTH, YEAR) From: To:	EXACT TITLE OF YOUR POSITION
NAME OF FIRM OR ORGANIZATION	ADDRESS AND PHONE OF EMPLOYER
TYPE OF BUSINESS OR ORGANIZATION	NAME AND TITLE OF IMMEDIATE SUPERVISOR
SALARY Starting $ Per Final $ Per	REASON FOR LEAVING

DATES OF EMPLOYMENT (MONTH, YEAR) From: To:	EXACT TITLE OF YOUR POSITION
NAME OF FIRM OR ORGANIZATION	ADDRESS AND PHONE OF EMPLOYER
TYPE OF BUSINESS OR ORGANIZATION	NAME AND TITLE OF IMMEDIATE SUPERVISOR
SALARY Starting $ Per Final $ Per	REASON FOR LEAVING

DATES OF EMPLOYMENT (MONTH, YEAR) From: To:	EXACT TITLE OF YOUR POSITION
NAME OF FIRM OR ORGANIZATION	ADDRESS AND PHONE OF EMPLOYER
TYPE OF BUSINESS OR ORGANIZATION	NAME AND TITLE OF IMMEDIATE SUPERVISOR
SALARY Starting $ Per Final $ Per	REASON FOR LEAVING

Read the following statements carefully before signing. If you have any questions regarding these statements, please ask for clarification before signing:

1. The facts I have set forth in my application for employment are true and complete. I hereby grant the Hospital permission to investigate and verify all statements which I have made on the application. I also understand that any material false statements, misrepresentation or omission on this application shall be sufficient cause for disqualification for employment or dismissal if employed.

2. I authorize the employers, organizations, schools or persons named in this application to give any information regarding my employment or education. I release said employers, organizations, schools or persons from any and all liability from any damage issuing this information.

3. I understand my employment is contingent upon the passing of a routine pre-employment health check provided by the Hospital.

4. I understand that I will be required to follow the personnel policies and rules of the Hospital and that infractions of said rules may lead to dismissal.

5. I understand that my employment can be terminated at any time, with or without cause and with or without notice, for reasons which either the Hospital or myself, as the case may be, considers sufficient. I also understand that employment does not constitute any agreement for employment for any specified period of time and that completion of a probationary period in no way alters the above employment relationship.

I verify that I have read, understand and consent to the above:

_____   _____
Signature of Applicant   Date

FOR PERSONNEL USE ONLY

START DATE _____   RATE _____
DEPARTMENT_____
CLASSIFICATION _____
STATUS _____
SHIFT _____

Two-Letter State Abbreviations

Alabama	AL		Montana	MT
Alaska	AK		Nebraska	NE
American Samoa	AS		Nevada	NV
Arizona	AZ		New Hampshire	NH
Arkansas	AR		New Jersey	NJ
California	CA		New Mexico	NM
Canal Zone	CZ		New York	NY
Colorado	CO		North Carolina	NC
Connecticut	CT		North Dakota	ND
Delaware	DE		Ohio	OH
District of Columbia	DC		Oklahoma	OK
Florida	FL		Oregon	OR
Georgia	GA		Pennsylvania	PA
Guam	GU		Puerto Rico	PR
Hawaii	HI		Rhode Island	RI
Idaho	ID		South Carolina	SC
Illinois	IL		South Dakota	SD
Indiana	IN		Tennessee	TN
Iowa	IA		Texas	TX
Kansas	KS		Trust Territory	TT
Kentucky	KY		Utah	UT
Louisiana	LA		Vermont	VT
Maine	ME		Virgin Islands	VI
Maryland	MD		Virginia	VA
Massachusetts	MA		Washington	WA
Michigan	MI		West Virginia	WV
Minnesota	MN		Wisconsin	WI
Mississippi	MS		Wyoming	WY
Missouri	MO			

Prescription Abbreviations and Symbols

Abbreviation	Meaning	Abbreviation	Meaning
ac	before meals	lb	pound
ad lib	as much as needed	μg	microgram
agi	shake; stir	m	minum
amt	amount	mEq	milliequivalent
ante	before	mg	milligram
aq	water	mL	milliliter
bid	two times a day	noct	night
$\bar{c}$	with	NPO	nothing by mouth
caps	capsules	N/S	normal saline
cc	cubic centimeter	OD	right eye
comp	compound	OS	left eye
contra	against	oz	ounce
dc	discontinue	pc	after meals
dil	dilute	per	by
disp	dispense	po	by mouth
dos	doses	prn	whenever necessary
dr	dram	pt	pint
elix	elixir	pulv	powder
emul	emulsion	q	every
et	and	qam	every morning
fl	fluid	qd	every day
garg	gargle	q4h	every four hours
gm	gram	qh	every hour
gr	grain	qid	four times a day
gt	drop	qn	every night
gtt	drops	qs	quantity sufficient
h, H	hypodermic	R	right
hr	hour	Rx	take (recipe)
hs	hour of sleep	rep	let it be repeated
id	intradermal	$\bar{s}$	without
im	intramuscular	sat	saturated
inj	injection	sc	subcutaneous
IV	intravenous	sig	write on label
kg	kilogram	sol	solution
L	liter	sos	once if necessary
L	left	ss	one-half

Abbreviation	Meaning	Abbreviation	Meaning
stat	immediately	tsp	teaspoon
suppos	suppository	TX	treatment
syr	syrup	u	unit
tab	tablet	UD	as directed
tbsp	tablespoon	VO	verbal order
tid	three times a day	5″, 10″	5 minutes, 10 minutes
tinct or tr	tincture	5′, 10′	5 hours, 10 hours
TO	telephone order	x	times
troc	lozenge	#	number

References

American Medical Association. *CPT/RVU 2001 Codes.* Chicago: American Medical Association, 2001.

Badasch, S., & D. Chesebro, *Introduction to Health Occupations,* 5th ed. Upper Saddle River, NJ: Prentice Hall, 2000.

Boyle, P. (Ed.), E.R. Dubose, S.J. Ellingson, D. Guinn, L.J. O'Connell, & D.B. McCurdy, *Organizational Ethics in Health Care: Principles, Cases, and Practical Solutions.* New York: Jossey-Bass, 2001.

Cohen, B., & D.L. Wood, *Memmler's The Human Body in Health and Disease,* 8th ed. Philadelphia: Lippincott-Raven, 2000.

Cox-Stevens, K., *Being a Health Unit Coordinator,* 5th ed. Upper Saddle River, NJ: Prentice Hall, 2002.

Fordney, M.T., & J.J. Follis, *Administrative Medical Assisting,* 4th ed. Albany, NY: Delmar Publishers, 1997.

Garrett, T.M., H.W. Baillie, & R.M. Garrett, *Health Care Ethics: Principles and Problems,* 4th ed. Upper Saddle River, NJ: Prentice Hall, 2000.

ICD-9-CM 2002. International Classification of Diseases, 9th Revision Clinical Modification. Hospital Edition Volumes 1–3, 2002. Los Angeles: Practice Management Information Corporation, 2002.

Keir, L., B.A. Wise, C. Krebs, & B. Krebs, *Medical Assisting: Administrative and Clinical Competencies,* 4th ed. Albany, NY: Delmar Publishers, 1997.

Lindh, W.Q., M.S. Pooler, C.D. Tamparo, & J.W. Cerrato, *Delmar's Comprehensive Medical Assisting,* 2nd ed. Albany, NY: Delmar/Thomson Learning, 2002.

Marieb, E.N., *Essentials of Human Anatomy and Physiology,* 7th ed. San Francisco: Benjamin/Cummings, 2002.

Noble, D.F., *Gallery of Best Resumes,* 2nd ed. Indianapolis: Jist Works, 2000.

Pullman, J., *The Nursing Assistant,* 3rd ed. Upper Saddle River, NJ: Prentice Hall, 2002.

Purtilo, R., & A.M. Haddad, *Health Professionals and Patient Interaction,* 6th ed. Gaithersburg, MD: W.B. Saunders, 2002.

Rowell, J.C., & M.A. Green, *Understanding Health Insurance: A Guide to Professional Billing,* 6th ed. Albany, NY: Delmar Publishers, 2002.

Taber, C.W. *Taber's Cyclopedic Medical Dictionary,* 19th ed. Philadelphia: F.A. Davis, 2001.

Turley, S.J., *Understanding Pharmacology,* 2nd ed. Upper Saddle River, NJ: Prentice Hall, 1999.

Wilson, M., *Medical Terminology Concepts,* 2nd ed. Upper Saddle River, NJ: Prentice Hall, 2002.

Index

Medical professional liability, 22
Medical records, 26, 115
  computerized, 122
  in the doctor's office, 118–120
  hospital, 116–118
  laboratory report, 114, 115
  as legal property, 120–121
  patient, 26
  problem-oriented (POMR), 122
  purposes of, 115–116
  source-oriented (SOMR), 122
  systems for maintaining, 122–123
Medical records department, 114, 116
Medical report, 114
Medical specialties, 9–12
  table, 10, 60
Medical terminology, 29–37
  abbreviations, 35–37
  pronunciation of, 34
  word elements, 30–34
  word variation, 34–35
Medical test, pre-employment testing, 251
Medical transcription, 121
Medicare, 169, 172–173, 195
Medication orders, prescription(s), 129–142;
    see also Drug(s)
  laws/regulations, 132–133
  responsibilities of handling, 131–132
MEDLARS, 159, 164
Memorandum, 98, 105
Metastasis, 56, 65
Microbiology, 144, 148
Microcomputers, 159, 162
Midsagittal, 63
Midsagittal plane, 56
Minicomputers, 159, 162
Mixed punctuation, 98
Mobile communications, 90–91
  cellular phones/pagers, 90
Modified block style letter, 98, 101,
    103–104
Money market account, 217, 219
Monthly itemized statement, 207
MRI (magnetic resonance imaging), 152
Multibutton key telephone, 79, 89–90
Muscle tissue, 58

N
National ZIP Code Directory, 108
Negligence, 16, 21
Neoplasm, 56, 65
Nephrology/nephrologist, defined, 10
Nervous tissue, 59
Net worth, 184, 186
Neurological surgery/neurosurgeon, defined, 10
Neurology/neurologist, 10, 11
  defined, 10
  as a nursing unit, 11

Nonverbal communication, 67, 73–74
Nosocomial infection, 39, 44
Nuclear imaging, 144, 152–153
Nucleus, 56, 57
Numerical filing, 114, 124
Nurse practitioner, 10
Nursery, defined, 11
Nursing, 9–11
  units, 11

O
Objective symptoms, 114
Obstetrics/obstetrician, 10, 11
  defined, 10
  as a nursing unit, 11
Occupational Safety and Health Administration
    (OSHA), 234
Office area, maintenance of, 233
Office equipment, 235–238
  inventory records, 236
  maintenance of, 235–236
  ordering, 236–238
Office maintenance, 231–243
  cleaning, 232–234
  flooring, 232
  hazardous waste management, 234–235
  lighting, 232
  soundproofing, 232
  temperature controls, 232
Office management, 242
Office manager, 239–243
  duties of, 240–243
  qualities of, 239–240
  role in marketing, 242
Office procedure manual, 231, 241–242
Office security, 238
Office supplies, ordering, 236–238
Old Age Survivors Insurance (OASI), 195
Oncology/oncologist, defined, 10
Open punctuation, 98
Ophthalmology/ophthalmologist, defined, 10
Optical scanner, 98, 110
Optometry/optometrist, defined, 10
Order transcription, 121
Organs, 56
Organs/systems, 59–61
Orthopedics/orthopedist, defined, 10, 11
  defined, 10
  as a nursing unit, 11
OSHA (Occupational Safety and Health
    Administration), 39
  bloodborne pathogens exposure controls,
    45–46
Otolaryngology/otolaryngologist, defined,
    10
Outdated files, 121
Output devices, 159, 163
Overdrawn accounts, 222